Content Area Literacy

Learners in Context

Second Edition

Mark W. Conley
University of Memphis

Boston   Columbus   Indianapolis   New York   San Francisco   Upper Saddle River
Amsterdam   Cape Town   Dubai   London   Madrid   Milan   Munich   Paris   Montreal   Toronto
Delhi   Mexico City   Sao Paulo   Sydney   Hong Kong   Seoul   Singapore   Taipei   Tokyo

Vice President and Editor-in-Chief: *Aurora Martínez Ramos*
Editor: *Erin K. L. Grelak*
Editorial Assistant: *Michelle Hochberg*
Vice President, Director of Marketing: *Margaret Waples*
Executive Marketing Manager: *Krista Clark*
Production Editor: *Mary Beth Finch*
Editorial Production Service: *Nesbitt Graphics, Inc.*
Manufacturing Buyer: *Megan Cochran*
Electronic Composition: *Nesbitt Graphics, Inc.*
Interior Design: *Jerilyn Bockorick, Nesbitt Graphics, Inc.*
Photo Researcher: *Kate Cebik*
Cover Designer: *Jennifer Hart*

Credits and acknowledgments borrowed from other sources and reproduced, with permission, in this textbook appear on appropriate page within text. Photo credits appear on page 424.

Library of Congress Cataloging-in-Publication Data

Conley, Mark William.
  Content area literacy : learners in context / Mark W. Conley. — 2nd ed.
    p. cm.
  ISBN 0-13-269012-8
  1. Language arts—Correlation with content subjects. 2. Content area reading. I. Title.

LB1576.C59 2011
428.0071'2—dc22

2011009645

10 9 8 7 6 5 4 3 2 1 EB 15 14 13 12 11

www.pearsonhighered.com

ISBN-10: 0-132-69012-8
ISBN-13: 978-0-13-269012-6

About the Author

Mark W. Conley, a professor in the in the College of Education at the University of Memphis, is a highly regarded academician, researcher, and author in the field of literacy. His cutting-edge research efforts focus on the relationships between adolescent literacy and new demands for accountability, developing learning strategies in content area classrooms, and teaching beginning and practicing teachers how to implement learning strategies within their curricula. As an accomplished author, Dr. Conley has published several books and numerous articles on literacy assessment, content area literacy, and literacy policy, including *Connecting Standards and Assessment through Literacy*. With this publication of *Content Area Literacy: Learners in Context*, Dr. Conley connects content area literacy teaching and assessment practices to research-based learning strategies within the context of today's challenges of assessment and accountability combined with new insights about adolescents and literacy.

Dr. Conley previously served as the coordinator of the doctoral program within the Department of Teacher Education at Michigan State University. Currently, Dr. Conley maintains a close connection with the practices and practitioners in today's schools as a professor at the University of Memphis and with Memphis City Schools, having designed the Memphis Literacy Corps curriculum, a literacy tutoring program involving 900 college age tutors and three thousand children. He has also created online and live professional development experiences for some of the district's seven thousand teachers. As an outgrowth of his research on adolescents and literacy in urban contexts, Dr. Conley directs an adolescent literacy tutoring program in urban schools staffed by beginning teachers. Dr. Conley also served on the Board of Directors for the National Reading Conference, 2006–2008. He recently served on the Quality Undergraduate Elementary and Secondary Teacher Education in Reading Task Force and Literacy Coach Task Force for the International Reading Association.

Dr. Mark Conley lives with his wife, Tami, an architect, in Memphis, Tennessee . . . except for one week each summer when he follows his passion for bicycling to take part in RAGBRAI, a weeklong bike ride across Iowa.

Brief Contents

Contents

2 Adolescent Literacy, Diversity, and Teaching Today's Learners 32

3 How to Pursue High Expectations for Teaching and Learning in an Era of Standards and Accountability 64

4 Alternative Ways to Plan and Teach Lessons   90

SECTION 2 Content Area Literacy: Teaching Today's Learners

5 Understanding and Using Texts   124

6 Ongoing Assessment 158

7 Activating Prior Knowledge and Increasing Motivation Before Reading 200

8 Building Vocabulary Knowledge and Strategies 228

9 Guiding Students during Reading 262

10 Guiding Students' Critical Literacy   298

11 Developing Content Area Writers 330

12 Building Literacy and Community from Inside and Outside the Classroom 370

Features

Research Brief

How to Plan

Teaching Today's Learners

Action Research

Connecting Standards and Assessment

Preface

This book is very purposefully entitled *Content Area Literacy: Learners in Context*. First and foremost, it is about Content Area Literacy, the area within education concerned with helping adolescents become more skillful with reading, writing, speaking, listening, viewing, and performing in all content areas. *Content Area Literacy* contains many useful techniques for teaching students how to gain knowledge about these skills while becoming more knowledgeable in each content area discipline.

Content Area Literacy: Learners in Context is also about today's educational context. The technological revolution has invaded adolescents' leisure time activities while presenting profound implications for their future. No Child Left Behind has increased pressure on teachers and students to perform with regard to higher educational standards and increasingly sophisticated state assessments. This is happening at the same time as researchers are sharing a more complete and complex account of the needs and challenges in the lives of adolescents—to form an identity, to make good decisions, to test their limits, and to be acknowledged for who they are and what they know. Teachers are at the center of this picture, characterized by increasing demands for accountability balanced against the struggles of adolescence, particularly for students with special educational needs, English language learners, and other struggling learners.

How This Book Is Organized

The first section of *Content Area Literacy: Learners in Context*, "Promoting Learning for Today's Challenges," confronts the need to fully understand today's educational landscape. Chapter 1, "Content Area Literacy: Helping All Adolescents Learn in New Times" reviews today's educational challenges and introduces content area literacy as the best way to promote learning. Chapter 2, "Adolescent Literacy, Diversity, and Teaching Today's Learners," discusses the diverse needs of adolescents and what it takes to base your teaching on individual differences. Chapter 3, "How to Pursue High Expectations for Teaching and Learning in an Era of Standards and Accountability," illustrates research-based principles for teaching and learning in this era of high-stakes testing and accountability. The section concludes with Chapter 4, "Alternative Ways to Plan and Teach Lessons," which explores assessment as the foundation for making decisions about diverse adolescents and content area literacy.

Section 2, "Teaching Today's Learners," focuses on the specifics of how to plan and teach, using principles of content area literacy. Chapter 5, "Understanding and Using Texts," consists of methods for understanding, evaluating, and teaching with texts. Chapter 6, "Ongoing Assessment," presents some alternatives for planning and teaching, using principles of content area literacy. Chapter 7, "Activating Prior Knowledge and Increasing Motivation," considers two important issues critical to enhancing students' understanding. Chapter 8, "Building Vocabulary Knowledge and Strategies," details teaching practices that encourage students skills to build and comprehend vocabulary knowledge across the curriculum. Chapter 9, "Guiding Students' Reading to Learn," demonstrates how to guide students' reading in content areas. Chapter 10, "Guiding Students' Critical Literacy," discusses a topic not often touched on in Content Area Literacy—how to help students become *critical* readers, no matter the discipline. Chapter 11, "Developing Content Area Writers," presents strategies for helping students develop the various writing skills required across the disciplines, as well in everyday life. The book concludes with Chapter 12, "Building Literacy and Community from Inside and Outside the Classroom," an especially crucial topic. This last chapter serves as the glue that holds all of the other chapters together by demonstrating ways to enlist students' cooperation while reaching out to parents and the community to support teaching and learning.

New to this Edition

Many changes have occurred across the educational landscape since the first edition. Politically, No Child Left Behind has not disappeared. Most of the reforms that impact literacy are still in place in schools, such as requirements that schools meet Adequate Yearly Progress. The standards reform movement has shifted from the states to a national effort, called the Common Core State Standards, which attempts to make state standards more consistent with one another. State assessments are being revised to reflect new and more rigorous standards. And teachers are under more pressure than ever to teach content and literacy in ways that impact students' achievements. With these changes in mind, the second edition:

▶ Updates information on the policy, standards, and assessment scene to encompass the new standards and reforms coming out of the Race to the Top program

▶ Reorganizes and re-titles the chapters so that it is easier to see connections between high expectations, standards based teaching, and alternative ways to plan

▶ Adds more specific examples about assessment, evaluation, and grading

▶ Updates citations references and citations, including adding more recommended readings

▶ Adds a feature called Praxis Practice to help beginning teachers prepare for the Praxis II test in reading across the curriculum

▶ Incorporates the popular A+ Rise strategies for teaching English Language Learners to align with relevant concepts

Special Features

Throughout *Content Area Literacy: Learners in Context*, special features have been provided to focus on issues of recurring importance, as well as to aid with review and understanding of key concepts in *Content Area Literacy*.

▶ Unique chapters, not found in other texts, on **"Guiding Students' Critical Literacy"** (Chapter 10) and **"Building Community from Inside and Outside the Classroom"** (Chapter 12) explore content literacy from a worldview, providing a perspective that reaches out to parents and the community for promoting literacy and learning.

▶ The strategy-based **How to Plan . . .** features in every chapter consist of practical instructional ideas that illustrate the principles in the book.

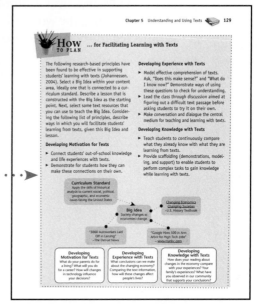

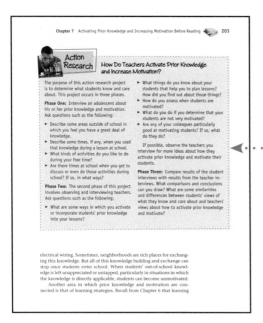

▶ **Action Research** features in every chapter offer prospective teachers practical suggestions for addressing specific content area literacy skills with students. Skills such as activating prior knowledge, improving comprehension, improving critical literacy, and writing for the real world are discussed.

▶ A **Teaching Today's Learners** feature in every chapter focuses on the diverse nature of students, and how to meet their needs. Each feature provides practical examples—what motivates students, the world of technology—connected to today's adolescents.

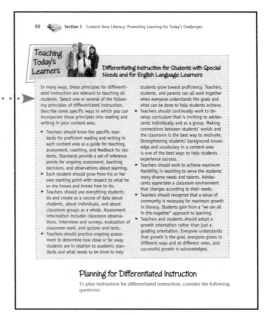

▶ **Connecting Standards and Assessment** features discuss important topics in the high-stakes, standards-based environment of today's schools and discuss how to work within this environment to use state standards to plan instruction. Each feature is correlated to Conley's *Connecting Standards and Assessment through Literacy* text, also published by Pearson.

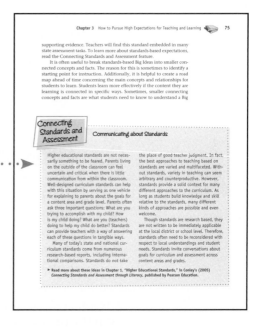

▶ At various points in each chapter, **Research Briefs** present important data and conclusions about student learning and effective teaching strategies based on the latest research.

▶ Throughout, the book **emphasizes home and school contexts** that influence learning, providing an overview of modern literacy challenges, including No Child Left Behind, changing technology, the diversity of students, and the central role of assessment.

▶ **Additional Pedagogical Aids** in each chapter include:

- A *Graphic Organizer* at the start of every chapter to help the reader organize his or her thinking before reading.

- A *Summary* that provides concluding thoughts on the overall message.

- *Special Projects* that encourage the readers to apply the concepts that have been introduced throughout the chapter.

- *Suggested Readings* that encourage further reading on the topics introduced in the chapter and that provide readers with a ready-made list of materials to obtain when creating their own resource library.

Supplements and Learning Aids

Instructor's Manual and Test Bank *Prepared by Mark Conley, Michigan State University, and Jaime Puccioni and Cathleen Clara, graduate students at Michigan State University.* The Instructor's Manual and Test Bank provides a wealth of interesting ideas and activities designed to help instructors teach the course. Each chapter includes a chapter-at-a-glance grid, a chapter overview, lecture outlines, discussion topics, activities, additional resources, plus test questions for each chapter. (Available for download from the Instructor's Resource Center at www.pearsonhighered.com/irc.)

Pearson MyTest The Test Bank is also available through our computerized testing system, MyTest, a powerful assessment generation program that helps instructors easily create and print quizzes and exams. Questions and tests are authored online, allowing ultimate flexibility and the ability to efficiently create and print assessments anytime, anywhere! Instructors can access Pearson MyTest and their test bank files by going to *www.pearsonmytest.com* to log in, register, or request access. Features of Pearson MyTest include:

Premium assessment content

▶ Draw from a rich library of assessments that complement your Pearson textbook and your course's learning objectives.

▶ Edit questions or tests to fit your specific teaching needs.

Instructor-friendly resources

▶ Easily create and store your own questions, including images, diagrams, and charts using simple drag-and-drop and word-like controls.

▶ Use additional information provided by Pearson, such as the question's difficulty level or learning objective, to help you quickly build your test.

Time-saving enhancements

▶ Add headers or footers and easily scramble questions and answer choices—all from one simple toolbar.

▶ Quickly create multiple versions of your test or answer key, and when ready, simply save to Microsoft-Word or PDF format and print!

▶ Export your exams for import to Blackboard 6.0, CE (WebCT), or Vista (WebCT)!

PowerPoint™ Presentation Designed for teachers using the text, the PowerPoint™ Presentation consists of a series of slides that can be shown as is or used to make handouts or overhead transparencies. The presentation highlights key concepts and major topics for each chapter. (Available for download from the Instructor Resource Center at www.pearsonhighered.com/irc.)

MyEducationLab

The power of classroom practice.

In *Preparing Teachers for a Changing World*, Linda Darling-Hammond and her colleagues point out that grounding teacher education in real classrooms—among real teachers and students and among actual examples of students' and teachers' work—is an important, and perhaps even an essential, part of training teachers for the complexities of teaching in today's classrooms. MyEducationLab is an online learning solution that provides contextualized interactive exercises, simulations, and other resources designed to help develop the knowledge and skills teachers need. All of the activities and exercises in MyEducationLab are built around essential learning outcomes for teachers and are mapped to professional teaching standards. Utilizing classroom video, authentic student and teacher artifacts, case studies, and other resources and assessments, the scaffolded learning experiences in MyEducationLab offer pre-service teachers and those who teach them a unique and valuable education tool.

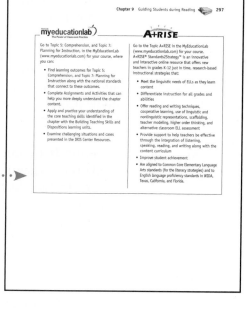

For each topic covered in the course you will find most or all of the following features and resources:

Connection to National Standards

Now it is easier than ever to see how coursework is connected to national standards. Each topic on MyEducationLab lists intended learning outcomes connected to the appropriate national standards. All of the activities and exercises in MyEducationLab are mapped to the appropriate national standards and learning outcomes as well.

Assignments and Activities

Designed to enhance student understanding of concepts covered in class and save instructors preparation and grading time, these assignable exercises show concepts in action (through video, cases, and/or student and teacher artifacts). They help students deepen content knowledge and synthesize and apply concepts and strategies they read about in the book. (Correct answers for these assignments are available to the instructor only under the Instructor Resource tab.)

Building Teaching Skills and Dispositions

These learning units help students practice and strengthen skills that are essential to quality teaching. After presenting the steps involved in a core teaching process, students are given an opportunity to practice applying this skill via videos, student and teacher artifacts, and/or case studies of authentic classrooms. Providing multiple opportunities to practice a single teaching concept, each activity encourages a deeper understanding and application of concepts, as well as the use of critical thinking skills.

As part of your access to MyEducationLab.

A+RISE®, developed by three-time Teacher of the Year and administrator, Evelyn Arroyo, gives new teachers in grades K-12 quick, research-based strategies that get to the "how" of targeting their instruction and making content accessible for all students, including English language learners.

A+RISE

A+RISE® Standards2Strategy™ is an innovative and interactive online resource that offers new teachers in grades K-12 just in time, research-based instructional strategies that:

▶ Meet the linguistic needs of ELLs as they learn content

▶ Differentiate instruction for all grades and abilities

▶ Offer reading and writing techniques, cooperative learning, use of linguistic and nonlinguistic representations, scaffolding, teacher modeling, higher order thinking, and alternative classroom ELL assessment

▶ Provide support to help teachers be effective through the integration of listening, speaking, reading, and writing along with the content curriculum

▶ Improve student achievement

▶ Are aligned to Common Core Elementary Language Arts standards (for the literacy strategies) and to English language proficiency standards in WIDA, Texas, California, and Florida.

Lesson Plan Builder Activities

The Online Lesson Plan builder is a tool that helps familiarize new and prospective teachers with the steps of a lesson plan, providing them a concrete structure that accounts for all the necessary elements, and allowing them quick access to important components including state and national standards.

Look for activities on the MyEducationLab for your course that link directly into the Online Lesson Plan Builder. You'll see video of a classroom and be offered the opportunity to determine a goal and craft a lesson for the group, scaffolded as you do to remember to focus on specific learning outcomes, incorporate Standards, and focus on the individual needs of learners.

IRIS Center Resources

The IRIS Center at Vanderbilt University (http://iris.peabody.vanderbilt .edu—funded by the U.S. Department of Education's Office of Special Education Programs (OSEP) develops training enhancement materials for pre-service and in-service teachers. The Center works with experts from across the country to create challenge-based interactive modules, case study units, and podcasts that provide research-validated information about working with students in inclusive settings. In your MyEducationLab course we have integrated this content where appropriate.

Study Plan Specific to Your Text

A MyEducationLab Study Plan is a multiple choice assessment tied to chapter objectives, supported by study material. A well-designed Study Plan offers multiple opportunities to fully master required course content as identified by the objectives in each chapter:

▶ *Chapter Objectives* identify the learning outcomes for the chapter and give students targets to shoot for as you read and study.

▶ *Multiple Choice Assessments* assess mastery of the content. These assessments are mapped to chapter objectives, and students can take the multiple choice quiz as many times as they want. Not only do these quizzes provide overall scores for each objective, but they also explain why responses to particular items are correct or incorrect.

▶ *Study Material: Review, Practice and Enrichment* give students a deeper understanding of what they do and do not know related to chapter content. This material includes text excerpts, activities that include hints and feedback, and interactive multi-media exercises built around videos, simulations, cases, or classroom artifacts.

Course Resources

The Course Resources section on MyEducationLab is designed to help students, put together an effective lesson plan, prepare for and begin their career, navigate their first year of teaching, and understand key educational standards, policies, and laws.

The Course Resources Tab includes the following:

▶ The **Lesson Plan Builder** is an effective and easy-to-use tool that students can use to create, update, and share quality lesson plans. The software also makes it easy to integrate state content standards into any lesson plan.

▶ The **Preparing a Portfolio** module provides guidelines for creating a high-quality teaching portfolio.

▶ **Beginning Your Career** offers tips, advice, and other valuable information on:

• *Resume Writing and Interviewing*: Includes expert advice on how to write impressive resumes and prepare for job interviews.

• *Your First Year of Teaching*: Provides practical tips to set up a first classroom, manage student behavior, and more easily organize for instruction and assessment.

• *Law and Public Policies*: Details specific directives and requirements teachers need to understand under the No Child Left Behind Act and the Individuals with Disabilities Education Improvement Act of 2004.

▶ **Longman Dictionary of Contemporary English Online** Make use of this online version of the CD-ROM of the Longman Dictionary of Contemporary English—the quickest and easiest way to look up any word while you are working on MyEducationLab.

Certification and Licensure

The Certification and Licensure section is designed to help students pass their licensure exam by giving them access to state test requirements, overviews of what tests cover, and sample test items.

The Certification and Licensure tab includes the following:

▶ **State Certification Test Requirements:** Here students can click on a state and will then be taken to a list of state certification tests.

▶ Students can click on the **Licensure Exams** they need to take to find:

- Basic information about each test

- Descriptions of what is covered on each test

- Sample test questions with explanations of correct answers

▶ **National Evaluation Series™ by Pearson:** Here students can see the tests in the NES, learn what is covered on each exam, and access sample test items with descriptions and rationales of correct answers. They can also purchase interactive online tutorials developed by Pearson Evaluation Systems and the Pearson Teacher Education and Development group.

▶ **ETS Online Praxis Tutorials:** Here students can purchase interactive online tutorials developed by ETS and by the Pearson Teacher Education and Development group. Tutorials are available for the Praxis I exams and for select Praxis II exams.

Visit www.myeducationlab.com for a demonstration of this exciting new online teaching resource.

Acknowledgments

Many individuals contributed to the vision that guides this book. Thanks to Laura Roehler and Patricia Edwards, for reminding me of the importance of students' and parents' perspectives; to Alfred Tatum and William Cumpiano, who renewed my understanding that literacy must help students find a place for themselves in life; to Hal and Joan Herber, who started me on this journey many years ago, and to Jaime Puccioni and Cathleen Clara for their assistance creating the Test Bank.

I appreciate the time my colleagues in the field took to review the second edition manuscript; thanks to Leif Fearn, San Diego State University; Rebecca L. Godwin, Barton College; Cynthia Sharp, Nevada Department of Education; and Terrell A. Young, Washington State University. Thanks also to those who reviewed the first edition: Suellen Alfred, Tennessee Tech; Freida Golden, Tarleton State; Leigh Hall, University of North Carolina, Chapel Hill; Stephenie M. Hewett, The Citadel; Nancy Kolodziej, Tennessee Tech University; Kathy Misulis, East Carolina University; Alyson Naquin, Nicholls State University; Olivia Saracho, University of Maryland; Carole Silva, California State University, Los Angeles; Mary W. Spor, Alabama A&M University; and Terrell Young, Washington State University. Members of a special advisory council include Suellen Alfred, Tennessee Tech; Martha Allen, Dominican College; Jean Benton, Southeast Missouri State University; Merry Boggs, Tarleton State University; Len Breen, Sam Houston State University; Donna Cooner, Colorado State University; David De Weese, Southern Illinois University-Edwardsville; Mary Lou Gammon, Northern Arizona University; Betty Higgins, Sam Houston State University; Lois Huffman, North Carolina State University; Louise Kaltenabugh, Southern University at New Orleans; Marilyn Leuer, California State University-Fullerton; Emily Long, University of North Carolina-Pembroke; Edith Mayers, University of Louisiana-Lafayette; Cheryl Slattery, Shippensburg University; and Beth Tope, Louisiana State University.

A special thank you to all the people at Allyn & Bacon, beginning with Vice President and Editor-in-Chief Aurora Martínez Ramos, Editor Erin Grelak, Senior Development Editor Mary Kriener, and Executive Marketing Manager Krista Clark for believing in the project and encouraging my thinking. I am also grateful to the production department of Production Editor Mary Beth Finch; Photo Editor Kate Cebik; and packager Susan McNally of Nesbitt Graphics for seeing this book through to the end.

And, of course, thanks go out to my family, to my daughters, Kelly and Erin, who always distract me in good ways; and to my wife, Tami, the eighth-grade math teacher turned school architect who not only supported me through the writing of this book but who is also responsible for many of the mathematics examples that appear throughout the book.

Mark Conley
Memphis

Foreword

The drumbeat for altering the course that many U.S. high schools are following is quickening and growing louder. For example, at the 2005 National Educational Summit on High Schools in Washington, DC, a spate of new reports underscored the pivotal role that high schools play in developing the intellectual capital for our country's future and how our high schools need to be transformed to fulfill that expectation. Two common threads ran through these reports and others that fill the secondary school reform landscape: *Standards must be raised to enable graduates to compete in the new economy, and the achievement gap must be closed for the growing number of struggling adolescent learners*. Not surprisingly, the goals of "raising the bar" and "closing the gap" can be very difficult to address simultaneously. Successfully doing so often requires dramatically different learning experiences and classroom instructional strategies for students as well as emphasizing different competencies for teachers through varying professional development experiences.

Mark Conley demonstrates throughout this book that he clearly understands the underlying tensions that exist for educators who are trying to raise the bar for students who should be challenged and stretched to achieve higher standards at the same time that they are attempting to close the gap for those who haven't acquired the foundational skills to enable them to excel in the core curriculum. Dr. Conley has done a brilliant job of describing the context within which educational solutions must be generated and the form that these solutions must take in order to be embraced by teachers as well as to be sufficiently powerful to significantly improve student outcomes. The first three chapters of the book present information that teachers need to make informed curriculum planning and instructional decisions. This is done by carefully weaving together emerging trends that are impacting schooling now and in the future with the unique learning attributes of adolescent learners and the complex curriculum demands that all students are expected to meet. At the end of Section One, the reader has gathered the necessary backdrop against which to understand the detailed presentation of instructional methods in Section Two.

The heart and soul of this book is the information presented in Section Two related to strategies for teaching adolescents in today's secondary schools. Dr. Conley has accomplished what others who have tried to figure out how to effectively improve literacy skills of adolescents *within* the context of demanding subject matter classes have not. Specifically, he presents a broad array of highly practical suggestions about how to teach high-leverage learning strategies within subject matter classes in ways that ensure mastery *and* generalization of the strategies to improve outcomes in content area classes and to demands students face in non-academic settings.

In light of the way that this book is structured and written, I am convinced that secondary teachers will find it to be one of the most valuable resources in their teaching toolbox for the following reasons:

▶ It is grounded in the empirical literature—hence, the instructional suggestions can be used with confidence of getting good outcomes.

▶ It is hands-on, providing clear, step-by-step instructions for how to implement various teaching strategies.

▶ It supplies specific examples from actual classroom situations to illustrate each learning point and instructional procedure.

▶ It is principle-based.

▶ It is comprehensive in scope, including a broad array of related resources for extended study of key topical areas.

The instructional framework used in this book is both logical and empirically based. One of the most distinguishing attributes of this book is its comprehensive nature. Specific instructional strategies related to curriculum planning, formative assessments, using text structure, building vocabulary and prior knowledge, and reading and writing methods are presented.

This book is the extraordinary resource that it is because of its author, Mark Conley. Dr. Conley has had extensive experience as a teacher, program developer, researcher, and writer. He has a deep understanding of the complexities of secondary schools, the needs of adolescents and teachers, and the dynamics that exist between them. I consider Mark Conley to be one of the brightest and most insightful educators of our time. His professional work has been devoted to improving the quality of environments in schools and enabling teachers and students alike to thrive. I believe that he is being extraordinarily successful in that quest.

While the clear focus of this book is achieving successful academic outcomes for students, Dr. Conley recognizes that the overall growth, development, and well-being of adolescents involve much more than acquiring academic proficiency alone. The final chapter of this book underscores this fact as it describes the vital role of developing safe and supportive learning communities in which students and their teachers can grow and develop.

In short, I believe that this book will provide teachers with the foundation that they will need to successfully create the kinds of environments and cultures of learning in their classroom that will promote optimal academic success. This very readable book is written with passion, vivid examples, and countless practical suggestions that can be readily implemented. This book will add greatly to my abilities as an educator in secondary schools, and it will be a resource to which I will frequently turn.

Donald D. Deshler
Director
University of Kansas
Center for Research on Learning

Content Area Literacy: Helping All Adolescents Learn in New Times

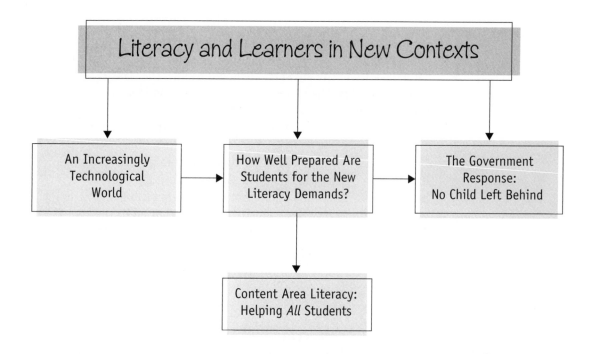

Literacy and Learners in New Contexts

- An Increasingly Technological World
- How Well Prepared Are Students for the New Literacy Demands?
- The Government Response: No Child Left Behind
- Content Area Literacy: Helping *All* Students

David Dolata, a prospective mathematics teacher at Michigan State University, shares his struggles over learning how to help students. As you read Dave's story, a common one for beginning teachers, consider your own experiences with teaching. Have you had experiences with students that are in any way similar to Dave's?

Dave's Story: What Does It Mean to Help Your Students?

I really struggle with what it means to give help to my students. I have some experience now, helping with assignments and quizzes. But I wonder, what does it really mean to help them? I know what I want them to learn in mathematics. Understanding means seeing the big picture, knowing the meaning behind the concepts and the procedures but also talking and writing about what they know. I want them to be able to tell how things work and why they work the way that they do.

When I first started teaching, many of my students fooled me for quite some time. This is how I was fooled. The whole time I was working on math concepts that are basic stuff for math geeks like me—factoring equations, for example. But these ideas are somewhat complicated for students who are not so mathematically inclined. Every time I would go over a new problem, I jumped in and showed them what to do. The students hung back until I basically gave them the answers. Little did I know that the whole time I was doing this, the students had absolutely no idea about what I was teaching them. They just nodded their heads at the right times when I asked them if they understood and waited for me to give them the answers.

Of course, the proof of my students' learning came when they had to take a test. They failed miserably. The true test of learning in any content area should be that the students can demonstrate what they know on their own. So, I learned that all of the "help" I was giving my students was really hurting them because they could not do anything on their own.

I changed in how I see "helping." At first, I thought helping means just doing everything you can do to help students get the right answer. Now, I realize that it means representing and interacting with the material in many different ways—through reading, writing, viewing, and discussing. Now, I show my students little tricks for how I read mathematics, things that have worked for me. We write all the time, telling what we know, drawing pictures sometimes, and exploring the ideas on the web. And we talk. We talk about the "whats" and the "hows" and the "whys" behind all of the ideas. I've even learned a few things about mathematical history that I never knew! This change from delivering the right answers to using all the tools—reading, writing, viewing, and discussing—has transformed my students from sleepy robots into hungry learners.

For some teachers, this discovery—that students learn best not from just presenting the information but by being helped to learn many different ways to find their own answers—can take many years. The purpose of this book is to promote your own discovery of how to transform your students into independent learners. The vehicle for this transformation is literacy: helping students learn how to make the best use of reading, writing, viewing, and discussing to gain knowledge in your content area. For many students, going through the school day means wrestling with subtle but important differences in concepts teachers take for granted. For example, consider how the meaning of a vocabulary term such as *scale* changes as students move from mathematics to science to social studies—from units of measurement to different assessments for weight to a key term for studying economics. Content area literacy is a field in education that integrates teaching and assessment practices that focus on reading, writing, viewing, and discussing into content areas so that students can more effectively gain knowledge. The added benefit of using these practices is that students also gain in their ability to practice their own literacy skills, which helps them to understand how they can apply their skills in different ways, depending on the challenges they encounter across the curriculum.

The focus throughout this book is on learners—you and your students. Through your experiences with this book and in your class, you will learn how to successfully understand and apply the research-based practices of content area literacy. This is the reason for the first half of the book's title: *Content Area Literacy*. The second half of the title— *Learners in Context*—refers to the fact that the teaching and assessment practices described here are applied in classrooms, with students who are diverse in language and literacy, family and community. The modern context of changing technological demands, high standards, and rigorous state and national assessments is another important part of this real-life context. This book was written to help teachers use content area literacy to balance the challenges and opportunities that accompany the context of modern, high expectations with the needs of diverse learners. The book begins with the context, by describing the new demands for education and accountability.

The Literacy Challenges of an Increasingly Technological World

We see the challenges of an increasingly technological world in the news every day. Global economic competition is based on the effective use of information and communication. Designers and engineers from several different parts of the world collaborate on plans and specifications for manufacturing in another part of the world. The Internet has emerged as the engine that drives information and communication. From a truly global perspective, there are greater numbers of people competing intensely for resources and markets. Workplaces cannot survive unless they become more productive and responsive to the needs of their customers. Technology and skill with technology are key (Leu et al., 2004).

Elements of the old manufacturing-based system are in decline. Companies and factories that used to thrive on rigid management styles must yield to new ways of working. New high-performance workplaces stress collaboration, seeking out information to solve problems, critically evaluating information, and communicating solutions with others (Mikulecky & Kirley, 1998).

These changes in the world and the workplace have important implications for the kinds and types of literacy required. First, literacy is no longer a matter of just looking up information in a book. Our increasingly technological world requires that students be prepared to seek out information from print as well as technological resources related to a full range of topics, issues, needs, and problems. Knowing how, when, and where to locate important information is as important as knowing how to manage, interpret, and critically evaluate the information. With the Internet at the center of these activities, the need exists for students to sort out accurate from less accurate information and essential from less essential information. Students must also be well prepared to synthesize and communicate information.

The technological world surrounds us even in our leisure activities, with Internet-based games, instant messaging, email, blogs, word processors, music and movie stores, listservs, and virtual worlds. However, it would be a mistake to assume that by mere participation in these activities, all students learn the literacy skills necessary to thrive in an increasingly technological world. Technological changes are so rapid and continuous that it is impossible to predict the new technologies that will emerge across the time it takes for a child to go from kindergarten to high school graduation. So besides the literacy skills of understanding important problems and seeking out and evaluating relevant information, our students need to know how to adapt to continual change. How can teachers help students with this enormous challenge?

The Government Response

Governments around the world have reacted with policies and laws to ensure that all students attain higher levels of literacy achievement. From 2001 until 2008, the **No Child Left Behind (NCLB)** Act was the initiative in the United States that was dedicated to producing higher achievement in all content areas, particularly in literacy. Though references to NCLB have largely disappeared from the popular media, many of the reforms are still deeply embedded in the daily workings of schools and districts. In a part of the law termed **Adequate Yearly Progress (AYP)**, NCLB mandated that students increase their knowledge and performance every year in every content area. Under NCLB, states developed target achievement goals each year that define AYP. The bar is raised in gradual increments each year until 100 percent of the students in the state are proficient on state assessments by 2013–2014. Meeting AYP requires that students thoroughly develop knowledge within a content area while using reading and writing to answer increasingly demanding test questions and other content area tasks. Students who are not up to the challenges of new high-stakes tests under these reforms do not get diplomas. Schools that do not adequately prepare their students can lose funding, teachers can be reassigned or fired, and schools can be closed.

The vehicle for determining adequate yearly progress is extensive state testing. Most, if not all, of this testing places a high priority on students' abilities to read and write well (Conley, 2005). NCLB laws mandated that *all students* improve in their test performance each year. In the past, schools could compute an average for all of their students and were deemed successful if the average of all students increased. However, NCLB requires results reported for all subgroups—broken down by ethnicity, special education, English language learners, and the economically disadvantaged. The new higher standard is that the performance of every one of these subgroups must improve each year. The changes ushered in by NCLB are significant: No longer can patterns of poor student performance be lost or disguised. The success of every student matters.

In 2009, a new government initiative was launched termed **Race to the Top**. Through Race to the Top, states have been encouraged through the promise of large funding awards to create educational reforms around four specific areas (U.S. Department of Education, 2010):

▼ **High-stakes testing has placed even more attention on student performance.**

- ▶ Adopting standards and assessments that prepare students to succeed in college and the workplace and to compete in the global economy
- ▶ Building data systems that measure student growth and success, and inform teachers and principals about how they can improve instruction
- ▶ Recruiting, developing, rewarding, and retaining effective teachers and principals, especially where they are needed most
- ▶ Turning around the lowest-achieving schools

The combined emphasis on preparing students to succeed and analyzing teacher effectiveness has raised the bar considerably. Teachers who effectively foster higher levels of achievement in their students will be rewarded. Teachers who possess the tools for increasing literacy as well as promoting preparing students well in a content area classroom will be among the most successful. This book has been written to help teachers accomplish these goals.

How Well Prepared Are Students for the New Literacy Demands?

Many students develop literacy successfully in some very general ways. However, this does not mean that even traditionally successful students are well prepared for our technological world and accompanying higher educational standards. And not all students develop literacy successfully.

Successful Reading and Writing

Stop and consider what happens when an individual reads and writes. In an instant, various kinds of special information about language are translated, connected, and applied to create meaning from or with a text, including these **foundational literacy skills** (Pressley, 2000):

► The **alphabetic principle:** understanding the ways in which the alphabet represents spoken sounds

► **Phonemics:** understanding the systematic ways in which letters and sounds combine to form syllables and words

► **Word recognition:** putting into practice understandings of sounds and letters to pronounce words

► **Comprehension:** relating prior knowledge about language and the world to text information, using vocabulary knowledge, constructing word and sentence meanings, and reading for specific purposes and to complete specific tasks

Click on A+RISE – WIDA ELP Standard Strategy in the MyEducationLab (www.myeducationlab .com) for your course. Next, select the Strategy Card Index tab, scroll to Fluency for Grades 6–12 and select the Circle of Friends strategy.

The first three factors—the alphabetic principle, phonemics, and word recognition—are necessary for **fluency,** or the automatic recognition of words without having to stop and figure out each letter or sound. With fluency, adolescents can read and write well without getting hung up on the details of letters and words. Experienced and successful readers and writers apply this complex knowledge automatically without having to stop and think about it.

How readers and writers use this knowledge has been a matter of debate. One research perspective suggests that literacy is a **bottom-up** process (Carver, 1990; Gough, 1984; Perfetti, 1985). This position emphasizes the importance of the text and a reader's fluency with the text as the most important factors. Students sound out and combine letters, syllables, and words, eventually building meaning from texts or through texts with their writing.

Another perspective is that literacy is **top-down** (Anderson & Pearson, 1984). This perspective gives more credit to readers and writers actively using their prior knowledge to create meaning from or with a text. On the basis of their knowledge and experience, readers and writers process texts selectively and with multiple interpretations. This perspective accounts for the fact that meanings surrounding a text can vary from person to person. For example, consider the different meanings that can be applied to this sentence:

Students hate annoying teachers.

Do students hate teachers who are annoying? Or do they hate to annoy teachers? The same sentence has two plausible but different meanings or interpretations. This perspective also accounts for the fact that sometimes, individuals do not bother to read or attend to all of the words, relying instead on the gist or general idea of a topic to make meaning through reading or writing.

A third perspective combines the bottom-up and top-down points of view. This is called an **interactive** approach (Rumelhart, 1994). Sometimes, especially when the reading is abstract and complex, readers and writers slow down and pay close attention to the words. Other times, when a topic is familiar and less complex, individuals skim, skipping words, sentences, and even entire paragraphs and write quickly without thinking because they can rely on their knowledge.

For most people, successful reading and writing are represented by a combination of these perspectives—part reliance on the language of a text, using knowledge and experience to shape understanding, and considering the context for making decisions about how to read and write. Think about the differences in your reading when you read the newspaper or a favorite book and when you read a complex chapter or article full of numbers, symbols, and graphics. Think about times when you have been writing about something very familiar and when you have been grappling with an unfamiliar, abstract topic. Successful individuals skim and pause at will, taking in or writing freely when the reading or writing is familiar and easy. Successful individuals also slow down and deliberate to increase their understanding when the reading or writing gets more challenging.

Consider your own reading process. Is it more bottom-up (depending on the text or the content area)? More top-down (guided by knowledge and experience)? Interactive (faster or slower, more or less in-depth, shaped by the complexity and familiarity of the topic)? Consider situations in which you adjusted your approach, depending on the text and the task at hand. Successful reading and writing involve considerable flexibility and self-awareness in using reading and writing to make meaning. Consider times when you were reading and writing in your content area and you felt particularly powerful and nimble in understanding and composing, when the meanings and words just flowed. Consider other times when you slowed down to grasp or create meaning. The fact that you were able to approach reading and writing in both of these ways is reflective of your proficiency as a reader and a writer.

These views of what it means to be a successful reader and writer have been challenged by more recent research involving literacy and technology (Leu et al., 2004). Students who are generally proficient in print-based reading and writing may be at a loss when it comes to the demands of seeking out, interpreting, evaluating, and communicating the information that is so common in digital environments. The new challenge to teachers concerns how to help even traditionally successful students develop the literacy skills necessary for success in our increasingly technological world.

Why Students Struggle with Reading and Writing

No matter how literacy is viewed or how expectations change, some students struggle. An important question is: Why do some students develop so much power and flexibility in reading and writing while others struggle over every word? There are many reasons. As you read this section, compare your own experiences with reading and writing. What were the times and circumstances when you struggled with reading and writing? Consider and share your own experiences in working with students who struggle with the following factors.

Speech and Language Development. Students develop differently in their ability to speak and connect their oral language to reading and writing. Some students grow up experiencing a great deal of difficulty learning word-level skills. Some of these students start out with language problems such as being unable to discriminate among different speech sounds. This can make it extremely difficult for them to connect letters and sounds or separate words into their individual sounds (Espy et al., 2004). When they figure out that they cannot use clues from letters and words to read or write, many of these students try to guess, using pictures or the beginning letters of words. Many of the guesses these students make result in errors.

▼ With a sense of urgency to help underachieving students do better, more and more communities reach out to the schools with special community tutoring and leadership programs. Many communities have seen their schools' scores rise as a result.

Dyslexia. A very small percentage of struggling students suffer from some form of **dyslexia**, a problem with perceiving or working with language. In the most familiar type of dyslexia, students perceive letters and words in reverse; these students have difficulty pronouncing or reading and writing words. Some estimates indicate that only about 1 percent or so of the struggling readers and writers actually experience some form of dyslexia (Vellutino & Scanlon, 2001). Many of these students are served through special education. A controversial issue concerns the numbers of students who have dyslexia who are served by special education compared to students who experience other kinds of learning difficulties caused, for example, by inexperience

with reading and writing and/or problems in developing knowledge about reading and writing or mismatched instruction. Although the percentages of students identified for services within special education can fluctuate greatly, from 10 percent to 20 percent of public school enrollment in each state nationwide (National Center for Education Statistics, 2005), only a very small number of these students may actually experience dyslexia. We will explore issues related to students in special education, often referred to as **special needs learners**, in the next chapter.

Knowledge about Reading and Writing. Struggling students know less about how to read and write. From their years of feeling unsuccessful and unmotivated, many are inexperienced with reading and writing. They do not know how to actively engage themselves with texts, monitor ways in which they are making meaning, or figure out what to do when things do not make sense, such as looking back, rereading, or revising (Cain & Oakhill, 2004). Struggling students can be severely limited in strategies to figure out what they are trying to read or write in comparison with skilled readers and writers (Pressley, 2006).

When a skilled student encounters a word, she or he recognizes it quickly and zeroes in on the appropriate meaning. For instance, in the sentence *The thief lifted the rock from the jewelry case*, a skilled reader likely can tell immediately from the context that *the rock* refers to a precious gem. Struggling students will make inefficient guesses at the letter-sound, word, and meaning level that produce lots of irrelevant associations. They are unable to pare down these associations to make appropriate sense of what they are reading or writing (Pressley, 2006). Not surprisingly, the development of writing relies on many of the same abilities as reading: understanding how letters and sounds work, understanding how letters and words combine into sentences and larger pieces of text and meaning, using vocabulary and prior knowledge, and writing for different purposes (Shanahan, 2006). Students who expend all of their effort figuring out letters, words, and sentences are limited in ways they are able to attend to the sense or message of what they are writing.

Consider what happens when you come upon a word or term you do not know when you are reading and writing, such as *alektorophobia*. Make a list of the options you would use to find what you need to know, such as looking up the word in a dictionary or encyclopedia, conducting an Internet search of the term, or asking someone you think might know the answer. If you are like most successful readers and writers, you probably have quite a list. You also know how to select just the right option for what you need in a particular situation, and you know what to do if the choice you have made is not working. Less skilled readers and writers often fall back on less effective strategies when they are stuck, including reading and rereading without a particular purpose. Less skilled individuals will try and retry using the same approach, sometimes just pronouncing a word over and over again, without understanding that the approach will not help them understand.

The Research Brief identifies just how prevalent problems with reading are today with many high schoolers. It also depicts some of the issues that can arise when students do not develop effective strategies as readers.

Research Brief

How Serious Is the Problem of Fluency among Adolescents?

In a recent study of 300 ninth graders in one urban high school, none of the students achieved a level of fluency that would be considered normal or average for their age. In fact, 12 percent read at a below-average reading rate, indicating that it would take them 150 percent longer to read a class assignment in comparison with average students. The lack of fluency experienced by these students was highly correlated to their poor performance on a high school graduation test (Rasinski et al., 2005). How will the results of this research likely affect your role as a teacher? What practices might you need to consider as you encounter these fluency patterns in your own classroom?

Language Differences. Cultural and language differences can play a role in whether or not a student struggles with reading and writing. First, it needs to be stated that every student is an individual, not just a clone of all of the members of a cultural or linguistic group. Not every student from another culture or every English language learner (a student whose first language is other than English) is a struggling reader or writer in English.

Indeed, some English language learners are from middle-class families with extensive schooling. Many read and write above grade level in their own language. However, although having a great deal of proficiency in a first language is helpful for learning to read and write in a second language, it is by no means a guarantee that the process will be easy for a student. If a student is unmotivated, the transfer of skills from one language to another may be as difficult as it is for an unmotivated native speaker to learn to read. Further, as the curriculum increases in complexity from elementary school to middle and high school, many of these students may find the challenges of reading and writing in English too difficult to overcome.

Some students come from backgrounds of poverty. These students' first language skills might be limited because they have not had widespread opportunity for education. They might have experienced serious interruptions in the schooling in their native language and arrive in the

A+RISE

Click on A+RISE – WIDA ELP Standard Strategy in the MyEducationLab (www.myeducationlab .com) for your course. Next, select the Strategy Card Index tab, scroll to Language and Content for Grades 6–12 and select the Language and Content Development strategy.

United States with very little or no English or content area knowledge. Many are not progressing satisfactorily in school or receiving the necessary help to become more skilled (Short & Echevarria, 2005).

Some students, whose first language does not employ an alphabetic writing system, such as Chinese and Arabic language systems, experience problems decoding English texts. Although they might read and comprehend pretty well in their first language, they can experience difficulty with reading English because they do not understand the alphabetic letters and the relationships of these letters with sounds in English. Without fluency in reading letters, sounds, and words, these students are blocked from gaining any meaning from their reading.

Differences in Cultural Knowledge. Still other students experience difficulty with reading and writing because of differences in cultural knowledge. For example, consider the following simple sentences (Eskey, 2005):

> It was the day of the big party. Mary wondered if Johnny would like a kite. She ran to her bedroom, picked up her piggy bank, and shook it. There was no sound!

It might be relatively straightforward for a nonnative speaker to understand some of the more literal aspects of these words and sentences, such as the fact that Mary wondered whether Johnny would like a kite or that she went to her bank for money. On the other hand, students from another culture might understand notions of a birthday party and giving gifts from a completely different, non-Western point of view.

Problems especially emerge when culturally shaped concepts such as *justice*, *revenge*, *worship*, or *love* appear on state tests and Westernized definitions of these concepts are treated as the correct answers. Rather than assessing a student's ability to read and write, the tests instead measure and mismeasure cultural differences. The language of assessment itself—words such as *explain your answers*, *justify your response*, and *take a stand*—can be unfamiliar to people from a different culture. All of this suggests that teachers should interpret assessment information about students from other cultures whose first language is not English with a great deal of caution. Read the How to Plan feature for some tips and an example for how to include linguistically and culturally diverse students in your lesson planning.

HOW
TO PLAN . . . for the Needs of Linguistically and Culturally Different Learners

A goal of working with all students should be to include everyone in while creating many different opportunities to participate and learn. This is particularly important for English language learners who reflect differences in language and culture. There are many options at a teacher's disposal for including all students and presenting multiple learning activities.

Consider this lesson from science. The idea is to begin a lesson with students' experiences instead of just diving into a textbook. For example, the California State Standards say that students must know how to analyze changes in an ecosystem resulting from changes in climate, human activity, introduction of nonnative species, or changes in population size. Planning for student involvement takes the form of these steps, asking students to do the following:

▶ Make observations about the natural world around them
▶ Discuss the interaction of humans and animals within nature
▶ Think about ways in which nature strives to maintain a balance in the environment
▶ Examine ways in which nature becomes affected by increases in population and/ or the introduction of nonnative plants, animals, and marine life

Rather than having students start their investigation with a boring lecture based on a textbook description, teachers and students can discuss the "ecosystems" in their lives—from nature, within their families, within society. The focus of this discussion is how individuals and nature strive for balance and what happens when things are out of balance. The advantage of this approach is that all students—even those who are linguistically and culturally different—potentially have something to say about their experiences that can lead to learning the science content.

Other ways of including linguistically and culturally different learners include the following:

▶ Using a mixture of oral language, reading, writing, and viewing to learn lesson content (if English language learners are inexperienced readers, they can become engaged through oral language experiences)
▶ Pairing students to work on class projects so that each student—the native speaker and the English language learner—takes turns participating based on his or her knowledge and experience
▶ Designing lessons that invite different kinds of input from students and their families (for example, sharing instances of mathematics, reading, writing, and scientific thinking from daily family life)

Poverty. Poverty and problems with reading and writing go hand in hand. In some communities, poverty is the reason that students move from school to school, sometimes as many as ten times during a student's elementary school career (Payne, 2001). When students move around this much, it can be difficult for them to receive consistent instruction in reading and writing or for teachers to consistently assess their progress. Poverty can also mean that students are not exposed to many enriching experiences, such as taking books out of the library, visiting a bookstore, or being exposed to educational media, including television and magazines, or the Internet. Poverty can be one of the reasons students arrive in middle and high school unable to read or write very well or not ready to learn in your content area. Although it is impossible for teachers to erase poverty from their students' lives, what are some ways in which teachers could help students who come from poverty feel a sense of belonging in school while progressing academically?

Motivation. For many students, experiences with reading and writing are just too flawed and require too much effort for what they are able to accomplish. Not knowing how to make sense of letters, sounds, and words ends the possibility of much, if any, comprehension or effective writing. Students who do manage to become fluent can face even more problems with comprehension and writing. For example, because they are unable to read very much or very flexibly, struggling students still have little knowledge about constructing meaning in comparison with more skilled readers (Cipielewski & Stanovich, 1992). A common experience of struggling students is that they do not know when they do not know, and they have few, if any, options available in knowing what to do about it. Faced with achieving little, if any, success for their effort and having little understanding of how to target their effort to get results, many struggling students simply give up (Pressley et al., 2003).

Increasing Curriculum Changes and Demands. As students grow older, especially as they enter the fourth grade, the school curriculum becomes much more complex, emphasizing comprehension to a greater degree as well as a broad range of subject matter materials and tasks. The job of reading and writing shifts from learning to read and write to reading and writing *to learn* in content areas. This important shift takes the form of increasing demands to learn more and more with text-based material while responding to a widening array of classroom tasks, such as questions, hands-on activities, and assessments. Instead of learning *about* reading and writing, older students must *use* reading and writing to build knowledge and perform. As this happens, students who struggle to read can fall behind in their achievement in all content areas. As they fall behind and experience more and more failure, they may become increasingly unmotivated.

Mismatched Instruction. The majority of students who struggle, in fact, do so as a result of varying skills and poor or mismatched instruction. Some students require more intensive instruction to develop strategies that work for them before they "get" the ways in which language works in reading and writing. There are many different ways to teach someone how to read, including immersing students in oral reading experiences; directly teaching about phonics, word recognition, and comprehension; and helping students to make use of pictures and language contexts to make meaning. When given reading materials and tasks that are appropriate to the ways in which individual students learn, many catch on and learn to read and write quite readily. A tragedy for far too many students is that schools sometimes wrongly assume that these students have dyslexia and place them in remedial reading or special education program in which they might or might not receive instruction that is appropriate for their needs (Allington, 2001). Unfortunately, some schools may not have the expertise to figure out what a struggling student needs or how to shape instruction to teach them (Pressley, 2006).

The reality is that most classrooms today reflect a full range of students—those who are proficient and those who struggle with reading and writing. A purpose of this book is to help you get ready to teach them. The Teaching Today's Learners feature offers some ideas about how teachers can include parents as partners in supporting their children's literacy learning. We will return to this important topic in Chapter 12, "Building Literacy and Community from Inside and Outside the Classroom."

A Persistent Achievement Gap

With so many reasons for why students might struggle with reading and writing, it should come as no surprise that big differences exist in performance and achievement among students. The **achievement gap** between different groups of students is the greatest force behind the reforms under No Child Left Behind. After decades of school reform and much money spent on promising instructional techniques and programs, an achievement gap persists between privileged and not-so-privileged middle and

Teaching Today's Learners

Enlisting Parents' Support

Struggling readers and writers benefit when their parents can support their literacy development. Parents of struggling readers and writers often feel relieved when they have some strategies for helping their children. An ongoing myth is that adolescents rebel against any parental involvement. In reality, most adolescents, like anyone, appreciate attention and effort on their behalf, even—or perhaps especially—if it comes from teachers and parents. Here is a list of activities that teachers can share with parents to help with reading and writing (Learning Disabilities Association of America, 2005):

▶ Present a good example. If possible, model good reading habits. Keep lots of reading material around the house. Every so often, turn off the television and read.

▶ Read the same book your adolescent child is reading and discuss it. This is a way to share an enjoyable experience and build conversations around reading.

▶ Let adolescents choose what they want to read. Take them to a bookstore or library and let them browse. Do not turn your nose up at popular fiction and magazines. Encourage connections between reading and enjoyment.

▶ Purchase or rent books on tape, especially for long family trips. While valuable for all students, this can be particularly helpful for English language learners or other students who are struggling with reading.

▶ Subscribe in your child's name to magazines such as *Sports Illustrated*, *Seventeen*, or *National Geographic*. Encourage reading of newspapers and current events magazines such as *Time* and *Newsweek*. Ask your children what they think about what they have read, and listen to what they say.

▶ Encourage your child to keep a summer scrapbook. Tape in souvenirs of your family's activities, such as pictures, postcards, ticket stubs, and photos. Have your child write captions and illustrate pictures that represent your vacation.

high school students (Snow & Biancarosa, 2003). Certain groups of students, particularly students living in poverty, some African Americans and Latinos, and some students whose first language is not English, continue to perform significantly below expectations, especially with reading and writing. These underperforming students are referred to as *at-risk students*, short for "at-risk of school failure." Many at-risk students fail to pass their state's reading test; others do not pass the state tests in one or more subject areas. Despite satisfying all other local graduation requirements, many of these students either fail to earn a diploma or drop out altogether (Barton, 2005).

Although the personal costs to individual underperforming students are difficult to imagine or calculate, the achievement gap costs society dearly. A constant drumbeat about increasing dropout rates, declining opportunities for low-skilled workers (Barton, 2005), worries over declining performance in mathematics and the sciences (National Center for Education Statistics, 1999), and the shift of jobs overseas (Brown, 2004) all reflect the costs of our students not performing well. There is little disagreement about the urgency for schools to do better, especially with students who underperform in reading and writing, a foundation for successful performance in all content areas.

Many national programs have been developed to help with the problem of the achievement gap with older students. Read about some of them in the Action Research feature.

Content Area Literacy: Helping All Students with Literacy in Content Areas

Our changing technological world and higher educational standards mean increased literacy challenges for all students. Traditionally successful students still need to become even more literate in ways that are more flexible and expand into a range of print and digital contexts. Students who struggled before face even more literacy challenges than ever. So what can teachers do to ensure that all students become more literate in more powerful ways? Recall Dave's question at the beginning of this chapter: How can teachers help students in this new era of ongoing literacy challenges? The answer lies in content area literacy.

Content area literacy is "the ability to use reading and writing for the acquisition of new content in a given discipline" (McKenna & Robinson, 1990). This definition has several implications for the issues discussed so far. To be content literate means having the ability to exercise a range of literacy skills, including strategies for understanding new vocabulary and for seeking out, interpreting, critically evaluating, and communicating information. Being content literate means being fully prepared to respond to the challenges of increasingly demanding state and national tests. Content area literacy represents a set of goals and tools for teachers to employ for shrinking the achievement gap while helping all students to become more literate and learn in more powerful ways in content areas.

A+RISE

Click on A+RISE – WIDA ELP Standard Strategy in the MyEducationLab (www.myeducationlab .com) for your course. Next, select the Strategy Card Index tab, scroll to Language and Content for Grades 6–12 and select the Language Acquisition and Content Knowledge strategy.

Action Research

What Is an Effective Program for Struggling Readers and Writers?

An important initiative from the federal government for older readers is the Striving Readers Program. (Review the program at www2 .ed.gov/programs/strivingreaders/index.html) The goals of the Striving Readers Program are to improve the overall level of reading achievement in middle and high schools, improve the literacy skills of struggling adolescent readers, and build a strong, scientific research base around specific strategies that improve adolescent literacy skills. Conduct a web search using the terms "struggling readers" "adolescents" "striving readers," and "literacy programs." Select one of the programs that you find and list its characteristics. What assumptions are made about struggling readers, and adolescents and about what works for them?

A number of blue-ribbon reports have been released concerning what should happen in effective literacy programs for adolescents, including:

► **Reading Next: A Vision for Action and Research in Middle and High School Literacy, from the Carnegie Corporation** www.all4ed.org/publications/ReadingNext/ReadingNext.pdf

► **Creating a Culture of Literacy, from the National Association of Secondary School Principals** www.principals.org/Content.aspx?topic=52936

► **All About Adolescent Literacy**, a website full of reports on adolescent literacy, the achievement gap and what to do about it, sponsored by the Carnegie Foundation. www.adlit.org/

Many reports and websites like these contain information that is freely downloadable. Select one report and read for what it says about effective programs for adolescents. Compare the findings of the blue-ribbon report with the literacy program you investigated. What common understandings do you find? Make a list of recommendations based on these documents for how schools can help adolescents become more literate.

Content Area Literacy and Our Technological World

Recent research on the literacy required for success in a technological world identifies five important strategies for learning in both print and online environments (Leu et al., 2007). As examples throughout this book demonstrate, content area literacy can help your students learn how to use these strategies.

Identifying Important Questions. This strategy involves reading and writing to solve problems and answer questions. There are large questions such as: How do we stop global warming? And there are smaller questions such as: What time is the matinee showing of a movie we want to see? Teachers often decide what is important before posing questions as part of a lesson or unit plan. It is equally essential to show students how to ask important questions on their own. This is a recurring theme throughout this book.

Locating Information. Whereas students used to be restricted to print resources, the Internet contains nearly infinite amounts of information. Although it is still important for students to know how to search through a variety of print-based sources, they also need to know how to seek out information through search engines, online libraries, blogs, and wikis (online encyclopedias). The range of resources and how to use them are the theme of Chapter 5, "Understanding and Using Texts."

Critical Thinking and Evaluation. Some skills for critical thinking and evaluation work well with both print and online texts. For example, students can benefit from asking the following evaluation questions for both print and online texts (Coiro, 2006):

▶ Does this make sense to me?

▶ Does this meet my needs (for information, solving a problem, etc.)?

▶ Can I verify this information?

▶ Can I trust this information?

▶ How does the author shape the message?

Online contexts offer a variety of tools for asking these questions, such as search engines. However, anyone can publish texts, so greater scrutiny of online texts is often necessary. Ways to help students ask and answer these questions in both print and online environments are the subject of Chapter 10, "Guiding Students' Critical Literacy."

Synthesis. Synthesis involves constructing meaning with texts. Sometimes, this means making connections among essential vocabulary terms. Other times, this means making choices about what to emphasize among the words and sentences on a page, which websites to visit, which links to follow, and ways of communicating one's understanding. Chapter 8, "Building Vocabulary Knowledge and Strategies," focuses on ways to develop students' abilities with vocabulary, including the technical language that is unique to each content area. Chapter 9, "Guiding Students' Reading to Learn," illustrates many ways to help students comprehend and learn with texts.

Communication. Sometimes, when we focus only on classrooms and schools, it is easy to forget that there are purposes and reasons for reading and writing. At the top of the list is communication. Reading and writing in the content areas should always help students make connections with real purposes and audiences. Of course, the Internet has expanded this view to include email, instant messages, blogs, discussion boards, and chats. Chapter 11, "Developing Content Area Writers," contains many useful ideas for stimulating students' communication.

Content Area Literacy and the Challenges of Accountability

Content area literacy is an essential tool for successfully confronting the challenges posed by accountability. Recall that governmental inspired reforms like NCLB and Race to the Top have produced much greater pressure for students to successfully perform on state tests and for teachers to teach well. To gain a better picture of both the reading and writing demands of state tests and ways in which content area literacy can be indispensable for meeting those demands, let's examine some content area questions from several state tests.

As these examples illustrate, content literacy is about a variety of factors, including a reader's prior knowledge; ability to read and use different kinds of vocabulary for different purposes; the language and complexity of the reading material; and the nature and complexity of what students are required to do, say, or write. Notice also how some of these tasks are more or less interesting or motivating for you. Consider how students, with their varied interests, would also vary in their motivation toward each of the tasks. Ways to promote greater motivation in your students are the topic of Chapter 7, "Activating Prior Knowledge and Increasing Motivation."

Content Area Literacy and Mathematics. Suppose students were required to respond to the following test item in mathematics (Figure 1.1):

Graphing a Player's Performance

Each number below represents the total points scored per game by one high school basketball player.

15, 44, 32, 18, 22, 41, 29, 23, 34, 21, 20, 33, 60, 19, 28

    A Organize the data in a box plot.
    B Identify the minimum, maximum, quartile 1, quartile 2, and quartile 3.
    C Use 1.5 times the interquartile range (quartile 3 minus quartile 1) to identify any existing outliers.

Explain your answers, including supporting calculations, tables, diagrams, charts, drawings, or graphs, in your answer booklet.

Source: Michigan Educational Assessment Program.

Figure 1.1

A mathematics item from a state test.

Notice the extent of special, subject-specific vocabulary necessary to understand this question: *box plot, quartile 1,* and *interquartile.* Notice also the commonplace words that have special meanings in this context—*minimum* and *maximum,* for example. The writing involved with this task is unique: creating a box plot and identifying specific points on the box plot. Finally, students are required to explain their answers through supporting calculations, diagrams, or graphs.

Although understanding the mathematics involved with this test item is certainly essential, being able to read, understand, and respond in writing to the item in specialized ways is also crucial. Content area literacy involves showing students how to adjust their reading and writing to the specific demands of different kinds of knowledge and tasks.

Content Area Literacy and Social Studies. Students taking a social studies state test might encounter an item like the one in Figure 1.2.

Again, the vocabulary of the test item is important: core democratic values, and supporting knowledge from history, geography, civics, or economics. As in a mathematics test item, students are required to support their answer. This time, rather than providing graphical support, students must supply in writing numerous kinds of social studies content knowledge that is specifically related to the position they take on the issue in the question. Notice also how this item has a particular requirement for prior knowledge. Students must know something about fuel-efficient cars and the issues surrounding them to be able to answer the question.

Figure 1.2

A social studies item from a state test.

ESSAY
Time – 25 minutes

Turn to page 2 of your answer sheet to write your ESSAY.

State High School Test in Social Studies

You will now take a stand on the following public policy issue:

Should the United States government require manufacturers to produce more fuel-efficient vehicles?

You may either support or oppose the manufacture of more fuel-efficient vehicles. Write a letter to your senator.

You will be graded on the following criteria. Your letter must include
- a clear and supported statement of your position;
- supporting information using a core democratic value of American constitutional democracy;
- supporting knowledge from history, geography, civics (other than the core democratic values), or economics (it is NOT enough to only state your opinion);
- a credible argument someone with the opposite point of view could use and an explanation that reveals the flaw in his or her argument.

Remember to:
- Use complete sentences.
- Explain your reasons in detail.
- Explain how the core democratic value you use connects to your position.
- Write or print neatly on the lines provided in your answer booklet.

Source: Michigan Educational Assessment Program.

Being content literate in social studies often involves comparing different kinds of information while developing and supporting critical points of view. Content area literacy provides numerous tools for helping students learn how to do these things on their own.

Content Area Literacy and Science. Let's change the focus again and examine this task from science (Figure 1.3).

There are fewer vocabulary items in comparison with the other content areas, but the ones that appear are extremely important—the nature of a circuit, for example. Reading the question carefully and understanding what makes a complete circuit are crucial for responding to this science task. The explanation required here is quite reflective of many

Testing Batteries

Julia wants to determine which of her batteries have little or no power remaining. She gathers the following materials: a flashlight bulb, two pieces of copper wire, and some tape.

- Describe a circuit or create a drawing, complete with labels, using only the above materials, that can be used to test which batteries have power remaining.
- Explain how one could test the batteries.

Source: Michigan Educational Assessment Program.

Figure 1.3

A science item from a state test.

science tasks. Students need to write about a procedure: creating a circuit between the ends of a battery and the base and metal side of a light-bulb and then determining the strength of the battery by the brightness of the bulb. Alternatively, they can write about how to use a battery tester or voltmeter to accomplish the same ends. The goal here is to depict the procedure accurately without introducing any misconceptions.

Science learning engages students in observations and interpretations based on their experiences with the natural world. Content area literacy can be used to support these activities in science through strategies for acquiring new vocabulary knowledge, observation and interpretation, prediction, and communication.

▲ Content area literacy reaches out far beyond just reading and writing. Students also must be able to connect understanding and performance.

Content Area Literacy and Art. Consider the instructions posed for students in an art class as shown in Figure 1.4.

Notice how this task, like the others we have examined, requires subject-specific understandings of vocabulary—elements of atmospheric space and using a viewfinder to adjust the arrangement. Some knowledge of portfolios and self-portraits is also required. Though no writing is required, one could argue that the act of composing pictures to convey a message is comparable to writing purposefully.

A common misconception is that activity- or performance-oriented content areas such as art, music, and physical education are neither academic nor involve reading and writing. On the contrary, these content

Figure 1.4

An art item from a state test.

> **Self-Portrait Portfolio Cover**
>
> A respected advertising company is providing one mentorship to a high school art student. Your selection for the mentorship will be based on the company's review of your portfolio. The company requires you to develop a self-portrait that shows things about yourself for the front of your portfolio. Leaf through the magazines, tearing out photographs of different things that you feel in some way represent things about you: hobbies, favorite colors, activities, favorite foods, talents, etc. Carefully trim 5 or more photographs and arrange them so that two elements of atmospheric space are established in the work. Using a view finder, adjust the arrangement, if necessary, so that the work demonstrates unified colors, and textures and balance. Carefully clean off any smudges or glue on the cover sheet and mount the self-portrait on the sheet provided for you.
>
> *Source: Missouri Assessment Program.*

areas encourage connections between thinking, reading and writing, and performing. Content area literacy, broadly defined as reading, writing, speaking, listening, and viewing, provides numerous ways of supporting learning that connects the understanding and performance.

To be literate in a content area, students must be able to adapt to many different kinds of reading and writing demands across the curriculum. As a successful student yourself, you already have a great deal of practice within your own content area in what it means to be adaptable. As such, you are the content specialist who can not only help your students gain knowledge in your content area, but also assist them in using reading and writing as important tools. You are in a unique position to improve the reading and writing performance of all of the students in your care. To find out how more about how to help your students deal with the literacy demands of high-stakes state tests, read the Connecting Standards and Assessment feature.

Principles for Teaching Content Area Literacy

Going back to Dave's question at the beginning of this chapter, what does it mean to help your students? Good teaching from a content area literacy perspective focuses on developing skilled reading and writing in multiple ways. These are the principles that will guide your work throughout this book:

> ▶ **Focus students' attention on words, patterns, and rules in their reading and writing.** For struggling readers and writers, the classroom can represent a cacophony of sounds, words, and symbols. Create opportunities for students, especially those who struggle with

Connecting Standards and Assessment

Content Area Literacy and High-Stakes State Assessment

High-stakes state tests are demanding higher levels of literacy from students. Though the appearance of these tests has not changed much from the multiple-choice, short answer, constructed response, and extended response formats, the content has changed dramatically. It is obviously important for teachers to learn about these tests to help students pass them. One way to learn about the tests is to examine released items. Released items can be found on many state department of education websites.

Individual content area tests reveal a range of reading and writing activities, from reading passages, problems, and experiments to evaluating and responding to information. Some of the more challenging test items require students to read multiple passages and then answer sweeping thematic questions that encompass the full range of the reading. Teachers often struggle separately in content area and grade-level groups to identify the skills that are necessary to succeed on the tests. This often yields long lists of objectives and activities. Imagine being a student going through the school day responding to a myriad of activities designed to teach to the state tests.

There is a difference between item teaching and curriculum teaching. In item teaching, teachers blindly rehearse students through sample test items in hopes that students will do well on the actual tests. Curriculum teaching involves discovering valuable curriculum goals and skills through a careful analysis of the tests and then teaching to those goals and skills. However, doing this separately for every test can be needlessly complicated and confusing. A better approach would be to discover the goals and skills that are held in common by all of the tests and then embed those goals and skills in the curriculum. One analysis of testing skills across tests yielded the following list of essential test-taking skills:

► Understanding and distinguishing between big and small ideas
► Analyzing questions
► Getting organized for a response
► Thinking about what you already know
► Taking a stand on content
► Proving your point
► Applying processes of selection and elimination

Of course, just identifying these skills does not completely solve the problem of embedding them into your teaching. Design a lesson in your content area based on one or more of these skills. Point out ways in which you will use reading and writing in your lesson to involve all of your students.

► **Read more about these ideas in Chapter 6, "When Teaching to the Test Is Just Good Curriculum," in** Conley's (2005) *Connecting Standards and Assessment through Literacy*, **published by Pearson Education.**

reading and writing, to study and learn new words and to discern patterns that will help them build meaning.

▶ **Provide students with lots of practice with oral and written language.** Classrooms that are rich in a variety of language activities—including reading, writing, speaking, listening, and viewing or observing—provide better opportunities for learning for varieties of readers and writers than classrooms that only emphasize reading or taking notes from PowerPoint presentations.

▶ **Show students how to make meaning with their texts and construct meaning through their writing.** Do not be satisfied only with students understanding the content. Make sure they develop strategies for comprehending and writing on their own. This is a recurring theme throughout this book.

▶ **Help students to develop multiple strategies for reading and writing.** Skilled students know many different ways to figure out what they need to know, especially when they get stuck.

▶ **Teach students to adapt their reading and writing strategies appropriately.** As a successful learner, you know that every strategy has its own time and place. A strategy that works perfectly well in an English class might not work well at all in a math class. Sometimes, a strategy that you select does not work for a particular situation, whether reading, writing, or problem solving. As you develop knowledge about learning strategies with your students, work with them to understand how to apply them appropriately for different contexts.

▶ **Teach students to become good critical thinkers.** This requires practice with understanding and evaluating different perspectives and the kinds of reasoning and evidence presented in various print, media, and technological contexts (Internet, television, movies, magazines, etc.).

Summary

It used to be a cliché to say that the world is constantly changing, but with today's technology, this cliché happens to be true. Governmental programs such as No Child Left Behind and Race to the Top provide ample evidence of the importance of our changing world for education and the economy. As state and national standards and tests are revised to reflect these changes, the demands increase for students to be literate in a variety of ways across the curriculum and beyond school. Unfortunately, neither traditionally successful nor struggling readers and writers might be up to meeting the demands of our changing technological world. More unsettling is the persistent achievement gap between successful and struggling readers and writers, particularly among various ethnic groups and the poor. Taken together, these factors combine to present some mighty challenges for today's teachers and their students.

The teaching practices of content area literacy are essential tools for today's teachers. For the new demands of reading and writing online, there are practices that support students' in locating and evaluating information. For the increased reading and writing demands in the content areas due to greater testing and accountability, there are practices that can help students to develop success and independence. This book is about how to use content area literacy to confront this new world while responding to the diverse literacy needs and capabilities of your students and, ultimately, to answer Dave's question at the beginning of this chapter: how you can help *all* students to become better content area readers, writers, and learners.

Special Projects

1. What are the new demands for learning in this technological age? Do a web search about some of the issues mentioned in this chapter. Record the skills and tools you use while conducting this search, such as locating information, analyzing and evaluating, synthesizing, and communicating, as well as the use of tools such as search engines, websites, and links. Which of these skills and tools would you expect to teach your students? Describe some ways in which you will teach them.

2. No Child Left Behind is a research-driven reform movement. No Child Left Behind is based on *Preventing Reading Difficulties in Young Children* (Snow et al., 1998) and the *National Reading Panel Report* (National Reading Panel, 2000), two blue-ribbon panel research reports. Later reports on adolescent literacy have helped to expand the goals of NCLB into middle and high schools, especially *Reading Next: A Vision for Action and Research in Middle and High School* (Biancarosa & Snow, 2004). These reports can be found in their entirety on the web. Review one of these reports and find out what it means for NCLB to be grounded in *scientifically based research*. Describe what these reports say about the role of literacy in reducing the achievement gap. What do these reports say about the characteristics of programs that successfully tackle literacy problems in students of all ages?

3. How is your state doing with the achievement gap? Do a web search for data with respect to test performance and dropout rates in your state. How might difficulties with reading and writing play a role in these data?

4. Write your literacy biography. Start with how you learned to read and write. Describe your experiences in school with reading and writing. What were the challenges and disappointments? What were your successes? How did you overcome any of the challenges you faced? Tell your story up through your college experiences.

5. Look up No Child Left Behind on your state department of education website. How does your state define Adequate Yearly Progress? What programs exist in your state that respond to No Child Left Behind? Which of these programs deal with struggling readers and writers?

6. Has your state filled out a Race to the Top application? Go to your state department of education website and find out. Alternatively, visit the Race to the Top website at the U.S. Department of Education www2.ed.gov/programs/racetothetop/index.html. Report on what some states are doing to reform education in order to participate in the program. What will these reforms mean to your future as a teacher?

7. Identify the tests that are used to determine Adequate Yearly Progress in your state. Gather some sample test items from these tests. In what ways are reading and writing skills required to perform well on these tests?

8. Interview a friend or relative about his or her experiences with literacy. How did they learn to read and write? What were this person's experiences with literacy like in school? How does the person use reading and writing at work?

9. Gather information about programs in local schools or in the community for adolescents who struggle with reading and writing. Conduct a web search or interview some local teachers or administrators. What evidence can you find that these programs are based on research? How are these programs designed to have an impact?

Suggested Readings

Allington, R. (2005). *What really matters for struggling readers: Designing research-based programs*. New York: Longman.

Conley, M., & Hinchman, K. (2004). No child left behind: What it means for adolescent literacy and what we can do about it. *Journal of Adolescent and Adult Literacy, 48*(1), 42–51.

Leu, D., Zawilinski, J., Castek, J, Banerjee, M., Housand, B., Liu, Y., & O'Niel, M. (2007). What is new about the new literacies of online reading comprehension? In A. Berger, L. Rush, & J. Eakle (Eds.), *Secondary school reading and writing: What research reveals for classroom practice*. Chicago, IL: National Council of Teachers of English.

Morrell, E. (2004). *Linking literacy and popular culture*. Norwood, MA: Christopher Gordon.

Rasinski, T., Padak, N., McKeon, C., Wilfong, L., Friedauer, J., & Heim, P. (2005). Is reading fluency a key to successful high school reading? *Journal of Adolescent and Adult Literacy, 49*(1), 22–28.

U.S. Department of Education. (2009). *The nation's report card: Reading 2009*. Washington, DC: National Center for Education Statistics. Download at: http://nces.ed.gov/pubsearch/pubsinfo.asp?pubid=2010458

U.S. Department of Education. (2010). Race to the Top Program Description. Washington, D.C: U.S. Department of Education, Office of Elementary and Secondary Education. www2.ed.gov/programs/racetothetop/index.html

Go to Topic 3: Motivation, Topic 9: Integrating Technology, and Topic 10: Struggling Readers in the MyEducationLab (www.myeducationlab.com) for your course, where you can:

- Find learning outcomes for Topic 3: Motivation, Topic 9: Integrating Technology, and Topic 10: Struggling Readers along with the national standards that connect to these outcomes.

- Complete Assignments and Activities that can help you more deeply understand the chapter content.

- Apply and practice your understanding of the core teaching skills identified in the chapter with the Building Teaching Skills and Dispositions learning units.

- Examine challenging situations and cases presented in the IRIS Center Resources.

Go to the Topic A+RISE in the MyEducationLab (www.myeducationlab.com) for your course. A+RISE® Standards2Strategy™ is an innovative and interactive online resource that offers new teachers in grades K-12 just in time, research-based instructional strategies that:

- Meet the linguistic needs of ELLs as they learn content

- Differentiate instruction for all grades and abilities

- Offer reading and writing techniques, cooperative learning, use of linguistic and nonlinguistic representations, scaffolding, teacher modeling, higher order thinking, and alternative classroom ELL assessment

- Provide support to help teachers be effective through the integration of listening, speaking, reading, and writing along with the content curriculum

- Improve student achievement

- Are aligned to Common Core Elementary Language Arts standards (for the literacy strategies) and to English language proficiency standards in WIDA, Texas, California, and Florida.

2 Adolescent Literacy, Diversity, and Teaching Today's Learners

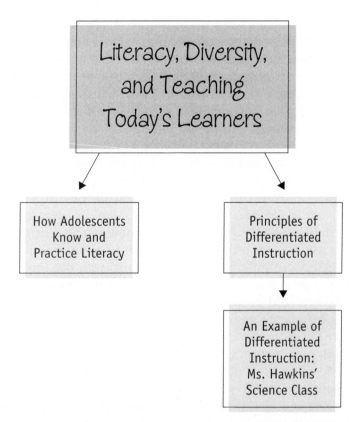

Adolescence has been depicted in a variety of ways. For example, some people see adolescence as a time when individuals reject everything adults say and do. Another view is that adolescence is a time of becoming, where adolescents seek out an identity and a place for themselves for now and later in life. Still others observe that adolescence is a time of constant change as adolescents interact with the world around them. Yet another view is that adolescence is very much a social and cultural phenomenon, with adolescents shifting and shaping their identities and actions as they move between home and neighborhood, work and school, peer group and popular culture (Moje, 2002).

All of these statements may be true at some point or another in the life of an adolescent. Take a moment to recall what adolescence was like for you. Most people remember adolescence as a time of reaching out, pushing forward, and pushing away while searching to define oneself. This chapter was originally intended to be about adolescent literacy. However, it would be more accurate to say that this chapter is about adolescents and their **multiple literacies**, since adolescents engage in many different kinds of literacy in every phase and circumstance (Gee, 2003).

Observe a group of adolescents in conversation, in person, or online, and you may very quickly learn that their reading and writing traverses many different worlds, from books and music to the Internet, television, and video games. Some of the ways in which adolescents are literate in these activities are comparable to literacy in school-based activities; others are very different.

These days, adolescents write volumes about themselves in online environments such as Myspace (www.myspace.com) and Facebook (www.facebook.com). Many adolescents are creating their own websites on places like Ning (www.ning.com) and Wetpaint (www.wetpaint.com). The place to explore identity while make social connections has moved online. Some of this writing makes it into the classroom—as responses to assignments, for example. However, not all of the written or digital expressions from the Internet will surface or ever be acknowledged in the classroom. These days, adolescents can be involved in entire universes of literacy outside the classroom. These literate activities could be a starting point for lessons if teachers were aware of them and adolescents felt safe and encouraged to share them (Moje & Tysvaer, 2010).

Adolescents are not identical in their literate practices. Some adolescents are skillful at moving from situation to situation, for example, from content area to content area, communicating and learning in a variety of ways. Some define themselves mostly through interactions with peers in school and in the community, engaging themselves in many different kinds of oral language while avoiding reading and writing. Some adolescents struggle with the kinds of literacy that are valued at school. Some prefer digital worlds, engaging themselves skillfully in electronic communication while tuning out school.

Diversity among adolescents and their literate practices poses an enduring dilemma for teachers: how to incorporate and build on adolescents' multiple and diverse literacies. Teaching today's learners requires varying instruction according to adolescents' varying literate practices. The notion of devising and adapting instruction according to students' strengths and needs is a recurring theme throughout this book. This chapter describes the diverse and multiple literacies adolescents bring to the classroom and introduces instruction designed to help today's adolescents expand their worlds of literacy.

How Adolescents Know and Practice Literacy

The past several decades of research have produced entirely new understandings about adolescents' ways of knowing and practicing literacy. Figure 2.1 depicts a research-based model of adolescent literacy (Moje et al., 2004). Consider this picture of adolescents and their literacies as you read the following discussion.

Adolescent Identity

Identity consists of preferences, styles of learning, and things we like and dislike. Identity includes ways of talking, believing, valuing, and even learning (Gee, 1996). Adolescence is the time for individuals to build a personal identity (Sadowski, 2003). Can you recall any groups that were important to establishing your own adolescent identity? What were some of the labels you encountered as other people attempted to characterize your own identity? How did your identity influence your choices about reading and writing? About participating at school? Consider these questions as

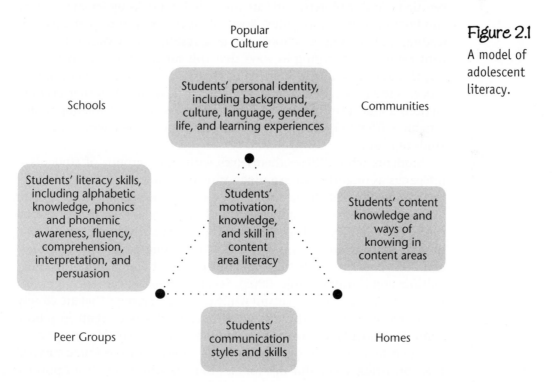

Figure 2.1

A model of adolescent literacy.

you read about the factors that influence adolescent identity and ways in which identity shapes adolescent literacy.

Not surprisingly, adolescents construct identity largely through social relationships. This is particularly true for groups of adolescents—athletes, band students, gangstas, geeks, goths, and computer nerds. Adolescent identity can also be the result of an individual's connections with a language or cultural group, such as Latinos, immigrants from eastern Africa, or other groups consisting of English language learners. Parents, teachers, and others apply labels to adolescents—average students, honors students, students in special education, and English language learners—that can also influence and adolescent's identity.

There are numerous examples in which personal identity and related literate practices conflict with school-based literacy. Gender-based practices and stereotypes can be sources of alienation and may lead to opting out of the kinds of literacy that are valued at school. Adolescent boys and girls have very different reading and writing habits and preferences (Brozo, 2002; Pipher, 1994). Adolescent boys tend to not read very much, preferring to watch television or play video games. Girls read more than boys do. Boys are interested in nonfiction and informational books written specifically for them, such as real-life accounts of athletes, heroes, adventurers, and explorers. Girls are interested in books by female authors and books about relationships. Boys might choose not to participate in reading and writing at school and, as a result, fail to gain experience with reading and writing in ways that will support them as they progress through middle and high school. Girls, on the other hand, might suppress their own literacy achievement, particularly when they become anxious about relationships with boys (Finders, 1997). Girls might also turn away from informational books because of their preferences for other kinds of reading.

Students who affiliate themselves with some groups of students—the gangstas or goths, for example—sometimes adopt the belief that being literate or street smart outside of school far outweighs being literate in school. Students who underperform in reading and writing might be those who identify with gangs. Ironically, these students often engage in very sophisticated forms of literacy, including gang writings, rules, and dress codes, though they remain indifferent about school reading, writing, and learning (Moje, 2002). Second language learners might feel more comfortable and successful while they are in groups that are closely associated with their ethnic identity outside of school than in school contexts. Students who come from families that are experiencing poverty are often more focused on their family's struggle for economic survival than on being successful in school. Students who come from poverty often experience tension in their family relationships and a fear of leaving their families behind through educational success (Payne, 2001).

Students who have been labeled by the school system as struggling—another kind of affiliation—can assume that their levels of literacy are insufficient to warrant much, if any, effort. In each of these cases, ways in which adolescents construct personal identity can lead to low or negative expectations about literacy and learning in school. Many adolescents feel that teachers and schools just do not care about them, so they never learn to value school-based

▲ Your students' personal identities are often very culturally based. These identities can be incorporated into the classroom in some way to enrich learning for everyone.

literacy practices. An important question is: How can teachers help all students develop a personal identity that is more closely associated with literacy and success at school?

Teachers need to learn as much as possible about adolescents' personal identities. Knowing a great deal about students and their personal identities can help teachers to make personal connections while inviting students into school-based literacy and practice. Personal identities are accompanied by many different kinds of literacy. Computer nerds might be experts with technology, gangsta students might be accomplished street poets, goths might be experts on punk music. Culturally based personal identities may be accompanied by heroes and role models who have made contributions in various content areas. For example, many geometric principles come from Arabic-speaking cultures as well as Greek mathematicians. The Latino culture provides many outstanding writers. African and Asian cultures are represented by many interesting artists and writers. Tapping into personal and cultural affiliations like these can be an effective way to motivate students and provide a foundation expanding opportunities with literacy.

When designing a unit of study on the Internet or one that requires use of the Internet, for example, engage the computer experts in your class in sharing their literate experiences and helping other students. When preparing students for observations about the world around them in science, ask students to share their own observations in text, digital, visual, or musical form. The greater the range of possible options for research and sharing, the more likely it is that students will be able and willing to use a literacy related to their personal identity to participate in school based literate activities. The How to Plan feature demonstrates one way in which a social studies teacher incorporated students' cultural identities into her work with a curriculum standard about diversity in cultural heritage.

Can teachers really affect an adolescent's personal identity and expand an adolescent's range of literacy options? Figure 2.1 illustrates that there are many influences on an adolescent's identity. Still, there are many opportunities to build literacy and learning in a content area, once teachers understand adolescents' personal identities and how to use that understanding to involve students in meaningful ways.

How ... for Building on Students' Personal Identities
TO PLAN

Suppose a teacher wanted to build upon students' cultural identities? Here is one teacher's approach with the Michigan Curriculum Standard from Social Studies: *Students will gain knowledge about the past to construct meaningful understandings of our diverse cultural heritage.*

The teacher started her lesson planning by thinking about the cultural backgrounds of her students. Puerto Ricans, Italian Americans, and African Americans were the largest groups. Next, she ran some test Google searches using terms such as "cultural heritage," "music," "art," "literature," and "inventions" along with descriptors such as + Italian, + Puerto Rico (or Puerto Rican), and + African American. She found the following websites:

The Cuatro Project Website
www.cuatro-pr.org/Home/Eng/english.htm

The Leonardo Museum
www.leonet.it/comuni/vinci

African American Art on the Internet
www.liu.edu/cwis/cwp/library/
aavawww.htm

In class, students were given the task of investigating their cultural heritage on one of the listed websites and additional websites of their choosing. They were asked to choose two aspects (artists, musicians, inventors, artwork, or inventions) of cultural heritage from each website for further research. For example, students who chose to investigate their Puerto Rican heritage decided to compare the older and the younger cuatristas (cuatro players). Next, students were asked to research and describe the connections of the artists or inventors with society (popularity among people of different ages, relationships with other arts such as painting, dancing, and performing). Students took notes about major artists and inventors, their backgrounds, and their major works or accomplishments. Students downloaded pictures for use in their final reports, which consisted of (1) an individual report on a favorite artist, inventor, or performer and (2) a group PowerPoint presentation. Students were asked to include their personal reflections on how the artist

Adolescents' Literacy Skills

It is extremely important to resist making sweeping generalizations about students' literacy skills. As was discussed in Chapter 1, there are many ways in which literacy skills are shaped for individual students, including speech and language development, different kinds of knowledge and experience with reading and writing, differences in language, family and cultural knowledge, poverty, motivation, and effective versus sometimes mismatched instruction. Read the Research Brief to gain an idea for what these factors might look like in the average classroom.

or inventor relates to their own interests. They were also asked what they would ask if they could travel to meet and talk with an individual artist or inventor.

The group investigating the Puerto Rican heritage compared Ladislao Martinez, a traditional cuatro player, with Alvin Medina, a modern cuatro player specializing in cuatro renditions of classical music. They compared the two players, using sound clips downloaded from the cuatro project website, and described differences in the cultures and societies of the different time periods for each player. They were particularly interested in comparisons with the cuatro music and modern-day popular music in the United States. They described the efforts of William Cumpiano to reintroduce the cuatro as a national instrument in Puerto Rico.

Working from a website depicting the inventions of Leonardo da Vinci (www.leonet .it/comuni/vinci), the group investigating the Italian American heritage demonstrated

how many modern machines actually started within da Vinci's drawings and artwork. They created an imaginary dialogue with da Vinci and presented a story about a society without da Vinci's inventions.

The group exploring the African American heritage focused on drums and drum performances from different regions of Africa. Using downloaded music clips, the students demonstrated differences in drums and rhythms from eastern, western, and southern Africa. They combined these sounds with images from African dance. Finally, they showed how some African drumbeats are still in use in modern African American music.

Following the example of this teacher and her class, can you think of ways to build from students' personal identities—cultural backgrounds, personal affiliations and interests, and role models—to teach an idea in your content area?

Research Brief

Students in an "Average" Classroom

Based on national statistics, there are twenty-four students in this class. Of the students in this class, nine are below basic in their reading ability, eight are average or basic readers, five are pretty good readers, and two are advanced readers. The females in the room are reading just a bit better than the males. In this classroom representing national averages, four students qualify for free and reduced lunch. Students who come to school hungry are reading well below the reading levels of their classmates. Two of these students are English language learners. Three of these students are struggling as students with special needs or learning difficulties. Percentages of students living in poverty who are English language learners or experiencing learning difficulties can be as high as 50 percent, or twelve students, in the data from across the country.

Source: National Center for Educational Statistics: **www.nces.ed.gov.**

Recall from Chapter 1 that students need foundational literacy skills, consisting of the knowledge and practice that are basic to reading and writing, such as knowing the alphabet; understanding how letters, words, and sounds go together through phonics and phonemic awareness; fluency; and comprehension. Adolescents require additional skills in content area literacy—reading, writing, listening, speaking, and viewing—to learn in English, mathematics, science, social studies, the arts, and physical education. Adolescents can be literate in many out-of-school ways too—with computers and video games (Gee, 2003), for example, and with popular media and culture (Alvermann & Hagood, 2000; Alvermann et al., 1999).

Adolescents can differ considerably in their comfort and success with literacy. Some struggle with foundational literacies; some are proficient in school-based literacies, including foundational and content area literacy; and some are more or less prepared to deal with the different challenges of using literacy in each content area. Teachers are the important mediators between adolescents, their literacies, and the demands of each content area. Assessment, the topic of Chapter 4, provides critical information about the literacies adolescents bring with them for teachers to support students in responding to the literacy challenges of each content area.

Diversity in Literacy among Students with Special Needs. There is often great variation in literacy among adolescents with special needs, especially with respect to what they are able to achieve academically, socially, and emotionally. Students who experience learning difficulties can reflect an entire range of talents as well as needs:

▶ There are adolescents who have very high IQ scores, whom some would call "gifted" students on the basis of their intelligence. Some of these students have well-honed social and leadership skills but nonetheless read and write many grades below level. Some of these students may experience dyslexia and are often poor spellers and do not comprehend what they read very well (Lyon et al., 2003). However, these problems do not keep many of these students from becoming leaders, popular with their peers, or successful athletes.

▶ Some adolescents with special needs have severe problems with language processing—speaking, reading, writing, and listening. They take so long to deal with information from language that they appear to be extremely slow learners. For these students, not only is their academic progress hindered, but they also experience difficulty in interacting socially (Leonard, 1998).

▶ Some adolescents experience emotional or behavioral disorders. Because of high proportions of inappropriate behavior compared with positive behaviors, they may be aggressive and disruptive, socially isolated, and/or behind academically (Landrum et al., 2003). Not all students with emotional or behavioral disorders experience problems with learning. Some are extremely gifted in reading and writing, but their emotional or behavioral disorders make it difficult for them to make friends (Mayer et al., 2001). Students with emotional impairments are not necessarily socially isolated. Some students suffer emotional impairments only in high-stress situations, such as classrooms, but are perfectly fine with friends outside school.

Diversity in Literacy among English Language Learners. Learning a new language while learning in a content area presents very complicated challenges. It is not as simple as the students just learning the correct names for things, the grammar, and the spellings. Words and meanings change from situation to situation. English language learners possess many different profiles with respect to their literacy skills and readiness to learn in each content area:

▶ Some adolescents arrive with literacy skills in their primary language sufficient to propel them quickly into learning in English. Students who have received a high-quality education in their primary language in their country of origin are often in a better position to learn

Click on A+RISE – WIDA ELP Standard Strategy in the MyEducationLab (www.myeducationlab .com) for your course. Next, select the Strategy Card Index tab, scroll to Language and Content for Grades 6–12 and select the LSRW strategy.

English than are students who come from more disadvantaged backgrounds (Krashen, 1996).

▶ Some adolescents arrive with a completely different background in oral language, different writing systems, and different concepts of sound-symbol relationships. There are students who represent every conceivable variation. Some communicate well orally and do not comprehend their reading in English very well; others read and speak well but cannot write well; and still others read and speak English reasonably well but are encountering the concepts in your content area for the first time (Ovando et al., 2003).

Teachers should not be surprised if some students appear with an abundance of literacy skills sufficient to support learning in a content area while others appear without many or only very limited literacy skills. Of course, there are many different students within this continuum, some of whom are highly literate in ways that are not necessarily valued at school—popular music and Internet interests, for example—yet they choose not to participate in literate activities while at school. There are other students who are proficient with literacy in some content areas and struggle in others. Later in this chapter, the discussion will turn to how to adapt teaching to this potentially wide array of needs in today's classrooms.

Adolescents' Content Knowledge and Ways of Knowing in a Content Area

There are many ways for adolescents to "know" in a content area. These include their knowledge about the content, knowledge gained from everyday experience, knowledge from popular culture, and ways of knowing in a content area. There are also many ways of "knowing" in a content area.

"Knowing" Content. Recent research in the various content areas has produced new understandings about what it means to know in a content area. Research on mathematics, literacy, and learning, for example, emphasizes knowing significant mathematical ideas and practicing high levels of mathematical reasoning (Cobb, 2004). Likewise, science educators stress knowing the "Big Ideas" in science but, perhaps more importantly, the ways of knowing—inquiry, argument, and criticism—that are central to knowing science (Yore et al., 2004). In the arts, teachers and researchers consider art and ways of knowing art as a process of developing personal identity, engaging in play, or a form of problem solving (Heath, 2004). History education is often concerned with knowing history as study of complex historical incidents and a place for students to find their own place in the study of history (Vansledright, 2004).

In many ways, educators in the content areas have turned away from traditional notions of what it means to know—just the facts, please— toward views that stress knowing important content and the ways of exploring, understanding, and inquiring about the world. Language and literacy are the natural foundation for these activities—reading, writing, speaking, listening, and viewing—and integrating these activities into pathways for knowing content.

Funds of Knowledge. Adolescents bring many different kinds of knowledge with them just from living rich lives with their families and in the community. Researchers have coined the term **funds of knowledge** to reflect the knowledge that students bring from their everyday life experiences (Moll, 1992a, 1992b). The main lesson from this research is that families often have surprising networks of knowledge and experiences— funds of knowledge—that can be useful for involving students in content area learning, particularly students from diverse cultures and with diverse languages. For example, many families engage in a wide variety of mathematical activities by maintaining a household budget. Many families experience science through gardening and household cleaning and repair. Literature, history, and various kinds of communication are often wrapped up in religious activity. The term *funds of knowledge* is very carefully chosen to reflect the belief that many students come to school with assets based on these and other family experiences. Unfortunately, these assets are often hidden, ignored by teachers, or—worse—treated as deficits. Furthermore, just as families and communities are diverse, the funds of knowledge that students bring to class are equally diverse.

Knowledge from Popular Culture. Another important source of what adolescents know and believe concerns popular culture. Music, movies, television, and the news media exert a powerful influence on adolescents. Popular culture provides an array of productive and healthy as well as violent and degrading images and messages. Some notable negative examples include Barbie dolls spouting, "Math is hard!," that liking school is for geeks, that science and math are certainly not for girls, or that anyone can be a well-paid musician or athlete with very little preparation. But there are also many positive examples in the form of role models for a healthy and active lifestyle, music, and the arts. As in the case of funds of knowledge from families and the community, teachers should build on adolescents' knowledge about popular culture and its messages. Do not make the mistake of assuming what students know and appreciate, however. Students' preferences are always changing. So too does popular culture. Still,

conceptions based on popular culture can be a fertile starting point for any content area lesson by making connections with what students have experienced. You will read many examples for how to do this in Chapter 10, "Guiding Students' Critical Literacy."

Think about how popular culture influenced your own experiences as an adolescent and, no doubt, continues to influence you. What are some connections that you can see between popular culture and teaching in your content area? Action Research presents one way of exploring and building upon students' knowledge of and experience with popular culture.

▲ Your students bring to your classroom funds of knowledge that often can be incorporated into your instruction. For example, to be able to work effectively with hand tools, these students likely have some understanding of geometry and even engineering.

Adolescents' Knowledge about How to Learn. It is also important to understand what adolescents know about how to learn in a content area. Each content area has its own ways of organizing and representing knowledge, its own language, its own ways of knowing, and different ways in which students come to understand and apply what they know. Some students may have picked up some particularly ineffective ways to learn in a content area, relying on memorized facts or formulas, for example, when they really need to know how to apply their knowledge in more creative ways.

Struggling students especially are not sensitive to different ways of knowing in the content areas. They often apply the same ineffective approach, such as rereading without any purpose, across all content areas. Students who are knowledgeable and understand various ways of knowing are well prepared for later study and to engage in careers that are grounded in the content areas. This need is particularly evident with the high expectations found in curriculum standards and on high-stakes content area tests. Consider some ways in which you "know" in your content area. Make a list of the ways that you have learned how to learn in your content area. What are some ideas or techniques that you could share with your students that have worked for you?

Adolescents' Communication Styles and Skills

Because of family and school experiences, some adolescents are effective with the communication styles and skills that are valued at school—practices such as taking turns, or waiting for directions before starting an activity (Heath, 1983, 1991). Some adolescents communicate in ways that are different from school communication. Knowing about these differences makes it possible for teachers to find ways to involve all students in content area lessons.

Culturally Based Communication Styles. The communicative styles of many cultures, including those of African American, Latino, and immigrant students, can be different from what is recognized or valued

Connecting Standards and Assessment

The Language of State Standards and State Tests

A frequent barrier for teachers and students concerns the language of state standards and state tests. Federal policies under No Child Left Behind require students to perform well with regard to state standards as measured by state tests. Unfortunately, many standards and tests are replete with educational jargon and specialized content area vocabulary. Students do poorly when standards and assessments contain language that is unfamiliar to them.

What are some possible solutions? Translating standards into plain language is a start. Consider an audience of students and their parents. How could a teacher respond appropriately to the question: What are the new goals for teaching in your content area? A teacher's response should be understandable to a layperson or student. For the language of tests, teachers can teach important testing vocabulary such as *describe, explain,* and *support.*

Another solution is to select and commit to a few standards at a time. Some standards documents contain one hundred or more individual standards and/or benchmarks. Teachers who try to teach them all risk confusing students or covering content superficially. Another approach is to seek out standards that apply across content areas. Some multidisciplinary teaching teams have applied this approach successfully with curriculum units devoted to real-world issues such as environmentalism, the global marketplace, and musical traditions. These teams emphasize such skills as learning how to gather appropriate information, analyzing issues, organizing and communicating information, and independent learning, all embedded in various ways within curriculum standards.

Finally, it is important to prioritize teaching and learning according to a small set of comprehensible standards and state assessment goals. Teaching and learning activities need to be consistent with standards and assessment goals if students are to be successful.

▶ Read more about these ideas in Chapter 3, "Clarifying and Communicating about Standards," in Conley's (2005) *Connecting Standards and Assessment through Literacy*, published by Pearson Education.

Researching and Responding to Adolescents and the Popular Media

A frequent struggle for most teachers throughout their careers is to keep in touch with adolescents' personal identities, including what adolescents know and care about. A reason this is important is so that teachers can facilitate connections between students and reading and writing in a content area. Of course, adolescence is a time of ongoing change and exploration. So how can teachers keep up with adolescents, their literacies, and their interests?

One way to keep up is to explore popular culture and its relationship with and impact upon adolescents. Popular culture, particularly television, is most often aimed at adolescents and young adults. Recent studies have found that as many as two-thirds of young people from age 8 to 18 years old have a television set in their bedrooms, many of which are connected to cable television, VCRs, and DVD players (Roberts, 2000). Television programmers attempt to reach the greatest number of adolescents by developing categories: age, race, gender, interests, and favorite activities. By presenting a variety of programs, the programmers hope to appeal to the full range of adolescent interests. Another assumption is that this approach to programming will increase chances that adolescent viewers will choose programs about people, situations, and dilemmas similar to their own.

Adolescent viewing preferences do divide along age, racial, and gender lines. Older adolescents are less interested in cartoons than are younger adolescents. Adolescents gravitate toward television characters who look like themselves and have lifestyles they admire. For instance, Black adolescents express strong preferences for Black television programming and characters. Females rate music, quiz and talk shows, and soap operas higher than do males, who prefer sports, movies, and science/technology programs (Roe, 1998).

at school. Differences often arise from different ways of participating in communication (Gay, 2000). Mainstream students, accustomed to school-like communication at home, complete with bedtime stories and teacher-like questions and students' responses, may find it relatively easy to understand and use the communication styles that are valued at school (Heath, 1991). Because of experiences with communication at home and in the community, some students might choose to converse with a teacher at the exact same time that the teacher is asking a question (Ladson-Billings, 1994). Sometimes, teachers view this behavior as disruptive, where as the student might view it as completely acceptable conversation. English language learners face the dual challenge of learning how to communicate at school while learning everything else (Short & Echevarria, 2005). Many students who communicate in

Some researchers have criticized this approach because it divides adolescents into discrete categories without taking into account individual adolescents and their preferences (Brown & Pardun, 2004). So what about individual adolescent preferences toward television? Obtain a copy of your local television viewing guide. Then select and copy a few samples of after-school and evening listings—for a Monday, Tuesday, and/or Wednesday, for example. Interview several adolescents about their viewing preferences. These could be relatives, neighbors, or, if you are teaching, your students. Ask them to circle their favorite television shows and explain why they like them. Is it the stories? The characters? The actors? Are reality, music, or sports shows better than shows based on stories? What appeals to them and why?

Describe the patterns in your data. What conclusions can be drawn? How do the findings from your investigation compare with previous research? Describe some ways to build on these findings to create reading and writing opportunities in your content area.

For example, a mathematics teacher learned that her students really liked the show *NUMB3RS*. She and her students watched an episode of the show and discussed ways in which mathematics was employed to solve crimes. Students then wrote mini-episodes of their own television shows, using the mathematical ideas from their class. A biology teacher demonstrated how the show *CSI* uses principles of cell biology to solve crimes. Students responded by writing about crime solving with clues from biological science. An English teacher focused on storytelling by having her students describe plot sequences from *Everybody Hates Chris*. How can you take advantage of your students' media knowledge and experiences?

ways that are different from school communication can feel isolated or even ignored. What they really need is appreciation and support. Listen carefully for the communication styles of your students. Chapter 12, "Building Literacy and Community from Inside and Outside the Classroom," addresses how to help all students to feel a sense of belonging no matter how they communicate.

Communication in Content Areas. Every content area has unique communication requirements, including using vocabulary, representing concepts and ideas in certain ways, and expressing thinking. To be able to participate in each content area, including developing and applying knowledge, adolescents need to acquire skills for communicating in each content area (Savignon, 2005). Students whose communicative styles are more closely aligned with school communication are not necessarily well prepared for communication in every content area. Students who have learned to sit passively, for example, waiting for teachers to produce answers for them, will not automatically understand how to engage in scientific inquiry or relate literature to their own lives. Sharing ways in which you have learned to communicate in a content area is one of the many ways to help students learn how to communicate more effectively.

Inviting Communication. Classrooms that invite adolescent participation in multiple ways increase the potential for teachers to learn about their students' communication styles and skills and, as a result, for teachers to invite communication. For instance, by varying classroom participation from whole class to small group and student pairings, teachers can observe students practicing different kinds of communication. Through support, explanations, modeling, and role-playing, students can improve their communication skills in every content area. A key principle in this effort needs to be respect for the communication styles and skills students bring with them as well as taking advantage of opportunities to teach students how to communicate well.

Make a list of some ways in which you and others communicate uniquely in your content area. What are some ways to show students how to communicate effectively? Examples for how to build students' communication capabilities in every content area are presented throughout this text.

Adolescents' Motivation, Knowledge, and Skill in Content Area Literacy

The previous discussion about students' personal identities, their literacy skills, their content knowledge and ways of knowing in content areas, and their communication styles and skills provides many ways of understanding students' motivation, knowledge, and skill in content area literacy. Students who carry strong personal affiliations from peers, family, and the community that are acknowledged in the classroom stand a better chance of being motivated; they understand that who they are and what they care about connect to what they are learning. Students who have a firm foundation in basic literacy skills are in a good position to be able to apply those skills to learning in content areas. Students' success with literacy in content areas, however, is also dependent on having or developing a rich knowledge base in a content area along with many alternatives for ways of knowing in a content area. Finally, students whose communication styles are considered and included tend to be more motivated for developing greater skill and literacy in a content area. How much of your own learning resembles this picture?

Any classroom full of adolescents represents a range of motivation, knowledge, and skill. Consider how the Research Brief on page 40 depicts this continuum for a so-called average classroom. Adolescents vary in their sense of belonging in a classroom, some feeling completely cut off from any appreciation for who they are. Some, having struggled their entire school career with reading and writing, will not even try to learn. Some lack much knowledge or experience in a content area and have few, if any, clues for how to improve their efforts. Still others are hindered when their communication styles are ignored or misunderstood. How much of your own education resembles this picture?

This book is designed to help teachers understand and respond to the diversity of adolescent motivation, knowledge, and skill, ultimately helping all students grow in their content area literacy. Let's start on this journey by examining one research-based example: the teaching and learning practices associated with differentiated instruction.

Differentiated Instruction

Differentiated instruction involves varying instruction according to the diverse needs of adolescents (Tomlinson, 2004). Differentiated instruction is not necessarily new. Teachers have long varied their instructional approach, using different kinds of texts and emphasizing diverse kinds of discussion practices and different groupings (e.g., small group, pairs, individual feedback), for example, according to differences in adolescents' interests, styles of learning, experiences, and life circumstances. Adapting instruction according to individual needs is also an important perspective within content area literacy (Conley, 2007). The principles of differentiated instruction guide many of the ideas that are presented in this book.

Research on differentiated instruction shows that students learn more effectively when teachers vary instruction and materials on the basis of consideration of individual needs rather than using the same approach for all students (Lou et al., 1996; Tomlinson, 2004). Differentiated instruction is particularly effective for students with special needs and English language learners. The Teaching Today's Learners feature on page 50 lists selected research-based guidelines for differentiating instruction for students with special needs (Tomlinson, 2004) and for English language learners (Short & Echevarria, 2005).

Teaching Today's Learners

Differentiating Instruction for Students with Special Needs and for English Language Learners

In many ways, these principles for differentiated instruction are relevant to teaching all students. Select one or several of the following principles of differentiated instruction. Describe some specific ways in which you can incorporate these principles into reading and writing in your content area.

▶ Teachers should know the specific standards for proficient reading and writing in each content area as a guide for teaching, assessment, coaching, and feedback for students. Standards provide a set of reference points for ongoing assessment, teaching decisions, and observations about learning.

▶ Each student should grow from his or her own starting point with respect to what he or she knows and knows how to do.

▶ Teachers should use everything students do and create as a source of data about students, about individuals, and about classroom groups as a whole. Assessment information includes classroom observations, interviews and surveys, evaluation of classroom work, and quizzes and tests.

▶ Teachers should practice ongoing assessment to determine how close or far away students are in relation to academic standards and what needs to be done to help

students grow toward proficiency. Teachers, students, and parents can all work together when everyone understands the goals and what can be done to help students achieve.

▶ Teachers should continually work to develop curriculum that is inviting to adolescents individually and as a group. Making connections between students' worlds and the classroom is the best way to motivate. Strengthening students' background knowledge and vocabulary in a content area is one of the best ways to help students experience success.

▶ Teachers should work to achieve maximum flexibility in teaching to serve the students' many diverse needs and talents. Adolescents appreciate a classroom environment that changes according to their needs.

▶ Teachers should recognize that a sense of community is necessary for maximum growth in literacy. Students gain from a "we are all in this together" approach to learning.

▶ Teachers and students should adopt a growth orientation rather than just a grading orientation. Everyone understands that growth is the goal, everyone grows in different ways and at different rates, and successful growth is acknowledged.

Planning for Differentiated Instruction

To plan instruction for differentiated instruction, consider the following questions:

► How can I relate what students are learning to their personal identities? To personal affiliations? To families and communities? To popular culture?

► How can I build on each student's multiple literacies? What are some areas of student expertise that can be used in teaching?

► What do students already know? What are their funds of knowledge? What can be used from students' knowledge about the content? From everyday experience? From popular culture?

► How can I respect students' informal home language and experiences while connecting with standard English and the school curriculum?

► How can I adapt my curriculum to the particular needs, interests, and learning styles of all students, particularly those with special needs?

► How can I invite communication from and with all students?

► How can I plan to teach students how to learn in my content area?

A social studies teacher who was teaching her students about responsible citizenship, with a particular emphasis on voting, considered these questions. Her students, she observed, were eighth-grade adolescents who cared a great deal about their rights and making choices. Many cared about their community and were particularly distressed when anyone spoke badly about the community or harmed the community in any way. She observed that her students knew about voting for political candidates or community issues only from the perspective of parents and older siblings going to the polls to vote. But this teacher also observed that her students were tremendous fans of reality television shows such as *American Idol,* in which the winners are selected through voting by the television audience. As a result, this social studies teacher chose to start her teaching about voting by asking students about their experiences with voting on television reality shows. Did anyone ever participate? Did they always agree with the results of the voting? The discussion about reality television shows became the basis for students to consider voting in the political sense on candidates and issues that affected their community. Planning the lesson this way—using principles of differentiated instruction—made it possible for all students to participate and to share their individual experiences, knowledge, and perspectives.

Teaching with Differentiated Instruction

Three particularly significant principles—a focused approach to the content, making clear but flexible teaching decisions, and learning based on varied expectations for student performance—are essential for teaching with differentiated instruction.

A Focused Approach to the Content. Differentiated instruction requires a clear focus on goals for learning content. Rather than emphasizing minute facts and details, differentiated content teaching involves emphasizing broad-based concepts and principles, referred to as **Big Ideas**. Big Ideas are principles such as the following:

▶ Grasping the significance of important themes in literature

▶ Using estimation in problem solving and computation

▶ Conveying feelings through musical expression

▶ Understanding connections between language and culture in a foreign language

▶ Demonstrating responsible personal and social relationships during physical activity

These ideas represent clear goals for teaching and learning the content of a lesson or unit of study. Teachers who are explicit about goals and use them to make decisions about teaching and learning provide greater opportunity for understanding the content than do teachers who focus on minutiae or are vague or ambiguous (Deshler et al., 2001). Chapter 3 depicts ways to develop Big Ideas for instruction.

A focused approach to the content also involves the varied use of many different kinds of texts, including textbooks, trade books, magazines, multimedia, digital texts, and the Internet, all in service of learning the Big Ideas. The principle here is that the greater the variation in texts, the more access and potential motivation students will have for learning. Chapter 6 addresses how to make responsible decisions about including and using many different kinds of texts.

Clear but Flexible Decisions about Teaching. Think back to your school experiences. Were you seated in rows listening to a teacher? This vision of teaching is in direct opposition to what works for the greatest range of learners. Differentiated instruction involves **flexible grouping**. Although teachers may still conduct whole-class introductory discussions about Big Ideas, the principle behind flexible grouping is to vary groupings to include whole class, small groups, pairs, and individual work for completing assigned tasks.

The value of this approach is to maximize students' opportunities for reading, writing, speaking, and listening within various grouping formats. Consider, for example, a whole-class lecture: The teacher is speaking while students merely listen or answer questions from time to time.

Now consider the pattern of communication within small groups: Students are engaged in speaking and listening. With pairs, students can help one another without competing for attention as they might in whole-class or small-group settings. Individual seatwork, guided by the teacher, offers yet another set of opportunities.

Decisions about flexible grouping depend on the task at hand and the teacher's assessment of which groupings are desirable. For example, some groupings consist of students who have different kinds of expertise that, combined, provide for greater learning. Some groupings are devised on the basis of mutual need, for example, an English language learner who has expertise about the content, such as culture and customs in a particular part of the world, and a native English speaker who needs to learn the content. Ways for teaching students how to learn in the context of flexible groupings are presented throughout this book.

Varied Expectations about Assessment and Learning. Differentiated learning requires ongoing assessment. Teachers need to find out early on in the planning process what students know, care about, and can do with regard to the content. However, assessment does not end there. Teachers need to continuously assess students' performance through ongoing assessment. **Ongoing assessment**, as the name implies, happens all the time using such varied techniques as classroom observation, interviews, reading and writing tasks, and many kinds of informal (journaling, quick writes, and quick summaries) as well as formal (quizzes and paper-and-pencil tests) assessments. Through ongoing assessment, teachers can develop an array of choices about the best ways to teach and for students to learn, how students are performing, and when students have learned. Chapter 6 is about ongoing assessment.

▲ Working with small groups of students allows you to learn their communication styles, to get a feel for their individual skills and needs, and to give them the individualized attention they may need.

Another important principle within differentiated instruction, as well as good assessment, is that students should be intimately involved in their own assessment (Stiggins, 2005; Tomlinson, 2004). Teachers are responsible for creating assignments that are interesting, engaging, and challenging for students. Students are more likely to be successful in doing those assignments if they understand what it will take, in terms of knowledge, effort, and skill, to do them well.

Finally, teachers need to create varied expectations for how students can demonstrate success. Well-designed assignments allow varied ways for students to respond—through writing, discussion, conversation, artwork, and other kinds of projects. These alternatives necessarily require different kinds of thinking about evaluation, scoring, and grading. The more varied the assignments, involving reading, writing, speaking, listening, viewing, and drawing, for example, the more varied are opportunities for student response. As a result, a wider range of students will be able to express their understanding.

An Example of Differentiated Instruction: Ms. Hawkins' Science Class

As you read this classroom example, consider how this teacher uses principles of differentiated instruction to address the needs of all of her students. Ms. Hawkins teaches ninth-grade science in a changing suburban school in Florida. Through schools of choice options in recent years, a number of students with special needs have moved into the middle school in which she works. In addition, the school has increased in the number of English language learners, mostly children of Cuban immigrants. Ms. Hawkins learned about differentiated instruction in a graduate school course about content area literacy.

Developing a Content Focus. Ms. Hawkins understands that one of her most important tasks is to identify Big Ideas. Her science teacher colleagues have already identified a Big Idea for the first marking period from the Florida curriculum standards: that separate parts of the body communicate with each other using electrical and/or chemical signals. This Big Idea fits into a larger idea for the entire semester of having students understand human body systems. A related goal, set by Ms. Hawkins and her colleagues, is to give students opportunities to read and write original scientific studies.

Ms. Hawkins decided to focus the content of her next lesson on learning how to comprehend and critique a scientific article about the human sense of taste. She chose the article in Figure 2.2 because it reflects a combination of scientific theory and conjecture and she knows her students are curious about the workings of the human body, including the senses. Using this text, she planned to model ways to engage in scientific thinking and read scientific writing. She selected several other texts for student application and practice.

Assessing Students. Ms. Hawkins actively assesses her students' motivation, knowledge, and skill. An important reading and writing problem

Today's Science Spring 2007 Issue

WHAT'S IN A TASTE?

What is a sense of taste and how does it work in our bodies?

This has been a mystery to scientists. Some people report that a sense of taste comes from different chemicals in the foods we encounter. Some report that it comes from our sense of smell. The reason they think smell is involved is that taste is sometimes disrupted by severe colds accompanied by stuffy noses. Most scientists hypothesize that our sense of taste comes not from the outside world, but from taste buds embedded in our tongues.

According to scientists, the human sense of taste is mediated by groups of cells inside our taste buds. These cells sample oral concentrations of large numbers of small molecules from a variety of outside influences — food and other substances — and report a sensation of taste. This process is called signal transduction, since cells in the taste buds transmit signals to centers in the brainstem.

In most animals, including humans, taste buds are most commonly found on small pegs of epithelium on the tongue called fungiform papillae. Taste buds are too small to see without a microscope, but fungiform papillae are easily observed as white dots on the tongue's surface. Among humans, there can be substantial differences in taste sensitivity. The number of fungiform papillae on

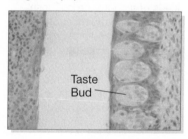

Taste Bud

16

Figure 2.2

A scientific article.

emerged at the heart of Ms. Hawkins' observations and planning: Many of her students have little, if any, experience with—if not downright fear about—reading and writing based on original scientific research articles. Ms. Hawkins understands this from observing her students' reading and writing with science texts earlier in the marking period. Ms. Hawkins conducted interviews with several of her students to find out how they were approaching their texts and related assignments. Many of her students lacked confidence to take risks with scientific ideas. Some of her students skipped over entire sections of text when reading became too difficult for them. Others were puzzled by important charts and graphs.

Figure 2.2
(continued)

the tongue reflects the strength of a person's sense of taste. Roughly one in four people is a "supertaster," someone with an extremely strong sense of taste. Supertasters are several times more sensitive to bitter and other tastes than most other individuals because they have many more fungiform papillae on their tongues. Supertasters inherit their strong sense of taste.

Scientists believe that a person's sense of taste comes directly from excitation of taste receptors in the fungiform papillae. Receptors for a large number of specific substances have been identified that contribute to the perception of taste. There are nearly 10,000 different kinds of receptor cells. These include receptors for such chemicals as sodium, potassium, chloride, glutamate, and adenosine. Despite the apparent complexity of the taste receptor process, only five types of tastes are commonly recognized: salty, sour, sweet, bitter, and umami.

The umami taste is that of monosodium glutamate and has recently been recognized as a unique taste, as it cannot be elicited by any combination of the other four taste types. Glutamate is present in a variety of protein-rich foods and is particularly abundant in aged cheese.

Based on reports from people with colds, scientists believe but have not yet proven that the sense of smell affects the sensation of taste. Scientists also believe that thermal stimulation of the tongue influences a person's sense of taste. In some people, warming the front of the tongue produces a clear sweet sensation, while cooling leads to a salty or sour sensation. More research needs to be done to establish these connections.

17

Some students believed that they needed to meticulously read every word to gain meaning. Many students demonstrated difficulty in knowing how to connect a particular assignment to information in the text.

Though she observed that many students engaged in thinking very similar to scientific inquiry—making observations, forming and testing hunches, examining evidence, and drawing conclusions—few of them connected their thinking in everyday situations to scientific inquiry. Ms. Hawkins considered these observations as she made teaching decisions.

Figure 2.3

Documenting students' ideas about the senses.

Certain—Facts or Theories	Beliefs or Hypotheses	Uncertain—Needs Research

Ears are for hearing
Eyes are for seeing
Tongue is for sense of taste
Skin is for feeling
Nose is for smelling
	Organs send signals to the
	  brain
	The nose is involved with taste
	The senses work together
	Sounds make noise and the
	  ear just hears the sounds
	Eyes need light to see
		Does the brain send
		  signals back (?)
		Food has a taste of its
		  own. The tongue just
		  interprets it.

Teaching Decisions. Ms. Hawkins decided to begin a discussion by asking students about their observations about their senses: seeing, hearing, smelling, feeling, and hearing. How did their senses work? What parts of the body are involved in each sense? Are there signals involved? She listed their observations. Next she asked students to divide their observations into three columns: (1) those they were certain about, (2) those they believed were true but could not yet back up with facts, and (3) those they were uncertain about. The results of their work appear in Figure 2.3.

Ms. Hawkins explained that the class was going to explore the human sense of taste and, in doing so, might answer some of their questions about all of the senses. She asked her students how they might investigate taste. They responded by reporting that they enjoyed television shows on the Discovery Channel and learned some things from television news. Some students said that they enjoyed visiting websites that answered their questions about how the human body works. One student reported that her mother worked as a dental hygienist and that she knows a great deal about the human tongue and people's sense of taste.

Next, Ms. Hawkins asked her students what they know about how scientists might investigate taste. The students responded with ideas such as "set up experiments" and "make observations." Ms. Hawkins introduced the scientific inquiry chart in Figure 2.4. She took some time to explain important vocabulary, such as *hypothesis* (a guess or a hunch), and how scientists use hypotheses to make predictions. She and her students returned to the senses chart and added hypothesis as a term to use for beliefs or hunches.

Ms. Hawkins shared her own experiences as a student learning about science and with scientific inquiry, acknowledging that sometimes

Figure 2.4 A model of scientific inquiry.

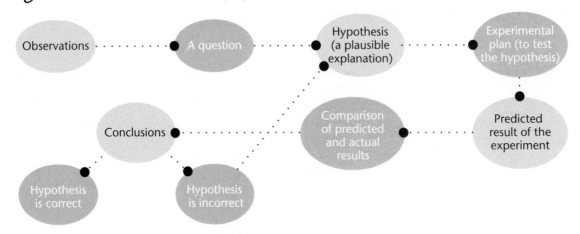

scientific thinking and writing can be very challenging. Ms. Hawkins read the article about human taste to her students. Before she read the article, she asked her students to listen carefully for examples of scientific hypotheses about the sense of taste. As she read the article, Ms. Hawkins demonstrated strategies that she uses regularly to read complicated science texts. These strategies include considering what she already knows about the topic, not worrying that she does not know every word, stopping and asking herself, "Does this make sense?" and thinking about a brief summary at the end of each paragraph or section.

After reading, Ms. Hawkins and her students compared what the article said about the sense of taste with their earlier observations about the senses. They verified some of their earlier observations, including the idea that the tongue is involved with taste. They noted new learning about structures in the tongue responsible for taste. They raised questions about how much scientists know about the interaction of taste and smell.

Ms. Hawkins paired students as partners to look for hypotheses about the sense of taste in other kinds of scientific writing. Student partnerships were based on varied needs and interests. For example, she partnered one student who is a special needs learner with another student because they were both concerned about diseases and the sense of taste. Another partnership was formed on the basis of interests in foods and taste. One of these students is a recently arrived immigrant who speaks mostly Spanish; the other is a second-generation Cuban American with proficient English skills. Ms. Hawkins also made available a wide variety of texts matched to her students' interests, from scientific journals, scientific websites, and reports from news magazines. Ms. Hawkins asked students to list hypotheses that scientists entertained as well as any evidence to support their hypotheses. While students worked, Ms. Hawkins circulated and observed how well her students appeared to understand scientific thinking while working through scientific writing. She would watch for signs of frustration or misconceptions and would guide students when they got stuck.

After discussing findings from their scientific reading and fine-tuning their approach to reading scientific texts, the class listened to an invited guest: the mother of one of the students who works as a dental hygienist. She shared her knowledge about the tongue. She described her experiences with health care for the tongue and how a healthy tongue is responsible for sense of taste. She also described diseases of the tongue and how different diseases inhibit or even destroy the sense of taste. She concluded by sharing practices for keeping tongues and mouths healthy, demonstrating proper tongue cleaning. Ms. Hawkins noted the motivation in her students for this real-world presentation through their questions and attentiveness throughout.

Varied Expectations for Teaching and Learning. Ms. Hawkins assumed that her students would vary with respect to how well they would comprehend scientific thinking and writing. For example, some students might cling to some of the inefficient ways they had approached texts in the past, such as getting bogged down with the vocabulary without keeping track of the meaning. Some students still struggled with what it means to make an observation and a hypothesis. When this happened, Ms. Hawkins reviewed important concepts and demonstrated alternatives in approaching difficult texts, such as reading for the gist and summarizing. To promote multiple ways of communicating about the texts, Ms. Hawkins encouraged students to talk about the texts in their own words, often translating observations and hypotheses into their own words. While doing so, she reminded students that scientists use specialized language to be precise in their observations. In this way, Ms. Hawkins sought to connect students' language to the language of science.

Ms. Hawkins asked her students to make separate lists about what scientists know and what they only believe to be true about the sense of taste. She also asked them to list their own observations, along with a possible experiment to check on one of their own hypotheses. Experiments could be in the form of descriptions, complete with hypotheses and procedures for doing the research. They could also be in the form of lists of steps or even drawings and illustrations of how an experiment could be performed. Ms. Hawkins involved her students in their own assessment by asking how they would know that they had created a reasonably well-planned experiment. Students responded with descriptions of how they would use the scientific inquiry chart to design and explain their experiments. They would know that they had done well if they could relate different parts of their experiment to the components on the scientific inquiry chart.

Throughout this series of activities, which took place over several days, Ms. Hawkins could see the many different ways in which her students comprehended scientific thinking and writing. The walls of her classroom were replete with various examples of students' hypotheses and designs for experiments. Students demonstrated a grasp of the basic concepts of Ms. Hawkins' lesson as evident in the many different ways students expressed their new knowledge and skill with scientific texts. She could tell that some students were still struggling with the ideas in the lesson and would probably need continued assistance with reading and writing. She planned to create more opportunities for these and other students to explore scientific reading and writing, supported by her guidance and feedback.

Summary

Teachers can create many opportunities for student achievement if the diversity of students' personal identities, literacies, everyday knowledge, experiences, and ways of communicating are valued at school. Unfortunately, in many classrooms, the diversity of today's learners is overlooked, ignored, or misunderstood in favor of rote learning from textbooks. The result can be poor motivation, with students alienated from school knowledge, skills, and expectations and showing very little learning. A guiding premise of this book is that the diversity of today's students presents many challenges but also many opportunities. The challenges are that students can be very different in the motivation, knowledge, and skill that they bring to school. The opportunities are to design lessons and units of study that solidly build upon what students know and care about.

Special Projects

1. This chapter introduced the term *multiple literacies*. Describe the multiple literacies that you have in your content area and in life. Think about all of the ways in which you use reading, writing, speaking, and listening in knowledgeable and skillful ways. How did you learn to be literate in so many different ways? What are some ways in which you can help your students gain the same level and diversity of literacies?

2. Find out more about adolescents in your community. What after-school activities are available? How do adolescents in your community spend their free time? What does participation in these activities suggest about these

adolescents' personal identities? About their literacies outside of school and multiple literacies?

3. Download the report, *Adolescent Literacy Development in Out of School Time* at www.carnegie.org/fileadmin/Media/Publications/PDF/tta_Moje.pdf. Report on how you can use some of the ideas from this report to incorporate students' after-school literacy activities into your classroom instruction.

4. Much has recently been written about the differences in literacy preferences between adolescent males and females. Read the following articles and compare what they say about gender differences. Describe how you will incorporate this research into your planning and teaching decisions.

   Cavasos-Kottke, S. (2005). Tuned out but turned on: Boys' (dis)engaged reading in and out of school. *Journal of Adolescent and Adult Literacy, 49*(3), 180–184.

   Guzzetti, B., & Gamboa, M. (2004). Zines for social justice: Adolescent girls writing on their own. *Reading Research Quarterly, 39*(4), 408–437.

5. Observe a teacher teaching in your content area, and, if possible, interview the teacher after the lesson. In what ways does this teacher practice differentiated instruction (even if he or she does not use the label)? For example, how does the teacher focus on the content? Make teaching decisions based on understandings of individual students? Conduct assessment based on an understanding of variations among students?

6. Assessment is sometimes a hotly debated issue when it comes to taking into account the diversity of students. For example, some argue that students should get a good grade when they finally demonstrate knowledge or skill. Others argue that students should get a good grade when they demonstrate growth from where they started. A third view is that both perspectives are important, that students definitely achieve some knowledge and skill but that they also grow from where they started. What are your beliefs? Take a position using information provided in this chapter.

Praxis Practice

Working with Questions for to Prepare for the Praxis Reading across the Curriculum Test

Multiple Choice Questions

1. Which is a most important feature of adolescents' literacy skills?

   a. They are learned in school hierarchically, from phonics to comprehension.

   b. They must be learned in school, especially during the elementary grades.

c. They are shaped by adolescent identity and out of school activities.

    d. Schools are not always well prepared to teach them well.

2. How do students demonstrate understanding in a content area?

    a. Students can recite the facts, concepts, and principles that make up important ideas.

    b. Students can communicate what they know effectively, relating to what they already know.

    c. Students can report on the information they have found in their textbook.

    d. Students can satisfactorily pass their end of unit examination.

3. What is differentiated instruction?

    a. Making up different assignments, including content and questions, for different kinds of students.

    b. Rewriting text information and changing assignments so that all of the students can read and write successfully.

    c. Lowering standards for students who respond to assignments more slowly while focusing on their growth.

    d. Targeting the same content specifically but adapting expectations and instruction in varied ways.

Constructed Response Questions

1. Ms. Jenkins always starts the year by surveying her students about their use of the Internet, including social interaction websites, website preferences, and even if they use blogs or have their own website. Explain Ms. Jenkins's approach and how she is contributing to the literacy development of her students.

2. Mr. Lloyd plans every lesson by first selecting a Big Idea he finds in the curriculum standards for his state and school. Next, he considers ways for selecting and adapting assignments in his social studies classroom for the differences among all of his students. Name and explain what Mr. Lloyd is doing, including the specific steps he needs to take in order to be successful with this approach.

Suggested Readings

Alvermann, D., Moon, J., & Hagood, M. (1999). *Popular culture in the classroom: Teaching and researching critical media literacy*. Newark, DE: International Reading Association.

Cavasos-Kottke, S. (2005). Tuned out but turned on: Boys' (dis)engaged reading in and out of school. *Journal of Adolescent and Adult Literacy, 49*(3), 180–184.

Gay, G. (2000). *Culturally responsive teaching: Theory, research, and practice.* New York: Teachers College Press.

Guzzetti, B., & Gamboa, M. (2004). Zines for social justice: Adolescent girls writing on their own. *Reading Research Quarterly, 39*(4), 408–437.

Moje, E. (2000). *All the stories that we have: Adolescents' insights about literacy and learning in secondary schools.* Newark, DE: International Reading Association.

Moje, E., & Tysvaer, N. (2010). *Adolescent literacy development in out of school time: A practitioner's guidebook.* New York: Carnegie.

Tomlinson, C., & Eidson, C. (2003). *Differentiation in practice: A resource guide for differentiating curriculum, grades 5–9.* Alexandria, VA: Association for Supervision and Curriculum Development.

Go to Topic 1: Diversity, Culture, and Literacy, and Topic 10: Struggling Readers, in the MyEducationLab (www.myeducationlab.com) for your course, where you can:

- Find learning outcomes for Topic 1: Diversity, Culture, and Literacy, and Topic 10: Struggling Readers along with the national standards that connect to these outcomes.

- Complete Assignments and Activities that can help you more deeply understand the chapter content.

- Apply and practice your understanding of the core teaching skills identified in the chapter with the Building Teaching Skills and Dispositions learning units.

- Examine challenging situations and cases presented in the IRIS Center Resources.

Go to the Topic A+RISE in the MyEducationLab (www.myeducationlab.com) for your course. A+RISE® Standards2Strategy™ is an innovative and interactive online resource that offers new teachers in grades K-12 just in time, research-based instructional strategies that:

- Meet the linguistic needs of ELLs as they learn content

- Differentiate instruction for all grades and abilities

- Offer reading and writing techniques, cooperative learning, use of linguistic and nonlinguistic representations, scaffolding, teacher modeling, higher order thinking, and alternative classroom ELL assessment

- Provide support to help teachers be effective through the integration of listening, speaking, reading, and writing along with the content curriculum

- Improve student achievement

- Are aligned to Common Core Elementary Language Arts standards (for the literacy strategies) and to English language proficiency standards in WIDA, Texas, California, and Florida.

3

How to Pursue High Expectations for Teaching and Learning in an Era of Standards and Accountability

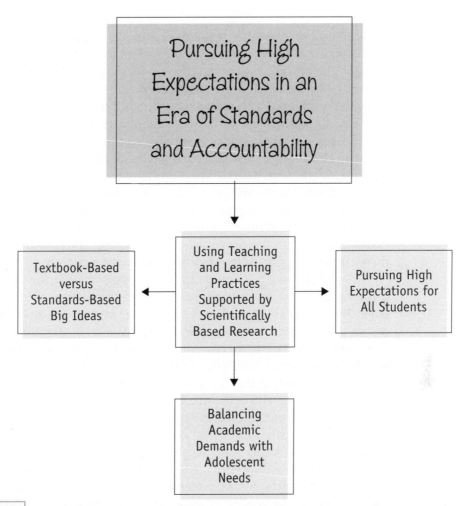

Pursuing High Expectations in an Era of Standards and Accountability

Textbook-Based versus Standards-Based Big Ideas

Using Teaching and Learning Practices Supported by Scientifically Based Research

Pursuing High Expectations for All Students

Balancing Academic Demands with Adolescent Needs

As explained in Chapter 1, many challenges affect today's teachers and adolescents, including new demands related to increasingly technological workplaces and worldwide competition. No Child Left Behind and now Race to the Top are the educational responses to this era, a time not only of technological change but also of higher standards and increased concern for educational accountability. The Common Core State Standards Initiative www.corestandards.org/ seeks to unify the various state standards into a single set of high standards and benchmarks that provide teachers and parents with a common understanding of what students are expected to learn, regardless of where they live. In short, against the reality of adolescents—some who succeed and many who struggle—teachers are expected more than ever to produce specific kinds of achievement for all students. What does this new era mean for the teachers?

The spirit of all of these initiatives is that all students will receive the same opportunities for successful achievement with rigorous academic goals. In the past, it was enough for schools to get by with only average student performance. It was almost accepted that there would always be struggling students. Unfortunately, this traditional approach leaves many students out, particularly those who might underperform in comparison with others, including students with special needs or English language learners. The average performance of a school can improve, while many students still perform poorly. This new era mandates that students within individual subgroups—the poor, minority students, students with special needs, and English language learners—must improve in their achievement just as high-performing students improve. The mandates also demand that teachers use proven effective teaching and learning practices, those that are supported by **scientifically based research.**

Chapter 2 posed a dilemma for teachers in meeting the demands of this new era: If adolescents are so diverse in their personal identities, in what they know about reading and writing, in their multiple literacies, and in their content knowledge and their knowledge about how to learn in a content area, how can teachers help all students to successfully pursue high standards? Principles of differentiating instruction provide a vehicle for answering this question by encouraging diverse and flexible teaching, learning, and assessment practices.

This chapter builds on the discussion so far about content area literacy through instruction based on Big Ideas. Recall that Big Ideas are principles and concepts that focus on the content. Here, we will explore different ways for identifying Big Ideas, including text materials, curriculum standards, and state assessments. The chapter demonstrates ways to use Big Ideas to set goals and make teaching and assessment decisions. Next, the chapter presents principles of teaching and learning that are supported by scientifically based research. The chapter concludes with a discussion of ways to balance the demands for high standards and accountability with the adolescents' authentic needs and interests.

Textbook-Based versus Standards-Based Big Ideas

The emphasis on curriculum standards and related state assessments within No Child Left Behind and the more recent move to create a national set of rigorous standards has increased pressure for students to know particular kinds of content and to use reading and writing in specific ways to meet high curriculum standards and pass state assessments.

It is not enough anymore for teachers to rely solely on a textbook in deciding what students should learn. In this era of increased state and national accountability (see the Research Brief), teachers need to develop standards-based Big Ideas. Let's compare the two approaches: textbook versus standards-based.

Research Brief

Higher Expectations from Governors for Adolescent Literacy Achievement

Research best practices identified by the National Governors Association Center for Best Practices, Adolescent Literacy Advisory Panel, and suggest five strategies to improve adolescent literacy achievement (National Governor's Association Center for Best Practices, 2005):

▶ Build support for a state focus on adolescent literacy.
▶ Raise literacy expectations across grades and curricula.

▶ Encourage and support school and district literacy plans.
▶ Build educators' capacity to provide adolescent literacy instruction.
▶ Measure progress in adolescent literacy at the school, district, and state levels.

These principles are being applied to develop support for the Common Core Curriculum Standards initiative www.corestandards.org/

Textbook-Based Big Ideas

It used to be easy to recommend that teachers simply pick up a textbook, select a topic or chapter, and then zero in on a content focus. To develop expectations for learning from a text, teachers ask: What should students understand by the end of a lesson involving this textbook selection? Or: What would students say after the lesson if the teacher asked them what they had learned from the text selection? Within content area literacy, this text-based approach has been called developing an **organizing idea** (Herber, 1978), **organizing principle** (Vacca & Vacca, 2004), or **content objective** (Conley, 1995). What these terms have in common is the goal of zeroing in on the principles and concepts that are important for teachers to teach and for students to learn. Figure 3.1 depicts a set of concepts that come from focusing on the content of a textbook selection.

Figure 3.1

Big Ideas based on looking at textbook selections.

Science

A single cell carries on all the same life functions that humans do.

English

You don't have to fight someone to keep your self-respect.

Mathematics

A fraction really represents division between two numbers.

Foreign Language

Shopping in France differs from shopping in the United States.

Physical Education

Warm-up and cool-down activities are essential for good training.

Social Studies

A democratic government is based on a balance of rights and responsibilities.

Health

Mental health is an illness that can affect anyone.

Art

An artist uses form and color to express feelings.

Music

A rap tune is as good as classical music.

Vocational Education

Shop safety requires a cool head and knowledge about first aid.

Business Education

It takes more than money to run a successful small business.

Identifying a concept from a textbook, however, does not equal consistency with state, district, or school standards and assessments. Teachers who focus on textbooks while ignoring state standards and assessments gamble with their students' performance in ways that matter for national and state funding for schools, students' academic progress, and even graduation. Sometimes, textbooks can be extremely limited in their coverage of national and state standards and assessments. For example, an eighth-grade social studies text might emphasize the responsibilities of good citizenship, including rights such as voting, due process, freedom of religion, freedom of the press, and freedom of assembly and responsibilities such as voting, paying taxes, and serving on a jury. State standards and tests, in comparison, might emphasize citizenship but also include history, civics, geography, and economics. Many texts are insufficient alone to prepare students for performing well according to state expectations and state tests.

▲ Mapping out the Big Ideas with students will help them make the connections between related concepts.

Standards-Based Big Ideas

The more effective starting point for teaching and learning consists of **standards-based Big Ideas.** Standards-based Big Ideas are identified in this way: Teachers examine standards in the form curriculum standards, published on state websites, and consider standards implied by state tests, also represented on state websites in the form of released test items. These standards are the foundation of Big Ideas that are used for making important decisions about students, teaching, and learning.

Figure 3.2 depicts a range of curriculum standards from many different content areas. Notice how many of these standards involve high levels of reading, writing, and speaking as well as interpreting, explaining, and evaluating in order for students to be successful.

Figure 3.3 presents a range of multiple-choice state assessment questions across several content areas. Consider how these assessment questions suggest standards-based expectations. Notice how each question asks students to use their content area knowledge to analyze readings, make comparisons, and select from among different hypotheses and themes. Notice also how many of these questions are located in real-world situations. These questions demonstrate how standards-based Big Ideas are responsible for varied ways of understanding, conveying knowledge, and manipulating information. The Action Research feature on pages 72–73 will guide you in further study of standards-based Big Ideas in your content area.

Figure 3.2

State standards: Big Ideas across the curriculum.

Number Sense Concepts and Operations

- The student understands the different ways numbers are represented and used in the real world.
- The student understands number systems.
- The student understands the effects of operations on numbers and relationships among these operations, and computes for problem solving.
- The student uses estimation in problem solving and computation.
- The student understands and applies theories related to numbers.

Source: Florida Sunshine State Standards.

Informational Materials in English

- Find similarities and differences between texts in the treatment, scope, or organization of ideas.
- Compare the original text to a summary to determine whether the summary accurately captures the main ideas, includes critical details, and conveys the underlying meaning.
- Use information from a variety of consumer, workplace, and public documents to explain a situation or decision and to solve a problem.
- Evaluate the unity, coherence, logic, internal consistency, and structural patterns of text.

Source: California English Language Arts Content Standards.

Art

- A student shall interpret and evaluate a variety of artworks, performances, or presentations, including elements, principles, and styles of the art forms and the social, historical, and cultural context of each work of art by:
- Analyzing artworks using the elements, principles, and styles of the art form;
- Evaluating works of art according to preestablished criteria;
- Describing personal reaction to the work of art;
- Explaining the connection between the work of art and its social, cultural, or historical context.

Source: Minnesota Content Standards.

Physical Education/Kinesiology

- The student demonstrates competency in many movement forms of physical activity.
- The student applies concepts and principles of human movement to the development of motor skills and the learning of new skills.
- The student analyzes the benefits of regular participation in physical activity.

Source: Florida Sunshine State Standards.

Using a Non-English Language

- Understand the main idea and some details of connected discourse.
- Narrate orally and in writing (present, past, and future) events in areas of personal and public interest.
- Derive meaning from oral, visual, and limited written stimuli and respond appropriately.
- Initiate, sustain, and bring closure to a variety of communicative tasks or situations.
- Express thoughts, ideas, preferences, and opinions in oral and written form.

Source: Michigan Standards for World Languages.

Middle School Science Standards

- The student conducts field and laboratory investigations using safe, environmentally appropriate, and ethical practices.
- The student uses scientific inquiry methods during field and laboratory investigations.
- The student uses critical thinking and scientific problem solving to make informed decisions.
- The student knows how to use a variety of tools and methods to conduct science inquiry.
- The student knows that systems may combine with other systems to form a larger system.

Source: Texas Essential Knowledge and Skills for Science.

Social Studies Test

Which of the following BEST describes the conditions that existed at the time these passages (about the American colonies) were written?

A. The British Empire was crumbling all over the world.

B. The colonists had won the Revolutionary War.

C. The British government ignored the actions of the colonists.

D. The United States did not yet exist as a nation.

Source: Michigan Department of Education.

Mathematics Test

A popular word processing software package costs $120.00. It costs $25.00 more than twice the cost of a less popular software package. The cost of the less popular package (c) can be represented by 2c + 25 = 120. What is the price of the less popular software package?

A. $190.00

B. $107.50

C. $72.50

D. $47.50

Source: Florida Comprehensive Assessment Test.

Science Test

A rabbit population has increased noticeably in the past ten years. Which of the following is a reasonable hypothesis for this population growth?

A. Competition for food has increased among rabbits.

B. The rabbit's main predator has been eliminated by human development.

C. Abnormal weather conditions have decreased water levels of the local ponds.

D. An organism that relies on similar food sources has migrated into the area.

Source: Massachusetts Department of Education.

English Test

Which one of the following themes is developed in the article about dolphins?

A. the conflict between art and science

B. the importance of technology

C. the joy of exploration

D. the difficulty of being true to oneself

Source: California High School Exit Exam.

Figure 3.3

Sample assessment questions on state tests.

Backwards mapping is a process that teachers can use to derive standards information from state test items (Conley & Gritter, 2007). Backwards mapping is based on the idea that every test item represents a set of cognitive steps that students need to follow to answer appropriately. Backwards mapping involves three steps:

1. Read the question. Figure out what kind of question it is and what it is asking. Determine the number of parts to the question. For multiple-choice questions, this might be very straightforward—a question and a fixed number of choices. Questions that require lengthier

Researching Standards-Based Expectations

Find your state in the list below. Then visit your state's Department of Education online and locate your state's curriculum standards. Next, locate any descriptions and released test items for your state's assessment in your content area (although many content areas are reflected in state standards, not all content areas are represented by state tests). Now select one or two grade levels in which you would like to teach. Describe the standards-based expectations for your content area and grade level. Make a list of the Big Ideas. Explain how skill in reading and writing might play a role in students' performance with respect to these content expectations.

Alabama
Alabama Department of Education
Website: www.alsde.edu/html/home.asp

Alaska
Alaska Department of Education and Early Development
Website: www.eed.state.ak.us/

Arizona
Arizona Department of Education
Website: www.ade.az.gov/

Arkansas
Arkansas Department of Education
Website: www.arkansased.org/

California
California Department of Education
Website: www.cde.ca.gov/

Colorado
Colorado Department of Education
Website: www.cde.state.co.us/

Connecticut
Connecticut Department of Education
Website: www.state.ct.us/sde/

Delaware
Delaware Department of Education
Website: www.doe.state.de.us/

District of Columbia
District of Columbia Public Schools
Website: www.k12.dc.us/dcps/home.html

Florida
Florida Department of Education
Website: www.fldoe.org/

Georgia
Georgia Department of Education
Website: www.doe.k12.ga.us/

Hawaii
Hawaii Department of Education
Website: www.doe.k12.hi.us/

Idaho
Idaho Department of Education
Website: www.sde.state.id.us/Dept/

Illinois
Illinois State Board of Education
Website: www.isbe.net/

Indiana
Indiana Department of Education
Website: www.doe.state.in.us/

Iowa
Iowa Department of Education
Website: www.state.ia.us/educate/

Kansas
Kansas Department of Education
Website: www.ksde.org/

Kentucky
Kentucky Department of Education
Website: www.education.ky.gov/KDE/Default.htm

Louisiana
Louisiana Department of Education
Website: www.louisianaschools.net/lde/index.html

Maine
Maine Department of Education
Website: www.maine.gov/education/index.shtml

Maryland
Maryland Department of Education
Website: www.msde.state.md.us/

Massachusetts
Massachusetts Department of Education
Website: www.doe.mass.edu/

Michigan
Michigan Department of Education
Website: www.michigan.gov/mde/

Minnesota
Minnesota Department of Education
Website: www.education.state.mn.us

Mississippi
Mississippi State Department of Education
Website: www.mde.k12.ms.us/

Missouri
Missouri Department of Elementary and Secondary Education
Website: http://dese.mo.gov/

Montana
Montana Office of Public Instruction
Website: www.opi.mt.gov/

Nebraska
Nebraska Department of Education
Website: www.nde.state.ne.us/

Nevada
Nevada Department of Education
Website: www.doe.nv.gov/

New Jersey
New Jersey Department of Education
Website: www.state.nj.us/education/

New Mexico
New Mexico Public Education Department
Website: www.ped.state.nm.us/

New York
New York Education Department
Website: www.nysed.gov/

North Carolina
North Carolina Department of Public Instruction
Website: www.ncpublicschools.org/

North Dakota
North Dakota Department of Public Instruction
Website: www.dpi.state.nd.us/

Ohio
Ohio Department of Education
Website: www.ode.state.oh.us/

Oklahoma
Oklahoma State Department of Education
Website: sde.state.ok.us/

Oregon
Oregon Department of Education
Website: www.ode.state.or.us/

Pennsylvania
Pennsylvania Department of Education
Website: www.pde.state.pa.us/

Rhode Island
Rhode Island Department of Elementary and Secondary Education
Website: www.ridoe.net/

South Carolina
South Carolina Department of Education
Website: www.myscschools.com/

South Dakota
South Dakota Department of Education
Website: doe.sd.gov/

Tennessee
Tennessee State Department of Education
Website: www.state.tn.us/education/

Texas
Texas Education Agency
Website: www.tea.state.tx.us/

Utah
Utah State Office of Education
Website: www.schools.utah.gov/

Vermont
Vermont Department of Education
Website: www.state.vt.us/educ/

Virginia
Virginia Department of Education
Website: www.pen.k12.va.us/

Washington
Office of Superintendent of Public Instruction (Washington)
Website: www.k12.wa.us/

West Virginia
West Virginia Department of Education
Website: wvde.state.wv.us/

Wisconsin
Wisconsin Department of Public Instruction
Website: www.dpi.state.wi.us/

Wyoming
Wyoming Department of Education
Website: www.k12.wy.us/

responses frequently have several parts that require many different kinds of responses. Note the parts and what is being asked in each.

2. Answer the question. Provide a response to each part of the question. Consider what the question is asking for and respond, taking note of the steps you are taking inside your head to generate answers.

3. Map or record the steps you took to read and answer the question. Do a think-aloud reflection, recapping what you did to answer the question. Write down the steps.

Figure 3.4 demonstrates backwards mapping with a persuasive essay. Notice how this process illuminates the need for teachers to address persuasion in a particular way: by taking a stand, providing reasons, and

Figure 3.4

Backwards mapping of a state test item to identify standards-based Big Ideas.

Tourism committees spend a great deal of money each year advocating natural landmarks of states and countries.

By using media such as posters, magazine advertisements, television commercials, and radio advertisements,

committees are able to send a message about beautiful places and, they hope, convince some tourists to travel to

those places.

> This is the audience.

Suppose you have been hired by a tourism committee. Write a persuasive essay

> Part One: Identify a special place.

in which you identify a place in the world that has something tourists might find

interesting. Explain precisely what makes that particular place so special. Develop

> Part Two: Explain what makes this place special.

your ideas so that a potential tourist would be persuaded to visit the place you

> Part Three: Add reasons and supporting details for what is special about the place.

have identified.

Source: California State Assessment.

Backwards Mapping

1. There are three parts to the question: the special place, why it is special, and reasons and supporting evidence for the specialness of the place.

2. I will select Disney World as my special place. I have had the most fun with my family there.

3. I picked the place. Now I need to select the reasons. Let's see, there are the rides, the food, and the shopping. I can say something special about each of those things.

supporting evidence. Teachers will find this standard embedded in many state assessment tasks. To learn more about standards-based expectations, read the Connecting Standards and Assessment feature.

It is often useful to break standards-based Big Ideas into smaller connected concepts and facts. The reason for this is sometimes to identify a starting point for instruction. Additionally, it is helpful to create a road map ahead of time concerning the main concepts and relationships for students to learn. Students learn more effectively if the content they are learning is connected in specific ways. Sometimes, smaller connecting concepts and facts are what students need to know to understand a Big

Connecting Standards and Assessment

Communicating about Standards

Higher educational standards are not necessarily something to be feared. Parents living on the outside of the classroom can feel uncertain and critical when there is little communication from within the classroom. Well-designed curriculum standards can help with this situation by serving as one vehicle for explaining to parents about the goals for a content area and grade level. Parents often ask three important questions: What are you trying to accomplish with my child? How is my child doing? What are you (teachers) doing to help my child do better? Standards can provide teachers with a way of answering each of these questions in tangible ways.

Many of today's state and national curriculum standards come from numerous research-based reports, including international comparisons. Standards do not take the place of good teacher judgment. In fact, the best approaches to teaching based on standards are varied and multifaceted. Without standards, variety in teaching can seem arbitrary and counterproductive. However, standards provide a solid context for many different approaches to the curriculum. As long as students build knowledge and skill relative to the standards, many different kinds of approaches are possible and even welcome.

Though standards are research based, they are not written to be immediately applicable at the local district or school level. Therefore, standards often need to be reconsidered with respect to local understandings and student needs. Standards invite conversations about goals for curriculum and assessment across content areas and grades.

▶ **Read more about these ideas in Chapter 1, "Higher Educational Standards," in Conley's (2005)** *Connecting Standards and Assessment through Literacy,* **published by Pearson Education.**

Figure 3.5

Considering Big Ideas and connecting concepts.

> **Mathematics**
>
> **Big Idea:** Find the surface area of an irregular three-dimensional figure where the outer faces do not have the same area (such as a shoebox or computer monitor).
>
> **Connecting concepts:**
>
> What *area* means
>
> How to find area
>
> Understand how to look at a three-dimensional figure on a two-dimensional piece of paper
>
> Identifying all of the faces of the figure
>
> Calculating the area of all of the faces of the figure
>
> **Social Studies**
>
> **Big Idea:** Understand monarchies as a form of government in the Elizabethan era.
>
> **Connecting concepts:**
>
> Knowing the historical period, time, and era
>
> Understanding the idea of *government*
>
> Understanding the unique features of monarchies

Idea. Some Big Ideas and connecting concepts appear in Figure 3.5. We will work more with the design of Big Ideas and connecting concepts in Chapter 4, "Planning for Teaching and Learning."

Using Standards-Based Big Ideas

Standards-based Big Ideas are used for a variety of important tasks, from setting specific goals for thinking about content to assessing students and selecting text and other kinds of curriculum resources.

Setting Goals for Thinking about the Content. Once teachers have identified the Big Ideas for a unit or lesson, it is important to consider the kinds of thinking students will be required to do in learning the Big Ideas. As was demonstrated in the previous section, not all standards-inspired Big Ideas are alike. Some focus on *comprehending* a set of concepts; others require *comparisons, critical reflection,* and *evaluation.* For instance, identifying ways in which numbers are represented is a different activity from comparing a fraction and a decimal. Following the procedures for a scientific experiment is a different activity from using scientific knowledge to make informed decisions. And retracing the plotline of a story is a different activity from justifying a theme. Big Ideas are not the same as ways of thinking about them, but they are certainly related. Students need help not only with understanding the Big Ideas but also with the appropriate ways of thinking with and about them.

Critical literacy, for example, is a term coined to describe the goal of helping students read, write, and learn with a critical eye (Fehring & Green, 2001). Critical literacy means weighing evidence across multiple texts, images, sounds, and multimedia. It consists of deliberations about others' agendas, perspectives, identities, and biases. Critical literacy could take as simple a form as comparing students' lives with the lives of characters in a novel. However, it could also entail asking critical questions about perspectives that we often take for granted as being fixed and unbiased, such as those from science and mathematics. More about critical literacy and how to promote it with Big Ideas and your students appears in Chapter 10, "Guiding Students' Critical Literacy."

Assessing Students. There are a number of good reasons for assessing students in light of Big Ideas. One of the most important is to build on what students know. Assessing students also helps teachers to personalize the curriculum by making real-life connections between students and the content. Yet another purpose is to facilitate choices for students in their learning. The more teachers gain knowledge about what students know and are able to do, the more teachers can offer assignments that vary in requirements for content knowledge and literacy demands.

Assessing students' knowledge about Big Ideas is more than a yes/no (students know it or they do not know it) proposition. Recall the number of examples so far in which some students already know the content while others do not, often in surprising ways. Rather than asking: Do students know about Big Ideas? a better question might be: What do students know and care about when it comes to the Big Ideas?

One way to answer this question is to identify which Big Ideas and connected concepts teachers have attempted to teach students. What curriculum standards are addressed in previous grades and content areas? What have students learned? Teachers often discover through this process that students have strong backgrounds in some areas but significant gaps in other areas that were either not covered or not fully learned. A fairly common example in mathematics, for example, concerns ongoing problems with understanding fractions and even numbers in upper

▲ **Students often need to understand how to learn. Providing direct attention can help you assess their comprehension.**

elementary, middle school, and high school grades. In science, students may be turned off because they have yet to connect science to their everyday observations. Students in high school often demonstrate problems with persuasive writing, a skill that is emphasized on many required state tests. And students who are taking a foreign language can experience considerable difficulty if they are not very proficient in their first language (Ridgway, 2003). These issues concerning assessing are addressed in Chapter 6, "Ongoing Assessment."

Planning and Teaching Lessons. A major use of Big Ideas is to plan and teach lessons. It is relatively easy for beginning teachers to fall into the trap of focusing mostly on filling time for students. Although keeping students occupied is a concern for well-managed classrooms, an equally important concern is to have students engaged in learning interesting and important content (Weinstein, 2003). That's where Big Ideas come in.

Big Ideas can be used to assess what students know and what they need to know and then to plan teaching and learning activities, including those involving literacy. Big Ideas can also be used to assess how teachers will know that students have gained the knowledge and skill related to a Big Idea. A very simple planning chart can be used as a brainstorming device, once Big Ideas have been identified. The How to Plan feature demonstrates a planning chart used to brainstorm a lesson in response to a social studies standard.

Selecting Texts and Other Resources. Big Ideas are also a useful device for considering and selecting the materials available for teaching. Some state standards are connected to required texts. Some are accompanied by lists of supplemental materials, such as trade books, DVDs and videos, websites, games, and even puzzles. It is always useful to conduct a web search for Internet sources of support for teaching a particular Big Idea, using Google (www.google.com), AOL search (www.search.aol.com), Yahoo search (www.search.yahoo.com), or Altavista (www.altavista.com).

How
TO PLAN

... by Building Lessons and Units around Standards-Based Big Ideas

How can teachers use Big Ideas to plan and teach lessons? Consider this approach. A planning chart can be constructed to aid in brainstorming about teaching and assessment related to a Big Idea. The following planning chart has been filled out to reflect one teacher's approach to Kansas Curriculum Standards in social studies.

Using the same approach, complete a planning chart for a Big Idea in your content area.

Big Idea: The student identifies and examines the rights, privileges, and responsibilities in becoming an active civic participant (from the Kansas Curricular Standards for History and Government; Economics and Geography).

PLANNING CHART

What Do Students Know about the Big Idea?	What Activities Will I Use to Teach the Big Idea?	How Will I Know That Students Have Learned the Big Idea?
Voting Serving in the government (representatives, mayor, etc.) **What Do Students Need to Know about the Big Idea?** The role(s) of political parties How public policy is formed Political and economic rights Civic responsibilities Civil disobedience Special interest groups	Form political parties in class and run a mock election for a class council. Identify special interest groups who lobby the council (more time off, snacks in class, etc.). Hold a civil disobedience day in class. Identify class issues worthy of protest. **Ways in Which Students Will Use Reading, Writing, Viewing, and/or Speaking to Learn the Big Idea:** Read *Martin Luther King's letter from the Birmingham Jail* http://www.almaz.com/nobel/peace/MLK-jail.html Read *Juror—Your Rights and Duties from the Kansas Bar Association* http://www.ksbar.org/public/public_resources/pamphlets/juror.shtml Research a local political party and/or interest group. Interview a local judge about jury duty. Write a persuasive essay about why individuals should be active participants in civic responsibilities. The essay should combine ideas from the lessons as well as students' personal perspectives and experiences.	Classroom observations focused on students' discussions about their roles as civic participants. Students' written reactions to the MLK letter and the juror description. Students' reports on the activities of a local political party and/or interest group. The quality of students' persuasive essays, reflecting knowledge about the Big Idea.

Keep in mind that students count in any search for text and other resources. Textbook writers and writers of other supporting materials did not have *your* particular students in mind when they wrote their materials. They had no way of knowing about students' lives in and out of school; what they like to read, talk, and learn about; and their strengths and needs. Any decisions about texts and other materials need to be combined with thoughtful concern for students, including what they know, what they can already do, and what they care about. Chapter 5, "Understanding and Using Texts," focuses on the issue of making connections between texts and students.

Building Community. Big Ideas and all of the ways of using them for assessing students, planning for teaching, and learning and selecting texts place teachers in an excellent position to explain curriculum to students, parents, and others outside the classroom. For students, Big Ideas represent the desired goals for learning. As many assessment experts argue, the more students know about the goals for learning, the better the students will be in achieving them (Stiggins, 2005). For parents, Big Ideas answer questions about what teachers are trying to accomplish. Many teachers capitalize on Big Ideas and parents as resources by offering parents tips on how to help their children with their homework. In short, using Big Ideas to keep everyone informed—especially students and parents—is a way of building a sense of community around what students are learning. Chapter 12, "Building Community from Inside and Outside the Classroom," shares many ideas for how to make this happen.

Using Teaching and Learning Practices Supported by Scientifically Based Research

This era of standards and accountability includes a mandate for teaching practices supported by scientifically based research. *Reading Next,* a report sponsored by the Carnegie Corporation, is a review of scientifically based research on adolescents and literacy (Biancarosa & Snow, 2004). These principles and practices are the result of this review:

1. Direct, explicit comprehension instruction, which is instruction in the strategies and processes that proficient readers use to understand what they read, including summarizing and keeping track of one's own understanding

2. Effective instructional principles embedded in content, including language arts teachers using content area texts and content area teachers providing instruction and practice in reading and writing skills specific to their subject area

3. Motivation and self-directed learning, which includes building motivation to read and learn and providing students with the instruction and supports needed for independent learning tasks they will face after graduation

4. Text-based collaborative learning, which involves students interacting with one another around a variety of texts

5. Strategic tutoring, which provides students with intense individualized reading, writing, and content instruction as needed

6. Using diverse texts, which are texts at a variety of difficulty levels and on a variety of topics

7. Intensive writing, including instruction connected to the kinds of writing tasks students will have to perform well in high school and beyond

8. A technology component, which includes technology as a tool for and a topic of literacy instruction

9. Ongoing formative assessment of students, which is informal, often daily assessment of how students are progressing under current instructional practices

10. Extended time for literacy instruction and practice that takes place in language arts and content-area classes

11. Professional development for teachers and administrators that is both long term and ongoing

12. Ongoing summative assessment of students and programs, which is more formal and provides data that are reported for accountability and research purposes

13. Teacher teams, which are interdisciplinary teams that meet regularly to discuss students and align instruction with standards and state assessments

A+RISE

Click on A+RISE – WIDA ELP Standard Strategy in the MyEducationLab (www.myeducationlab .com) for your course. Next, select the Strategy Card Index tab, scroll to Language and Content for Grades 6–12 and select the Recommended Grouping Strategies.

Notice how these principles complement the principles of differentiated instruction, particularly with respect to building on students' interests and needs, the use of a variety of texts and instructional approaches and groupings. There are also several new ideas here that are worth considering. For example, it is important for teachers to directly explain ways for students to comprehend and learn. A simple way of thinking about this is to recall tricks or techniques, or approaches to learning, that you used in surviving a difficult course. Some students focus on a syllabus and individual assignments to guide their attention and effort. Some summarize what they know, either orally or on note cards. Knowing some ways in which you survived, comprehended, and learned, consider how to teach these techniques directly to your students.

Another important principle concerns using assessment to guide and evaluate your teaching. The central idea of scientifically based research is that only teaching practices that have been validated through evidence should be used. Although it is not always possible to emphasize research-based practices, it is important to ask: What is the purpose for the practices you have selected? and How will you know that a practice you have selected actually works? In the spirit of emphasizing scientifically based teaching practices, all of the practices that have been selected for this book are research-based. Each practice has been grouped according to expected learning outcomes, such as teaching students to get motivated, summarize, predict, or remember.

Pursuing High Expectations for All Students

On the basis of the philosophy that all adolescents benefit from being held to the same standards, no students are excluded from meeting high expectations, especially with the current government educational reforms. In the past, when students were excluded, such as students with special educational needs, they might not have received the same amount of attention as other students who were held to higher standards. The Individuals with Disabilities Education Act, for example, mandates inclusion of students with special educational needs, including students with disabilities, for access to, participation in, and making progress in the general education curriculum. This mandate includes assessment. Under the No Child Left Behind laws, students with special needs and English language learners are required to make regular improvements on state assessments for schools to make Adequate Yearly Progress. All students are counted.

Although this can seem like a daunting challenge, there are some useful principles to follow in trying to help all students achieve. Not surprisingly, the worst practice for teachers and diverse adolescents is to resort to the old model of teacher lecture, reading from and responding to textbooks and quizzes and tests that ask students to recall what they have learned. Instead, consider the following ideas (Abedi, 2004; Abedi et al., 2000; CAST, 2004). Again, compare these principles to those from differentiated instruction and from scientifically based research.

▶ Explain why it is important to learn various Big Ideas and concepts. Students will be more successful learners if they are motivated to learn. A key part of motivation comes from understanding why the knowledge students are gaining is important within the curriculum and for them personally.

▶ Help students to understand connections and patterns in the content they are learning. It is much harder to try to understand and remember hundreds of disconnected facts than to learn Big Ideas and related concepts and facts.

▶ Teach students about academic language. Some students, especially some English language learners, might be unfamiliar with the academic language (such as the technical vocabulary in a content area or the special language of teaching and assessment) even if they know a great deal about the content of the class. Help students to know the difference between questions that ask, for example, to explain, compare, calculate, or predict.

▶ Emphasize multiple, flexible pathways for engagement, learning, and expression, including reading, writing, speaking, listening, viewing, drawing, and touching. The more pathways teachers use while teaching, the more likely it will be that one will connect with the special strengths and needs of individual students.

▶ Provide ample amounts of time for students to complete assignments. Some English language learners or students with special needs might read more slowly than other students. With practice and experience, these students can learn to read more flexibly. Point out times when an assignment needs careful review and other times when assignments involve light skimming. Demonstrate the difference.

▶ Demonstrate strategies for students to use while learning. Do not make the mistake of assuming that teaching activities and assignments guarantee learning. For learning to happen, students often need to understand how to learn. Share examples of the learning strategies that have worked for you.

▶ Assess students' progress. All students benefit from a careful monitoring of their progress. This can be especially true for students with special needs, such as English language learners. Watch for signs of students falling behind—puzzled looks, poor performance, or frustration—and ask students about their experiences with learning.

A+RISE

Click on A+RISE – WIDA ELP Standard Strategy in the MyEducationLab (www.myeducationlab .com) for your course. Next, select the Strategy Card Index tab, scroll to Classroom Assessments for Grades 6–12 and select the Academic Vocabulary Word Wall strategy.

For more information about helping all students succeed in today's environment of high standards and rigorous assessments, visit the University of Minnesota's National Center on Educational Outcomes (www .cehd.umn.edu/nceo/), a website clearinghouse devoted to helping students with special needs to meet high educational standards in the general education classroom. The National Alternate Assessment Center

Teaching Today's Learners

Using Multiple Pathways to Pursue High Expectations for All Students

As the ideas in this chapter illustrate, reaching all students requires instructional approaches that are multifaceted, involving reading, writing, speaking, listening, viewing, drawing, manipulating, designing, and creating. Here is how one teacher followed this principle to teach the following Missouri curriculum standard: *Recognize and generate equivalent forms of fractions, decimals, and percents.* Understanding the relationships among fractions, decimals, and percents is particularly challenging for many students, even well into middle and high schools. Students experience many problems, including knowing the difference between a larger and a smaller amount; knowing how to add fractions, decimals, and percents together; and understanding equivalent numbers, such as ½, ⁴/8, 0.5, and 50 percent.

After struggling with these ideas with her students, Ms. Redburn came up with this teaching activity involving demonstrating, explaining, writing, and drawing. She cut out some circles. Next, she cut these whole circles into parts—halves, quarters, and eighths. Students were given a collection of parts, several whole circles, a number of half circles, some quarters, and many eighths.

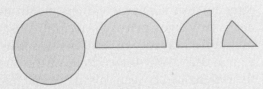

Ms. Redburn explained that this was a way to learn about fractions. The students would identify different parts or fractions, compare parts with respect to which were larger and smaller, and then add and subtract parts. She explained that this activity, breaking up a whole into parts, was not unlike what students do every day with money.

First, Ms. Redburn asked her students to identify the parts—half circles, quarter circles, and eighth circles. She suggested that a whole circle could be created using a specific number of parts and that the number of parts would differ, depending on the size of the parts. Students soon discovered that a circle could be made from two large parts, four smaller parts, and eight even smaller parts.

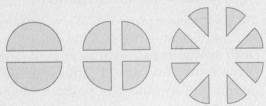

(www.naacpartners.org/) provides numerous examples of alternative instructional techniques and assessments for students with the most significant cognitive impairments. Read the Teaching Today's Learners feature about one mathematics teacher's approach to providing multiple pathways for teaching all students to learn.

Students drew each of the respective figures on a separate piece of paper, along with their observations about how many figures it took to create a whole circle—two, four, or eight. Ms. Redburn explained that these numbers corresponded to the names of fractions of the circle—½, ¼, and ⅛.

The next step was to help students understand relationships between smaller and larger parts. First, students observed that it took two one-half pieces, four one-quarter pieces, or eight one-eighth pieces to make a whole circle. They also concluded that one could combine two one-quarter pieces to make a half piece and four one-eighth pieces to make a half. Quarter pieces could be made up from two one-eighth pieces.

Now, the class moved on to learning how to add different pieces together. Ms. Redburn demonstrated: "Suppose we wanted to add ½ and ¼? Let's see how we might figure that out. Well, how many ¼ pieces are in a half?"

Students noticed that there were two quarter pieces in a half, and adding the other quarter, they arrived at ¾. After demonstrating one more addition example—⅜ plus ¼—Ms. Redburn asked her students to create as many addition combinations as they could.

Finally, Ms. Redburn demonstrated subtraction, using the circle figures: "Suppose we had a half and wanted to take away an eighth, kind of like cutting a piece of pie. How could we think about that?"

One student volunteered that a half was made up of four eighths. If you took one away, you would have three eighths. Again, Ms. Redburn demonstrated another subtraction problem—subtracting ¼ from ⅜—and then asked her students to come up with their own subtraction examples, using the circle figures.

In the days ahead, Ms. Redburn used the same examples to demonstrate relationships among decimals—0.125, 0.25, and 0.50—and percents—12.5, 25, and 50 percent. She demonstrated how to think about the figures and numbers, including identification, part-whole relationships, addition, and subtraction. Students wrote about their observations and conclusions and drew picture examples of how they could combine fractions, add, and subtract.

Balancing Academic Demands with Adolescent Needs

In this era of standards and accountability, a challenging dilemma has emerged, one that pits the academic curriculum of accountability and standards against the adolescent world (Morrell, 2004). On the one hand, teachers are responsible for teaching the standards and helping students to achieve on state tests. On the other hand, there is the adolescent world of out-of-school literacies and experiences. If teachers privilege the standards-based curriculum to the total exclusion of the students' world, they risk alienating students. Students might never bother with the standards or tests. Alternatively, if teachers completely acquiesce to adolescents' interests, students might feel valued without ever becoming successful with the standards and assessments for which they are to be held accountable. With this dilemma in mind, how can teachers strike a balance between academic demands and students' needs?

▲**By understanding students' insights and interests, you can personalize instruction to help them meet academic demands.**

Personalize Teaching and Learning

One possible answer to this question concerns using students' needs and interests to personalize teaching and learning. The fact that students are engaged in creating and operating within their own personal worlds presents teachers with an opportunity. Whenever possible, focus classroom conversations on students' experiences. Students' experiences—their observations about the world, their family lives, their encounters with the Internet and the media—provide a meaningful context for academic content. There are many examples of what this kind of classroom looks like, from connecting rap songs to poetry and literature anthologies to having students consider everyday uses and misuses of numbers and data; from connecting everyday observations of the world to scientific understandings to considering one's place in larger social, environmental, and political issues. These classrooms focus on real problems and, whenever possible, emphasize real texts and real inquiry. Teachers in these classrooms start and end with students' insights, their multiple literacies, and their personal experiences. Considering your own experiences, can you remember teachers who were particularly adept at personalizing teaching and learning to prepare students for meeting academic demands?

Teach Learning Strategies

Another way of balancing academic demands with students' needs involves showing students how to learn. Although it is critical for teachers to personalize knowledge in a content area, it is just as important for teachers to develop students' understanding of **learning strategies,** or ways to learn in a content area. To understand the idea of learning strategies, take a moment to reflect on your own approaches to learning. Consider any one of a number of situations you have experienced in which you had to figure out how to learn effectively and perhaps efficiently. Was it in a class where there were substantial demands to read a lot? Were the questions and assignments particularly difficult? What did you do? You probably focused on the expectations for the class and then selected and scanned the reading material to gather and digest the most information for particular assignments. Think about how you can communicate these tips or learning strategies for students in your content area.

Summary

Teaching in this era of standards and accountability can seem like a complex business compared to the tradition in secondary schools of teaching from the textbook. Standards-based Big Ideas present many opportunities for identifying and working with interesting and engaging content, designing standards-based lessons and assessments, and building community. As never before, teachers are the critical resource for balancing the demands of standards and mandates with students' interests and needs. Through flexible and varied approaches to the curriculum and texts, teachers can use content area literacy to help all of today's adolescents learn to be successful. How teachers do this is the subject of this book.

Special Projects

1. What are the standards-based expectations in your content area? Identify the standards for your content area, and complete a planning chart for how you would teach the standard. Be sure to include a number of reading and writing activities with your plan.

2. Visit the website of your state department of education and select some released test items for your content area. Use backwards mapping of the test items to uncover the standards. Describe how you could teach students to meet these standards.

3. Visit the Common Core State Standards website www.corestandards.org/ and review the standards in your content area. If your state has not adopted these standards yet, compare your state's standards with the Common Core standards. What are the implications of these standards for teaching and learning in your content area? What are the implications for the kinds of literacy your students will need in order to achieve successfully?

4. Describe a lesson in your content area in which you implement practices for helping students with special needs to meet high educational standards.

5. Describe a lesson in your content area in which you implement practices for helping English language learners to meet high educational standards.

Praxis Practice

Working with Questions to Prepare for the Praxis Reading across the Curriculum Test

Multiple Choice Questions

1. According to recent governmental education reforms, the best classroom practices in literacy are:

   a. Found to be effective based on scientifically based research

   b. Preferred by teachers and their students

   c. Fun and motivational for students

   d. Identified by national experts in literacy

2. Which is a reason why textbooks may not be good as the only source of lesson ideas?

   a. Textbooks are usually written in a boring manner.

   b. Textbooks can be written without a solid or consistent connection to standards.

   c. Textbooks are written in places far away from students.

   d. Textbooks are not always up to date.

3. What is a best way to pursue high expectations with students?

   a. Expect a lot from students as they do their work.

   b. Criticize students when they provide incorrect answers.

   c. Correct students' work, making sure they receive good feedback.

   d. Plan lessons starting with big ideas from state standards.

Constructed Response Question

1. Pursuing high standards with diverse students can be a challenging balancing act. Describe a lesson in which you identify high standards while considering the diverse needs of your students.

Suggested Readings

Conley, M. (2005). *Connecting standards and assessment through literacy.* New York: Pearson Education.

Go to Topic 7: Planning for Instruction in the MyEducationLab (www.myeducationlab.com) for your course, where you can:

- Find learning outcomes for Topic 7: Planning for Instruction along with the national standards that connect to these outcomes.

- Complete Assignments and Activities that can help you more deeply understand the chapter content.

- Apply and practice your understanding of the core teaching skills identified in the chapter with the Building Teaching Skills and Dispositions learning units.

- Examine challenging situations and cases presented in the IRIS Center Resources.

Go to the Topic A+RISE in the MyEducationLab (www.myeducationlab.com) for your course. A+RISE® Standards2Strategy™ is an innovative and interactive online resource that offers new teachers in grades K-12 just in time, research-based instructional strategies that:

- Meet the linguistic needs of ELLs as they learn content

- Differentiate instruction for all grades and abilities

- Offer reading and writing techniques, cooperative learning, use of linguistic and nonlinguistic representations, scaffolding, teacher modeling, higher order thinking, and alternative classroom ELL assessment

- Provide support to help teachers be effective through the integration of listening, speaking, reading, and writing along with the content curriculum

- Improve student achievement

- Are aligned to Common Core Elementary Language Arts standards (for the literacy strategies) and to English language proficiency standards in WIDA, Texas, California, and Florida.

4 Alternative Ways to Plan and Teach Lessons

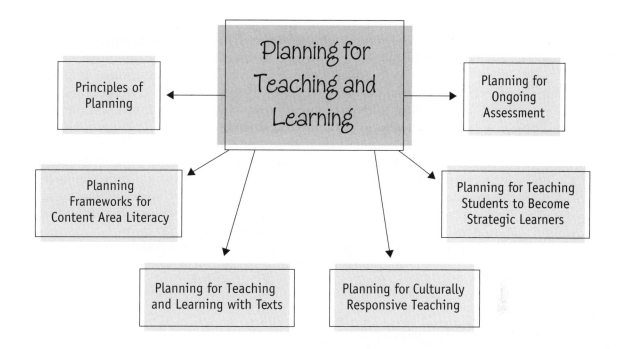

According to the research, the most successful classrooms look like this: Teachers hold clear and high expectations for students. The teachers in those classrooms are committed to their work, and they hold themselves and each other accountable for good work. The curriculum and teaching practices in these classrooms are powerful and challenging, meaning lots of reading, writing, speaking, listening, viewing, and performing. Teachers in these classrooms require meaningful understanding on the part of students as opposed to having students just memorize facts. These teachers work intentionally to motivate students, using positive "can-do" expectations rather than automatically expecting failure. They show students how to learn, and they show that they care. They praise students for good work in ways that help students to understand how their efforts lead to successful learning. There are positive relationships among teachers, administrators, parents, and students. These practices have been shown to be especially effective with minority students and students who are at risk of school failure, such as special needs students and English language learners, but they are equally effective with all students (Langer, 1999; Pressley et al., 2004; Reeves, 2000).

So how do classrooms get to be this effective? One answer involves thoughtful planning. Planning involves identifying important knowledge and skills and organizing instructional and assessment practices. It means thinking carefully about students and the resources that are available for teaching them. It means shifting and adapting on the basis of new insights gained from teaching.

The purpose of this chapter is to pull together many of the topics that have been discussed already: understanding students, working with high expectations, making good decisions about texts and other resources, and ongoing assessment. This chapter presents frameworks for lesson planning, including specific ways of working with texts, and a rationale for selecting teaching and learning strategies focused on literacy. This chapter is about the specifics of how to plan based on concerns for today's students and instruction in highly effective classrooms.

Principles of Planning

Planning is an extremely active process. To plan well, teachers need to entertain all of the possibilities: students and their literacies, texts and modern resources, and different effective approaches to teaching and learning. Planning is also an interactive process. Teachers confirm, adapt, or even abandon plans when confronted with new information while teaching. Read the Research Brief for some ideas for how to become an expert planner. For purposes of review and to lay a foundation for this chapter, consider the following principles of planning.

Effective Planning Requires Knowledge about Students: Who They Are, What They Know, and What They Care About

For the sake of planning, this knowledge needs to be specific to the content. So consider the content. What do students already know? What do they need to know? Avoid the trap of assuming that they know virtually nothing, though there may be occasions when that is truly the case. Instead, think about all of the different ways in which they might know a little bit, even misconceptions they might have.

Research Brief

Learning How to Plan

Recent research says that the best way to learn how to plan with today's students is in context—in real classrooms, with high curriculum expectations and diverse students (Lowery, 2002). Beginning teachers just do not learn how to plan as well when they practice planning only as part of university classes. Teachers learn to plan most effectively by converting what they know into instructional and assessment practices in the context of messy and constantly changing classrooms. What does this mean for your practice? Take approaches to planning, such as the ones in this chapter, as general guidelines and a starting point. Spend time in classrooms working with students, trying out plans, and assessing what works. Observe how students read, write, and perform when taught according to your plans and the plans of teachers you observe. Be especially observant for times when plans do not go as expected. Over time, experiences with planning in real live classroom contexts can help to make you an expert planner.

Another set of questions concerns what students care about. How motivated are they to learn the content? If they know very little or have misconceptions about the content, this question might be difficult to answer. On the other hand, if students have unsuccessfully tried to learn, their motivation might not be particularly high. Other factors, including students' own preferences and out-of-school experiences, can influence motivation. Students who care mostly about video games or hip-hop might become motivated if you can help them to make connections between their interests and the content.

Planning Needs to Be Grounded in High Expectations

Because of standards-based reforms and increased testing, adolescents face high expectations. Whenever planning a lesson or series of lessons, identify one or two curriculum standards to serve as Big Ideas, as the teacher in Figure 4.1 did while teaching her students about persuasive writing.

Figure 4.1

Lesson plan designed around a curriculum standard.

Curriculum Standard: *Students write coherent and focused texts that convey a well-defined perspective and tightly reasoned argument. The writing demonstrates students' awareness of the audience and purpose and progression through the stages of the writing process.*

Big Idea: *Persuasive writing involves taking a perspective and backing it up with good reasons.*

Preparation

1. Introduce the idea of persuasive writing.
2. Ask students to describe times when they have had to convince or persuade someone to do something.
3. Demonstrate ways to brainstorm for topics by taking a perspective (for example, current events). Make a list of topics that one might use to persuade an audience.
4. Discuss the role of the audience in persuasion. Compare an audience of peers and an audience of parents if the topic were "I should be able to stay out past midnight."
5. Discuss reasons used to support a perspective. Distinguish between good and not very effective reasons, depending on the audience.
6. Write a simple persuasive paragraph with the class, using one of the topics brainstormed earlier.

Guidance

1. Students brainstorm topics that they can use for persuasion.
2. Students write a simple persuasive paragraph.
3. The teacher walks around, providing help and feedback with students' writing.

Application

1. Introduce persuasive five-paragraph essays.
2. Examine persuasive writing prompts from state writing tests.

Source: English–Language Arts Content Standards for California Public Schools.

Examine state tests to determine additional expectations and skills. Referring to the tests does not mean that you need to blindly teach to a test. Do not forget to consider expectations within your local school district or school. Often, standards that are written at local levels offer a more detailed view of what students are expected to know and do. Incorporate the literacy demands posed by standards into your planning.

Consider the Potential for Various Kinds of Texts and Other Resources to Help Students Grow in Their Knowledge and Skill

Though it can be relatively easy as a beginning teacher to get pulled into the trap of teaching only from a text, remember that textbooks might offer only very imperfect representations of the knowledge students need to learn. Just reading from a textbook will not make connections between students and the content. Students often need to develop a variety of perspectives on the knowledge they are learning. Do not overlook the potential for using other materials—trade books, Internet resources, mass media, authentic documents—to supplement classroom texts. Problematic texts can be addressed in part by helping your students learn how to read them. The most successful schools, particularly in communities with large numbers of English language learners and children from poverty, are successful because they immerse students in lots of wide and varied reading and writing (Pressley et al., 2004). For a description of how to find out about using Internet resources for planning, read the Action Research feature.

When Planning, Teachers Need to Consider the Full Range of Instructional Possibilities

Every classroom contains a diverse set of learners with different personal identities, literacies, family and community influences, knowledge, skills, and motivation. Teachers who provide multiple pathways for learning, including reading, writing, speaking, listening, viewing, and performing, give all students the chance to learn the content, making it possible for the broadest range of students to become effective learners.

Planning Needs to Be Continuously Informed by Ongoing Assessment

Ongoing assessment means using many different kinds of assessment for many different assessment purposes: to understand students and their motivation, to sample content knowledge and skill, and to determine how and whether students have achieved, to name a few. Ongoing assessment also means frequent sampling of how students are doing, what they know and care about, and what they are able to do. Ongoing assessment is a powerful planning tool, helping teachers to plan for instruction but

Action Research — Using the Internet to Plan

The Internet can be a source for lesson and unit ideas, some of high quality and others of questionable value. Compile a list of Internet sites by doing a web search on the phrase *lesson planning*. Identify some websites that contain lesson plans for your content area. Evaluate the plans from the websites for how well they contain the following:

▶ Big Ideas linked to curriculum standards and assessments
▶ Appropriate teaching activities that improve content knowledge and literacy skill
▶ Opportunities for reading, writing, speaking, listening, viewing, and performing
▶ Teaching strategies that develop learning strategies
▶ Assessment of content knowledge, learning strategies, and motivation

Next, consider a plan that would use only Internet text materials. What would an Internet-based plan look like? What adjustments would you need to make for students if the resources for your plan were entirely on the Internet? Follow these steps and create an Internet-based lesson plan. Describe ways in which designing a lesson plan based on the Internet is similar to or different from basing a lesson plan on more conventional (text) resources.

1. Identify an audience of students.
2. Select a Big Idea for this audience (or a set of Big Ideas, for planning a unit). Remember to consult state and/or local curriculum standards and assessments.
3. Decide on the type of planning framework: direct instruction, problem-based, inquiry and research, unit plan.
4. List Internet resources (websites, links, etc.) for the lesson or unit.
5. List the teaching and learning strategies for the lesson or unit.
6. List the assessment activities for the lesson or unit.

also to reflect on how to improve instruction so that students learn more effectively. See Chapter 6, "Planning for Teaching and Learning," to learn more about ongoing assessment.

Planning Frameworks for Content Area Literacy

There are many different ways to plan. Each approach has with it particular challenges and opportunities for students. The following sections discuss some common **planning frameworks**: different structures for

Figure 4.2

Lesson and unit planning frameworks.

	Explanations, modeling, guiding, and providing feedback	Presenting students with an interesting and challenging problem and guiding them in solving it	Engaging students in making observations, gathering and reviewing data, and forming conclusions	Planning and teaching a series of lessons connected by Big Ideas or by a central Big Idea or question
Direct Instruction				
Problem-Based Learning				
Inquiry				
Unit Planning*				

*Can consist of one or various forms of lesson plan.

devising lesson and unit plans with different purposes. The descriptions and examples that follow provide a good starting point in thinking about how to approach planning. Figure 4.2 provides an overview of the planning frameworks discussed in the following sections.

Direct Instruction

Direct instruction consists of providing students with explicit explanations for new ideas, concepts, and skills, relating the new knowledge to what students know and providing opportunities for practice, feedback, and application. Direct instruction has received considerable research support (Gagne et al., 2004; Pressley, 1998). The effectiveness of direct instruction stems from ways in which teachers take explicit steps to ensure that students really learn.

Direct instruction should not be confused with a long-standing and fairly common practice: **recitation** (Gee, 1996). Recitation consists of telling students what they should know, quizzing students to see whether they "got it," and then moving on to new questions. A common misconception is that just because one student answers a question, all of the other students understand. Teaching as just recitation misses many opportunities to show students how to learn successfully.

In contrast to recitation, direct instruction involves specially planned **teacher explanations** designed to build on what students already know or know how to do to teach new knowledge and skill. Teachers who use direct instruction **model** or demonstrate for students how to use and apply new knowledge. Direct instruction also involves providing students with lots of opportunities for **practice** with new ideas. This is often referred to as **guided practice,** as teachers circulate and provide additional guidance, correcting misconceptions or elaborating, for example, as students explore new ideas. Finally, direct instruction consists of creating opportunities for **applying** new knowledge and skill by encouraging students to make connections with other ideas they have learned and ideas in the outside world.

Throughout the cycle of direct instruction, teachers should consider employing multiple kinds of literate practice, including reading, writing, speaking, listening, viewing, and performing. A simple model for direct instruction appears in Figure 4.3. Read the How to Plan feature on page 99 for ideas about how to use direct instruction to plan your own lessons.

Figure 4.3

Teaching and learning within direct instruction.

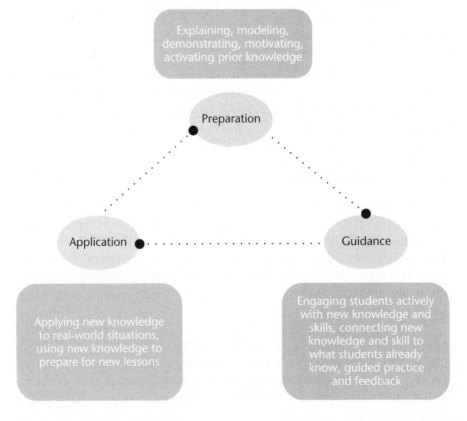

Explaining, modeling, demonstrating, motivating, activating prior knowledge

Preparation

Application

Guidance

Applying new knowledge to real-world situations, using new knowledge to prepare for new lessons

Engaging students actively with new knowledge and skills, connecting new knowledge and skill to what students already know, guided practice and feedback

How ...for a Lesson Employing Direct Instruction
TO PLAN

Consider these questions when preparing a lesson employing direct instruction (Gagne et al., 2004). Using these questions, design a lesson based on the direct instruction planning model.

Preparation
How will I gain students' attention about the Big Idea? What do students know or care about that can be used to start a conversation about the Big Idea for today's lesson? What are some ways to motivate students about learning the Big Idea? What connections can be made with the Big Idea right away?

How can I explain the objective(s) of the lesson? Sometimes, all this takes is a simple and direct explanation. Other times, a demonstration of new skills accompanied by an explanation will serve. Whatever your approach, make sure explanations explicitly state what students are about to learn.
This:
> Today, we are learning about the American pioneers, what motivated them, and how they made decisions about what to explore and where to travel.

Not this:
> Pioneers settled in new places, normally traveling by covered wagon. Let's read about the pioneers.

How can I connect the new lesson with previous learning? Identify previous Big Ideas and remind students about them. Provide opportunities throughout the lesson for students to recall important prior knowledge.

Guidance
How can I present, demonstrate, and discuss the new content? Consider ways to involve students in learning the new information. What experiences and skills do students have that could be used to learn the new content? How can students' experiences be used to shape their interpretations and, if appropriate, their evaluations of the new content? How will you provide multiple pathways to literacy, including reading, writing, speaking, listening, viewing, and performing, for students to learn? What accommodations need to be made for diverse learners, including students with special needs and English language learners?

How can I provide opportunities for students to practice ideas and skills from the new content? What in-school and out-of-school opportunities are available? What kinds of performances (such as conversations, research, and projects) could provide opportunities for practice?

How can I provide feedback? How can I deal with misconceptions? What further elaborations or demonstrations are necessary?

How can I assess students' performance? How will I determine that students have learned? How can I tell that they need further teaching? What kinds of reteaching will be necessary? How can I assess for later learning?

Application
How can I provide opportunities for students to apply newly acquired knowledge to new situations? How can I connect ideas from this lesson to ideas in the next lesson? How can I get students to connect in-school learning to out-of-school situations and contexts?

Figure 4.4

Problems for use in a problem-based approach to lesson planning.

Problem Solving in Mathematics

You are an architect planning a house for Mickey Bitsko, the pizza baron. This is Mr. Bitsko's summer home, so your budget is only a modest $1 million dollars. The house is being built on a small estate lot, so it cannot be any larger than 6000 square feet. You will need to plan for a kitchen, a dining room, an entertainment room, and six bedrooms: a master bedroom, four smaller bedrooms for each of Mr. Bitsko's children, and a guest room. The master bedroom needs to be larger than 200 square feet to accommodate Mr. Bitsko's exercise equipment. First, design the house to include all of the rooms. Next, calculate whether you have stayed within your budget of one million dollars, based on the building cost of $225 per square foot. Adjust your design for the house, depending on whether you are over or under your budget.

Problem Solving in English *(Based on* Roll of Thunder, Hear My Cry*)*

One of the students in your school is being ostracized and picked on because he dresses differently and talks differently from the other students. This student is constantly getting in fights with others. He sits alone in the cafeteria all the time and appears to have no friends. Thinking about the way the family is treated in *Roll of Thunder, Hear My Cry*, describe how you would act in this situation. What would you do, and what would you not do? How would you involve your friends? Family? Teachers?

Problem-Based Learning

In **problem-based learning** students are presented with an interesting and challenging problem and are guided through reasoning in how to solve it (Savoie & Hughes, 1994; Stepien & Gallagher, 1993). This approach is common in mathematics but also works well in English (moral and ethical dilemmas), history (resolving world conflicts), science (environmental issues), physical education (health and fitness issues), music (music appreciation and performance, art (art appreciation and performance), and foreign language (understanding and misunderstanding language and culture). For a problem-based lesson, teachers present a problem, such as the examples in Figure 4.4. Notice how the problems reflect real-world problems and/or problems directly connected to students' concerns.

To prepare students for problem solving, provide explanations and modeling, just as in direct instruction. This time, focus explanations and modeling on how to solve problems. Teachers can present a warm-up problem and model ways for students to approach problem solving. For instance, with the mathematics example, teachers could ask students to design and decorate a single room before asking them to work with the idea of an entire house. For the English example, teachers might ask students to work with a specific example from their reading before asking them to consider the moral dilemmas involving a student in their school. The full versions of the problems are occasions for students to practice their new understandings while teachers observe students' efforts and provide feedback. Application activities consist of solving a new problem or even having students write and solve a new problem. As should be evident, lessons that are organized around problem solving provide many opportunities for students to engage in many types of literate activities.

▲ Direct instruction involves more than simple "recitation." Direct instruction consists of explicit instruction of new knowledge and providing opportunities for practice and application to ensure understanding.

Inquiry

An **inquiry** focus for lesson planning engages students in using content knowledge as a means to research and inquire. Whereas gaining content knowledge itself can be the main focus with direct instruction and problem-solving lessons, inquiry involves students in *using and applying* content knowledge to learn more. A long-standing tradition within science teaching but more recently popular in many other content areas, inquiry consists of using content knowledge for making observations and gathering and reviewing data. (Collins, 1987; DeBoer, 1991; Rackow, 1986). Inquiry approaches work especially well in science when students make observations and predictions about the natural world, history when students examine historical and/or political data, and English, music, physical education, and family and consumer science when students ask questions concerning how people live their lives. These inquiries are often modeled on the work of people in society and the world—scientists, writers, lawyers, educators, and others—who actually engage in these activities. Inquiry lessons contain many opportunities for literate activity and learning.

A useful adaptation of our work with Big Ideas is the **Central Question.** Central Questions are open-ended questions that guide students' activities during inquiry-focused lessons. They can be adapted from curriculum standards, just like Big Ideas. The advantage of questions in contrast to

Figure 4.5

Examples of central questions for inquiry-focused lessons.

Science
How can I build big things?
What is the quality of air in my community?
What is the water like in my river?
Why do I have to wear a helmet when I ride my bike?
(From Marx et al., 2004)

Health, Physical Education, Recreation, and Dance
With so much attention on fitness, why is there an obesity epidemic?
Despite Title IX, why are some sports still called "masculine" while others are termed "feminine"?
What is a reasonable and doable plan for physical fitness?
Why is AIDS still an epidemic?
(From Daly, 1994)

Music
What do you feel and hear as you listen to the musical piece?
- Ask students to experiment and improvise on musical instruments as they listen to the musical piece once again.
- Ask students to improvise on percussion instruments and sing along as they listen to the musical piece a third time.
- Students start improvising with the recording, but then the recording is turned off, and students improvise without the recording.
- Students read the composer's description of his or her work, including the ideas and feelings the composer was trying to express.
- Ask students to improvise on musical instruments once again, this time trying to convey the feelings from the composer.
(From Allsup & Baxter, 2004)

Big Idea statements is their use as a vehicle to guide inquiry. Examples of Central Questions that are used for inquiry appear in Figure 4.5.

Again, it is helpful to consider this variation on lesson planning in the context of the direct instruction model. Many students are naturally curious about many of the topics in the world around them, and they certainly make many of their own observations. However, this does not mean that they know how to *do* inquiry, particularly in the ways in which people in society and the world do inquiry. This is where the teacher's role of explaining, modeling, and demonstrating comes in. As will be discussed in Chapter 7, "Activating Prior Knowledge and Increasing Motivation," one of the best things teachers can do to get students curious in a lesson is to provide experiences early on in which they can observe, feel, and record their experiences. For inquiry, this means such things as bringing an iguana to a science class, letting students explore a cartful of poetry books in an English class, or picking up an instrument just to make noise or to improvise or mimic a recorded song in a music class. Guided practice takes the form of shaping students' observations and helping them to make comparisons and conclusions. Focused Internet searches provide ways of elaborating and extending students' inquiry. Regular conversations throughout are a good way to keep inquiry-focused lessons on track.

Unit Planning

Unit planning consists of preparing a series of lessons connected by Big Ideas. Just as there are many different ways to design lessons, there are a number of ways to design units. There are also many ways to incorporate literate activities and practices. One of the simplest ways to devise a unit is to select one theme or core Big Idea such as the following:

- ▶ Four-sided figures
- ▶ Animals that cannot live without oxygen
- ▶ The color red in various media
- ▶ Physical conditioning needed for running sports
- ▶ Wars—why we have them and how we solve them
- ▶ Literature about death

Once a Big Idea for the unit has been identified, a next step is to make a list or map of all of the Big Ideas whose understanding contributes to the core idea for the unit. The mapping in Figure 4.6 is for a unit about physical conditioning for running sports.

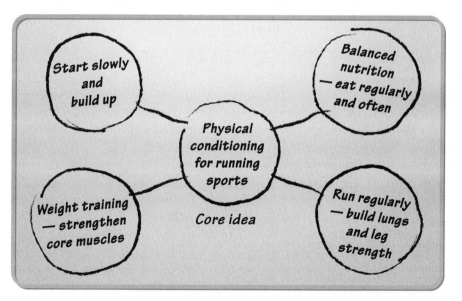

Figure 4.6
Big Idea web for unit planning.

One advantage of brainstorming and mapping out Big Ideas for a unit is that this helps students to anticipate and connect what they are about to learn. Research has shown that when teachers take the time create a unit organizer, understanding is improved, particularly for low-achieving students, students with learning disabilities, and even average-achieving students (Deshler et al., 2001). Figure 4.7 depicts a unit organizer for a unit on defending a position on current events along with a specific lesson dealing with a particular current event.

Units of study can reflect any one or a combination of planning frameworks, including direct instruction, problem-based learning, and inquiry. It is helpful to consider the nature of the Big Ideas in a unit in order to select particular frameworks. For example, a unit about six-sided three-dimensional figures might best be represented through hands-on inquiry, with students recording their observations of differently shaped quadrilaterals.

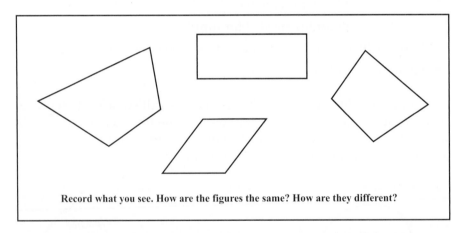

Record what you see. How are the figures the same? How are they different?

Teachers' understanding of students' knowledge might also influence the particular approach to a unit. If students have never considered alternative shapes other than a square, for example, inquiry might be the best approach to arouse their curiosity. Or a teacher might decide upon direct instruction because of students' inexperience.

A unit about animal respiration might best be approached through direct instruction. Again, students' knowledge could be a deciding factor. Though students have experience with their own respiration, the abstract nature of some of the Big Ideas and concepts might call for greater explanation and modeling of ways to think about the ideas. Or a teacher could approach the unit from a problem-solving perspective, knowing that students are concerned about the effects of smoking on lung health and lung cancer.

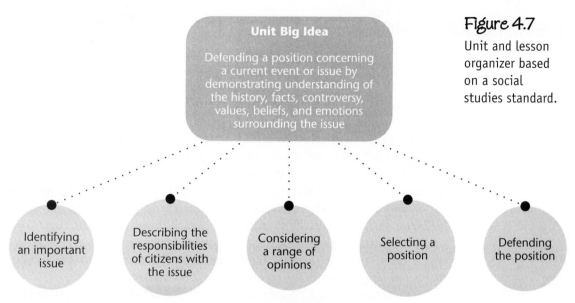

Lesson Big Idea
Society's difficult choices about life and death: The case of Terri Schiavo

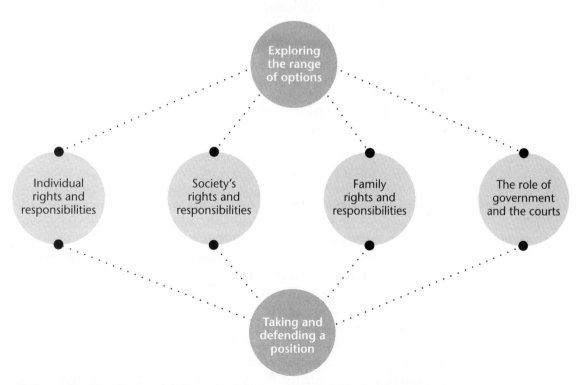

Challenge Question: Does society have the right to make end-of-life decisions, or is that up to the individual?

Planning for Teaching and Learning with Texts

Not all lessons are centered on texts, but many of them are. There are particular ways in which teachers need to think about planning for students' learning with texts. Many students attack texts with little sense of purpose. They just go through the motions of reading, sometimes not reading very much at all. As discussed in Chapter 5, "Understanding and Using Texts," there are many different possible purposes for using texts. One obvious purpose is for students to gain more knowledge. Another related purpose is for students to gain a variety of perspectives. One way to do this is for students to read and respond to a variety of texts. Yet another purpose is to help students become more aware of their own understanding as they read texts—in other words, to know more clearly what they know. A number of approaches to planning have been proposed to help students learn more effectively with texts.

The **instructional framework** (Herber, 1978; Herber & Nelson-Herber, 1993) is intended to address purposes for learning with texts before reading, during reading, and after reading. The components of the instructional framework mirror the elements of direct instruction. This is no accident. It is only logical to expect that learning is most effective when teachers explain, demonstrate, guide, and help students make connections, whether they are learning with texts or using any other representation of knowledge (magazine, multimedia, or digital, for example). Figure 4.8 presents the major components of the instructional framework for learning with texts: prereading, guiding reader-text interactions, and postreading.

Prereading

Prereading is literally getting ready to read texts. Activities within prereading can range from more teacher-directed to highly interactive with students. Teacher-directed approaches to prereading include providing students with a context for understanding the text to be read, leading a discussion about the topic of the reading, and providing information about the knowledge within the upcoming texts. More interactive approaches to prereading engage students in making observations, raising questions, forming predictions, and asking questions. The difference in choosing one approach versus the other depends on students' prior knowledge and motivation for the new learning along with the complexity and degree of students' familiarity with the text. With little knowledge, experience, or motivation, students benefit from greater teacher

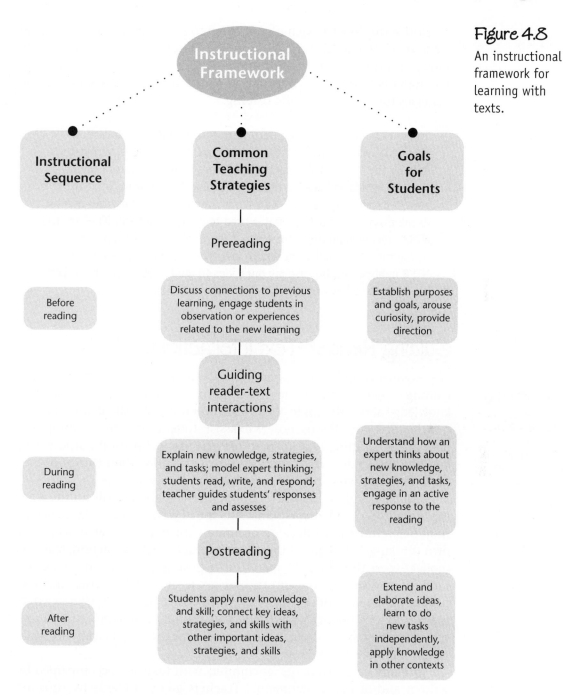

Figure 4.8
An instructional framework for learning with texts.

Instructional Framework

Instructional Sequence

Common Teaching Strategies

Goals for Students

Prereading

Discuss connections to previous learning, engage students in observation or experiences related to the new learning

Establish purposes and goals, arouse curiosity, provide direction

Guiding reader-text interactions

Explain new knowledge, strategies, and tasks; model expert thinking; students read, write, and respond; teacher guides students' responses and assesses

Understand how an expert thinks about new knowledge, strategies, and tasks, engage in an active response to the reading

Postreading

Students apply new knowledge and skill; connect key ideas, strategies, and skills with other important ideas, strategies, and skills

Extend and elaborate ideas, learn to do new tasks independently, apply knowledge in other contexts

Before reading

During reading

After reading

direction, at least at the start. In other cases in which students know a bit more and are curious, teachers can extend opportunities for students to discuss and ponder. In any case, prereading should effectively establish purpose for reading texts, arouse curiosity, and provide direction.

Notice this health teacher's approach to prereading. She is preparing her students to read and respond to some National Transportation Safety Bureau (NTSB) accident reports and statistics. Observe how she focuses her students' attention with guiding questions as well as some simple strategies for approaching the reading:

> "We're going to read some information today, and some statistics, about highway fatalities due to alcoholism. The statistics were gathered by the National Transportation Safety Board in a recent publication. Now, this will seem a little technical at first. But we want to zero in on three questions: How big is the problem of fatalities due to drunk driving? What have states tried to do about it? and What are the NTSB's recommendations for preventing problems with drunk drivers in the future? I don't want you to feel that you have to read the entire NTSB publication. But use my questions to guide you as you read. Let's see what they have to say about ending this horrible problem."

Guiding Reader-Text Interactions

Click on A+RISE – WIDA ELP Standard Strategy in the MyEducationLab (www.myeducationlab .com) for your course. Next, select the Strategy Card Index tab, scroll to Fluency for Grades 6–12 and select the Guided Reading with Read Alouds strategy.

The essence of **guiding** is *showing how*. There are several purposes for guiding reader-text interactions. One purpose is to help students develop knowledge about the topic of the text (and not just soak up and regurgitate the text). Another purpose is to assist students with monitoring their own understanding, to ask: Does this make sense? A third purpose is to develop knowledge in students about what to do when things do not make sense. So what does this look like in practice?

Teachers guide students by reminding them about goals for the reading. They offer students explanations for new knowledge. Even better, they help students to develop accurate explanations that reflect their own thinking. Throughout the period of reader-text interaction, teachers model expert thinking. They do this by posing questions, thinking out loud about ideas and concepts that are not clear, and demonstrating how to construct new understandings. An honest and useful acknowledgement is to let students know when you are not clear about an idea and concept. Then show them how you build meaning, especially in situations that are not very clear.

In many cases, students' encounters with texts are accompanied by written and/or oral assignments. Teachers guide students by showing them ways of connecting their assignments with meaning in the texts. Doing this requires special knowledge on the part of the teacher about the demands of different assignments, for example, answering questions versus gathering information for a report. Teachers guide students by sharing this special knowledge with students so that they can successfully engage in all kinds of responses to their reading. Consider how this music teacher does this for his students: "I remember the first time I studied musical time signatures, I got very confused. It helped me to think about fractions, particularly when I thought about dividing a pie into quarters. Once I figured out the whole-part relationships, then it all started to fall into place."

Postreading

Postreading is a time for recapping, organizing, remembering, and applying. A good practice throughout a text-centered lesson is to regularly ask: What do we know now? Postreading is an excellent time to ask that question, but it should not be the only time. Organizing the new knowledge can take many forms, from simple written summaries to maps and diagrams that show how the new knowledge is connected to other ideas students have learned. Sometimes, when teachers and students have arrived at this point and it seems that students know the new knowledge, teachers assume that the learning can stop. But this is the time in a lesson that is ripe for making new connections with old knowledge, world knowledge, and knowledge in upcoming lessons. Effective postreading activities extend and elaborate new ideas and apply the new knowledge to many other contexts. Notice how this science teacher does this with his students: "So now that we've read about efforts to physically clean up the rivers around Detroit—with publicly led volunteer cleanup efforts, for example—let's think about some ways that we, as scientists, could get involved."

Planning for Culturally Responsive Teaching

Earlier, we discussed planning for differentiated instruction, providing for differences in students' knowledge, motivation and skill. A related and equally important consideration for planning is **culturally responsive pedagogy** (Gay, 2000; Moje & Hinchman, 2004). Culturally responsive teaching consists of using the cultural knowledge, prior experiences, and performance styles of culturally diverse students and making learning more appropriate and effective for them. For planning, this means that teachers need to learn as much as possible about students' cultural backgrounds but also about their experiences as

▲ **In the culturally responsive classroom, students are active participants in all aspects of the classroom.**

individuals and members of a family and the community, all of which shapes students' knowledge, motivation, and skills.

These are research-based principles for practicing culturally responsive pedagogy with culturally diverse adolescents (Moje & Hinchman, 2004). Accompanying each principle is an idea or set of ideas for how to apply the principle. The Teaching Today's Learners feature provides a snapshot for how one teacher put these principles into practice.

1. **Culturally responsive teaching begins with forming a relationship between teachers and students.** Teachers can go to community events, get to know students' families, and get to know what students care about.

2. **Culturally responsive teaching recognizes and is respectful of the many different cultural experiences that any one person can embody.** Teachers need to understand that individuals do not in themselves represent cultural groups but that individuals are influenced by their cultural backgrounds.

3. **Culturally responsive teaching works with adolescents to develop applications of content knowledge that are relevant to them.** Teachers can organize instruction around questions that are of interest to students, including everyday observations.

4. **Culturally responsive teaching depends on developing in-depth understandings of content area knowledge.** Students do not benefit when curriculum content is either watered down or too focused solely on testing demands. Teachers need to help students build knowledge in ways that will help them be successful later on in life.

5. **Culturally responsive teaching invites adolescents to participate in multiple and varied content-specific experiences, including reading, writing, speaking, listening, and performing in the service of increasingly sophisticated knowledge construction.** Teachers need to help students learn to communicate in multiple ways within content area disciplines but also across different disciplines.

Teaching Today's Learners

Planning for Culturally Diverse Students

Read the following vignette about Ms. Appel and her students preparing to read *The Joy Luck Club*. How many principles of culturally responsive pedagogy can you identify from Ms. Appel's approach to teaching?

Ms. Appel, a high school English teacher, attends school events, such as band concerts and athletic events, because she gets to see her students in different settings. Sometimes, they are with their families, many of whom are Italian American or African American, and she gets to meet them. The families also enjoy meeting her. She shares stories of growing up in a different community as the daughter of a teacher and a retail sales clerk. Her visibility in the community is particularly helpful when students are struggling in her class or misbehaving or when there are reasons to celebrate their successes. Parents know that she is available and interested in their concerns.

One of the novel selections on the required book list is *The Joy Luck Club* by Amy Tan. Ms. Appel wants to use this novel rather than others such as *The Scarlet Letter* or *The Old Man and the Sea* because it bears more of a relationship to her students' lives. The novel is about four women who came to America many years ago to escape China's feudal society for the promise of democracy. Each woman has a daughter who belongs to the new generation, those of Chinese heritage who grew up speaking English and learning American customs. *The Joy Luck Club* tells of the varied difficulties and tragedies involved in the mother-daughter relationships. Ms. Appel notes similarities between the immigrant families in the novel and those in her community. She also notices comparisons with respect to life's challenges,

including parents' and children's struggles to understand one another.

Ms. Appel plans to start work with the novel by engaging students in a study of family history. Students will brainstorm interview questions and then interview selected family members, such as parents and grandparents. The focus of the interviews will be questions such as: What was it like for you growing up? What challenges did you face? How did you overcome the challenges? and What did you learn? After conducting their interviews, students would be instructed to turn the questions over to their interviewees and have them ask the same questions. Ms. Appel planned to teach her students strategies for recording and drawing themes from these interviews.

Once the interviews were gathered and interpreted by individual students, Ms. Appel planned to have students compare the results of their interviews across families. What was growing up like for everyone across the community? What were the common struggles? How did people overcome them? and How were parents' struggles the same or different from the students?

While this interview process would take up a good deal of time, Ms. Appel justified the time spent in a couple of ways. The interviews would engage in exploring relationships not unlike those portrayed in the novel. Also, the process would help students to understand the importance of appreciating multiple kinds of perspectives, not only in their families but also across the community. As students proceeded to read *The Joy Luck Club*, Ms. Appel could see many examples of how her planning paid off. Students noted many comparisons between the novel and their own lives.

6. **Culturally responsive teaching invites adolescents to develop and express new understandings of the world, merging mainstream content concepts with everyday knowledge in alternative forms.** Teachers need to provide many opportunities for students to explore multiple perspectives on information.

Planning for Teaching Students to Become Strategic Learners

Another critical part of planning concerns the development of learning strategies. Although it is important for students to grow in their knowledge of the content, it is equally essential for them to understand how to gain knowledge on their own. This section describes the nature of learning strategies and how to teach them.

The Nature of Learning Strategies

Webster's Third International Dictionary defines a strategy as a plan of action that is intended to accomplish a specific goal (Gove, 2002). A **learning strategy** is a plan of action to learn an idea, a concept, a skill, or any number of other things. Teaching students about learning strategies will not only increase students' knowledge in a content area but also show them how to learn independently (Nokes & Dole, 2004).

To consider your own use of learning strategies in the past, think about one of the most demanding courses you ever experienced, one with the most reading and the greatest number of complicated assignments. What did you do to get through that course? Did you focus on the assignments and read only those readings that related directly to the assignments? Did you learn to skim and summarize, looking for what was important to accomplish the assignments successfully? These are examples of learning strategies. A selection of research-based learning strategies and their use appears in Figure 4.9.

Many students are left to acquire learning strategies on their own, without any help from teachers. Research suggests that a very few students are able to attain learning strategies naturally from their experiences with learning but that many more are not (Pressley, 2006). These strategies have been found to be particularly effective with special needs students (Deshler et al., 2001) and English language learners (Krashen,

Learning Strategy	What it does
Getting yourself motivated	Establishes purposes, arouses curiosity
Activating prior knowledge	Simulates thinking about what you know
Connecting the known to the new	Connects new knowledge to what you already know
Using the context	Uses information from surrounding text or context to figure out unknown information
Building meaning from familiar word parts	Breaks down larger words into smaller, more recognizable parts
Using references	Connects questions and needs for information to sources of information
Extending and remembering	Elaborates new learning and organizes it for later recall
Predicting	Builds predictions based on prior knowledge, conversation, and/or text
Questioning	Developing questions that target attention, combine and integrate knowledge
Using imagery	Making pictures in your mind for what you are reading and/or learning
Summarizing	Taking larger selections of text and reducing them to their bare essentials
Considering, evaluating, and taking multiple perspectives	Establishing, comparing, and assessing points of view
Considering evidence	Connecting perspectives to supporting knowledge
Planning	Developing a course of action, such as in reading or writing
Writing	Setting down and organizing thoughts and ideas in written form
Reviewing and revising	Reconsidering, changing, modifying ideas and concepts

Figure 4.9

Research-based learning strategies and their uses.

2004), but all students can benefit from work with them. Learning strategies need to be taught, and they are taught most effectively in the contexts in which they are used: content area classrooms.

Teaching Learning Strategies

What are some effective ways of developing learning strategies? A first step is to identify the content for teaching and design a plan. Select text and other resources. Then step back and ask: What are some learning strategies that could assist students, given what students are about to learn? Consult the chart in Figure 4.9 for some answers to this question.

Different lessons provide opportunities for focusing on different learning strategies. For example, some lessons are characterized by substantial numbers of unfamiliar words. During these lessons, students could learn and practice with strategies for understanding unfamiliar words (connecting the new to the known, using the context, syllabication, or references). Other lessons are occasions for teaching strategies that develop comprehension (predicting, questioning, using imagery, summarizing). Still other lessons present opportunities for teaching learning strategies such as perspective taking and supporting a perspective through evidence (taking perspective, considering evidence). Some lessons are opportunities for teaching about writing strategies (planning, writing, reviewing, and revising). Teachers consider the characteristics of your intended lesson or even unit and then identify the learning strategies that make the most sense.

Once teachers have identified the learning strategy or strategies that are most appropriate for a particular lesson, it is time to consider the best ways to teach them. Figure 4.10 depicts a chart that relates research-based learning strategies to teaching strategies.

This chart will guide our work through the rest of this book. Like learning strategies, teaching strategies are ways of achieving a goal. Teaching strategies are a plan of action to develop content knowledge and learning strategies. Like learning strategies, there are often a number of teaching strategies from which to choose. The choice of an appropriate teaching strategy depends on the lesson.

Here's an example. A **semantic map** is a very popular teaching strategy for helping students connect what they already know to new knowledge, particularly new vocabulary concepts. A common use of semantic maps is for teachers to ask discussion questions and then draw a map, recording students' responses. The act of drawing a semantic map brings up important prior knowledge, but it does not teach students how to use that knowledge or create and use semantic maps on their own to learn new knowledge. For that to happen, teachers need to teach a learning strategy: *how to connect the known to the new.*

These are the steps for teaching a learning strategy (Pressley, 2006):

▶ Name the strategy and explain it to the students.

▶ Describe the use of the strategy.

▶ Model ways to use the strategy.

Click on A+RISE – Literacy Strategies in the MyEducationLab (www.myeducationlab. com) for your course. Next, select the Strategy Card Index tab, scroll to Vocabulary and select the Semantic or Concept Web for Upper Grades strategy.

Chapter	Learning Strategy	Teaching Strategies
Increasing Motivation and Activating Prior Knowledge	Getting motivated	Concept-oriented reading instruction
	Activating prior knowledge	Anticipation guides, PreP, K-W-L
Vocabulary	Connecting the known to the new	List-group-label, semantic mapping, graphic organizers
	Using the context	Context
	Syllabication	Word parts
	Using references	Dictionary, thesaurus, Internet
	Extending and remembering	Vocabulary self-collection, categorization, semantic feature analysis, word puzzles
Guiding Students' Reading to Learn	Predicting	Directed reading-thinking activity
	Questioning	Three-level guides, question-answer relationships, ReQuest
	Imagery	Guided imagery, visual imagery strategy
	Summarizing	Using text patterns to summarize, guided reading procedure
	Remembering	Note taking
Guiding Students' Critical Literacy	Constructing and evaluating perspectives	Questioning the author, critical media literacy lessons, taking a stand on content, web quests
	Considering and evaluating evidence	Reaction guides, discussion webs, critical media literacy lessons
Guiding Students' Writing	Planning	Analyzing writing assignments, brainstorming and organizing, gathering information
	Writing	Persuasive writing, journal writing and learning logs, writing to inquire (research), writing a report, writing a narrative
	Reviewing and revising	Self-evaluation checklist, peer evaluation, rubrics for evaluating writing

Figure 4.10

Research-based learning strategies and teaching strategies designed to teach them.

▶ Encourage students to use the strategy, especially during reading and writing.

▶ Provide students with opportunities to practice and apply the strategy.

▶ Point out occasions when students spontaneously use the strategy on their own.

The goal of the science teacher, Mr. Anderson, who employed the semantic map in Figure 4.11, was to help his seventh-grade students build an understanding of the Big Idea why airplanes fly based on their observations about airplanes and flying. But he also wanted to explicitly teach his students that an important learning strategy in science is connecting the known to the new. So he started his lesson by explaining the learning strategy and showing students how to use it. He described a time when learning about weather reporting how he considered what he already knew about the weather. Then, when he studied the science behind the weather, he was able to confirm some of the ideas but add others. He called this connecting the known to the new and explained that this is a good way to learn science. Next, he introduced the teaching activity, a semantic map, as a good way of recording the known information and connecting it to the new information. Students practiced creating maps of their own knowledge before Mr. Anderson led the class in a discussion and mapping activity devoted to why airplanes fly. The class continually referred back to this map as they read and researched more information related to the Big Idea. In subsequent lessons, Mr. Anderson reinforced students' use of connecting the known to the new by reminding them about the learning strategy and praising them when they used it on their own.

Figure 4.11

Using a semantic map to develop a learning strategy.

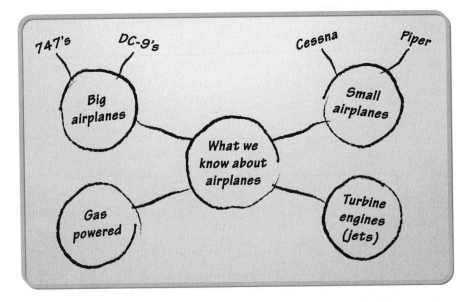

Planning for Ongoing Assessment

A well-crafted set of plans for a series of lessons or a unit presents many opportunities for assessment. Consider what has been discussed so far in this chapter. Planning needs to focus on students and their knowledge, skill, and motivation. Assessment can inform teachers' plans for students as well as help to reflect on lesson and unit outcomes. Planning must be grounded in high expectations. Assessment can be used to determine through multiple ways how students are meeting expectations. Planning involves thoughtful selection and use of texts and other resources. Assessment can help with text decisions as well as aiding in evaluating the appropriateness of those decisions. Planning should include considerations of how to help students learn from texts and develop learning strategies for them to learn on their own. Assessment can be employed to figure out what students have learned and how they have learned to apply knowledge and strategies. Consider these examples for assessing students' content knowledge, their development of learning strategies, and their motivation.

▲ An important part of planning for instruction includes planning for ongoing assessment of content knowledge as well as interest and involvement.

Assessing Content Knowledge

Consider this far-too-common scenario. Teachers develop a test based on the content of a lesson or unit, and most, if not all, of the students do poorly. What could be the reasons? Many times, the content from teaching and the content of assessment are similar, if not the same, yet the manner in which teachers teach and the questions on the test are not congruent. A good example of this mismatch concerns some hands-on, authentic lessons and units in which, for example, students plan an extended vacation to another country, measure air pollution using scientific measuring equipment, or propose solutions for an enduring community problem such as joblessness and poverty. Many teachers are surprised when their observations indicate that students are learning the intended concepts but a test later suggests that the students have not learned them.

Plan for assessing content knowledge in a variety of ways. For example, use opportunities for assessment that frequently occur, such as classroom conversations and observations, but also consider ways for making more formal assessments so that they reveal what students

Connecting Standards and Assessment

Classroom Assessment

Classroom assessments are excellent ways to capture the day-to-day growth of students. To do so, the assessments need to be rich, purposeful, and varied. Teachers need an ongoing picture of students' developing content knowledge, their skills, and their dispositions. Multiple and varied assessments provide new and different opportunities for students to revisit, rethink, and internalize what they are learning. And classroom assessments need to be seriously considered with respect to broader state standards and assessments.

Though it has a funny-sounding name, kidwatching is a time-honored form of informal student observation. Kidwatching can be adapted to a wide variety of classroom tasks and purposes, with the goal of observing how well students are learning. For younger students, oral reading performance will often provide clues to their oral reading fluency.

Students who struggle with oral reading will need additional help in other areas, such as comprehension. Sometimes, teachers can employ or design their own informal reading inventories to assess students' skills with reading and writing in a content area. A content area reading inventory is a useful device for determining how adolescents deal with content area texts. Portfolios are excellent for involving students in their own assessment.

Perhaps one of the most challenging aspects of classroom assessment involves interpreting students' performance. Looking for patterns in student performance across different kinds of tests is one way to make sense of all of the data. Teachers should also be ready to critically examine their own tests for flaws or misinterpretations on the part of their students.

▶ **Read more about these ideas in Chapter 11, "Selecting, Designing and Using Classroom Assessments" in Conley's (2005)** *Connecting Standards and Assessment through Literacy,* **published by Pearson Education.**

have learned. Sometimes, this requires making assessments more closely resemble the activities that occur during teaching. Other times, teachers should teach students specific strategies for completing assessments with which they are unfamiliar. The Connecting Standards and Assessment feature suggests ideas about how to plan for classroom assessment.

Assessing Learning Strategies

Another important aspect of planning for assessment should be determining whether students are acquiring and understanding learning strategies. Incorporate tasks on assessments that provide students with additional practice in applying learning strategies. For example, present students with a question or problem. Rather than simply being asked to answer the question or solve the problem, students are required to name a learning strategy they could use. For example, consider the unfinished detective story in Figure 4.12.

For *A Dark and Stormy Night,* students might use some combination of summarizing what happened, taking a perspective, and considering supporting evidence. Teachers can use assessment to strengthen students' understanding of learning strategies by provide opportunities for students to talk about their choices while teachers offer feedback and students learn from one another.

Describe a learning strategy that you could use to solve this murder mystery:

A Dark and Stormy Night

It was a dark and stormy night on the good ship Candy Bar. The seas were swelling up as the storm approached. Suddenly, a shot rang out. Everyone rushed to the sound of the gunfire, Cadbury's room. Inside the room, Cadbury lay dead, one shot through his heart. Everyone was a suspect, as the captain began his questioning. Penny Chocolate said that she was enjoying a glass of red wine in her cabin. There was a wine stain on her robe. The Southern gentleman, Mint Patty, said that he was on the upper deck enjoying a cigar. His breath reeked of cigars. Tootsie Roll, an entertainer from New York, produced a letter that she said she was writing when Cadbury was shot. The writing on the letter was perfectly formed. Who murdered Cadbury?

Figure 4.12

Choosing a strategy to find an answer: An unfinished detective story.

Assessing Motivation

Everyday conversations and occasional interviews and surveys are excellent ways to plan for assessing motivation. There are many different ways in which students signal that they value what they are learning, feel successful, and want to learn more. A key indicator concerns ways in which students connect effort with their motivation. Students who are motivated tend to be knowledgeable, skillful, and excited about learning more. The opposite is also true. Students who are struggling are usually unwilling to trudge on. Plan to watch for signs of students' increasing knowledge, skill, and confidence. Consider reasons why students might be motivated or unmotivated as clues to how future planning might need to be adjusted to improve motivation.

Summary

Highly effective classrooms are well planned, with many opportunities to read, write, and converse. These are classrooms where teachers improve students' content knowledge while respecting and incorporating students' backgrounds and also teaching students how to learn. Planning to help students learn with texts requires special considerations. Texts present opportunities to teach students about skilled reading and writing. Plans based on learning with texts provide occasions for teaching students about learning strategies. Finally, with any plan, do not neglect assessment. Every phase of planning and instruction invites assessment. Make sure that plans for assessment are varied yet consistent with teaching practices.

Special Projects

1. This chapter has presented many of the ingredients that go into lesson and unit planning. Now it is time to devise your own plan. Follow these steps:

   a. Identify an audience of students (e.g., a varied group of eighth graders or a group of eleventh graders).

   b. Select a Big Idea for this audience (or a set of Big Ideas, for planning a unit). Remember to consult state and/or local curriculum standards and assessments.

c. Decide on the type of planning framework: direct instruction, problem-based, inquiry and research, unit plan.

    d. List the texts and other resources for the lesson or unit.

    e. List the teaching and learning strategies for the lesson or unit.

    f. List the assessment activities for the lesson or unit.

2. Describe some learning strategies you have used in the past. In what situations did these strategies work best for you? What are some situations in which these strategies did not work as well? How could you teach someone else how to use a strategy that has worked for you?

Praxis Practice

Working with Questions to Prepare for the Praxis Reading Across the Curriculum Test

Multiple Choice Questions

1. Even though students can be very diverse in their literacy abilities, lessons should be planned around:

    a. Varied expectations

    b. High expectations

    c. Fun and motivation

    d. Important facts and details

2. An important framework for teaching from texts involves different activities for:

    a. Taking notes, asking questions and summarizing

    b. Learning vocabulary, comprehending and writing

    c. Decoding, spelling and speaking

    d. Pre-reading, during reading and post reading

3. Direct instruction that teaches literacy involves:

    a. Explanation, demonstrations, modeling and student practice

    b. Lecture, note-taking, testing and recitation

    c. Correcting students' work and handing it back for them to correct

    d. Explaining big ideas and then assigning book work

Constructed Response Question

1. Describe a lesson in which you employ direct instruction to teach content knowledge and literacy in your content area.

Suggested Readings

Gay, G. (2000). *Culturally responsive teaching: Theory, research, and practice.* New York: Teachers College Press.

Lenz, K., & Deshler, D. (2004). *Teaching content to all: Evidence-based inclusive practices in middle and secondary schools.* Boston: Allyn and Bacon.

Moje, E., & Hinchman, K. (2004). Culturally responsive practices for youth literacy learning. In T. Jetton & J. Dole (Eds.), *Adolescent literacy research and practice* (pp. 321–350). New York: Guilford.

Pressley, M. (2005). *Reading instruction that works: The case for balanced teaching.* New York: Guilford.

The Power of Classroom Practice

Go to Topic 7: Planning for Instruction in the MyEducationLab (www.myeducationlab.com) for your course, where you can:

- Find learning outcomes for Topic 7: Planning for Instruction along with the national standards that connect to these outcomes.
- Complete Assignments and Activities that can help you more deeply understand the chapter content.
- Apply and practice your understanding of the core teaching skills identified in the chapter with the Building Teaching Skills and Dispositions learning units.
- Examine challenging situations and cases presented in the IRIS Center Resources.

Go to the Topic A+RISE in the MyEducationLab (www.myeducationlab.com) for your course. A+RISE® Standards2Strategy™ is an innovative and interactive online resource that offers new teachers in grades K-12 just in time, research-based instructional strategies that:

- Meet the linguistic needs of ELLs as they learn content
- Differentiate instruction for all grades and abilities
- Offer reading and writing techniques, cooperative learning, use of linguistic and nonlinguistic representations, scaffolding, teacher modeling, higher order thinking, and alternative classroom ELL assessment
- Provide support to help teachers be effective through the integration of listening, speaking, reading, and writing along with the content curriculum
- Improve student achievement
- Are aligned to Common Core Elementary Language Arts standards (for the literacy strategies) and to English language proficiency standards in WIDA, Texas, California, and Florida.

5 Understanding and Using Texts

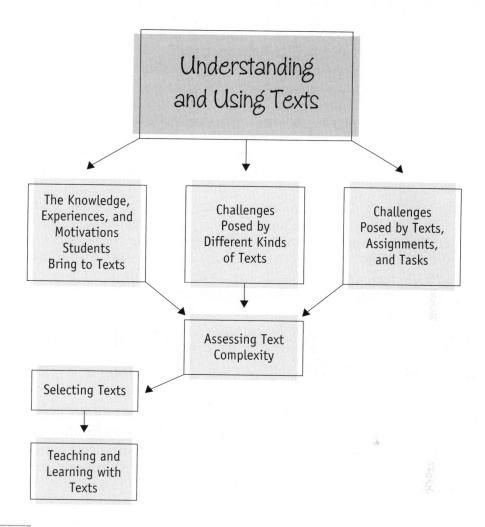

popular image of the classroom is of a teacher standing in front of rows of students, textbooks open and at the ready. Now consider the modern classroom. Sure, textbooks are still evident. Literature is sometimes the central focus, especially in English classes, but literature is used to broaden and enrich understandings in many other content areas. A growing trend is for classrooms to embrace texts from popular culture, including Internet web pages, trade books, music, movies and other media, magazines, and newspapers (Morrell, 2004). But there are also desktop computers, laptops, and iPods. Teachers, who in the past wrote their lessons on overhead projectors, now use PowerPoint and podcasts.

An ongoing dilemma, which started long before the Digital Age, concerns making the most effective use of textual resources. Decisions about texts rely in part on students—on their knowledge and experiences and their motivation. Students who have a strong sense of purpose about a text will read and respond to the most challenging texts. Consider instances in which students are told by adults that they are not allowed to read certain popular culture texts, such as comic books or teen magazines. Texts and their characteristics also play a role. Regardless of student motivation, some texts stop students from learning anything useful because of their complexity. Consider students who give up on playing Dungeons and Dragons or chess online because the rules are too hard to read and apply. At the heart of any discussion about texts are ways in which students are asked to perform different kinds of tasks or assignments with texts. Teachers play an important role in creating text-based assignments that invite motivation and engagement. This chapter is about the texts, how teachers can understand what students bring to their interactions with texts, and realizing the potential for various texts to help students learn in content areas.

The Knowledge, Experiences, and Motivations Students Bring to Texts

Any discussion of texts and their nature and complexity needs to begin with the motivation, knowledge, and experiences that students bring to texts (Alexander & Jetton, 2000). There is a long-standing image of students encountering complicated texts and stopping cold. For some students, this might be true for a variety of reasons. It is always a good idea to accurately assess students' knowledge throughout your teaching with texts. Knowledge about texts involves understanding the linguistic code—the sounds and how they go together into words and sentences—and the meanings. It also involves topical knowledge that comes from the outside world or from experience in a subject. Some students, particularly special needs students and English language learners, might be struggling with the language of the text, yet they may have world knowledge or even subject matter knowledge that could help them to compensate. Other students might understand the words and the basic meanings but have little knowledge or experience to help them out (Alexander & Jetton, 2000).

Students' Knowledge and Texts

Having a great deal of knowledge about a text's topic is one way in which students sometimes overcome complexity. Students who are widely read in an area or have relevant life experiences often build on

those experiences to confront complicated texts. For instance, in a social
studies unit devoted to researching the
Arctic, one student demonstrated considerable skill in locating and learning
from texts about Arctic explorations.
This student happened to have an uncle
whose role in the Army Corps of Engineers involved Arctic exploration! Now
consider the opposite situation, in which
students have little, if any, knowledge
about topics or texts. As the Teaching
Today's Learners feature demonstrates,
teachers need to be ready to help students
with diverse kinds of knowledge and experience, especially students with special
needs and English language learners.

▲ Some students
may struggle with
the language of
a text. Be sure
to assess their
comprehension
and provide help
when necessary.

Students' Experiences with Texts

Still another way in which students learn to deal with text complexity is
through experience and learning. Students sometimes encounter poorly
written texts—texts with murky purposes and mysterious organizational
schemes. Some poorly written texts do not bother to offer much by way
of explanation or example. Yet, over time and through experience, some
students learn to create their own purposes in reading and to develop
organization and coherence in poorly written texts through notes taken
about these texts. Think about similar experiences in which you com-
pensated for poorly written texts. What tools did you use to understand?
Outlining? Note taking? Consider teaching ways of using these techniques to help students learn with complicated and poorly written texts.

Motivation and Texts

To some extent, motivation can overcome problems that students encounter with texts. If a text contains knowledge that students really want to
gain, they might be persistent enough to overcome a text's problems. Alternatively, when students are not particularly motivated, teachers need to
find ways to help students see personal connections with texts. Even when
texts are not particularly complex, students might still need help with motivation. The How to Plan feature on page 129 offers ideas about building
students' knowledge, experience, and motivation for learning from texts.

Teaching Today's Learners

Using Texts with Students with Special Needs and English Language Learners

Consider these principles when planning to use texts with students with special needs and with English language learners. Describe a lesson in your content area in which these principles are operating.

Diverse Students and their Resources

Remember that diverse students come into encounters with texts with many resources, despite cognitive, social, and emotional challenges and/or language differences. Some of these resources include the following:

▶ **Knowledge and information:** from family experiences, about other countries and their cultures, customs, and resources
▶ **New and different perspectives:** about families and the community, the world, society, and beliefs
▶ **Opportunities for learning:** from sharing ways of thinking, exposure to other languages, and doing things that might otherwise be taken for granted

Instructional Accommodations

Plan for teaching diverse students with texts, using these research-based principles:

▶ Understand that some students need more time than others to engage in text-based activities.

▶ Understand that students learn with texts in different ways (such as reading, writing, listening, and communicating).
▶ Communicate clear expectations for students in learning with texts.
▶ Demonstrate and model for students how to meet high expectations.
▶ Whenever possible, combine conversation with learning with texts.
▶ Base instruction with texts within students' experiences.
▶ Whenever possible, involve students by actively engaging them with texts.
▶ Make instructional activities accompanying learning with texts structured and predictable.
▶ Ask questions that require extended responses (as opposed to brief yes-no responses).
▶ Build in-depth investigations of text content.

Employ a wide variety of groupings—pairs, small groups, and the whole class—to provide students with a variety of communication opportunities.

Source: The National Clearinghouse for Bilingual Education.

HOW TO PLAN

... for Facilitating Learning with Texts

The following research-based principles have been found to be effective in supporting students' learning with texts (Johannessen, 2004). Select a Big Idea within your content area, ideally one that is connected to a curriculum standard. Describe a lesson that is constructed with the Big Idea as the starting point. Next, select some text resources that you can use to teach the Big Idea. Considering the following list of principles, describe ways in which you will facilitate students' learning from texts, given this Big Idea and lesson.

Developing Motivation for Texts

▶ Connect students' out-of-school knowledge and life experiences with texts.
▶ Demonstrate for students how they can make these connections on their own.

Developing Experience with Texts

▶ Model effective comprehension of texts. Ask, "Does this make sense?" and "What do I know now?" Demonstrate ways of using these questions to check for understanding.
▶ Lead the class through discussion aimed at figuring out a difficult text passage before asking students to try it on their own.
▶ Make conversation and dialogue the central medium for teaching and learning with texts.

Developing Knowledge with Texts

▶ Teach students to continuously compare what they already know with what they are learning from texts.
▶ Provide scaffolding (demonstrations, modeling, and support) to enable students to perform complex tasks to gain knowledge while learning with texts.

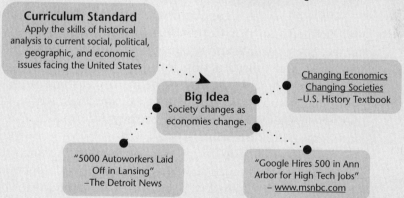

Curriculum Standard
Apply the skills of historical analysis to current social, political, geographic, and economic issues facing the United States

Big Idea
Society changes as economies change.

Changing Economics Changing Societies
–U.S. History Textbook

"5000 Autoworkers Laid Off in Lansing"
–The Detroit News

"Google Hires 500 in Ann Arbor for High Tech Jobs"
– www.msnbc.com

Developing Motivation for Texts
What do your parents do for a living? What will you do for a career? How will changes in technology influence your decisions?

Developing Experience with Texts
What conclusions can we make about the changing economy? Comparing the text information, how will these changes affect people's lives?

Developing Knowledge with Texts
How does your reading about changes in the economy compare with your experiences? Your family's experiences? What have you observed in our community that supports your conclusions?

Opportunities and Challenges Posed by Different Kinds of Texts

Different kinds of texts pose different kinds of opportunities and challenges. The following sections explain and compare informational, narrative, and digital texts and graphic novels.

Informational Texts

Informational texts are texts that are used to convey and represent information. The stereotype of informational texts is the school textbook, though informational texts can appear in all sorts of places outside of school: on billboards, lists, graphics and logos on food packages, and traffic and road signs. **Documents** are a special kind of informational text with their own advantages and challenges. Documents include forms, schedules, indexes, tables, charts, checks, deposit slips, labels, and even a music transcription (see Figure 5.1). Well-designed documents can represent a great deal of information in an efficient format. In any kind of informational text, the amount of information represented can become a liability when too much information is represented in too compact a form (Mosenthal & Kirsch, 1989).

Research says that good informational texts have clear purposes and a well-defined audience. Good informational texts are consistent in maintaining their purpose and message. They include plenty of explanation, examples, and substantiation for ideas. Effective writers of these texts create a well-organized network of main ideas and supporting details with clear connections throughout (Alexander & Jetton, 2000). Notice in the television listings in Figure 5.2 how information is well organized and immediately accessible.

Have you ever read an informational article in which the writer did not appear to know much about his or her topic and skipped around a lot? How about informational web pages that are intended for beginners but are full of jargon? These are cases in which the principles of well-written informational texts have been violated. Add to this description the problem of a text not exactly meeting a reader's needs to gain particular kinds of knowledge. The knowledge that readers gain from ill-formed, uninformative informational texts can be minimal at best.

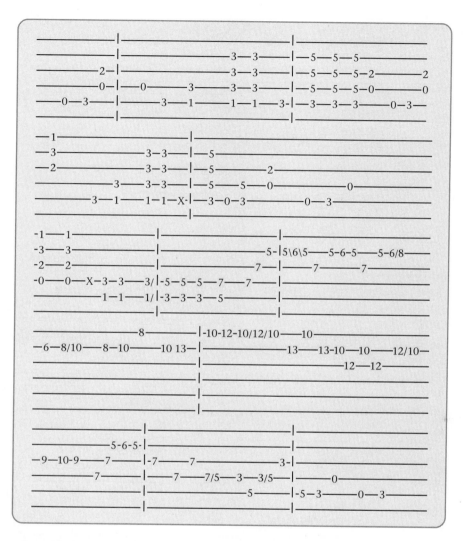

Figure 5.1
Music transcription for guitar.

Narrative Texts

Narrative texts are, in some ways, a bit more complicated than informational texts. The notion of good narrative texts is continually debated. A current perspective is that good narrative texts represent varied worlds, cultures, values, and beliefs in ways that challenge students' existing ideas and values (Marshall, 2000). Well-written narrative texts invite students to compare their own experiences with characters and situations reflected in the texts. In doing so, students gain knowledge about themselves and the people and worlds around them. This process works differently in each content area. In English, narrative texts connect readers to feelings, self-understanding, and knowledge about literature and writing.

Click on A+RISE –
Literacy Strategies in
the MyEducationLab
(www.myeducationlab
.com) for your course.
Next, select the Strategy
Card Index tab, scroll
to Comprehension with
Nonfictional Texts
and select the What?
So What? Now What?
strategy.

Figure 5.2

Example of a document text.

Television Listings for Your Local Area

	8:00 p.m.	8:30 p.m.	9:00 p.m.	9:30 p.m.	10:00 p.m.
HSN 2	Carolyn Strauss Fashions		Toni Tan Secret	Body Shaping by Rhonda Shear	Toni Tan Secret
CBS 3	Two and a Half Men TVPG, Repeat, CC	Two and a Half Men TVPG, Repeat, CC	College Basketball CC >		
PBS 4	Antiques Roadshow CC		American Experience TVPG, CC, DVS		
ABC 5	Extreme Makeover: Home Edi... TVPG, CC		The Bachelor TVPG, CC		Supernanny TVPG, CC >
WZPX 6	America's Funniest Home Videos TVPG, CC		Mary Higgins Clark's Lucky D... (PG13) TVPG		
FOX 7	Nanny 911 TVPG, CC		24 TV14, CC		Fox 47 News at 10 CC >
UPN 8	One on One TVPG, Repeat, CC	Cuts TVPG Repeat, CC	Girlfriends TVPG, Repeat, CC	Half & Half TVPG, Repeat, CC	Friends TVPG, CC
CBET 9	Dangerous Liaisons (2003) (NR), CC				The National CC
NBC 10	Fear Factor TVPG, Repeat, CC		Behind the Camera: The Unaut... (NR) TV14, CC		
WGNSAT 11	Home Improvement TVG, CC	Will & Grace TV14, CC	Will & Grace TV14, CC	Home Improvement TVG, CC	WGN News at Ten CC >
WBL 12	7th Heaven TVG, Repeat, CC		Summerland TVPG, CC		Cops TV14, CC
HBO 14	Reverse of the Curse of the... TVPG, CC		Scooby-Doo 2: Monsters Unlea... (PG), CC		
UPN 15	One on One TVPG, Repeat, CC	Cuts TVPG, Repeat, CC	Girlfriends TVPG, Repeat, CC	Half & Half TVPG, Repeat, CC	The King of Queens TVPG, CC
CSPAN 16	Prime Time Public Affairs				

Narrative texts are useful in telling the story of mathematics, creating a meaningful context for science, elaborating and personalizing historical events, and building appreciation for the arts and physical achievement. Challenges of narrative texts are also connected to matters of style—a writer's choice of words, the shaping of sentences, and the cadence and rhythm of the language. For example, students are often frustrated by writers who go on with a single sentence for many lines or a single paragraph for several pages. Students might also find narratives from earlier historical periods complex because of unfamiliar word choices and phrasings.

Digital Texts

Dealing with complexity within **digital texts**—photographs, the media (television, electronic newspapers, and cartoons), movies, and Internet images—can be even more challenging. Every digital text is constructed with a unique creative language—different genres, grammar, syntax, symbols, devices, and metaphor systems. Embedded in digital texts are values and multiple points of view. Many digital texts, such as websites and television images, are business-driven with a profit motive. Just as digital texts are represented in many ways, people experience digital texts in many different ways: mouse-clicking, viewing, and listening (Pailliotet, 2001).

Digital texts are noteworthy for their prevalence in students' lives. Digital images are everywhere, and they play a role in how people view reality. Digital texts enable adolescents to encounter all sorts of unofficial or even underground experiences with literacy, including web logs—better known as blogs—and fanzines, or zines, which are self-published magazines, either print or electronic. Today's adolescents can create and consume their own digital texts, many of which are unfamiliar to and complicated for adults. For a quick look at how digital texts have become more common in today's classrooms, read the Research Brief.

Some aspects of digital texts are like informational texts. Digital texts with a clear purpose, solid organizational structure, and consistency of language and imagery can be easier to understand than digital texts that are unfocused and disorganized. Digital texts also contain features that are unique. Consider Internet web pages. The simpler ones, like the school home page of a school shown in Figure 5.3, consist of basic information with perhaps a rudimentary menu bar: home page, email address, and résumé. The more complex web pages (see Figure 5.4) are three-dimensional, presenting multilevel menus and clickable buttons and images. Compared with merely turning a page, some digital texts represent labyrinths of information. Have you ever had the experience of being inside a complex web page and not knowing how to navigate your way out? By contrast, even the most complicated-appearing websites can sometimes be

▼ Digital texts are more and more common in schools today. A growing number of teachers around the country use podcasts as teaching tools.

Research Brief

How Prevalent Are Computers and Technology Texts in Today's Classrooms?

► In fall 2003, nearly 100 percent of public schools in the United States had access to the Internet, compared with 35 percent in 1994.

► In 2003, 93 percent of public school instructional rooms had Internet access, compared with 3 percent in 1994.

► In 2003, 95 percent of public schools with Internet access used broadband connections to access the Internet. In 1996, dial-up Internet connections were used by about 74 percent of public schools that had Internet access.

► The likelihood of using broadband connections increases with school size, from 90 percent for small schools to nearly 100 percent for large schools in 2003.

► In 2003, rural schools were less likely (90 percent) than both urban schools (98 percent) and suburban schools (97 percent) to have broadband Internet access.

► In 2003, 32 percent of public schools with Internet access had wireless connections, an increase from 23 percent in 2002.

► In 2003, the ratio of students to instructional computers with Internet access in public schools was 4.4 to 1, a decrease from the 12.1 to 1 ratio in 1998, when it was first measured.

► The ratio of students to instructional computers with Internet access was higher in schools with the highest poverty concentration (percentage of students eligible for free or reduced-price lunch) than in schools with the lowest poverty concentration.

Source: National Center for Education Statistics: www.nces.ed.gov.

easy to navigate because the designers employed a user-friendly organizational scheme.

Graphic Novels

Graphic novels are an increasingly popular medium, particularly with adolescents. A graphic novel is not quite comic book and not quite novel. It is a lightly bound book with colorful graphics, sometimes wordless and sometimes with sparse words used to tell a story or convey meaning. The genre can encompass informational or narrative text

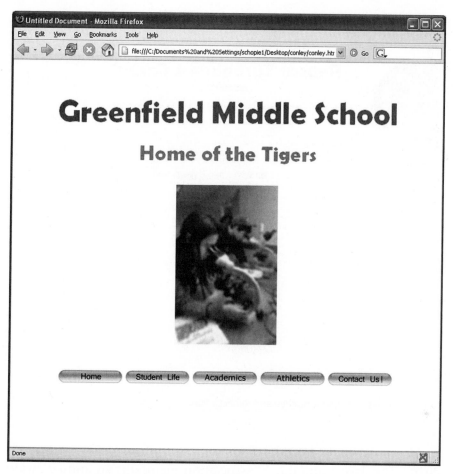

Figure 5.3

Example of a simple website.

*Special thanks to Carnella Hughey and Rebecca Parker.

and can appear in digital formats online. They have become so popular with adolescents that many adolescents like to create their own graphic novels. Teachers can use graphic novels to their advantage not only because of their motivation value but also because of their application to diverse topics. For example, a number of graphic novels are useful in social studies covering issues surrounding immigration, such as *The Arrival* (Tan, 2007), *Persepolis: The Story of Childhood* (Satrapi, 2003), *Persepolis 2: The Story of Return* (Satrapi, 2004), *The Four Immigrants: A Japanese Experience in San Francisco* (Kiyama, 1999) and *American Born Chinese* (Yang, 2006). Because of their format, many teachers combine graphic novel in order to compare experiences and connect to students' experiences. Many teachers use graphic novels to supplement more

Figure 5.4

Example of a complex website.

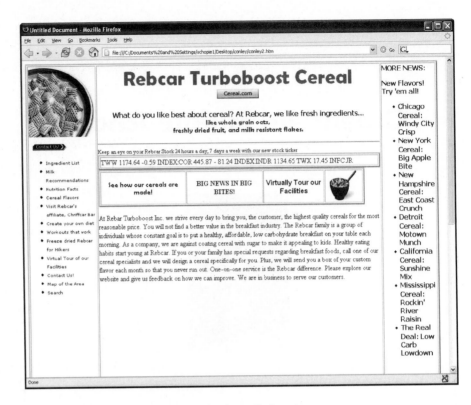

*Special thanks to Carnella Hughey and Rebecca Parker.

conventional texts for added motivation and relevance (Boatright, 2010). The American Library Association maintains an annual award website about Great Graphic Novels for Teens http://www.ala.org/ala/mgrps/divs/yalsa/booklistsawards/greatgraphicnovelsforteens/gn.cfm and there are many other websites with free downloadable graphic novels. Because they are a popular media, there are sometimes few restrictions on the content of graphic novels, so teachers should always thoroughly review graphic novels or online content for appropriateness.

Assessing Text Complexity

Researchers have spent many years trying to figure out what makes various texts more or less complicated for text users. Early efforts focused on simple text features, such as word and sentence length. More recent research emphasizes the specific characteristics of well-written or well-designed informational, narrative, and digital texts. Textbook companies and other commercial publishers often conduct their own textbook assessments so that they can market books, other media, and software appropriately. However, beware of claims that certain materials are "right on level" for students. Usually, this means that the publishers have used a readability formula to derive a crude grade level score. The best way of assessing text complexity consists of evaluating how students are experiencing a text. The Action Research lists some ideas about how to evaluate multiple kinds of experiences with texts.

Action Research

Assessing Texts, Tasks, and Complexity from Multiple Perspectives

Conduct this simple experiment to research texts, tasks, and individual points of view about what makes texts easy and complex.

1. Gather a sample of five or six text selections that you regularly encounter in school, at work, or during your recreational reading. Select texts that you consider complex and other texts that you consider relatively easy. Rank-order these texts from easiest to most difficult. Using the text assessments presented in this chapter, measure the complexity of these texts. Describe how these measurements support or conflict with your own impressions of the complexity of these texts.

2. Now write a description of tasks that you regularly perform with each of these texts (e.g., read, interpret, apply, respond, write, research, inquire, evaluate, or critique). Rank-order these tasks from easy to most difficult. Describe how these tasks interact with the texts to make the experience of reading more or less difficult.

3. Next, make a list of websites that you regularly visit. Rank-order these websites from easy to most complex. How are these websites the same or different from the text studied earlier? How do the tasks involved with these websites compare with the tasks accompanying the texts?

4. Compare your experiences with these print and digital texts and tasks with the experiences of others in your class. Pay particular attention to situations in which you found texts and tasks very complex whereas others found them relatively easy. Also examine situations in which the texts and tasks were easy for you but very complex for others.

5. Report on your findings, using these questions as a guide. How do individual motivations, knowledge, and experiences account for these differences? Given the potential for diverse responses to texts, including complexity, describe some ways in which you will need to adapt your approach to teaching with texts so that all students can learn.

Readability Formulas

An early attempt to assess text complexity, still in use today, involves **readability formulas**. The Fry formula in Figure 5.5 is one example. Readability formulas are based on the notion that text complexity lies in the length of the words and sentences. Put simply, the shorter the words and sentences, the easier the reading, and the longer the words and sentences, the more difficult the reading. Formulas like this are often used as a marketing technique for texts ("These books are all on the seventh-grade reading level—perfect for your students!"). Many formulas have been computerized so that teachers can enter texts with unknown readability levels and derive a number representing the text's complexity. Using a word processor such as Microsoft Word, check the tools option. Most word processing programs offer the option of providing readability statistics for text selections.

Just a few examples demonstrate how limiting readability is as a concept that reflects a reader's experiences with modern-day texts. For example, analyzing a text by itself leaves out many other important features of using texts, such as what the reader already knows and prefers. The notion of readability also leaves out what readers are asked to *do* with texts. Consider the differences in complexity among these tasks:

▶ Write down all of the words in the text.

▶ Restate the words in the text in your own words.

▶ Interpret what the words in the text mean.

▶ Apply the words in the text to a situation that is similar to one in your life.

Notice how these tasks vary from very simple to more complex. The differences lie in requirements to gather up and integrate more and more information. The last task, applying the words to personal experience, can be extremely complex for individuals who have never experienced anything like what is in the text.

Readability Checklists

Readability checklists acknowledge that text complexity concerns more than counting the length of words and sentences. In fact, the readability checklist in Figure 5.6 has been modified from the original checklist (Irwin & Davis, 1980) for use with evaluating digital as well as printed texts. Teachers use readability checklists like this one to make predictions

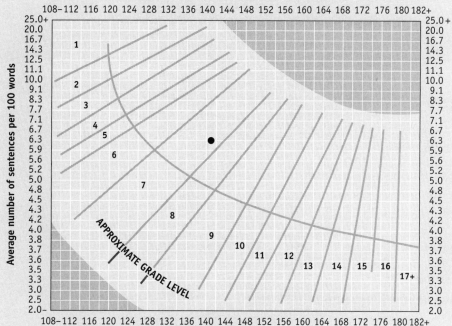

Graph for Estimating Readability—Extended

Average number of syllables per 100 words

Source: E. Fry (1977). Fry's readability graph: Clarifications, validity, and extensions to Level 17. *Journal of Reading, 21,* 242–252.

Figure 5.5

A popular readability measure.

Expanded Directions for Working the Readability Graph

1. Randomly select three sample passages and count out exactly 100 words each, starting with the beginning of a sentence. Do count proper nouns, initializations, and numerals.

2. Count the number of sentences in the 100 words, estimating length of the fraction of the last sentence to the nearest one-tenth.

3. Count the total number of syllables in the 100-word passage. If you don't have a hand counter available, an easy way is simply to put a mark above every syllable over one in each word, then when you get to the end of the passage, count the number of marks and add 100. Small calculators can also be used as counters by pushing numeral 1, then pushing the + sign for each word or syllable when counting.

4. Enter graph with *average* sentence length and *average* number of syllables; plot dot where the two lines intersect. The area where the dot is plotted will give you the approximate grade level.

5. If a great deal of variability is found in syllable count or sentence count, putting more samples into the average is desirable.

6. A word is defined as a group of symbols with a space on either side; thus, *Joe, IRA, 1945,* and *&* are each one word.

7. A syllable is defined as a phonetic symbol. Generally, there are as many syllables as vowel sounds. For example, *stopped* is one syllable and *wanted* is two syllables. When counting syllables for numerals and initializations, count one syllable for each symbol. For example, *1945* is four syllables, *IRA* is three syllables, and *&* is one syllable.

Figure 5.6 A readability checklist.

In the blank before each item, indicate **Y** for "yes," **S** for "Sort of," or **N** for "no." An N or S next to any of the items under AUTHORITY or ACCURACY AND BIAS means that the text or website should either be used with caution or not be used at all.

AUTHORITY

_____ 1. The organization or person responsible for the text/website is identified, along with a way of verifying the identity (via email, a phone number, and a postal address).

_____ 2. The organization or person's qualifications for creating the text/website are clearly stated or evident.

ACCURACY AND BIAS

_____ 1. Sources for information are clearly listed so that they can be verified.

_____ 2. Text and images of people, places, and events are accurate and fair.

_____ 3. Points of view and opinions are clearly labeled or are evident and distinguished from factual information.

UNDERSTANDABILITY

_____ 1. The assumptions about students' vocabulary knowledge are appropriate.

_____ 2. The assumptions about students' prior knowledge are appropriate.

_____ 3. The text/website explicitly states complex relationships among ideas and concepts.

_____ 4. New ideas and concepts are linked to students' prior knowledge.

_____ 5. Abstract concepts are accompanied by concrete explanations and examples.

_____ 6. New ideas are introduced one at a time with sufficient explanation and examples.

_____ 7. Definitions are understandable. It is not necessary to look things up or follow hyperlinks to understand new concepts.

_____ 8. The text/website avoids irrelevant details.

_____ 9. The text/website pages are well formatted (graphics, menus, links, and so on enhance and do not interfere with reading).

USABILITY

_____ 1. Titles, headings, and subheadings represent the content of the text/website.

_____ 2. Any charts and graphs are easy to read and are supportive of text/website information.

_____ 3. Illustrations and pictures are of high quality and are supportive of text/website information.

_____ 4. The print size of the text/website is appropriate for the level of the readers and for good readability.

_____ 5. Important terms are in italic, boldface, or hyperlink text.

_____ 6. Color combinations of text and background are well coordinated, making the text/website easy to read.

continued

continued

INTERESTABILITY

_____ 1. Titles, headings, and subheadings are interesting and capture the reader's attention.

_____ 2. The writing style of the text/website is appealing to the students.

_____ 3. The layout and overall appearance of the text/website are interesting (e.g., the author uses colorful language and/or humor).

_____ 4. Color and graphics are used to make the text/website more appealing.

_____ 5. The text/website provides positive and motivating models for both sexes as well as for other racial, ethnic, and socioeconomic groups.

SUMMARY RATING

Circle one choice for each item

The website rates highest in /understandability/ /usability/ /interest/

The website rates the lowest in /understandability/ /usability/ /interest/

STATEMENT OF STRENGTHS

STATEMENT OF WEAKNESSES

Source: Adapted with permission from Irwin, J and C. Davis (1980). "Assessing readability: The checklist approach." Journal of Reading 24: 124–130.

about their students' experiences with texts, ideally based on the teacher's prior experiences with teaching and learning with texts.

The checklist has five categories. The first two categories, *authority* and *accuracy and bias,* stem from concerns that the digital age has made it much more difficult to distinguish between legitimate texts and those that purvey libelous portrayals, falsehoods, inaccurate information, and even hatred (Bruce, 2003). The prevalence of desktop publishing, web publishing software, and access to server space has made it all the more important to assess whether or not a text can be trusted to provide reliable information. Even though a text is judged to be reliable, teachers will still want to engage students in critical examinations of writers' qualifications and perspectives, the subject of Chapter 10, "Guiding Students' Critical Literacy."

The third category concerns *understandability.* Understandability involves predictions about students' vocabulary and prior knowledge and the explicitness of the purposes, ideas, and connections within the text under consideration. The fourth category, *usability,* focuses on the organizational features of a text, including the clarity of the print, charts and graphs, and graphics, including pictures. Taken together, understandability and usability describe the characteristics of text that tend to make them well written or poorly written. The final category, *Interestability,* involves predictions about text features designed to arouse students' curiosity and motivate. Note the emphasis here on varied, positive, and motivating role models.

Predictions based on a readability checklist are made most appropriately with a particular group of students in mind. Teachers can practice using a readability checklist by selecting a text or a digital image, selecting an audience of students, and reviewing the text using the analysis categories.

FLIP Readability Assessment

A FLIP assessment improves on readability formulas and the readability checklist with students responding directly to a text (see Figure 5.7). *FLIP* stands for *friendliness, language, interest,* and *prior knowledge* (Schumm &

Figure 5.7

A FLIP assessment for *Sheet Metal Forming Processes and Die Design* intended for use in an industrial technology class.

Friendliness	
How friendly is the text/website? What is the text/website's purpose? Does the text/website carry out its purpose, using lots of explanations and examples?	The purpose of the book is very clear—it's about sheet metal forming! It has many examples to show how to do things.
Language	
How many new words do you see in this text/website? How difficult does the writing look to you?	There were a lot of new words for me. That helped a lot. The writing is pretty complicated, but it has lots of pictures.
Interest	
In what way does this text/website look interesting to you? Why? Why not?	It reminds me of my dad's job—lots of machines and metal. I think I'll like reading about that.
Prior Knowledge	
What do you already know about this text/website?	I've worked on my car before, and I've visited websites about this topic.

Mangrum, 1991). This assessment is relatively easy to prepare and administer. A disadvantage is that students might provide only very general reactions to their experiences with a text. To use this assessment effectively, teachers need to discuss the meanings behind FLIP categories with students.

For example, to help students with the friendliness portion of the assessment, it would be useful to discuss their notions of what makes a text friendly or challenging. The second part of the assessment, *language,* focuses on students' judgments about the relative number of new or unfamiliar words in the text. Consequently, a useful conversation to have around the issue of language concerns what it means to "know" a word or "kind of know" a word and what happens when the sheer number of new and unfamiliar words becomes a problem. The third part of the assessment, *interest,* addresses the extent to which the text engages students and arouses their interest. A useful discussion here would be about what sorts of texts and features of texts students tend to view as inviting. Finally, the FLIP assessment asks students to consider their *prior knowledge.* A useful discussion concerns what it means to "sort of know" versus "have little clue" about the knowledge represented by the text.

Challenges Posed by Texts, Assignments, and Tasks

As was mentioned earlier, from the student's perspective, not all questions or assignments are alike. Some tasks ask very little of students, such as identifying or selecting words or images. Other tasks ask a great deal, requiring students to search for, think about, and integrate text information and images. Figure 5.8 depicts one way to think about the complexity of teachers' assignments, from asking students to identify facts and concepts all the way to asking them to take a stand and support it while sorting out accurate and misleading information (Mosenthal & Kirsch, 1998). Some texts are accompanied by multiple tasks. Students' knowledge about the texts and about the tasks combine in meeting the challenges posed by text-based assignments and tasks. For instance, consider the experience of a student responding to the complicated state language arts assessment question in Figure 5.9. Students who have experience in writing about only a single text at a time would find this question more challenging than would students who have experience in writing about several texts at a time.

Whenever possible, be careful when pairing unfamiliar and complex texts with complicated assignments. The effects on students tend to be cumulative. When preparing to assign a complicated text and assignment,

Figure 5.8

The complexity of what teachers ask students to *do* with texts.

	Complexity Scale for Reading Material and Assignments	**Sample Assignments**
Identify concrete facts and concepts (Whats)	**Easy** Tasks in this level require students to identify information that is quite concrete, such as a **person**, **place** or **thing**, or an **amount**, **time frame**, or **characteristic**. The information is usually presented in relatively short texts. Students are asked to locate a single piece of information that is synonymous with information in a question.	List all of the ingredients in the winning barbeque sauce. Locate the algebraic equation on page 36. List the steps in a scientific experiment from page 22. Tell the parts of speech for the Spanish language (from page 10). Identify the key signature for Stars and Stripes. List the names of the athletes on page 44.
Identify procedures (How to's)	**Moderately Easy** Tasks in this level require students to identify information that is fairly concrete, usually **procedures**. Sometimes, tasks at this level ask students to make low-level or obvious interpretations.	How did Anne Frank's family escape arrest for so long? How do you add two numbers together? How do you use a graduated cylinder to measure liquids? How is the government organized?
Identify a reason or explanation (Whys)	**Balanced Between Easy and Complex** Tasks in this level require students to identify a **reason** or **explanation**. This often starts with identifying several pieces of information and forming interpretations. Questions tend to consist of several phrases or sentences. Required answers tend to be in the form of multiple responses.	Based on your reading of the unsolved mystery *Murder on Board*, select the most likely murder suspect. Based on your reading, explain in detail the roles that lift, thrust, and gravity play in propelling the space shuttle through the air.
Compare and contrast, cause and effect	**Somewhat Complex** Tasks on this level require students to identify rather abstract information, including **reasons**, **evidence**, **explanations**, **causes**, **results**, **comparisons**, and **contrasts**. These tasks require students to compare and integrate information. Multiple responses may be required. Distracting information may be present.	Why did the mountain climbers continue their trek, despite the enormous hardships? How did their decision to carry on affect what eventually happened to them? How do plants get their nutrition? How is this different from the way animals get their nutrition? Compare $3x^2 = 2x + 8$ with $(3x - 4)(x - 2)$. Are these equivalent? How do you know?
Take a stand or perspective and support it	**Very Complex** Tasks in this level require students to identify quite abstract information. Students are required to **locate**, **compare**, **integrate**, and **generate information**. Specialized prior knowledge may be required to complete the task. The reading almost always contains distracting or misleading information.	Take a stand about whether the Civil War was a just war. Support your stand with facts from the period and your own knowledge about wars throughout history. Examining the data on smoking, illness and death rates, insurance costs due to smoking, and workers' rights, determine whether smokers should be banned from the workplace.

Figure 5.9

An example of a complicated text-based task on a state test.

Response to the Reading Selections

Write a response to the scenario question that is stated in the box below. Your own ideas and experiences may be used in your response, but you MUST refer to information and/or examples from both of the reading selections you have just completed to be considered for full credit. You may look back at both of the reading selections to help you answer the question at the end of the following scenario.

Scenario Question: At a recent assembly, a guest speaker offered his views on what it takes to achieve the American dream. At the core of his beliefs is the view that in the United States, anyone can achieve the American dream. All it takes, he said, "is commitment, dedication, and hard work." He further believes that individuals are in control of their own futures and it is up to them to succeed or fail.

SCENARIO RESPONSE

Do you AGREE or DISAGREE with the speaker? Why? Give details and examples from BOTH reading selections in support of your response.

Source: Michigan English Language Arts Assessment.

it helps to break down the assignment into smaller steps or tasks, demonstrating for students how they can approach the complicated text and assignment. Specific ways to do this are addressed throughout this book.

Selecting Texts

Before selecting texts of any kind, it is important to think about, map out, or list the knowledge students need to learn. As was discussed in earlier chapters, a good place to start is with state and local curriculum standards and assessments. This will help to identify the Big Ideas, connecting concepts and related practices and performances that students should learn. The next question to ask is: Which text and other resources are available to teach the Big Ideas and concepts?

Big Ideas and Texts

Creating a chart like the one in Figure 5.10 is one way to answer the question of selecting texts and other resources to teach Big Ideas. On the left side of the chart, list the desired knowledge and practices. On the right

Figure 5.10

Desired knowledge and practices and text assessment.

Standards, Big Ideas, and Connecting Concepts	Texts That Represent Desired Knowledge and Practices
Processes of Life The student knows that organisms respond to internal and external stimuli. Big Idea: Plant respiration and growth is affected by light. - Light is needed for chemical reactions within photosynthesis. - Photosynthesis is responsible for plant nutrition and growth in the leaves.	Textbook: *Biology: The Web of Life*—plant respiration section Website: Arizona State University Center for the Study of Early Events in Photosynthesis *Newton's Apple* television program about photosynthesis
Knowledge Necessary for Practices and Performances	**Texts That Represent and Demonstrate Desired Practices and Performances**
The student describes patterns of structure and function in living things. Comparing changes in plants when light is and is not available.	Scientific research guide: What happens when you change a plant's light source? Logging changes in plants that have been placed in different lighting conditions (high versus low) Logging changes in plants that have had paper shapes paper clipped to their leaves (light deprivation)

Source: Florida Sunshine State Standards in Science.

side of the chart, list the text resources that could best be used to develop students' knowledge. In cases in which school or district requires the use of certain materials, scan those materials for the most appropriate segments or sections that can be used to increase students' knowledge. Completing this step helps teachers to focus on desired knowledge rather than just on what texts by themselves have to offer. Notice in the example how many different texts are often necessary to develop students' knowledge.

Yet another criterion for selecting texts consists of the practices and performances students need to learn to become expert in a content area (Kintsch, 1989). In other words, texts are used in content areas not only to develop knowledge about Big Ideas, but also to practice various skills in content areas. Scientific knowledge, for example, is accompanied by skills for scientific inquiry. Knowledge about literature in English coincides with understanding how to engage in writing for different purposes and audiences. In short, knowledge in content areas is rarely about just knowing something; it is about knowing *and* doing. Figure 5.11 depicts various ways of thinking about Big Ideas and skilled practices across the content areas. Notice how each area defines Big Ideas and skilled

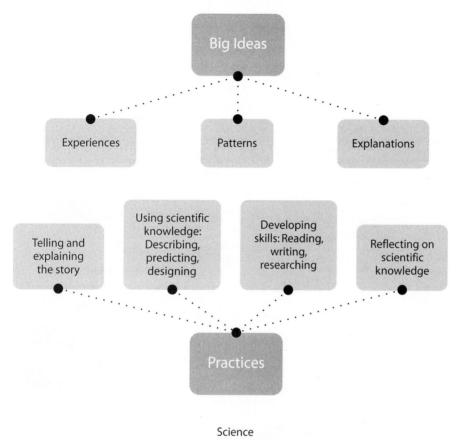

Figure 5.11
Models of
knowledge and
skilled practices
in content areas.

practices in different ways. Teachers need to consider selecting texts that will address the need to develop knowledge *and* skilled practice in content areas. The Connecting Standards and Assessment feature on page 150 offers additional ideas about selecting texts based on Big Ideas and skilled practice with testing skills.

Finding a Variety of Texts

Having a variety of texts available is interesting and enriching for students. The traditional school textbook or literature anthology approach runs the risk of alienating students who otherwise spend a great deal of their time engaged with the Internet and the popular media. Teachers can find out a great deal about different kinds of texts by using search engines like Google (www.google.com), Yahoo (www.yahoo.com), Answers.com (www.answers.com), and Dogpile (www.dogpile.com). For instance, the

Figure 5.11
(continued)

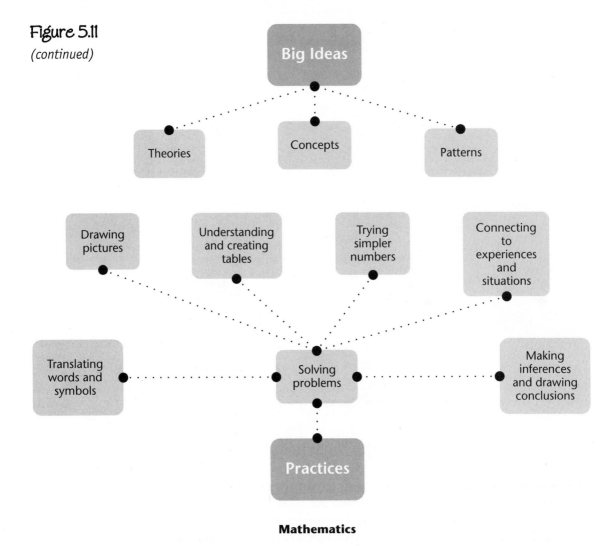

Mathematics

following supplemental trade books in mathematics were found by typing into Google the phrase *"young adult literature" + mathematics:*

Devil's Arithmetic: A Unit Plan by Janine H. Sherman
The Grapes of Math: Mind Stretching Math Riddles by Greg Tang and Harry Briggs
The Joy of Mathematics by Theoni Pappas
Math Curse by Jon Scieszka
Math Is Language Too: Talking and Writing in the Mathematic Classroom by Phyllis and Dave Whitin
Math Talk: Mathematical Ideas in Poems for Two Voices by Theoni Pappas

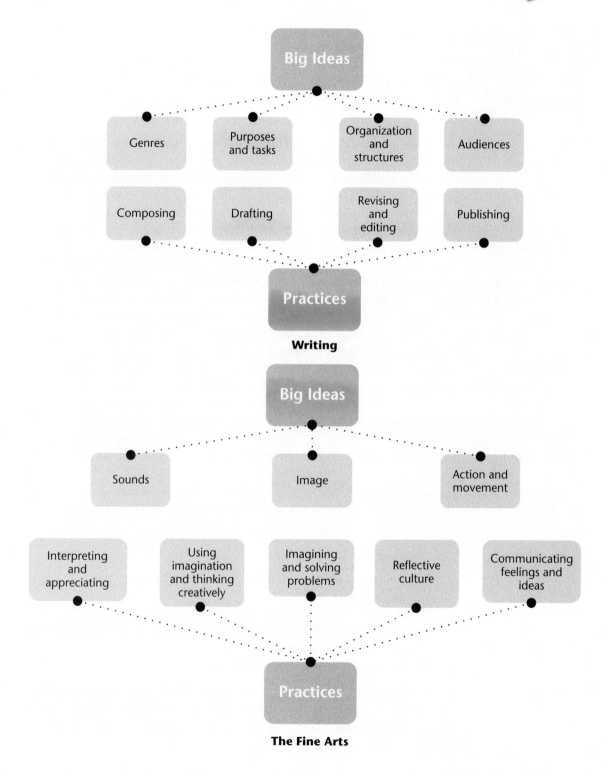

Writing

The Fine Arts

Connecting Standards and Assessment

Meeting Content and Test-Taking Needs

Texts are typically used to teach many different kinds of Big Ideas and for all kinds of purposes. Sometimes, it can be challenging to find texts that relate to curriculum ideas and test taking skills at the same time. One way to do this is to chart out the standards-based Big Ideas for a lesson and then select one or two testing skills. For instance, in social studies, a common standard concerns ways in which geography shapes the human environment. The standard lends itself to many types of exploration, including ways in which the geography of the United States shaped patterns of settlement, industrial and economic patterns, farming, and even culture and religion.

A related test-taking skill concerns thinking about what you already know. Many students rush through tests without considering their knowledge very carefully. The importance of considering prior knowledge before answering cannot be underestimated. In this case—considering how geography plays a role in people's life decisions—students are provided with an excellent opportunity to think about where they live, why people live there, and how the geography of their own immediate environment impacts people's lives. In this way, there is a good match between the standards-based Big Idea (geography and life decisions) and the test-taking skill (thinking about what you know).

Once this connection has been identified, teachers can create integrated lessons involving texts of various kinds. Some of these lessons can involve revising and redesigning published materials. Some revisions can incorporate reading, writing, and reasoning.

▶ Read more about these ideas in Chapter 8, "Integrating Standards and Assessment through Daily Practice," in *Connecting Standards and Assessment through Literacy* (Conley, 2005), published by Pearson Education.

The Number Devil: A Mathematical Adventure by Hans Magnus Enzensberger et al.
The Phantom Tollbooth by Norton Juster
Sir Cumference and the Great Knight of Angleland: A Math Adventure by Cindy Neuschwander
The Westing Game by Ellen Raskin

Figure 5.12 has useful websites for teachers. The lists and bibliographies were found by searching on terms such as *young adult literature, trade books,* and *biographies* with the delimiters + *English,* + *social studies,* + *health,* or + *music.*

Teachers can also search Amazon (www.amazon.com) for specialty books such as biographies and autobiographies. Figure 5.12 also has websites consisting of resources and links to resources within various content areas. Many of these websites were found by searching Discoveryschool.com (www.discoveryschool.com) under Kathy Schrock's Guide for Educators.

Teaching and Learning with Texts

The remainder of this book consists of teaching activities and learning strategies for learning with texts. For now, remember these principles and practices for creating the right conditions for conditions for teaching and learning with texts.

Be Knowledgeable about What Students Bring with Them for Understanding Texts—Their Motivation, Interests, Knowledge, and Skills. It should be clear by now that text complexity is not just a matter of looking at the prototypical school textbook and making isolated judgments about the complexity of a text. What matters far more are the students—the knowledge, skills, and motivation they bring to a text and their experiences with texts. Be especially sensitive to the challenges faced by special needs learners and English language learners who might still be struggling with the language of texts. Don't overlook the advantages that prior knowledge and experience can bring to learning from texts. Sometimes, even when students are struggling with basic language issues, teachers can still draw them into the conversation and the learning by helping the students to make connections.

▼ Students tap into a variety of resources to complete their work. Successful schools provide access to texts of all kinds—both print and digital.

Carefully Assess Students' Experience and Understandings of Assignments and Tasks That Accompany Texts. Observe students while they work, and look for signs that assignments are interacting with texts in problematic ways—hands raised, multiple questions and concerns, even frustration and boredom. When this happens, be prepared to

Figure 5.12 Useful Websites

Lists and bibliographies of content area texts.

Outstanding trade books—National Science Teachers Association
http://www.nsta.org/ostbc

Notable Trade Books for Young People—National Council for the Social Studies
http://www.socialstudies.org/resources/notable

Making Multicultural Connections through Trade Books (Montgomery County Public Schools)
http://www.mcps.k12.md.us/curriculum/socialstd/MBD/Books_Begin.html

Booklist
http://www.ala.org/ala/booklist/booklist.htm
Reviews of both adult and children's books from the American Library Association's Booklist magazine.

TeenLit.com
http://www.teenlit.com
Promotes adolescent literacy with online publishing of teen poetry, short stories, and essays, book reviews, and teacher resources

Teen Reading (sponsored by the American Library Association)
http://www.ala.org/ala/yalsa/teenreading/teenreading.htm
Includes recommended reading and resources for librarians, parents, and teachers

Quick Picks for Reluctant Young Adult Readers (sponsored by the American Library Association)
http://www.ala.org/ala/yalsa/booklistsawards/quickpicks/quickpicksreluctant.htm

Scholastic Trade Books
http://teacher.scholastic.com/products/tradebooks/index.htm
Large publisher of trade books

Random House Young Adult Books
http://www.randomhouse.com/teachers
Large publisher of trade books

International Reading Association Children's Book Awards
http://www.reading.org/association/awards/childrens_ira.html
Annual awards for quality children's and adolescent literature

International Reading Association Book Reviews
http://www.readingonline.org/past/past_index.asp?HREF=/reviews/literature/lit_index.html

continued

continued

No Flying, No Tights

http://www.noflyingnotights.com/index2.html

A website for reviewing graphic novels for teens

Comic Book Resources

http://www.comicbookresources.com

A collection of Web links covering hundreds of resources about comic books.

The ALAN Review

http://scholar.lib.vt.edu/ejournals/ALAN/alan-review.html

Online review of and ideas for using young adult literature across the content areas

Links and resources for content area teaching and learning

Social Studies for Kids

http://www.socialstudiesforkids.com

**Office of Mathematics, Science and Technology Education,
List of Web Resources for Math Educators**

http://www.mste.uiuc.edu/mathed/mathedlinks.html

Basic Steps in Writing a Research Paper

http://www.crlsresearchguide.org

Don't Buy It! Get Media Smart!

http://pbskids.org/dontbuyit

Paradigm Online Writing Assistant

http://www.powa.org

Agricultural Ideas for Science Fair Projects

http://www.ars.usda.gov/is/kids/fair/ideasframe.htm

Nutrition Explorations

http://www.nutritionexplorations.org

Music Educators Resource

http://www.edgate.com/musichall/educator/index.html

Health Teacher Links

http://www.healthteacher.com/teachersupports/weblinks/default.asp

modify assignments, sometimes breaking them down into smaller parts, to support the challenges students are confronting with texts.

Use a Wide Variety of Texts and Literature, Including Published Texts, Informal Texts, and Student-Generated Texts. Research has shown that the most successful schools are literally awash in books of all

kinds—textbooks, trade books, and media—while students are engaged in all sorts of digital texts and communication: websites, email, instant messages, and blogging (Pressley et al., 2004). Teachers should aspire to making available as many kinds of texts as possible.

Be Aware of and Address the Challenges That Texts Present for Students—Topic Familiarity, Clearly Stated Purposes, Explicit Text Organization, Connectedness among Ideas and Concepts, Explanations, and Examples—and Support Them in These Challenges.

▶ Think about ways that you—as a student—have learned how to learn from texts and share those techniques with your students.

▶ Teach students how to use texts, especially in ways that students are expected to use texts in their assignments and on various kinds of tests.

▶ Modify your assignments used with texts so that students are not overwhelmed with the complexity of both the texts and the assignments.

▶ Help students to make connections with the concepts in texts so that they can grow in their knowledge, skill, and motivation.

Summary

The world of texts has changed dramatically to include informational materials, narratives, and endless assortments of digital texts. While students are continually exposed to reading and even creating this new world, they still need help in getting the most out of their encounters with texts. Teachers can play a substantial role in guiding students in their work with texts by carefully assessing and selecting texts that reflect important Big Ideas and skills; assessing students and their motivation, knowledge, and skill for learning with texts; and demonstrating effective strategies in learning from texts.

Special Projects

1. Visit your state department of education's website and locate the curriculum standards in your content area. Select a standard or two and identify the Big Ideas. Next, locate a text (print and/or digital) that is appropriate for teaching a lesson in your content area. Imagine an audience of students (e.g., seventh graders, tenth graders). Evaluate this text with regard to (a) suitability to develop students' understanding of the content of the curriculum standard(s), (b) complexity as measured by any of the assessment tools found in this chapter, and (c) interest and motivation of your audience of students.

2. Develop a list of teaching activities for the Big Ideas and text materials in Special Project 1. Evaluate these activities using the complexity scale in Figure 5.8. For the more complex activities, describe some ways in which you could break them into smaller parts so that students can be successful.

3. Do a web search for web-based resources to use in your content area. Make a list of young adult books that would be appropriate for your use. Visit a local bookstore and examine these books while locating others. Prepare an annotated bibliography of text resources for use in your content area. Include print resources (informational texts, biographies, and/or young adult literature) as well as electronic (websites) sources.

Praxis Practice

Working with Questions to Prepare for the Praxis Reading across the Curriculum Test

Multiple Choice Questions

1. Readability is a matter of:

   a. The number of long sentences found in a text

   b. The number of hard words found in a text

   c. What students bring to the text and features of the text

   d. Students' knowledge of the topic of a text

2. The main categories of different types of text are:

    a. Friendly, familiar, and frustrating

    b. Information, narrative, digital, and graphic

    c. Frustrating, instructional, and independent

    d. Books, textbooks, and magazines

3. Which is a good instructional practice to promote learning from texts?

    a. Use a wide variety of texts

    b. Use easy, readable texts

    c. Use difficult or slightly harder to read texts

    d. Use the mandated school textbook

Constructed Response Question

1. Select a Big Idea in your content area. Next, select at least three texts that you could use to teach that Big Idea. Describe how you would analyze the texts for their suitability for you students. Then explain how you might use the texts to teach students an understanding of the Big Idea.

Suggested Readings

Bruce, B. (2003). *Literacy in the information age.* Newark, DE: International Reading Association.

Koss, M., & Teale, W. (2009). What's happening in YA literature: Trends in books for adolescents. *Journal of Adolescent and Adult Literacy, 52*(7), 563–572.

Morrell, E. (2004). *Linking literacy and popular culture.* Norwood, MA: Christopher Gordon.

Schmidt, P., & Pailliotet, A. (2001). *Exploring values through literature, multimedia, and literacy events.* Newark, DE: International Reading Association.

Go to Topic 5: Comprehension in the MyEducationLab (www.myeducationlab.com) for your course, where you can:

- Find learning outcomes for Topic 5: Comprehension along with the national standards that connect to these outcomes.

- Complete Assignments and Activities that can help you more deeply understand the chapter content.

- Apply and practice your understanding of the core teaching skills identified in the chapter with the Building Teaching Skills and Dispositions learning units.

- Examine challenging situations and cases presented in the IRIS Center Resources.

Go to the Topic A+RISE in the MyEducationLab (www.myeducationlab.com) for your course. A+RISE® Standards2Strategy™ is an innovative and interactive online resource that offers new teachers in grades K-12 just in time, research-based instructional strategies that:

- Meet the linguistic needs of ELLs as they learn content

- Differentiate instruction for all grades and abilities

- Offer reading and writing techniques, cooperative learning, use of linguistic and nonlinguistic representations, scaffolding, teacher modeling, higher order thinking, and alternative classroom ELL assessment

- Provide support to help teachers be effective through the integration of listening, speaking, reading, and writing along with the content curriculum

- Improve student achievement

- Are aligned to Common Core Elementary Language Arts standards (for the literacy strategies) and to English language proficiency standards in WIDA, Texas, California, and Florida.

6

Ongoing Assessment

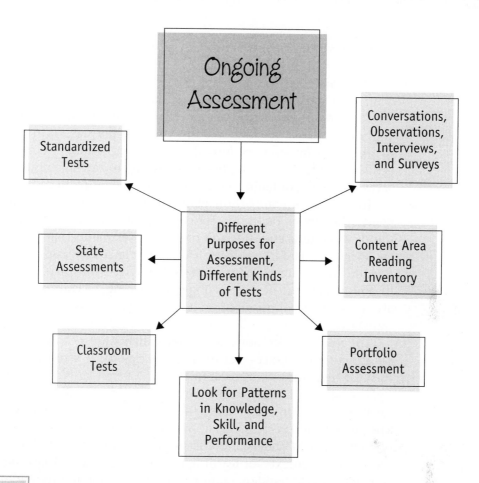

Ongoing Assessment

Standardized Tests

Conversations, Observations, Interviews, and Surveys

Different Purposes for Assessment, Different Kinds of Tests

State Assessments

Content Area Reading Inventory

Classroom Tests

Portfolio Assessment

Look for Patterns in Knowledge, Skill, and Performance

Ongoing assessment is a term that signals that assessment should be diverse and happening all the time. Through their own development and everyday experiences with literacy and learning but also through instruction, students change and learn all of the time. As a result, teachers need to continually update their knowledge about what students are experiencing in and out of school, what students know and can do, and how teachers can create contexts for students to become more literate and learn. The task of creating assessment that is ongoing and informative can be particularly challenging in this era of high standards and accountability.

Classroom assessments are particularly useful, including day-to-day conversations with students, observations, and reviews of classroom work and classroom test performance. These often overlooked kinds of assessment provide a rich, classroom-based picture of students' literacies and learning. Teachers use these tests to plan instruction as well as to determine how well students have learned.

Other kinds of assessment, such as state tests and standardized tests, are used for **high-stakes purposes**. The term *high-stakes* literally means that tests are employed to assess accountability—whether teachers, students, and schools are meeting high standards—and assign penalties if they are not. For example, because of the current educational reforms, poor performance on state assessments in some states can mean reassigning or firing teachers, loss of resources, or school closings. For students, performance on a high-stakes assessment can mean the difference between passing or failing a grade or even graduating from high school.

Ironically, in comparison with classroom observations and assessments, the general public tends to offer greater credibility to high-stakes, standardized tests and state and national assessments that are developed by using standard procedures. However, classroom assessments often provide immediate clues for what students need and what teachers need to do to create the best conditions for learning. Classroom assessments also provide useful information about how students might perform on state tests.

For teachers, decisions about assessments are not best represented by an either/or choice—between either classroom assessments or tests used for high-stakes purposes. In this era of standards and accountability, teachers need to use all of the assessment tools available, all the time, for a variety of purposes—hence the need for assessment that is ongoing. The purpose of this chapter is to help you develop and use assessment in ongoing ways to understand and meet students' literacy needs and create effective contexts for learning for today's learners. A key message of this chapter is to build on patterns within assessment information about students' motivation, knowledge, and skill in content area literacy. The Connecting Standards and Assessment feature identifies some ways to stay informed about different kinds of assessments, their purposes and applications.

Chapter 2 presented a model (Figure 2.1) for the many ways adolescents know and practice literacy. Here, that model will be used to construct a rationale for using different kinds of tests. Figure 6.1 depicts a chart comparing the ways in which adolescents know and practice literacy (from Figure 2.1) with various techniques available for assessing adolescent literacy, presented in this chapter. The shaded areas represent points of intersection—places where the characteristics of adolescents and their literacy learning are assessed by particular assessment techniques.

Of course, no single assessment is sufficient for determining what students care about, know, and are able to do with respect to their literacies, content knowledge, and practices. An important guideline is to use

Connecting Standards and Assessment

Clarifying Your Perspective about Testing

With so much emphasis on testing these days, it is challenging to keep up with all of the changes. It is particularly important for teachers to keep up with tests that are used for high-stakes purposes, such as state assessments used to meet the requirements of No Child Left Behind. Tests that are used for high-stakes purposes are often employed to reform schools, usually at a time of educational crisis. Knee-jerk reactions without much forethought are the unfortunate result of many high-stakes efforts. Assessments can be misinterpreted or applied inappropriately when used in crisis mode. The use of assessments tends to fall into two categories: those used to garner snapshots of students progress and those used to assess students' growth. Growth-oriented assessments involve multiple observations of a student's performance over time. An ongoing challenge is to integrate

many different kinds of assessments with curriculum standards, especially because state tests do not always accurately reflect state standards.

Other than the National Assessment of Educational Progress, there are few, if any, national tests. Most testing occurs at the state level to comply with No Child Left Behind. Many districts and schools employ a wide variety of local and classroom-based assessments for a variety of purposes. An effective plan for ongoing assessment is to emphasize growth *and* achievement. It is important to communicate about assessment with respect to appropriate purposes, and one-shot tests say little about growth, and multiple classroom observations may not say enough about achievement. Consider your audience carefully when communicating assessment information.

▶ **Read more about these ideas in Chapter 2, "High-Stakes Assessment," and Chapter 4, "Clarifying and Communicating about Testing," in Conley's (2005)** *Connecting Standards and Assessment through Literacy,* **published by Pearson Education.**

multiple assessments and look for patterns in students' performance. Do not over rely on results from any single test.

Another important point is to consider carefully how to assess in light of different students' needs. The Teaching Today's Learners feature on page 163 discusses how to make assessment accommodations for students with special educational needs and for English language learners.

In the following sections, assessments depicted in Figure 6.1 are described and illustrated. The chapter starts with assessments that help teachers to understand students—their personal identity, how they see themselves and their peers, and their academic performance. These assessments include conversations, interviews, surveys, and observations.

A+RISE

Click on A+RISE – WIDA ELP Standard Strategy in the MyEducationLab (www.myeducationlab.com) for your course. Next, select the Strategy Card Index tab, scroll to Classroom Assessments for Grades 6–12 and select the Alternative ELL Assessments: Introduction strategy.

Figure 6.1

Characteristics of adolescents, their literacies, and related forms of assessment.

	Conversations, Observations, Interviews, and Surveys	Content Area Reading Inventory	Classroom Tests	Portfolio Assessment	State Assessments	Standardized Tests
Personal Identity						
Literacy Skills						
Content Knowledge and Ways of Knowing						
Communication Styles and Skills						
Context (school, home, community, peers, and popular culture)						
Students' Motivation, Knowledge, and Skill in Content Area Literacy						

The next set of assessments is focused on academics—the content area reading inventory, classroom tests, and portfolio assessments. The chapter concludes with useful information about understanding, interpreting, and applying information from state tests and standardized tests.

Personal Assessments

Conversations, interviews, surveys, and observations are some of the best ways to get to know students as individuals, what their experiences are like in the classroom, how they approach learning, and how they view

Teaching Today's Learners

Making Assessment Accommodations

The following guidelines are for assessing students with special needs and English language learners respectively. Describe some ways of making accommodations like this for assessment in your content area.

For students with special educational needs (National Center on Educational Outcomes, 1997):

▶ Administer the test individually or to a small group in a separate location

▶ Administer the test in a location with minimal distractions

▶ Provide the test on audiotape

▶ Increase spacing between test items or reduce items per page or line

▶ Increase the size of answer spaces

▶ Highlight key words or phrases in the directions

▶ Provide cues (e.g., arrows and stop signs) on the answer form

▶ Allow a flexible schedule

▶ Extend the time allotted to complete the test

▶ Allow frequent breaks during testing

▶ Administer the test in several sessions, specifying the duration of each session

▶ Administer the test over several days, specifying the duration for each day's session

For English language learners (Butler & Stevens, 1997):

▶ Extra assessment time

▶ Breaks during the test

▶ Administration over several sessions

▶ Oral directions in the native language

▶ Small-group administration

▶ Use of dictionaries

▶ Reading aloud of questions in English

▶ Answers written directly in the test booklet

▶ Directions read aloud or explained

themselves in multiple ways in and outside of school. Knowing more about students as individuals will help with teaching and learning in at least three ways:

▶ Motivating students by bringing their backgrounds and prior knowledge into classroom lessons

▶ Helping students to make connections between their lives and academic texts and concepts

▶ Guiding students to use their backgrounds and life experiences to critically read and evaluate academic texts and texts from popular culture (mass media, film, music, sports, and the Internet)

For secondary teachers, knowing students individually can be a challenging task. For this reason, this section will address various ways of learning about students through daily opportunities for assessment.

Classroom Conversations

One of the most readily available ways of learning about students is through conversations. A prime opportunity for learning about students is by asking them questions while they work. Some sample questions to ask students while they work are the following:

▶ What are you thinking about as you work on this?

▶ What steps are you taking to get this done?

▶ How are you using reading or writing?

▶ How are you using research? How are you using the Internet?

Sometimes, conversational opportunities emerge when students are experiencing difficulty. When students experience difficulties with their work, ask: Where are you stuck? and What do you suppose you could do to solve this problem? Other times, teachers can create opportunities by asking students to guide them in their approach to their work. To get students to guide you in understanding their work, ask questions such as: How are you doing this? and What will you do if you get stuck on this?

Students who are uncertain about their approach to their work or who get stuck with little, if any, sense of their alternatives could be experiencing a number of problems, such as not knowing much about the content or being inexperienced in ways of knowing in the content area. They may even be struggling with reading, writing, and communicating. Be especially observant for signs that students are uncertain or stuck and have few, if any, options for solving their problems with learning.

Classroom Observations

Classroom observations nicely complement classroom conversations. In the course of an hour each day, students are called upon to perform in various ways—responding to questions, reading aloud, solving problems, doing labs, translating, interpreting, explaining, representing, and evaluating. During these performances, watch carefully not only for signs that students understand the content, but also for ways in which they engage in these learning activities.

For some students, it is no great stretch to move from one kind of text and task to another. For other students, anxiety, hesitation, and uncertainty during these activities can reflect problems with content knowledge, a lack of connection between a student's prior knowledge and the content, low motivation, and indecision about how to learn. Be cautious about making universal assumptions. Just because a student shows mastery of one topic or set of concepts is no guarantee of a repeat performance, just as problems in one content area are no reliable predictor of problems everywhere else. Watch for patterns of performance and compare with other teaching and learning situations and assessments.

Interviews

Some teachers find that interviews are the best way to learn about students in and out of school. However, with 140 or more students a day, it is unreasonable to expect that teachers can interview every students on a regular basis. Some teachers have found a useful compromise by interviewing focus groups of students, small groups that reflect a representative sample of students across the school day. Some useful student interview questions appear in Figure 6.2 (adapted from Moje et al., 2004).

For learning in your content area:

What is the last thing you learned in science? What have you learned so far in social studies? What was your favorite book last year in English? What do you like to do in art class? What is your favorite subject? What is your least favorite subject?

Are you a good reader in (content area)?

Are you a good writer in (content area)?

How do you feel about talking in front of the class? Participating in a group discussion?

Do you know anyone who is really good in (content area)? What does this person do that makes him or her so good in (content area)?

When you are reading/writing/studying in (content area), what do you do when you come to something you do not know?

Tell me about a time when you really felt successful in (content area).

Tell me about a time when you really felt unsuccessful in (content area).

For favorite outside-of-school literacy experiences:

What have you read lately? What are you writing? What music are you listening to? What music do you play? Tell me your favorite song. Why do you like it? What makes rap different from jazz? What is your favorite movie?

For goals for the future:

What do you want to do when you graduate from high school?

Figure 6.2

Useful student interview questions.

Figure 6.3

Questions to ask parents about their adolescent children (students).

> Tell me about (your student). What has it been like for him or her in school? What has it been like for him or her in (content area)?
>
> Does (your student) talk about any favorite subjects in school?
>
> What does (your student) like to do after school? Does it ever involve reading or writing?
>
> Does (your student) spend any time on the Internet? If so,what kinds of Internet sites does (your student) enjoy?

Parents can also provide useful insights about your students' literacy and approach to learning in your content area. Although parent conferences can be some of the most challenging experiences for beginning teachers, conferences are important opportunities to learn more about your students as well as to explain your curriculum, your classroom, and your expectations. Figure 6.3 depicts some useful interview questions for parents.

Reading Attitude and Interest Surveys

Yet another option consists of developing and administering reading attitude and interest surveys. Surveys are quick to administer and interpret. **Reading attitudes** are all about feelings of approaching or avoiding situations involving reading. Students' attitudes toward reading affect their engagement and reading practices. Poor attitudes can be responsible for students choosing not to read, regardless of their reading skill (McKenna et al., 1995). **Reading interests** involve preferences for reading different kinds of reading materials. Interest is often responsible for students' motivation to read specific kinds of materials. Lack of interest can be the reason for students' resistance to some kinds of materials. Research has suggested that schools need to do a much better job of making interesting reading materials available for middle and high school students (Worthy et al., 1999).

Success in promoting students' engagement in reading requires that teachers know as much as they can about students' reading attitudes and interests. Once teachers are aware of students' likes and dislikes and their preferences for different kinds of reading, the teachers are in a better position to use reading to start a unit of study, focus or stimulate discussion, or supplement classroom textbooks according to students' interests.

Many tools are available for assessing reading attitudes and interests. One is to simply observe students to find out about the reading materials they enjoy. Other techniques include observing comments students make about their reading preferences in their classroom writings. The techniques depicted here involve administering reading attitude surveys and interest inventories. For example, Figures 6.4 and 6.5

Figure 6.4

Surveying general attitudes about reading with open-ended questions.

When you are reading and you come to something you don't know, what do you do?

Do you ever do anything else?

Who do you know who is a good reader?

What makes him or her a good reader?

Do you think she or he ever comes to something she or he doesn't know when reading?

If your answer is yes, what do you think he or she does about it?

What do you think is the best way to help someone who doesn't read well?

How did you learn to read? What do you remember? What helped you to learn?

What would you like to do better as a reader?

Describe yourself as a reader.

Using a scale of 5 to 1, with 5 being a terrific reader, what overall rating would you give yourself as a reader?

Figure 6.5

Surveying general attitudes about reading using a simple scale.

	Yes	Not sure	No
I like reading stories.	___	___	___
I am not interested in books.	___	___	___
I like reading comics or magazines.	___	___	___
I like reading poems.	___	___	___
I think reading is difficult.	___	___	___
I like reading silently by myself.	___	___	___
I like watching TV better than reading books.	___	___	___
I don't like reading at home.	___	___	___
I like going to the library.	___	___	___
I like reading information books.	___	___	___
I like reading with an adult to help me.	___	___	___
I enjoy reading.	___	___	___
I think reading is boring.	___	___	___
Which of these do you read at home?	___	___	___
Storybooks	___	___	___
Comics	___	___	___
Magazines	___	___	___
Newspapers	___	___	___
Information books	___	___	___
Poems	___	___	___
Others at home read with me.	___	___	___

How often do you read at home?	Every day	Most days	Not often	Never

represent two different ways of constructing a reading attitude survey: one as an open-ended questionnaire (Goodman et al., 1987) and the other as a simple survey (Sainsbury & Schagen, 2004). There are advantages to both approaches. The open-ended questions invite students to share their feelings in their own words. This can be particularly beneficial in learning about students who struggle with reading. The simple attitude survey has the advantage of quick administration and easy interpretation.

Figure 6.6 depicts an attitude survey crafted for English language learners (Yamashita, 2004). Notice how the items have been adapted to reflect attitudes toward reading in a student's first language and then reading in English. This reflects the possibility that students might feel perfectly comfortable about reading in their first language yet feel anxiety about reading in English.

Figure 6.7 contains a survey for assessing students' reading interests (Worthy et al., 1999). Notice especially the way in which this survey is administered. Students might not know the terminology used on the survey, including *young adult adventure* or *biography*. To help students respond, the elements of the survey are read out loud and discussed so that students can answer on the basis of their experiences. Notice also how the interest inventory asks students to name some preferences for specific kinds of books. Knowing about students' favorite books and authors can help teachers to incorporate those reading materials into daily classroom practice.

Content Assessment

Content Area Reading Inventory

A **Content Area Literacy Inventory** is especially useful when teachers want to directly observe how students deal with content area readings and assignments, including writing (Vacca & Vacca, 2004). Designed as a dry run in interacting with a class textbook or other kinds of content area texts and classroom tasks, a Content Area Reading Inventory is a particularly good tool to determine how students understand classroom work and assignments in your class. Content Area Reading Inventories can be given to individual students, but they are most often administered to an entire class. The results of a Content Area Reading Inventory can provide teachers with an indication of how well prepared students might be for reading and writing in a content area and what steps teachers might need to take to help students.

Figure 6.6 Surveying the reading attitudes of English language learners.

	Strongly Agree	Agree	Undecided	Disagree	Strongly Disagree
I feel anxious if I don't know all of the words.	5	4	3	2	1
I feel anxious if I don't know all of the words in English.	5	4	3	2	1
If it is not necessary, I prefer to avoid reading as much as possible.	5	4	3	2	1
If it is not necessary, I prefer to avoid reading in English as much as possible.	5	4	3	2	1
I think reading many books is advantageous to getting a job.	5	4	3	2	1
I think reading many books in English is advantageous to getting a job.	5	4	3	2	1
Reading is enjoyable.	5	4	3	2	1
Reading in English is enjoyable.	5	4	3	2	1
Reading is my hobby.	5	4	3	2	1
Reading in English is my hobby.	5	4	3	2	1
I think reading many books is advantageous to the study of this subject.	5	4	3	2	1
I think reading many books in English is advantageous to the study of this subject.	5	4	3	2	1
I feel anxious if I am not sure whether I understand what I read.	5	4	3	2	1
I feel anxious if I am not sure whether I understand what I read in English.	5	4	3	2	1
I feel tired when I am presented with a long text.	5	4	3	2	1
I feel tired when I am presented with a long text in English.	5	4	3	2	1
I think reading many books enables us to gain more knowledge.	5	4	3	2	1
I think reading many books in English enables us to gain more knowledge.	5	4	3	2	1
I think reading is useful to shape my personality.	5	4	3	2	1
I think reading in English is useful to shape my personality.	5	4	3	2	1
I think I can read quickly.	5	4	3	2	1
I think I can read in English quickly.	5	4	3	2	1
I think my reading ability is advanced.	5	4	3	2	1
I think my reading ability in English is advanced.	5	4	3	2	1
I think I read a lot.					
I think I read in English a lot.	5	4	3	2	1

Figure 6.7 Surveying students' reading interests.

Part I: Which of the following kinds of reading material would you be most interested in reading? Please listen as each item is read and discussed. Then put a check by those materials that you would choose to read if they were available and you had time to read. If you have a comment or want to write in a title, you may do so underneath each item. Raise your hand if you have any questions.

1. ____ Young adult literature novels

2. ____ Young adult funny novels

3. ____ Young adult novels about things that happen to people

4. ____ Young adult novels about science fiction or fantasy

5. ____ Scary books

6. ____ Biography

7. ____ Series books

8. ____ Information books or magazines about sports

9. ____ Magazines about people

10. ____ Information books and magazines about cars and trucks

11. ____ Books that are mostly for adults

____ Write your favorite title(s) or author(s)

12. ____ Poetry books

13. ____ Encyclopedias or books that give information about different things

14. ____ Young adult novels about things that happen to people

15. ____ Almanacs or record books

16. ____ Cartoons or comics

17. ____ Drawing books

18. ____ Animals

19. ____ History or historical fiction

20. ____ Information books: science and math

21. ____ Picture books

22. ____ Other books or magazines

Part II: Please listen as the following questions are read. Then answer them. Raise your hand if you have any questions.

1. If you could read anything that you wanted to read, what would it be?

2. Who is your favorite author?

3. Where do you usually get your reading materials (circle one)

school library   public library   store _____

home   classroom   other_____

Preparing a Content Area Reading Inventory. To prepare a Content Area Reading Inventory, follow these steps:

1. **Select a reading assignment for students.** This can be just about anything, including reading pages from a book, doing math or science work, studying pages from a social studies text, or doing research in the library or on the Internet.

2. **Have the student or students read some of the assignment.** Ask: What do you need to do with this assignment? How will you get started? What will you need to do to be successful?

3. **After students complete the assignment, ask them to describe what they did and how they thought that it helped them.**

4. **Observe students' use of text aids, such as graphs, problems, and questions inserted in the text.** Most students, particularly struggling readers, skip text aids. Some good readers skip text aids because they can get enough meaning from the rest of the text. Select a text aid and ask the student or students to tell you what it is for and what it is telling him or her.

An alternative to this approach is to prepare specific questions about the classroom text, using a form like the one in Figure 6.8 (Vacca & Vacca, 2004).

Teachers in performance-oriented content areas might adapt this inventory to students' performance skills, such as speaking and writing in a foreign language, recognizing and responding to musical notation, explaining a method of physical conditioning, or demonstrating an artistic technique. All teachers can gain a great deal of insight from this form of assessment by having students talk about what they are doing while they are performing a particular skill.

Evaluating Students' Performance. Evaluating how students perform on a Content Area Reading Inventory involves following these steps:

1. **Observe problems with reading, writing, and other various ways of responding and performing.** For instance, does the student spend an inordinate amount of time trying to figure out the text or understand the task or assignment? Does the student gain much understanding for the effort she or he is expending on reading or writing? Does the student stumble over particular topics or kinds of tasks?

2. **Determine whether the students are more concerned with procedure or are engaged in the content.** Procedural concerns include pronouncing the words, filling in blanks, and just getting the assignment done. Signs of engagement in the content include talking about the content, asking questions about the content, or summarizing the important concepts.

Figure 6.8

Sample content area reading inventories.

Mathematics

Read pages 98–103 in your mathematics textbook. Then look up at the clock and record the time when you finished reading. Record this time in the space provided on the response sheet. Close your book and answer the first question. Then open your book and answer the remaining questions.

Finished reading time:_____

STUDENT RESPONSE FORM

Part I. Directions: Close your book. Answer the following question on the back of this sheet. What was this reading selection about? Use as much space on the back of this sheet as you need to complete your answer.

Part II.

A. Directions: Open your book and answer the following questions:

  1. The United States stayed only with the English system of measurement.
    a. True
    b. False
    c. Can't tell

  2. The metric system is used in many other fields besides science.
    a. True
    b. False
    c. Can't tell

  3. An inch is larger than a centimeter.
    a. True
    b. False
    c. Can't tell

  4. The ruler on page 99 uses two different kinds of measurements.
    a. True
    b. False
    c. Can't tell

B. Directions: Answers to these questions are not directly stated by the author. You will need to read between the lines to answer them.

  1. Why would it be more difficult to measure with inches, compared with centimeters? _____

  2. What is the reason for units of measurement to be divided up into smaller parts? _____

C. Directions: The following questions ask about the assignments in the reading selection.

  1. What do you suppose is the purpose for the questions in the section labeled *Covering the Reading*?

    _____

  2. How would you use the ruler on page 102 to answer questions 13, 14, and 15?

    _____

  3. Look at the questions in the section labeled *Exploration*. How would you answer those questions?

    _____

Foreign Language: French

Read pages 78–85 in your French textbook. Then look up at the clock and record the time when you finished reading. Record this time in the space provided on the response sheet. Close your book and answer the first question. Then open your book and answer the remaining questions.

Finished reading time:_____

STUDENT RESPONSE FORM

Part I. Directions: Close your book. Answer the following question on the back of this sheet. What was this reading selection about? Use as much space on the back of this sheet as you need to complete your answer.

Part II.

A. Directions: Open your book and answer the following questions:

1. French teenagers have coffee at the end of meals.
   a. True
   b. False
   c. Can't tell

2. The French never really like to eat out very much.
   a. True
   b. False
   c. Can't tell

3. The best response to "You get an 'A' on a math test" is *Trés bien!*
   a. True
   b. False
   c. Can't tell

4. *Il est neuf* is the proper way to say that it is nine o'clock.
   a. True
   b. False

B. Directions: Answers to these questions are not directly stated by the author. You will need to read between the lines to answer them.

1. In what ways are *Leçon B* and *Leçon C* different?

   _____

2. How would you answer the questions about money on page 82?

   _____

3. What kinds of experiences have you had that are like those in *Mise au point sur... la cuisine française*?

   _____

continued

Figure 6.8
(continued)

---

continued

C. Directions: These questions ask about the assignments in the reading selection.

1. What is the purpose of the section entitled *Enquête culturelle*?

_____

2. Describe what you would need to do to accomplish the activities under the section labeled *Communication*.

_____

3. What is the purpose of the section labeled *Pratique*?

_____

---

3. **Watch for students' ability to integrate text information.** Less proficient readers often ignore large chunks of important text information to the detriment of meaning. Proficient readers make strategic use of all of the text information they need to comprehend well and complete assignments successfully. Sometimes, proficient readers skip text information because they figure out that it is not necessary for completing an assignment.

Classroom Tests

Yet another approach to finding out about students is by observing their performance on well-designed classroom tests.

Well-Designed Classroom Tests. Rick Stiggins, a well-known assessment expert, defines sound classroom assessment this way (Stiggins, 2005):

▶ *Assessment targets are understandable and appropriate:* Goals, objectives, and outcomes are clear and appropriate.

▶ *Assessment methods are consistent with instruction and promote student learning:* Teaching, learning, and assessment tasks and procedures are complimentary; student performance with these assessment methods yields rich and significant information that helps teachers decide what to do next.

▶ *Evaluation and grading criteria are clear and consistent with targets and methods:* Evaluation and grading are connected directly to evidence of performance rather than being general impressions.

▶ *Communication about assessment is accurate and concerned with the interests of multiple audiences:* Students, teachers, parents, and administrators all have a stake in sound classroom assessment.

Whenever teachers administer a test or otherwise engage in assessment, they learn more about students and about their own assessment practices. When students do not do well on a test or student performance is difficult to interpret, that is a sign that it is time for teachers to revisit assumptions about the assessment. Students' test performance can also present numerous opportunities to learn more about students' content understandings, literacies, and skills in a content area.

▲ Authentic assessment includes observing how well students can apply concepts.

Gathering Information from Authentic Classroom Tests.
Authentic tests are a particularly good example of a classroom test from which teachers can learn a great deal about students, particularly their content knowledge and related literacies. Authentic tests engage students in reading and writing in a content area for real purposes, typically consisting of tasks that resemble messy, real-world challenges and situations faced by adults. Response to an authentic test often requires a sophisticated understanding of knowledge in your content area and good measure of skill in reading, writing, and communicating. For this reason, authentic tests are good preparation not only for standardized and state tests but also for challenges later in life. An authentic test can be used before teaching students about a Big Idea. Administering a test beforehand can provide information about students' prior knowledge. An authentic test can also be used after teaching, as an assessment of what students have learned and what they need to know more about. An example of an authentic test and an accompanying rubric used to evaluate students' performance appears in Figure 6.9.

Steps in Preparing an Authentic Classroom Test.
Preparing an authentic classroom test requires several steps:

▶ **First, it is a good idea to start with a clear goal or target for your assessment.** Recall our discussion of Big Ideas. A Big Idea is an excellent candidate for designing an authentic assessment.

Figure 6.9

An authentic assessment and an accompanying scoring rubric.

Getting Ready for the Bike Tour. You plan to bike the Register's Annual Great Bicycle Ride Across Iowa™ bike tour. The tour lasts 7 days and covers 500 miles. Each day, you will bike about 70 miles or so. Considering your current level of fitness, prepare a training plan that will get you ready. It is now January, and the bike tour is at the end of July. Your plan should contain specific details about how you will build up your physical readiness for the tour. Explain the principles of good conditioning that went into your plan. You will present your plan to a simulated medical review board, which will decide whether your plan is good enough for you to go on the tour.

Key Element	Desired Performance	No Evidence		Some Evidence		Substantial Evidence
Prepare a training plan	The plan demonstrates a reasonably safe development of conditioning from a beginning level.	1	2	3	4	5
Specific details	The plan contains details that will lead to levels of conditioning appropriate to the physical activity.	1	2	3	4	5
Principles of good conditioning	The plan connects details to clear and acceptable principles of physical conditioning.	1	2	3	4	5
Plan presentation	The presentation of the plan is clear and convincing.	1	2	3	4	5

▶ **Second, consider a real-life example related to your target or goal.** In the example provided in Figure 6.9, the target consists of assessing students' understanding of physical conditioning related to vigorous physical activity. The real-life example is about getting ready for a physically demanding bike tour.

▶ **The third step consists of asking questions that will require students to use their knowledge about the Big Idea to answer questions about the real-life situation.** Notice how, in our example, the required plan engages students in some very real writing—to prepare a plan that reflects principles of good conditioning.

The best authentic assessments are genuine, reflect the outside world, and immerse students in literate activity, such as reading, writing, and research.

Interpreting an Authentic Assessment. Designing an approach to scoring and interpreting for an authentic assessment involves some analysis of the question. First, identify the key elements of the question—What is the question asking for? In our example, there are four key elements:

preparing a training plan, providing specific details, connecting the plan to principles of good conditioning, and a clear and convincing presentation. Notice in Figure 6.9 how each of these key elements has been identified and connected to a five-point scale for analyzing students' responses. Taken together, this approach to interpreting students' performance is referred to as a **rubric**. Rubrics can be a great source of information about students' content knowledge, their ways of knowing the content, and their literacy skills. Read How to Plan for more examples of designing and learning from authentic assessments.

Portfolio Assessment

Portfolios are a gathering of students' work (Valencia, 1990). Often contained in a large, expandable file folder, a portfolio can hold the following:

▶ Samples of student work selected by the teacher and/or student

▶ Teacher observations, feedback, and notes

▶ Student's self-evaluations

▶ Notes about a student's progress, contributed by the teacher and the student

A primary goal of portfolios is to involve students in evaluating their own work. Portfolios also consist of a variety of indicators of learning so that teachers, administrators, students, and parents gain the most complete picture of a student's development. Of all of the assessments described so far, portfolios represent perhaps the greatest variety of choices to represent a student's personal identity, literacy skill, content knowledge and ways of knowing, communication and motivation, and knowledge and skill in content area literacy.

A distinguishing strength of portfolios, in comparison with other assessments discussed so far, consists of their potential for student involvement. Students can get involved in selecting their work and organizing and evaluating what they have accomplished. But teachers have to help students learn how to do these things. Teachers need to model each behavior—selecting, organizing, interpreting, and evaluating—so that students can learn to do these things on their own. There are many different ways to organize portfolios for different purposes. Here, we discuss three examples.

Personality Profile Portfolio. The simplest kind of portfolio—and a good place to start early in the academic year—is with a **personality profile portfolio**. A portfolio consisting of a personality profile asks

HOW
to Plan
... for Authentic Assessment

Study the sample authentic assessments in the examples of scoring rubrics that follow. Design your own authentic classroom assessment and scoring rubric. Compare your assessment and scoring rubric with others in your class. What are some differences across content areas? What are some common elements? Describe what you will determine about students' literacy and content area knowledge, using your authentic assessment.

Examples of Authentic Assessment

Mathematics Standard: solves real-world and mathematical problems involving estimates of measurements, including length, time, weight/mass, temperature, money, perimeter, area, and volume, and estimates the effects of measurement errors on calculations.

Getting Out of Credit Card Debt. Many financial experts are worried that the average American family now carries $8,000 dollars in credit card debt. With an average interest rate on credit cards at 13 percent, the experts are worried that bankruptcies may be on the rise as consumers fail to pay the balances on their credit cards. You are in a family with a monthly take-home income of $2,500. Your mortgage payment is $1,200 per month, your utility bills are $200, and you spend $400 on food and other household essentials. You have a $300 per month car payment. This leaves you with $400 per month. You have been using this cash and credit cards for clothing, entertainment (movies, CDs, etc.),

travel, car repairs, home maintenance, and vacations. But now you want to pay off your credit card. Create a plan for paying off your credit card in the shortest period possible, taking into account all of your expenses

English Standard: locates, gathers, analyzes, and evaluates written information for a variety of purposes, including research projects, real-world tasks, and self-improvement.

Documentary or Work of Fiction? Al Gore's film *An Inconvenient Truth* won an Oscar for best documentary. Your job is to write a movie review for the local newspaper. Form an informed opinion of the film, considering accusations that the work is more a work of fiction than a documentary. Your review should show evidence that you have carefully considered your audience: students in your age group and older, parents, businesspeople, and senior citizens in your community.

Science Standard: understands the interconnectedness of the earth's systems and quality of life.

Ratifying the Kyoto Treaty. The Kyoto Treaty commits industrialized nations to reducing emissions of greenhouse gases, principally carbon dioxide, over the next decade. Greenhouse gases are produced principally through manufacturing. However, there is a continuing debate among scientists about whether carbon dioxide levels are really increasing and the impact high CO_2 emissions might have on the world's environment. The

United States has chosen so far not to sign the Kyoto Treaty because of possible harmful effects of scaling back manufacturing on the economy and doubts about the real impact of greenhouse gases. You will write a report to Congress with your recommendations about greenhouse gases and the role of U.S. manufacturers.

Social Studies Standard: understands how social, cultural, economic, and environmental factors contribute to the dynamic nature of regions.

Tsunami Aid. The Asian tsunami of 2004 created unprecedented destruction of people and property in coastal areas of parts of Asia. You are part of a United Nations panel overseeing relief efforts in the region. Write a recommendation for the panel in which you describe: (1) the kinds of aid required to save people from further harm, (2) what needs to be done to rebuild in the region, including possible relocation of populated centers, and (3) early detection systems in case another tsunami occurs sometime in the future.

Music Standard: establishes a strategy for making informed, critical evaluations of the quality and/or the effectiveness of a performance.

The Grammy Awards. You are a member of the committee responsible for this year's Grammy Award nominations. Using what you have learned about musical performance and quality, prepare a slate of three nominees each for the categories Song of the Year,

Album of the Year, Best New Artist, and one other category of your choosing. You will defend your choices to a simulated group from the media (our class).

Foreign Language Standard: interacts in a variety of situations that reflect the activities of teenagers in the target culture, using appropriate verbal and nonverbal communication.

Living in France. You and a partner will construct a conversation about what it is like to live in your community in France. Your conversation must be in French. Include in your conversation your feelings about family, school, things that you do after school, and, of course, shopping, eating, and enjoying yourselves.

Visual Arts Standard: understands that works of art can communicate an idea and elicit a variety of responses through the use of selected media, techniques, and processes.

Select one of the visual arts we have been studying (painting, photography, collage, PhotoShop art, web page design). Next, consider a topic or idea about which you are passionate—the environment, politics, war, human rights, capital punishment, or gender in society, for instance. Communicate your idea in a way that will convince or persuade your audience (our class and parents on Parents' Night) about your point of view. Your work needs to stand on its own with minimal, if any, additional explanation.

(continued)

(continued)

Examples of Scoring Rubrics for Authentic Classroom Assessments

Mathematics

5 The plan appropriately balances credit card payments with living expenses and pays off the credit card debt within a limited amount of time (within five years).

4 The plan appropriately balances credit card payments with living expenses and pays off credit card debt over an extended period of time (more than five years).

3 The plan mostly balances credit card payments and living expenses but could be more aggressive in paying down credit card debt.

2 The plan does not lead to paying off the credit card debt and/or leads to increased debt or insufficient living expenses.

1 The plan contains insufficient details to determine its merits or potential in reducing the debt.

English

	No	A Little bit		Yes
The piece is written in the form of a movie review.	1	2	3	4	5
The review contains an informed opinion (evidence of outside research).	1	2	3	4	5
The opinion is supported with details from the film and relevant research.	1	2	3	4	5
The review considers the debate: documentary versus fiction.	1	2	3	4	5
The review shows evidence of considering the community as audience.	1	2	3	4	5

Visual Arts

	Exceptional	Admirable	Acceptable	Needs
Content	Topic or idea is portrayed with passion and energy.	Topic or idea is presented with enthusiasm.	Topic or idea is clearly represented.	Topic or idea is not very clear.
Visual Art	The visual art is uniquely and ideally matched with the message.	The visual art is well matched to the message.	The visual art is related to the message, though other visual arts may have worked more effectively.	The visual art is inappropriate for the message.
Persuasive/ Artistic Technique	The artist's technique powerfully persuades the audience.	The artist's technique offers the opportunity for persuasion.	The artist's technique is clear.	The artist's technique is not very clear.
Audience Response	The audience is overwhelmingly moved by the visual art.	The audience is variously swayed by the visual art.	The audience can understand the purpose of the visual art.	The audience is confused about the purpose of the artwork.

students to represent something about which they are the world's greatest experts—their personal identity (Wilhelm & Smith, 2002). To create a personality profile, students can use print media (magazines, books, and newspapers) and/or digital media (computers, scanners, word processors, and web publishing software) to represent their interests, favorite songs, important quotes, games, CDs, and movies. Students might want to include personal photos, provide links to favorite websites, or select and group web-based images of their favorite places. The products of this work can range from elaborately decorated folders to personal web pages and blogs. Figure 6.10 depicts an example of a portfolio entry in a personality profile portfolio.

The Best Time of My Life

The best time of my life was when I visited my aunt and uncle in Florida. My aunt, Ellie, and uncle, Henry, are two of the most colorful people I have ever met. They took me to many of their favorite places and showed me a great time.

My uncle is a real estate developer who builds hurricane-proof houses. He took me on a tour of his building sites one time. The houses are built of cinder block, with walls about a foot and a half thick. He is obviously very proud of his work. At one site, he told me how he worked hard to keep the landscape as natural as possible. Almost to prove his point, he pointed to an orange tree full of oranges. He directed me to pull off my shirt and fill it up with oranges! I did what he said and we had a feast on oranges for the rest of the day.

My aunt took me to Busch Gardens and spent the day with me. We walked around and saw all of the animals. When we were done, she took me out to Red Lobster. I never had scallops and shrimp that were so good!

Probably the best memory is the way my aunt and uncle treated me like one of their family. And although I was only 13, they treated me like an adult. They listened to me and took me seriously. I will never forget them.

Summary Statement

I chose this short essay to put in my portfolio because it tells a lot about me and my family. But it also shows how I can develop an idea in my writing, with an introduction, two main points and a conclusion. When I look back at the essay, it makes me remember my aunt and uncle and I feel proud that I am learning how to write better all of the time.

~Pete

Figure 6.10

A sample portfolio entry.

Academic Portfolio. **Academic portfolios** are collections of students' best work. Typically, academic portfolios consist of two parts: (1) classroom evidence, work samples, or test data that exemplify learning, and (2) summary statements that explain or help to synthesize the gathered work. Academic portfolios can be exhibits of students' literacy skills and their content knowledge and ways of knowing in a content area. Students might also wish to display evidence of their motivation and skill in a content area through examples of their academic achievements.

Growth Portfolio. **Growth portfolios** are exhibits of students' development from an earlier point to a later point. These portfolios are an important addition to any teacher's system of ongoing assessment since so many other kinds of assessment, just sample a single point in time—a pretest or posttest, a writing assignment, or a class project. In contrast, growth assessments take samples from multiple points, documenting students' growth in a particular area of content and skill.

▼ Demonstrating skills learned can highlight students' knowledge and development.

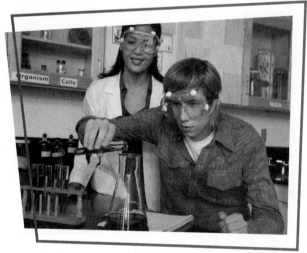

For example, English teachers can help students to develop growth-oriented portfolios around persuasive writing. Mathematics teachers might focus on growth in problem-solving strategies. Foreign language teachers might emphasize growth in language use. Physical education teachers might organize portfolios according to progress with physical challenges and fitness knowledge.

Getting Started with Portfolios. There are a number of ways to make portfolios a regular part of classroom assessment. First, consider curriculum goals, especially standards-based Big Ideas, and students. Ideally, portfolios should reflect students' development with respect to standards-based expectations and patterns of student performance appropriate for different age levels. Teachers can find clues to expected development for students within standards documents at the state, district, and school levels. Second, consider instruction—teaching and learning that are occurring to assist students in meeting the expectations. Instruction should be consistent with expectations, and assessment should be consistent with instruction.

Once teachers have identified Big Ideas and have selected and aligned instruction and assessment, it is time to organize and develop students' portfolios. To initiate portfolios, some teachers bring in their own examples—portfolios containing family pictures, professional portfolios, or covers of favorite books. Explain to students the significance of items in your own portfolio so that they get an idea of how portfolios uniquely portray things about individuals. In the beginning, students need lots of assistance in selecting examples and explaining their own selections. Continuous modeling of how to make choices and write explanations will help. Some teachers construct minilessons about how to make selections and the various reasons for selections. Easier reasons involve selecting the best work, as in an academic portfolio. Students can also choose something they have learned, something that took a long time, took a lot of effort, or involved interests outside of school. More sophisticated choices usually involve collaboration between teachers and students and focus on Big Ideas. These choices might focus on writing samples, results of content area tests, or student work samples, such as story maps, reader response, and class projects (Vizyak, 1999).

Evaluating Portfolios. A strength of portfolios concerns numerous opportunities to evaluate many different kinds of students' work. Teachers can evaluate portfolios by designing a simple rubric, such as the one in Figure 6.11. This rubric was designed by using Utah's core curriculum standards for health.

	No Evidence		Some Evidence		Exemplary
Comprehends concepts related to health promotion and disease prevention.	1	2	3	4	5
Knows how to access valid health information and health-promoting products and services.	1	2	3	4	5
Practices both health-enhancing and risk-reducing behaviors.	1	2	3	4	5
Analyzes the influences of society, culture, media, technology, and physical environment on health.	1	2	3	4	5
Practices and applies goal-setting, decision-making, problem-solving, and stress management skills to promote healthy behaviors.	1	2	3	4	5
Develops understanding and respect for self and others.	1	2	3	4	5
Advocates for personal, family, and community health.	1	2	3	4	5

Figure 6.11

A rubric for evaluating a portfolio in a health class.

Students' Self-Evaluations. Do not miss the opportunity to involve students in assessing their own portfolios. Students need help, however, in evaluating their choices and explanations. One way to help students evaluate portfolios is by introducing the idea of **high-quality work**. To evaluate portfolios effectively, students need to understand what it means to produce high-quality work in reading and writing performance and in response to classroom assignments and projects. Most students are accustomed to simply handing things in just to get a grade. To help students develop the idea of high-quality work, teachers ask students this question with every assignment:

> If we do high-quality work on this assignment, what will it look like?

Teachers and students then discuss what it means to do the best work on an assignment, even participating in creating the evaluation criteria and the grading for the assignment. Figure 6.12 depicts additional questions that are useful in helping students to evaluate the contents of their portfolio.

Portfolios and Parent Conferences. It has become popular in recent years to engage students in using portfolios to evaluate their work during parent conferences. The teacher should model each of the steps that students will need to know to do this. First, students will need to be intimately involved in making and explaining their own portfolio choices. Next, they need to have practice in evaluating and reflecting on their own work. Finally, teachers should organize and guide practice sessions for students so that they can converse comfortably with parents about what they have learned. Read Chapter 12, "Building Community," for more suggestions about communicating with parents about assessment information.

Figure 6.12

Questions to help students evaluate their own portfolios.

- What is your favorite piece (or the best piece) in your portfolio?
- Why is this piece your favorite (or the best)?
- Do you think your writing (or your reading, math, science, social studies, foreign language, physical education, or music) has improved? How?
- How can you improve your writing (or your reading, math, science, social studies, foreign language, physical education, or music)?
- How can teachers help you improve your writing (or your reading, math, science, social studies, foreign language, physical education, or music)?

Mandated Assessments

· ·

State Assessments

State-level assessments have been around for more than half a century but have acquired much more importance in the past few years. Many states are using and revising state assessments to meet the requirements of No Child Left Behind. With only a few exceptions, most state tests are not standardized. Validating a test to make it standardized is costly and labor intensive, so many states have ignored standardization (Popham, 2003). Because of this, comparisons of student performance on state tests from one year to another are normally not recommended.

No Child Left Behind requirements for students to demonstrate Adequate Yearly Progress have changed this picture. Some states are either replacing state tests with standardized tests, such as the Metropolitan or the ACT, or revising and reviewing existing state tests so that they become standardized. Some states are designing and implementing new tests called **exit examinations** to assess how well students are prepared for college and the workplace. Read the Research Brief for information on these new state testing initiatives. This section provides an in-depth picture of state tests and their implications for students and literacy.

Increased Challenges for Reading and Writing in Content Areas. As was discussed in Chapter 3, recent revisions to state content area tests have created increased challenges for reading and writing in content areas. Consider the examples of test items in Figure 6.13. Notice how each of the test items emphasizes not only subject matter knowledge but also the use of reading and writing to take a stand and defend it, analyze, make predictions and explanations using available information, and synthesize and interpret, combining readings and life experiences. When state tests were originally conceived, they were used to assess only the most basic skills, such as finding main ideas and simple computation (Conley, 2005). The newer tests represent higher standards and higher stakes for students, teachers, and schools. Not only are these tests often tied to graduation requirements, but schools that fail to demonstrate Adequate Yearly Progress are subject to No Child Left Behind penalties. Because of these policies, it is important for teachers to learn as much as they can about the state tests and the challenges these tests represent for students. Read the Action Research feature on page 189 to find out more about different kinds of content area tests and their demands for skill in reading and writing.

Research Brief

Assessment and High School Performance

These statistics provide an indication about how important assessment has become for high school performance (National Center for Education Statistics, 2005a).

► Students in twenty states, accounting for more than half of all public school students in the United States, are required to pass exit examinations in order to graduate from high school.

► Of the twenty states, seven had minimum competency examinations, ten had standards-based examinations, and three had end-of-course examinations. Five additional states—Arizona, California, Idaho, Utah, and Washington—are phasing in exit examinations. Of these five states, only Utah will institute a minimum competency examination. The other four will institute standards-based examinations.

► By 2009, of the twenty-five states with exit examinations in place, all but six—Maryland, Minnesota, New Mexico, North Carolina, Texas, and Utah—will use these examinations to meet the accountability requirements of No Child Left Behind.

► All twenty of the states with mandatory exit examinations in 2004 tested both English/language arts and mathematics ability.

► Ten states also tested science knowledge. Nine of the ten states also tested social studies knowledge.

► All twenty states included multiple-choice questions on their examinations, though only Alabama used these questions exclusively. The other states included various types of extended responses, the most common of which asked students to compose a written response.

► The percentage of students who passed their exit examinations on their first try ranged from 36 percent in Arizona to 91 percent in Georgia in mathematics and from 40 percent in Maryland to 95 percent in Georgia in English/language arts.

► Although the percentage of students who passed exit examinations varied greatly by race and ethnicity across states, Asian and White students were more likely to pass their mathematics and English/language arts exit examinations on their first try than Black or Hispanic students.

Problems with Interpreting State Tests. Some teachers are fortunate enough to receive results from the tests that pinpoint the areas of student's strengths—taking a stand, interpretation, defending a point of view, for example—and areas of need: critical analysis, prediction, and explanation. However, results are sometimes presented in confusing ways, using terminology such as *percent satisfactory, percent moderate,* and *percent low* and using unconventional scoring scales that are unlike any that teachers encounter in a classroom, such as *a scaled score of 245,* or *10 points above the state performance target.* Again, the best way to understand students' state test performance is to visit the state department of education's website to learn more about the tests and their interpretation.

State Assessments Tell Only a Partial Story.

Though state assessments are increasingly important with policies under No Child Left Behind, remember that the results tell only a partial story about students. If students believe that the tests have real consequences for them and they try hard, then test performance may say something about what they know or know how to do in a content area. Do your students perceive that the tests count? Do they believe that test performance will help or hinder their progress in school or later in life? Are the tests in any way

---

State High School Test in Social Studies

You will now take a stand on the following public policy issue: **Should the U.S. Congress pass a law that requires political candidates to release a list of all organizations that contribute over $100?** You may either support or oppose a law requiring political candidates to release a list of these contributors. Write a letter to your congressional representative. You will be graded on the following criteria.

Your letter must include:

- a clear and supported statement of your position;
- supporting information using a Core Democratic Value of American constitutional democracy;
- supporting knowledge from history, geography, civics (other than the Core Democratic Values), or economics (it is not enough to state only your opinion);
- supporting information from the Data Section; and
- a credible argument someone with the opposite point of view could use and an explanation that reveals the flaw in his or her argument.

Remember to: Use complete sentences.
Explain your reasons in detail.

> Explain how the Core Democratic Value you use connects to your position.
>
> Write or print neatly on the lines provided in your Answer Folder.

State High School Test in Mathematics

Gertrude is doing pushups as part of her exercise program. She did 2 the first day, 3 the second day, and 5 the third day. Each day she wants to do as many pushups as on the previous two days combined.

Part A. Based on the information above, how many pushups would she have to do on the sixth day? Extend the pattern through day six to support your answer.

Part B. Is it realistic for Gertrude to continue this program for pushups? Explain your answer. You may extend the pattern further to support your explanation.

Figure 6.13

Sample items from state assessment tests.

Figure 6.13

(continued)

State High School Test in Science

Provide three predictions for how the weather will change in Madison over the next several hours. Explain your predictions using what you know about the movement of air and moisture between high- and low-pressure systems.

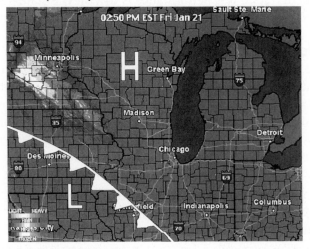

High School Test in Reading

Write a two-page response to the scenario question that is stated in the box below. Your own ideas and experiences may be used in your response, but you MUST reference information and/or examples from ALL THREE reading selections to be considered for full credit (4 points). You may go back and reread or skim the selections at any time.

Scenario

On Halloween night, you plan to attend a school-sponsored party. Parents in the school district planned the party as a safe, alcohol-free alternative to unsupervised parties. A local band will be playing, and you expect to have a good time with your friends. One of your best friends invites you to go out drinking and spending the night terrorizing little trick-or-treaters and vandalizing houses.

Scenario Question

Even though you know it would be better to go to the school party, you really like your friend and enjoy hanging out. Should you go with your friend and try to keep things tame or convince your friend to go with you to the school party? Why?

---

relevant to how they see themselves now and where they see they are going? If the answer to these questions is no, then it might be unreasonable to expect students to perform very well. Their performance could have more to do with their apathy toward the tests than with their content knowledge or ways of knowing and communicating in a content area.

There are a number of relatively simple ways to determine students' motivation and understandings about state assessments. One way is to work

Action Research | Reviewing Test Items

Each of the following websites contains content area test items from state tests, classroom tests, and even tests used for international comparisons. Alternatively, obtain some sample tests from a local middle or high school in your content area. Review test items from your content area. What demands do these tests make with respect to reading and writing skill? Describe ways in which you can prepare your students to meet the demands of these tests.

Released items from all state tests
http://www.edinformatics.com/testing/testing.htm

Mathematics
http://www.edinformatics.com/testing/ny_math.htm

Social Studies
http://www.tea.state.tx.us/student.assessment/
resources/online/2003/grade8/socialstudies.htm

http://www.tea.state.tx.us/student.assessment/
resources/online/2003/grade10/socialstudies.htm

Science
http://www.tea.state.tx.us/student.assessment/
resources/online/2002/eoc/biology.html

http://www.tea.state.tx.us/student.assessment/
resources/online/2003/grade10/science.htm

Reading/English
http://www.tea.state.tx.us/student.assessment/
resources/online/2003/grade11/read.htm

Science, Mathematics and Technology
http://education.jlab.org/solquiz/index.html

Fine Arts/Music
http://www.coe.missouri.edu/~map/mapcd/items/
other/theme.pdf

Physical Education
http://www.coe.missouri.edu/~map/mapcd/items/
other/fitness.pdf

Foreign Language
http://www.coe.missouri.edu/~map/
mapcd/5th_edition/mein_leben.pdf

---

with students on a few practice items. As students work on the items, ask them to describe how they are responding to the items. What knowledge are they using? What steps are they following to answer the questions? Watch for occasions when students get stuck—for items on which they are unable to analyze what the questions are asking, how and whether they are able to take a stand and defend it. Watch for signs that students are really engaging themselves rather than just plugging in answers.

Standardized Tests

Standardized tests in middle and high schools are often used to assess achievement with literacy and content area learning, to determine whether a student is experiencing problems with learning, or to assess a person's potential for learning. Not all tests are standardized. To become standardized, a test must be subjected to rigorous, long-term study. The performance of various subgroups of students is examined and compared over a period of time. Subgroups of students are usually identified by socioeconomic status; race or ethnicity; and urban, suburban, and rural locations. A goal of standardizing a test is to enable reasonable predictions about how individuals with certain characteristics tend to perform. This principle is central to the No Child Left Behind requirements that students from all subgroups need to demonstrate regular improvement (Conley, 2005).

Types of Standardized Tests. There are many different types of standardized tests. **Achievement tests** measure a student's acquired knowledge and skills, such as literacy. **Diagnostic tests** are used to identify learning difficulties, particularly with reading and writing. **Intelligence tests** are used to indicate an individual's potential for learning (McGraw-Hill, 2003).

Figure 6.14 depicts the names of many standardized tests that are used with adolescents, including the skill areas that these tests measure. As the figure illustrates, many standardized tests focus on foundational literacy and mathematics skills and, to some extent, on content knowledge, ways of knowing, and communicating in content areas.

Remember the standardized tests that you took for college entrance purposes? These include the ACT and SAT tests. The ACT test consists of multiple-choice items that cover four content areas: English, mathematics, reading, and science. An optional subtest consists of a writing task. The SAT tests include a reasoning test, consisting of verbal reasoning (literal comprehension, vocabulary knowledge, and extended reasoning) and mathematical reasoning (arithmetic, algebraic, and geometric); a writing test that assesses ability to express ideas in standard written English, recognize faults in language usage and sense changes in meaning; and an entire battery of subject area tests such as literature, U.S. and world history, biology, chemistry, physics, and foreign languages. Like IQ tests, only more specifically focused on performance in subject areas, these tests are designed to assess a student's potential. These tests typically consist of heavy demands for skill in literacy along with requirements for content knowledge and content area literacy.

Reporting Student Performance. Student performance on standardized tests is reported in a number of ways (see Figure 6.15). Raw scores are almost never reported. The reason is that most standardized tests are concerned with representing an individual's performance only in reference to the performance of individuals within a larger group. If a student receives a score of six correct items out of ten, it says nothing

Figure 6.14 Examples of commonly used standardized tests.

Achievement Tests

Tests	Content/Skills Tested	Grade Levels	Publisher
California Achievement Tests	Vocabulary, reading comprehension, language mechanics and expression, math computation, math concepts and application, science, social studies, spelling, and study skills	5–12	CTB/McGraw-Hill
Iowa Test of Basic Skills	Vocabulary, reading comprehension, spelling, capitalization, punctuation, usage and expression, math concepts and estimation, math problem solving and data interpretation, math computation, social studies, science, maps and diagrams, reference materials, word analysis, listening	3–8	Psychological Corporation
Metropolitan Achievement Test	Reading comprehension, math concepts, math problem solving and computation, language, science, and social studies	3–12	Harcourt Educational Measurement
Stanford Achievement Test	Word study, reading skills/comprehension, vocabulary, mathematics, language, spelling, social studies, listening	1–9	Harcourt Educational Measurement

Diagnostic Tests

Tests	Content/Skills Tested	Grade Levels	Publisher
Stanford Diagnostic Test	Vocabulary, comprehension, and scanning skills	4–10	Harcourt Educational Measurement

Intelligence Tests

Tests	Grade Levels	Publisher
Slosson Intelligence Test	Infants through adults	Slosson Educational Publications
Stanford-Binet Intelligence Scale	Ages 2 through adult	Riverside Publishing Company

about how the student performed with respect to the larger group. It is more likely that the score will be converted to a *grade equivalent,* a *percentile,* a *stanine,* or some other scale so that the student's performance can be interpreted relative to the group's performance. As a result, the student scoring a 6 might actually be performing on a par with other students in tenth grade (a grade equivalent), or in the fiftieth percentile (in the middle of all students taking the test), or in the eighth stanine (in the upper levels of achievement).

Criticisms of Standardized Tests. Although school districts use standardized tests for a variety of important purposes, the tests are not

Figure 6.15

Ways of reporting data from large-scale tests.

Raw score: The number of correct answers. This is the basis for all other scores.

Grade equivalent: These scores place students on the continuum of grade levels and months within grade levels. For instance, a student might achieve a score of 4.1. This translates into a score of Fourth Grade, First Month. This might not be a concern if the student is a fourth grader in the early part of the year, but it can be a concern if the student is a sixth or eighth grader.

Percentile rank: Tells the percent of the norm group students your student outscored. The norm group is the group of students used to develop the test. This is the group that is always used in comparisons with your student's performance. A student with a percentile rank of 85 outscored 85 percent of the students in the norm group who took the test before.

Scaled score: Raw scores are converted to a single scale with intervals of equal size.

Stanine: Raw scores are converted so that students' scores are placed on a 1 through 9 scale. Scores in the upper third are said to be superior. Those in the lower third are below average. Students who score in the midrange, 4 through 6, are said to be average.

without their critics. Many educators rightfully point out that a score from a standardized test is only a snapshot of what students know or know "how to do." Other critics point out that because standardized tests are developed on such a large scale, for entire regions or countries, they say little about students' performance with respect to the local curriculum or locally required assessments (Kohn, 2000). Notice in Figure 6.1 on page 162 the areas that standardized tests do not test very well, including students' personal identity and contextual sources of knowledge and communication, including families, peers, and the community. In many ways, students' performance on standardized tests only poorly reflects the contexts in which students live and learn. Yet standardized tests, with their scientific aura, can have a powerful impact on students' lives and the decisions that schools make.

It is important to remember that test performance, particularly on standardized tests, represents only one of life's experiences and not a student's entire identity (Gay, 2000). In fact, overreliance on standardized testing sometimes leads to bad decisions, such as placing students in educational programs that are poorly matched to students' needs. Can you remember your own experiences with standardized tests as a student? Can you remember any ways in which standardized tests were used to make decisions about your education or future? Looking back, were the decisions good ones?

Using Standardized Test Scores. School districts and schools use standardized tests for a variety of purposes, from gaining a big-picture perspective on how students are doing to making decisions about which courses will be available to students, such as honors and advanced placement classes. Schools and districts are interested in scores for answering questions such as: How are the tenth graders doing in reading and mathematics? and Are students getting better? For example, one school district recently reported that 50 percent of the eighth graders were reading below the fiftieth percentile, which translates into reading two or more years below grade level. Imagine a class in which half of the students were slow or poor readers. How would that influence your teaching? What modifications would need to be made for these students in instruction? In assessment?

Sometimes standardized tests are used to place students in remedial or lower-track classes. Other purposes include gathering data for important decisions such as identifying students who are in need of special educational services. For these purposes, teachers and consultants look for patterns in the test data, comparing a student's potential with his or her actual performance, to determine, for instance, whether or not a student is performing up to his or her potential. If students are not performing as expected, then further study is usually undertaken, and special educational services might be provided.

Every teacher should find out what standardized tests are being used in a school and district and what data are available from the tests. Educate yourself about the purposes, the scoring, and the interpretations related to the tests. Get a copy of the tests, if possible, and explore the kinds of skills that are tested. Ask administrators, colleagues, and parents about the tests so that you understand how the tests are used to make decisions about your students. Be watchful for ways in which the tests and test performance are combined with other assessments—classroom assessments, observations, and conversations, for instance—in order for everyone to gain a complete picture of students' performance. At times, teachers find themselves in the position of providing additional information that either supports or conflicts with the results of a standardized test. Become knowledgeable and proactive about standardized tests so that you can advocate effectively for the needs of your students.

Interpreting Assessment

One of the modern-day frustrations for many teachers concerns the need to take time to interpret assessment information. The view of this chapter has been that assessment should be occurring all the time—through less formal conversations, interviews and surveys, structured Content Area Reading Inventories and classroom tests, and student-centered portfolios. Teachers can also count on information from state assessments and standardized tests to regularly enter the mix. An important question is: How can teachers make sense of all of this information? One answer to this question is to look for patterns.

▼ When a student feels good about his or her classwork, the feeling can be contagious and motivate the student to continue striving to achieve.

Personal Identity

Through conversations with students and observations, teachers might notice specific kinds of personal preferences for certain kinds of Big Ideas in the curriculum (such as "I like studying about different parts of the world. My mom is a travel agent." or "I want to learn about the new word-processing program. My dad runs the computers at his work."). In contrast, some students might voice an aversion to some subjects or ideas (such as "Algebra is hard!" or "I hate writing essays!"). Observing these patterns can help teachers to decide to investigate further, asking why students view some ideas as better than others. Or teachers can choose to use some students as resources for the class.

Literacy Skills

Assessment patterns can also say a great deal about students' literacy skills. Teaches may observe some students who require more time to complete assessments or who make consistent kinds of errors while reading, writing, or performing. For instance, some students might experience difficulty with reading and writing because they have not yet mastered basic fluency skills necessary to put words together and understand them. These patterns can assist teachers with making special accommodations during instruction or assessment (see Teaching Today's Learners on page 163) or referring students to special education teachers or literacy coaches for tutoring and extra help.

Content Knowledge and Ways of Knowing

Patterns in the data can also reveal a great deal about students' content knowledge and ways of knowing. Remember that it is not the level of students' knowledge that is most useful or revealing. Look for patterns that show which individuals know different kinds of information. Do not be fooled into thinking that entire classes of students have mastered the content if only a few students truly understand while others still suffer from misconceptions. Assessments of content knowledge can be a teacher's most important resource with decisions about whether students finally "get it" or need reteaching.

Communication Styles and Skills

A fairly common and challenging pattern is for students to reveal their literacy and knowledge through oral communication yet fail to perform well on paper-and-pencil or computer-based tests. The reverse can also be true—some students are great on paper, yet falter when challenged to explain their thinking. With either of these patterns, teachers need to demonstrate the desired performances—reading, writing, and speaking—and provide students with guided practice and feedback. In this way and over time, teachers can help students to expand their abilities to communicate what they know.

Context

Assessment patterns related to school and community contexts concern connections. To what extent do students feel that their family experiences are important and valued? Do students have opportunities to participate using their knowledge about popular culture and the media? The more students feel connected, the more willing they are to participate and learn.

Students' Motivation, Knowledge, and Skill in Content Area Literacy

This is where all of the patterns come together. What does the assessment information say about students' motivation to learn? What does it say about students' capacity with the unique literacies required in each content area? How do their knowledge and literacy support their skill in content area learning? Of course, students will differ in ways in which the assessment information represents answers to these questions. Some students will struggle with motivation. Some will be unfamiliar with the language of a content area. Some will experience difficulties with comprehension and writing. Others will be unable to critically reflect on what they are learning. Each of these areas is covered in a separate chapter later in this book.

Summary

Although today's assessment spotlight is mostly on state tests and standardized tests, it is important not to underestimate the role of informal conversations, observations and interviews, and classroom assessments in supporting teachers' ongoing assessment. No single assessment can possibly deliver all of the kinds of assessment information that are important and useful. Teachers need good assessment information to see patterns in students' performance and to make decisions about students' literacy; content knowledge and ways of knowing; communication styles; and motivation, knowledge, and skill in content area literacy. Teachers need good assessment information to create contexts for students to become more literate, increasingly knowledgeable in a content area, and, ultimately, successful learners.

Special Projects

1. Prepare a set of interview questions or a survey that you would use with students in your class. If possible, try your interview or survey out on some students. What did you learn?

2. Design a reading attitude or a reading interest survey for your content area. Adapt the surveys depicted in this chapter to focus on reading attitudes and interests in your content area. If possible, administer the survey to a group of students. What patterns in reading attitudes and interests did you discover? How can you use this information in your teaching (for instance, selecting texts to use in your instruction)?

3. Using the guidelines in this chapter, create a Content Area Reading Inventory for a text or other kinds of reading material in your content area.

4. Describe your system of ongoing assessment, using the techniques described in this chapter and/or others that you know about or can find, for example, on the Internet. Remember to start with Big Ideas. Next, consider the kinds of instruction you will use to teach the Big Ideas. Describe assessments for (a) learning about students' personal identities, (b) students' knowledge about Big Ideas and ways of knowing, (c) students' communication styles and skills, and (d) understanding students' motivation, knowledge, and skill in content area literacy.

Praxis Practice

Working with Questions to Prepare for the Praxis Reading Across the Curriculum Test

Multiple Choice Questions

1. Which are some examples of assessments teachers can use to keep track of their students' growth in literacy:

   a. attitude and interest surveys.

   b. classroom tests for content knowledge.

   c. classroom observations, Content Area Reading Inventory, classroom tests.

   d. motivation surveys, classroom tests and interest inventories.

2. Which is an example of good assessment practice in your classroom:

   a. Always review unit tests with students.

   b. Have students self-correct any assessments.

   c. Use only written tests.

   d. Test often using multiple kinds of assessments.

3. How often should you employ assessments in your classroom?

   a. At the beginning of a unit.

   b. At the end of a unit.

   c. All of the time.

   d. At the beginning and the end of a unit.

Constructed Response Question

1. Describe how you would go about designing a Content Area Reading Inventory to assess students' reading for a particular topic in your content area.

Suggested Readings

Kohn, A. (2000). *The case against standardized testing: Raising the scores, ruining the schools.* Portsmouth, NH: Heinemann.

Ravitch, D. (2010). The death and life of the great American school system: How testing and choice are undermining education. New York: Basic Books.

Stiggins, R. (2005). *Student-involved assessment for learning.* Upper Saddle River, NJ: Prentice Hall.

Scott, T. (2005). "Consensus through accountability? The benefits and drawbacks of building community with accountability." *Journal of Adolescent and Adult Literacy 49*(1), 48–60.

Williams, B. (2005). "Standardized students: The problems with writing for tests instead of people." *Journal of Adolescent and Adult Literacy 49*(2), 152–159.

The Power of Classroom Practice

Go to Topic 2: Assessment in the MyEducationLab (www.myeducationlab.com) for your course, where you can:

- Find learning outcomes for Topic 2: Assessment along with the national standards that connect to these outcomes.

- Complete Assignments and Activities that can help you more deeply understand the chapter content.

- Apply and practice your understanding of the core teaching skills identified in the chapter with the Building Teaching Skills and Dispositions learning units.

Go to the Topic A+RISE in the MyEducationLab (www.myeducationlab.com) for your course. A+RISE® Standards2Strategy™ is an innovative and interactive online resource that offers new teachers in grades K-12 just in time, research-based instructional strategies that:

- Meet the linguistic needs of ELLs as they learn content

- Differentiate instruction for all grades and abilities

- Offer reading and writing techniques, cooperative learning, use of linguistic and nonlinguistic representations, scaffolding, teacher modeling, higher order thinking, and alternative classroom ELL assessment

- Provide support to help teachers be effective through the integration of listening, speaking, reading, and writing along with the content curriculum

- Improve student achievement

- Are aligned to Common Core Elementary Language Arts standards (for the literacy strategies) and to English language proficiency standards in WIDA, Texas, California, and Florida.

7

Activating Prior Knowledge and Increasing Motivation Before Reading

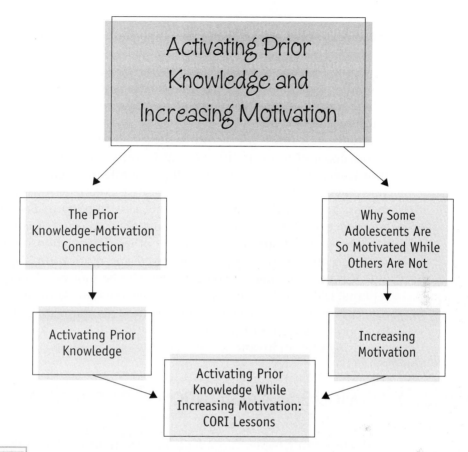

Consider this picture of a successful student (Guthrie et al., 2004): The student is working in a subject or area in which the student feels that he or she has some knowledge and skills that can be used for further learning. The student knows just the right questions to ask and makes choices about what information is important and what is not. The student searches for needed information in places that are familiar (such as in the library or on the Internet). When the sources of information are unfamiliar, the student knows what to do to gain the needed knowledge. This student has been successful in putting forth effort in this area before, so he or she is willing to work hard to learn now. The student regularly summarizes the knowledge along the way and continually monitors progress in reaching the learning goals. Does this picture resemble your own experiences with motivation in any way?

Contrast this picture of a successful student with one of a disengaged student, every teacher's fear. This student might feel that every content area topic is unfamiliar and boring. He or she has a defeatist attitude about learning anything new. This student refuses to persist in the face of difficulty, feeling that the information has to be readily available or not at all. This student often prefers to work alone, if he or she works at all, hiding the lack of skill and poor motivation from others. Often, such students are the ones who turn their mental energy away from academics and toward driving teachers and everyone around them totally crazy (Guthrie et al., 2004).

Notice how much the picture of success depends on a student's prior knowledge and motivation. Personal identity, an individual's content knowledge, and past experiences all play a role in whether students are motivated in one situation or another. Past experiences with learning, success, and knowing how to learn are also important. Because prior knowledge and motivation are so intimately connected, it is nearly impossible to talk about one without the other. The relationship between activating and developing prior knowledge and motivation is also a close one. It is unreasonable to expect students to be motivated about a concept that is unfamiliar. On the other hand, activating knowledge about a concept might be just the way to motivate. This chapter considers ways to support students for learning by activating their prior knowledge and increasing their motivation.

The Prior Knowledge–Motivation Connection

A+RISE

Click on A+RISE – WIDA ELP Standard Strategy in the MyEducationLab (www.myeducationlab .com) for your course. Next, select the Strategy Card Index tab, scroll to Language and Content for Grades 6–12 and select Motivational Strategies.

As discussed in Chapter 2, students bring various kinds of prior knowledge with them, particularly from family, community, and school experiences. Teachers who are skillful in understanding their students as individuals and a product of their experiences are in a good position to motivate. When teachers fail to acknowledge what students know, they risk alienating them by ignoring a big part of their personal identity. This can be an especially important point for English language learners who need to feel included to further develop of their language skills and see connections between their world knowledge and new knowledge at school (Ovando et al., 2003). The Action Research feature suggests some ideas about exploring possible differences between students and teachers with respect to prior knowledge and motivation.

Some students may have substantial funds of knowledge related to academic areas such as economics, medicine, religion, culture, and science, all from experiences with their families and the community (Moll, 1992b). Depending on their parents' occupations, some students might know a great deal about computers and other forms of technology. Some might know about farming and gardening, carpentry, masonry, and

Action Research

How Do Teachers Activate Prior Knowledge and Increase Motivation?

The purpose of this action research project is to determine what students know and care about. This project occurs in three phases.

Phase One: Interview an adolescent about his or her prior knowledge and motivation. Ask questions such as the following:

▶ Describe some areas outside of school in which you feel you have a great deal of knowledge.

▶ Describe some times, if any, when you used that knowledge during a lesson at school.

▶ What kinds of activities do you like to do during your free time?

▶ Are there times at school when you get to discuss or even do those activities during school? If so, in what ways?

Phase Two: The second phase of this project involves observing and interviewing teachers. Ask questions such as the following:

▶ What are some ways in which you activate or incorporate students' prior knowledge into your lessons?

▶ What things do you know about your students that help you to plan lessons? How did you find out about those things?

▶ How do you assess when students are motivated?

▶ What do you do if you determine that your students are not very motivated?

▶ Are any of your colleagues particularly good at motivating students? If so, what do they do?

If possible, observe the teachers you interview for more ideas about how they activate prior knowledge and motivate their students.

Phase Three: Compare results of the student interviews with results from the teacher interviews. What comparisons and conclusions can you draw? What are some similarities and differences between students' views of what they know and care about and teachers' views about how to activate prior knowledge and motivate?

electrical wiring. Sometimes, neighborhoods are rich places for exchanging this knowledge. But all of this knowledge building and exchange can stop once students enter school. When students' out-of-school knowledge is left unappreciated or untapped, particularly in situations in which the knowledge is directly applicable, students can become unmotivated.

Another area in which prior knowledge and motivation are connected is that of learning strategies. Recall from Chapter 6 that learning strategies are specific approaches to learning, such as predicting or summarizing, that are selected appropriately for different kinds of situations, according to specific goals. Some students might have only very limited knowledge about learning strategies, repeatedly rereading things they do not understand, for example, without any other effective alternative. Other students have a much fuller understanding of learning strategies, knowing how to select the right strategy for a situation, tailoring the strategy to the situation, knowing how to assess whether or not the strategy is working, and selecting another strategy if it is not. Students who know about learning strategies and how to apply them effectively tend to be more motivated than are other students who lack this kind of important knowledge. Helping students to gain knowledge about learning strategies and how to apply them can build motivation, particularly with respect to students' willingness to put forth effort.

Why Some Adolescents Are Motivated and Others Are Not

Whenever teachers are faced with an angry, unmotivated student, it is important to remember that she or he might have plenty of reasons to feel that way. Repeated experiences with failure, dilemmas over how to succeed at home and at school, and treatment from teachers and peers can all conspire to make some students feel considerably unmotivated in middle and high school. Read Teaching Today's Learners on page 205 to develop some ideas about teaching practices that can address these issues.

Motivation and Prior Experiences with Success and Failure. Motivation can be deeply connected to students' prior experiences with success and failure. For instance, students who expend a great deal of effort trying to learn without any knowledge of learning strategies are often unsuccessful and unmotivated. When they get stuck, these students might not even know that they are in trouble. To their minds, they just get things wrong without knowing why. Failure and an unwillingness to try in school can then become integral to students' personal identities as well as their personal affiliations.

School practices conspire to reinforce students' experiences with success or failure. By the time students arrive in high school, they have already experienced many years of trying to be successful at school.

Teaching Today's Learners

Motivation and Adolescence Literacy Development

The following are research-based principles about motivation and adolescent literacy development (Reed et al., 2004). For each, describe a classroom practice where you can promote increased motivation and adolescent literacy. For example, one way to increase motivation and adolescent literacy is to provide more opportunities for choice with regard to what students read. Describe some other specific ways in which you can transform these principles into classroom practices.

▶ *Adolescence is a time for defining oneself. It is also a time for disidentification and disengagement.* When adolescents experience failure with literacy, for example, they might disengage from academics as a way of preserving their self-concept.

▶ *Adolescent identity changes all of the time because of different ways in which adolescents negotiate within different contexts.* Fluctuations in who they are have less to do with hormones than with their experiences in different contexts.

Many adolescents learn to take on different roles, depending on different goals and values necessary to succeed in or out of school, including literate and not-so-literate identities.

▶ *At a time when adolescents develop more complex roles and identities for themselves, they are often given less and less control over many aspects of their lives, including what it means to be literate.* School values around state tests and standards can overshadow students' multiple and out-of-school literacies.

▶ *Adolescent literacy thrives when adolescents feel that they have personal choice over what they are reading and doing.* Personal autonomy and control are very important for adolescents and their literacy development.

▶ *Adolescent literate activities out of school extend into using phones, cell phones, and pagers; computers, the Internet, instant messaging, and email; video games; and a variety of music and art forms.*

The lucky students have received affirmation and rewards for their hard work. Ratings of "excellent" and grades of "A" are almost always the result of their effort, even with the most challenging tasks. A competitive educational system, however, is based on the idea that not everyone will get "A" grades. Other students get "needs improvement" or "B" and "C" grades. In short, there are always winners and losers.

Years of feeling unsuccessful in certain subjects or even throughout a school career can take a heavy toll. Many of these students have tried hard in the past, only to view negative results for their efforts. For these students, the logical response to ongoing failure is to withdraw and stop valuing school. The message these students have received for their effort is not even to try. One very powerful reason why some adolescent students are so unmotivated is their continual failure to succeed. Classroom assessments are a way to keep in touch with how students are doing as well as their motivation related to success and failure. The Connecting Standards and Assessment feature provides information about designing classroom assessments.

Connecting Standards and Assessment

Designing and Using Classroom Assessments

Well-crafted classroom assessments are a way to keep in touch with students' prior knowledge and motivation. Good classroom assessment incorporates concerns for both growth and achievement. For instance, in starting a lesson or unit, it is important to understand what students already know and what they care about with regard to the Big Ideas. It is also important to know how students are growing in their knowledge and motivation as a result of your efforts and theirs. Finally, teachers need to understand students' achievement, how close they are to meeting curriculum standards, and their understanding of Big Ideas.

Classroom assessments should be varied. Teachers can learn a great deal from observations and from listening to students as they work. The work that students produce can be a great source of assessment information. Informal or impromptu interviews with students can help to shed light on how students are perceiving goals and assignments. And, of course, the more common formal quizzes and tests will illuminate students' achievement. Taken together, all of these assessments can be used to triangulate what students have learned and what they need to know more about.

Some reading assessments, such as the Content Area Reading Inventory, can be used to assess how students learn from classroom texts. Other reading assessments, especially those that involve oral reading performance, can help teachers to understand the role of fluency in their students' comprehension performance.

▶ To read more about the role of classroom assessment in activating prior knowledge and motivating students, read Chapter 11, "Selecting, Designing and Using Classroom Assessments," in *Connecting Standards and Assessment through Literacy* (Conley, 2005), published by Pearson Education.

Motivation and Differences between Home and School Values.
Sometimes, problems with motivation arise from complicated dilemmas that arise from different values around education at home and at school. For example, families living in poverty might actually fear education as a way of losing their relationships with their children (Payne, 2001). In contrast to the mainstream view of education as the way out of poverty, families living in poverty might fear what will happen to their children and their relationships if education succeeds. Adolescents from cultural backgrounds that are not acknowledged or included at school may feel like they are failing, arising from struggles with fitting in simultaneously at home, in the community, and at school (Gay, 2000; Moje & Hinchman, 2004). Sometimes, adolescents withdraw from the educational system entirely because school does not represent anything they value (Morrell, 2004).

Motivation and Teacher Expectations. Teachers sometimes unintentionally worsen feelings of failure, disaffection, and not wanting to try anymore. For instance, if a teacher believes that a student will be successful or unsuccessful on the basis of previous years' performance or daily classroom performance, those expectations often get communicated in various ways. The research demonstrates that some teachers do not wait as long for a response from low-achieving students as they do from high-achieving students. When low-achieving students hesitate to answer a question, the teacher is more likely to give them the answer or call on someone else. Low-achieving students tend to receive more teacher criticism, less praise, and less helpful feedback than high-achieving students do. Some teachers pay less attention to and call less frequently on low-achieving students than high-achieving students. Some teachers also demand less academically from low-achieving students than from high-achieving students. Finally, some teachers are simply less friendly toward low-achieving students than high-achieving students (Brophy, 1985).

Activating Prior Knowledge

Teachers sometimes assume that students do not have any prior knowledge of certain topics. To be sure, students might not have much, if any, specific knowledge about more abstract or esoteric topics. In cases of little if any relevant knowledge, teachers have several choices. One is to present the new knowledge in small pieces, starting with simpler, possibly more accessible ideas and then building to the more abstract. Another option is to make comparisons to ideas that students might already know and then build into the new ideas. In most cases, teachers will need to help students activate what they do know in order to learn something new. More likely than not, students possess some knowledge about what they are learning. This prior knowledge is often referred to as a *schema* or a mental model representing what the student knows at the time. A student's schema for a topic is responsible for all sorts of mental operations, such as determining the importance of different kinds of information, summarizing ideas, making inferences, generating questions, and monitoring comprehension (Dole, Duffy, Roehler, & Pearson, 1991). The following teaching strategies represent different ways to help students engage in these activities to activate prior knowledge as a learning strategy. The Research Brief discusses what researchers have learned about the value of activating prior knowledge.

Research Brief

Activating Prior Knowledge

Activating prior knowledge means more than just having students think about what they know. Students need to learn how to mobilize their prior knowledge in specific ways to interact successfully with texts to get the most out of what they already know to learn new ideas. Students who have been unsuccessful in activating prior knowledge in the past might think only generally about what they know. Their thinking is not necessarily relevant to the lesson, texts, or tasks at hand. Prior knowledge for these students undermines rather than supports their learning. The goal for activating prior knowledge is to help all students employ their prior knowledge in strategic ways (Pressley, 2000). As more students experience success in activating their knowledge to learn, they will likely become more motivated.

Anticipation Guides. Anticipation guides consist of a series of statements to which students respond by agreeing or disagreeing. The statements represent themes or ideas from the reading, writing, listening, or viewing that students are about to do. When students respond to the statements, they are activating prior knowledge about what is ahead. Students are not only gaining familiarity with what they are about to learn, but also taking up a point of view and creating expectations for meaning that will help them through their reading.

Preparing an anticipation guide involves the following steps (Herber, 1978; Herber & Nelson-Herber, 1993; Vacca & Vacca, 2004):

▶ *Select a curriculum standard and/or the Big Idea(s) for a lesson.* As this book has advocated throughout, start with the knowledge you would like students to comprehend.

▶ *Identify the sources of information* (readings, other media, Internet material) you want students to consider.

▶ *Analyze the sources of information.* Decide what ideas are most important. Many of these ideas will appear explicitly. Some will be implicit (from combining different kinds of information).

▶ *Write the major ideas in brief, clear, declarative statements.* The best statements are generalizations from the sources of information that are accessible to your students, based on their experiences and prior knowledge. Avoid overly abstract or overly factual statements.

For example: Those who fail to study history are condemned to repeat it. (Good statement, applicable to every day)

Demographic irregularities underlie the results of most tests. (Nearly incomprehensible and boring)

Lots of people get killed in wars. (Too obvious and factual)

▶ *Discuss with students the meaning of each statement.* Clarify any misunderstandings or confusion before you ask students to predict.

▶ *Ask students to make their own predictions about whether the statements are true and why they think the way they do.* This is a good place to explain and model the process of prediction. Demonstrate, using one of the statements, how students can make predictions.

▶ *Assign the material.* Have students evaluate the statements with regard to the material for the lesson.

▶ *Contrast students' predictions with the author's intended meanings and messages.* Provide opportunities for students to practice and confirm their predictions based on the declarative statements.

A+RISE

Click on A+RISE – Literacy Strategies in the MyEducationLab (www.myeducationlab .com) for your course. Next, select the Strategy Card Index tab, scroll to Comprehension with Nonfictional Texts and select the Anticipation Guide strategy.

A science teacher followed these procedures and produced an anticipation guide about the future of the automobile engine. She started the lesson by asking students what they had heard or read in the news about piston engines, hybrid engines, and hydrogen engines (writing the words on the board). After students shared their opinions,

▲ Finding what interests your students and tapping into their prior knowledge can help students avoid falling through the cracks.

the teacher passed out the anticipation guide shown in Figure 7.1. Students worked in pairs and shared their predictions. After some whole-class comparisons, the students visited the website on the guide and tested their predictions.

A career development and occupational studies teacher wanted his students to look ahead at their intended careers and the educational experiences that their career choices would imply. He designed the anticipation guide in Figure 7.2. Notice how in this case, predicting is the key learning strategy, not only for reading the class textbook but also for thinking about careers.

Finally, an English teacher wanted her students to use their Internet experiences to make predications about the characteristics of unbiased and reliable websites. She created the statements in Figure 7.3 on page 213 with the idea of having students explore Wikipedia, the open architecture Internet encyclopedia. The prereading discussion indicated that students really did trust a lot of Internet content, though they also had their doubts. Their foray into Wikipedia introduced a discussion about how to tell in advance whether Internet-based information is reliable.

An anticipation guide provides an excellent opportunity to explain and demonstrate how students can activate their prior knowledge as a way to learn. Point out to students that the discussions they are having about the statements are helping them to think about what they know. Ask students to share how this influences their experiences of reading and learning. Explain to students ways in which they can activate their prior knowledge even when anticipation guides are not present, including brainstorming and asking their own questions. In this way, the goal of using of anticipation guides—activating prior knowledge—can be transformed into an independent learning strategy for students.

PReP. PReP stands for the **Pre Reading Plan**, a technique for assessing and activating prior knowledge (Langer, 1982). The assessment part of the technique involves learning about what students already know about a topic and the language they use to describe it. This helps teachers to make good decisions about how to increase students' knowledge. The activating knowledge part consists of building students' awareness of what they already know and elaborating and refining what they know through group discussions.

Figure 7.1

An anticipation guide about the future of the automobile engine.

Curriculum Standard: Students will use mathematical analysis, scientific inquiry, and engineering design, as appropriate, to pose questions, seek answers, and develop solutions.
(Source: Learning Standards for New York State)

The Future of the Automobile Engine
Directions: Each of the statements below represents a possible prediction you might make about the future of the automobile engine. Read each statement and decide whether you agree with it or not. Write A (Agree) or D (Disagree) in the blank before each.

A or D

1. Future automobile engines will be much more environmentally friendly.
2. The technology is already available for automobile engines that do not depend on gasoline.
3. The only thing stopping development of a new car engine is resistance from those who favor the gasoline engine.
4. Try as we might, scientists will probably never design the perfect and perfectly safe hydrogen-driven automobile engine.
5. Hybrid automobiles are just a temporary stepping stone to newer technologies for automobile engines.

Now read the article about hydrogen cars from Science Central News (www.sciencecentral.com). Go back to the statements above and see whether your prediction is true, or whether you have changed your mind. Write a reason for your answer in the space below each statement. If there are any statements for which you do not have enough information, do a web search to find information that will help you make a prediction.

Select a Big Idea for students to know, such as this one from the Texas Essential Knowledge and Skills for Mathematics:

Measurement. The student solves application problems involving estimation and measurement of length, area, time, temperature, capacity, weight, and angles.

PReP consists of three parts: brainstorming, associating, and elaborating. Think of this as asking three kinds of questions:

► What do you know? (brainstorming)

► What made you think about that? (associating)

► What else do you know? (elaborating)

Figure 7.2

An anticipation guide about career options.

Curriculum Standard: Students will be knowledgeable about the world of work, explore career options, and relate personal skills, aptitudes, and abilities to future career decisions.
(Source: Learning Standards for New York State.)

Knowing Your Career

Part I: We are going to do some reading and some Internet research about the relationship between education, personal knowledge, and abilities and future career decisions. Think about your own assumptions about what it takes to get into a good career. Read each of the following statements and then mark the appropriate column stating whether you agree or disagree with each prediction. Be ready to explain your choices.

Agree	Disagree	
_____	_____	1. You have to go to a four-year college to get a good job.
_____	_____	2. Students my age shouldn't worry too much about a career; there's plenty of time to decide.
_____	_____	3. Knowledge in math and science is as important as good communications skills.
_____	_____	4. There are plenty of jobs to go around, but not necessarily the best paying or most satisfying.
_____	_____	5. It is possible to go right from high school into a well-paying career.

Part II: Now read the information on pages 98–107 in your book. If what you read supports your predictions, place a check in the Yes column. If the text does not support your predictions, place a check in the No column. For each statement, write a reason for your decision.

Support from the Reading?

Yes	No	Reasons
_____	_____	1._____
_____	_____	2._____
_____	_____	3._____
_____	_____	4._____
_____	_____	5._____

For our example about measurement, a lesson might proceed this way: Ask students, "What do you know about measurement?" or "What are your experiences with measurement around your house or in school?" Answers might include observations about using rulers or tape measures. For each response, the teacher asks, "What made you think about that?"

Figure 7.3

An anticipation guide for critical analysis of websites.

Curriculum Standard: Students will listen, read, and write for critical analysis and evaluation. (Source: Learning Standards for New York State.)

Evaluating Websites

Part I: Read each of the following statements. Based on your experiences with the Internet, place a check under the column Agree or Disagree. Be ready to explain your choices.

Agree   **Disagree**

_____   _____   1. The only reliable websites are those where the authors, their qualifications, and contact information are listed.

_____   _____   2. Unbiased websites always list sources for their information.

_____   _____   3. You can trust websites where points of view are labeled separately from facts.

_____   _____   4. Only print-based encyclopedias are reliable and accurate.

_____   _____   5. The Internet has caused us to change our ideas about what is unbiased and accurate and what is not.

Part II: Now we are going to visit a website called Wikipedia (http://en.wikipedia.org). Wikipedia is a project to create an online encyclopedia. Anybody can log in and contribute, unlike print encyclopedias, which are written by established writers. After searching through and reading about Wikipedia, go back to the statements above and see whether you have changed your mind. Record some examples from Wikipedia to support your choices.

Students often respond with personal stories and experiences that often make their prior knowledge more evident and richer. Asking "What else do you know?" might elicit some ideas about measurement that were not immediately evident at first, such as measuring the temperature, the time of day, or hours passed.

An advantage of PReP is that it can give you a rapid assessment of what your students know both quantitatively (little, some, or lots of knowledge) and qualitatively (what they know, what they do not seem to know). Perhaps the greatest advantage is that this activity provides an opportunity to talk about activating prior knowledge as a learning strategy, what it is, and how to do it. For this to happen, make sure you thoroughly explain to students why and how you are using this technique and how they can use it to activate prior knowledge for themselves.

A+RISE

Click on A+RISE –
Literacy Strategies in
the MyEducationLab
(www.myeducationlab
.com) for your course.
Next, select the Strategy
Card Index tab, scroll
to Comprehension with
Nonfictional Texts and
select the Know – Want
to Know – Learn (K-W-L)
strategy.

K–W–L (Know, Want to Know, Learned). K–W–L is a teaching activity that activates students' prior knowledge, getting them ready to learn with texts. Like all of our teaching activities, it is important to start with a Big Idea such as this one:

Anyone can adopt a healthy lifestyle.

This idea comes from the national health education standards from the American Alliance for Health, Physical Education, Recreation and Dance (www.aahperd.org/aahe/pdf_files/standards.pdf).

Students start K–W–L by brainstorming everything they know about a topic. This information is recorded in the "Know" column of a K–W–L chart (Figure 7.4). Next, students generate a list of questions about what they want to know about the topic. These questions are listed in the "Want to Know" column of the chart. During or after their reading, students answer the questions that are in the "Want to Know" column. Answers to the questions, new information, and new questions are recorded in the "Learned" column of the K–W–L chart.

Teachers use the K–W–L chart by drawing it on the blackboard, printing it out for students to complete in pairs or small groups, or placing it on an overhead projector. It is important to keep in mind that students will not automatically know how to do the activities described here: making predictions and asking and answering questions. Demonstrate

Figure 7.4

A K–W–L guide about healthy lifestyles.

Know	Want to Know	Learned
Eating junk food does not help.	What does it mean to be healthy?	Healthy people live longer.
You shouldn't smoke.	How often should you have to exercise to be healthy?	Many illnesses can be prevented by eating healthy foods.
You need to exercise.	What happens to people who are drug addicts?	It is not only what you put in your mouth (protein, carbohydrates, fat), it is how much you put in your mouth (calories).
People are more overweight than ever before.	Can't doctors just fix an unhealthy lifestyle?	There is some disagreement about how much physical activity is enough.
Being unhealthy will kill you!	What are the effects of heredity?	How can I keep MYSELF healthy?

ways of using the chart a few times before you ask students to use the chart on their own. When first using this technique, teachers might need to prompt students a bit and provide some examples for the Know step. Rather than just asking, "What do you know?," engage students in a conversation about the topic. For the Want to Know step, be ready with a few sample questions and explain to students the reasoning behind them. For the Learned step, encourage students to answer their questions but also to be on the lookout for new questions or ideas that they have not yet considered. Though this approach was originally developed only for informational texts, it can be used for multiple kinds of texts, all brought together under the same Big Idea.

Though running through K–W–L will engage students in activating their prior knowledge, it will not teach students to activate their prior knowledge as a learning strategy for use apart from the K–W–L guide. For this to happen, teachers need to explain the strategy of activating prior knowledge and how to use it. The K–W–L guide provides a good foundation for this kind of explanation.

Increasing Motivation

Research suggests that there are several key factors for building motivation among students. Teachers need to model their own enthusiasm for learning. They need to arouse students' curiosity while presenting clear expectations for students' knowledge about content and expected performance. What is taught should be worth learning, moderately challenging, and engaging (Gambrell, 2001). Use the following research-based principles as a guide for increasing motivation (Pressley, 2000; Pressley et al., 2003).

Be Caring and Passionate

Many teachers, even beginning ones, are already very caring and passionate. Teachers who manage to motivate their students, however, know how to convert their care and passion into hard work on behalf of their students. They learn as much as they can about their students and build their teaching on this knowledge; they demonstrate and explain, show students how to learn, and provide guided practice and regular feedback. Teaching this way can be extraordinarily difficult to do with large classes, hour after hour. Only the most caring teachers put in this kind of passionate effort (Noddings, 1984).

Find and Put to Use Many Different Ways to Motivate

Not every student will be motivated in quite the same way. Who they are, what they know, and their preferences all play a role. As a result, it is important for teachers to tailor efforts at motivation to the individual needs of students. For some students, this means making connections between their prior knowledge and experiences. For other students, this means connecting to some understanding of where they see themselves going later in life. And do not forget the enormously influential roles that popular culture and the media (Alvermann, et al., 1999) play in students' lives (Morrell, 2004).

▲ Passionate teachers find new and interesting ways to present content and create enlivened classrooms.

Work with Interesting Content

Be observant for opportunities to incorporate interesting content into the curriculum. For instance, many curriculum standards are relevant to current events about which students are very passionate. For example, consider the following English Language Arts curriculum standard from California:

Critique the power, validity, and truthfulness of arguments set forth in public documents; their appeal to both friendly and hostile audiences; and the extent to which the arguments anticipate and address reader concerns and counterclaims (e.g., appeal to reason, to authority, to pathos and emotion).

This standard lends itself to working with interesting content, from misleading television and magazine ads to Internet content. Consider the guidelines for weight loss claims from the Federal Trade Commission (Figure 7.5). Students can read and review the guidelines to consider whether they agree with them. Next, they can apply the guidelines to ads they encounter in the media and on the Internet.

Weighing the Evidence in *Diet* Ads

Flip through a magazine, scan a newspaper, or channel surf and you see them everywhere: Ads that promise quick and easy weight loss without diet or exercise. Wouldn't it be nice if – as the ads claim – you could lose weight simply by taking a pill, wearing a patch, or rubbing in a cream? Too bad claims like that are almost always false.

Doctors, dieticians, and other experts agree that the best way to lose weight is to eat fewer calories and increase your physical activity so you burn more energy. A reasonable goal is to lose about a pound a week. For most people, that means cutting about 500 calories a day from your diet, eating a variety of nutritious foods, and exercising regularly.

When it comes to evaluating claims for weight loss products, the Federal Trade Commission (FTC) recommends a healthy portion of skepticism. Before you spend money on products that promise fast and easy results, weigh the claims carefully. Think twice before wasting your money on products that make any of these false claims:

"Lose weight without diet or exercise!" Achieving a healthy weight takes work. Take a pass on any product that promises miraculous results without the effort. Buy one and the only thing you'll lose is money.

"Lose weight no matter how much you eat of your favorite foods!" Beware of any product that claims that you can eat all you want of high-calorie foods and still lose weight. Losing weight requires sensible food choices. Filling up on healthy vegetables and fruits can make it easier to say no to fattening sweets and snacks.

"Lose weight permanently! Never diet again!" Even if you're successful in taking the weight off, permanent weight lost requires permanent lifestyle changes. Don't trust any product that promises once-and-for-all results without ongoing maintenance.

"Block the absorption of fat, carbs, or calories!" Doctors, dieticians, and other experts agree that there's simply no magic non-prescription pill that will allow you to block the absorption of fat, carbs, or calories. The key to curbing your craving for those "downfall foods" is portion control. Limit yourself to a smaller serving or a slimmer slice.

Figure 7.5

Working with interesting content.

Source: The Federal Trade Commission.

Present Content in Interesting Ways

Presenting content in interesting ways includes a passionate teacher who models interest in learning the content; thought-provoking and even hands-on or observational approaches to learning with clear connections to the real world; and multiple texts, including texts from the world outside of school, such as newspapers, magazines, videos, Internet web pages, downloaded images and documents, music, and other kind of performance. Content is interesting when it is accompanied by engaging activities—projects, discussions, and role-playing—and productions such as posters, collages, movies, artwork, and scale models.

Emphasize Prediction

Prediction is the act of applying appropriate prior knowledge and past experiences to various kinds of text or new experiences in order to imagine what comes next (Block & Pressley, 2003). From a motivation perspective, prediction is like a game; it is surprising when an individual's prediction is not quite accurate and fun to find out that a prediction is correct. So prediction can be engaging. Prediction is also an excellent way to activate prior knowledge. The act of thinking ahead helps students to zero in on relevant ideas and build knowledge.

Set Realistically High Expectations for Students

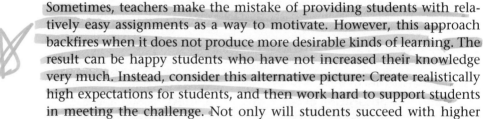

Sometimes, teachers make the mistake of providing students with relatively easy assignments as a way to motivate. However, this approach backfires when it does not produce more desirable kinds of learning. The result can be happy students who have not increased their knowledge very much. Instead, consider this alternative picture: Create realistically high expectations for students, and then work hard to support students in meeting the challenge. Not only will students succeed with higher expectations, but they also will have earned well-deserved praise and feelings of accomplishment.

Provide Regular Feedback and Timely Praise

An extremely important connection is that between effort and accomplishment. The more students know about what they need to do to succeed and the more they feel they are genuinely succeeding because of their effort, the more they will be motivated to succeed some more. Teachers play a key role in this equation. Focus praise on particularly praiseworthy actions and performances, pointing out how such actions in the future can lead to more success and praise. This will help students to connect their efforts with success. Watch for opportunities to help students see that their effort is paying off and what they need to do to continue a pattern of success.

Balance Competition with Cooperation

As discussed earlier, some adolescents have had many negative experiences with competition, particularly with grades, by the time they are in high school. At the same time, adolescents need experiences with cooperation, an important skill in many contexts, especially the world of work (Mikulecky & Kirley, 1998). It is therefore important to balance competition and cooperation for the sake of motivation as well as for what students need later in life.

Cooperative small groups are a good way to do this. Small-group discussions and projects can offer a more accessible and supportive context for special needs students and English language learners. Small groups working together can often accomplish a great deal more academically than whole-class groups working competitively can. Students in groups of three or four can be more motivated and engaged, provided that the group task requires every individual to contribute. Individual as well as group grades or rewards are especially useful to help the groups be productive (Johnson & Johnson, 1985). Now that testing has become so much a way of life, especially since passage of No Child Left Behind, competition is more a part of schooling than ever before. To provide balance and to create a supportive place for student work, consider using cooperative groups from time to time.

Promote Possible Selves

Think about where you are in life now and what you envision for yourself and your career. What about your family and friends? What will your life be like in five years or more? The answers to these questions are personal but can also be highly motivating. More likely than not, these are the questions that guide you in your decision making and persistence in many areas of your life.

For adolescents, answers to these questions can be elusive. Though adolescents can see their roles as adults just over the horizon, it can be difficult for them to connect what they are doing in the here and now with their possible selves. Help students to think about the long term. Guide them in asking the key questions about themselves and their possible futures: Will you be a scientist? A nurse or doctor? A historian? A lawyer? A reporter? How will you get there? The more teachers can invoke images in your students of possible selves and connect those images to knowledge in a content area, the more students will be motivated to learn.

Activating Prior Knowledge While Increasing Motivation: CORI Lessons

▲ Using the CORI approach to teaching encourages students to conduct their own research and observations, and to use multiple resources to gather information.

There are many different practices that can be brought to bear to activate prior knowledge and increase motivation. Read the How to Plan feature for ideas about increasing motivation for diverse students. However, only a few practices achieve both goals at the same time. In the following sections, read about CORI, an instructional practice that incorporates many of the principles of activating prior knowledge and increasing motivation from the previous sections. Consider ways in which you can use CORI in your own content area to accomplish the same goals.

Concept-Oriented Reading Instruction

Concept-oriented reading instruction (CORI) is a research-based lesson planning framework for increasing motivation (Guthrie et al., 2004; Swan, 2004). The approach was developed in elementary, middle, and high schools with low-achieving students. Rather than assuming that motivation comes from tricks or gimmicks, this approach assumes that motivation can be developed through student curiosity, social interaction, and engagement. This approach can be integrating as a whole or in parts to many different kinds of lessons and units.

CORI has several important phases, depicted in Figure 7.6. CORI proceeds a bit like a research project. It starts through real-world observation, during which students document their experiences and pose questions. The intent of this work, early in a lesson, is to arouse curiosity and personalize learning. Internet explorations, hands-on demonstrations, experiments, readings, audiotapes, and video clips of both the familiar and the strange can all be used to pull students into a lesson, engaging their interest and attention.

How
TO PLAN
... for Activating Prior Knowledge and Motivating Diverse Students

Research suggests specific principles to guide planning for activating prior knowledge and motivating diverse students (Landis, 2002). Notice how many of these principles involve multiple forms of literacy—reading, writing, and conversation. Notice also how many of these build knowledge about the content but also knowledge about how to learn. The goal is to help diverse students to feel a sense of belonging, success, and motivation in the class.

1. All students need to feel that they belong. This is especially true for students with special needs and English language learners, who might be struggling with learning in various ways.
2. All adolescents need to feel that they are doers in the classroom, free to take manageable risks and learn from their mistakes.
3. Teachers can help to establish a positive context for risk taking by modeling desirable behaviors, including risk taking and learning from mistakes.
4. Motivation builds from successful experiences with applying learning strategies,

such as activating prior knowledge. Teachers can help by teaching and modeling ways of using prior knowledge with texts and other resources.
5. Teachers need to provide a positive social and academic environment for diverse adolescents. For example, teachers can create conditions for all students to react to and contest the interpretations of other readers.
6. Teachers should encourage all students to share opinions about how to interpret texts, confront a writer's choice of words or ideas, and question a writer's motivation.
7. Teachers should engage students' prior knowledge about other texts, movies, or other personal experiences.
8. Teachers should promote prediction as a way to build understanding.
9. Teachers need to model ways for students to write about their opinions and support their opinions with evidence.

Describe how one or more of these principles could be used to plan a specific lesson for students in your content area.

The next stage in the CORI approach involves helping students to pursue their questions, hunches, and observations through research. Notice the range of strategies that students need to know to accomplish this phase—from selecting and evaluating texts to taking notes and outlining. Students will not automatically know how to do these things, so you will need to show them, through modeling, guided practice, and feedback. The same is true of the next phase: to comprehend and integrate.

Figure 7.6

A CORI approach to teaching and learning.

Observe and Personalize	Search and Retrieve	Comprehend and Integrate	Communicate with Others
Observe patterns Collect examples Perform experiments Record observations Identify critical features Formulate questions Activate prior knowledge Generate ideas Self-monitor (check your understanding)	Find texts (print and digital) Use reference sources (library and Internet) Evaluate texts Connect observations and resources Refine and narrow your search Skim for information Take notes Make outlines	Analyze texts Summarize Make interpretations Draw conclusions Identify main points or themes Select supporting details Use imagery Use text organization (patterns) Identify and evaluate points of view	Write in journals Create informational summaries or stories Participate in debates Make diagrams and charts Draw pictures and maps Create posters Write poetry Give presentations Report findings

Show students how to gather up their observations and research, look for patterns, summarize, and draw conclusions. The final phase is about communicating the results of this inquiry to others in multiple ways.

A CORI-inspired lesson could be just as boring as assigning students a dry, traditional research project. But consider what is really happening here to build motivation. The CORI approach to lesson planning consists of many elements that adolescents find appealing—multiple texts, personalized curriculum, choices, and control over what they are learning (Rycik & Irvin, 2001). Obviously, not every lesson could or should resemble every aspect of a CORI approach. However, when using or adapting CORI, remember to do the following:

▶ Build curiosity whenever possible according to students' interests.

▶ Support students with clear expectations.

▶ Teach them the learning strategies they will need to be successful.

▶ Provide consistent and timely feedback and praise.

These are all essential practices for increasing students' motivation. Here are several examples of using CORI in practice.

CORI and Social Studies

Consider this history standard from Indiana:

> Students examine the relationship and significance of themes, con-
> cepts, and movements in world and United States histories; learn
> methods for comprehension, analysis, and interpretation of histori-
> cal events and documents; and explore the resources available to
> them for research and problem solving.

Unfortunately, many state standards like this one are written in ways
that are hardly inspiring. So how can teachers turn a dry standard like
this one into a motivating lesson? The first step is to figure out how to
represent the knowledge in interesting ways. Solving this puzzle requires
knowing students well. Suppose students are intensely interested in the
ideas of fairness and justice. In that case, consider using this Big Idea:

> An individual's life story sometimes becomes a political movement.

To build an understanding of this idea, teachers can use a case study
approach involving a biography, selected web pages, and song lyrics. The
biography for this case is that of Rubin "Hurricane" Carter, an African
American who was imprisoned in 1967 after a conviction for murder.
Various web pages take sides as to Carter's innocence or guilt, presenting
facts and opinions. Bob Dylan's song "Hurricane" tells the story, with
a particular slant toward Carter's innocence. The combination of these
texts is designed to increase students' curiosity about Carter as an individual, his guilt or innocence, and how Carter was elevated to almost a
celebrity in the entertainment and political arenas. From this base of perspectives and information within a CORI framework, students conduct
their research, form their own opinions, and report on their findings.

Using CORI in Art

Consider another example from art, using the Big Idea:

> What is visual art?

This idea comes from Arizona's visual arts standards. To kick off this idea,
teachers and students could perform a web search (using www.google.com
or another search engine) for visual art images using the search term *art*.

Students can explore these images to build their own definitions of art. Other websites provide contrasting opinions, including www.whatisart .org, a website of links to visual artists' sites, and in the art and art history sections of www.about.com. Students could work in teams to create their own visual artworks—collages, posters, photo essays, sculptures, digital media presentations—consistent with their emerging definitions. Further research in the library, at museums, and on the Internet can expand students' conceptions of what art is or could be. The culminating project for this Big Idea could be an art exhibit, communicating students' multiple points of view about the question "What is visual art?"

Summary

Passion is an important element of successful teaching and learning, but it is not the only one. Knowing about prior knowledge and connections with motivation is also essential. Students bring a variety of past experiences with them that contribute to their motivation and their disengagement. It helps to be caring and passionate about teaching and to model interest in a content area. But teachers also need to act—creating a supportive environment, demonstrating how to learn, providing time for practice, and offering feedback and authentic praise—if students are to become motivated. Well-developed practices to activate prior knowledge as well as research-based, emerging practices such as CORI to increase motivation are good ways to pursue the connection between prior knowledge and motivation with students.

Special Projects

1. Select a Big Idea in your content area for which students might have some prior knowledge and/or even a little motivation. Now select one of the teaching activities described in this chapter and design an activity that is appropriate for the Big Idea. Finally, describe how you will use the teaching activity to help students become more aware of the need to activate their own prior knowledge and self-motivated.

2. Select a Big Idea from your content area. Create a lesson based on the CORI approach to lesson planning: observing and personalizing, searching and retrieving information, comprehending and integrating, and communicating with others. Be sure to include steps for demonstrating these activities for students.

Praxis Practice

Working with Questions to Prepare for the Praxis Reading across the Curriculum Test

Multiple Choice

1. Activating students' prior knowledge is classroom strategy used to motivate students. However educators should *not*:

   a. Activate prior knowledge at the beginning of a lesson.

   b. Assume students have little, or no, prior knowledge of a concept.

   c. Search for the best ways to activate prior knowledge within their classroom.

   d. Miss an opportunity to lecture students to make sure they "get it."

2. Which of the following recognizes the role of using a student's schema to understand new information:

   a. Identifying which information is important.

   b. Memorizing notes from the blackboard.

   c. Answering factual questions on a standardized test.

   d. Writing an report to capture what really happened at Gettysburg.

3. A teacher notices that students are bored with the content of a chapter in a textbook. Which of the following represents the best way for the teacher to address students' motivation challenges?

   a. Tell students that they should study because some day they will need the knowledge.

   b. Change teaching so that the content is presented in more interesting ways.

   c. Tell students that unless they read the material, you will quiz them.

   d. Change your approach so that you are emphasizing the pictures.

Constructed Response

Poison Frog Diversity Comes from the Andes Mountains

The Amazon basin has a wide variety of animal species. The mountains towering over the Amazon might have something to do with that diversity.

A new study discovered that poison frogs traveled from the Andes Mountains to the Amazon rainforest many times over the last millions of years. The mountains, scientist theorize, have long been responsible for the many plant and animal species that have found their way into the jungle. With each new movement from the mountains to the Amazon and back, the frogs evolved into new and different species.

Now that researchers have identified the source and characteristics of the poison frog differentiation, they can also begin to consider how to save different species. It may make more sense, for example, to save a species that is ancient and unique rather than one that evolved recently and has lots of close relatives.

—adapted from Sohn (2009), *Mountains Fed Amazon's Frog Diversity*

Below, under the headings "Motivation for Reading" and "Motivation for Writing," you will find two phrases that appear in this passage. For the phrase under "Motivation for Reading," describe one instructional strategy that you could use to facilitate students' motivation for reading about this particular topic. Then, while focusing on the sentence that appears under the heading "Motivation for Writing," describe one instructional strategy that could be used to motivate students to write about that topic.

Motivation for Reading

"With each new movement from the mountains to the Amazon and back, the frogs evolved into new and different species."

Motivation for Writing

"Now that researchers have identified the source and characteristics of the poison frog differentiation, they can also begin to consider how to save different species."

Explain how the instructional activities that you selected in Task 1 would help students develop their capacities within the areas of Motivation for Reading and Motivation for Writing, respectively.

Applying your knowledge of reading and writing as complex and interrelated ways of constructing meaning, explain how your chosen teaching strategies would effectively integrate reading and writing to motivate students to learn in the content areas.

Suggested Readings

Guthrie, J., & Alvermann, D. (1998). *Engaged reading: Processes, practices, and policy implications.* New York: Teachers College Press.

Guthrie, J., & Wigfield, A. (1997). *Reading engagement: Motivating readers through integrated instruction.* Newark, DE: International Reading Association.

Swan, E. (2004). Motivating adolescent readers through Concept-Oriented Reading Instruction. In T. Jetton & J. Dole (Eds.), *Adolescent literacy research and practice* (pp. 283–303). New York: Guilford.

Go to Topic 3: Motivation in the MyEducationLab (www.myeducationlab.com) for your course, where you can:

- Find learning outcomes for Topic 3: Motivation along with the national standards that connect to these outcomes.

- Complete Assignments and Activities that can help you more deeply understand the chapter content.

- Apply and practice your understanding of the core teaching skills identified in the chapter with the Building Teaching Skills and Dispositions learning units.

Go to the Topic A+RISE in the MyEducationLab (www.myeducationlab.com) for your course. A+RISE® Standards2Strategy™ is an innovative and interactive online resource that offers new teachers in grades K-12 just in time, research-based instructional strategies that:

- Meet the linguistic needs of ELLs as they learn content

- Differentiate instruction for all grades and abilities

- Offer reading and writing techniques, cooperative learning, use of linguistic and nonlinguistic representations, scaffolding, teacher modeling, higher order thinking, and alternative classroom ELL assessment

- Provide support to help teachers be effective through the integration of listening, speaking, reading, and writing along with the content curriculum

- Improve student achievement

- Are aligned to Common Core Elementary Language Arts standards (for the literacy strategies) and to English language proficiency standards in WIDA, Texas, California, and Florida.

8 Building Vocabulary Knowledge and Strategies

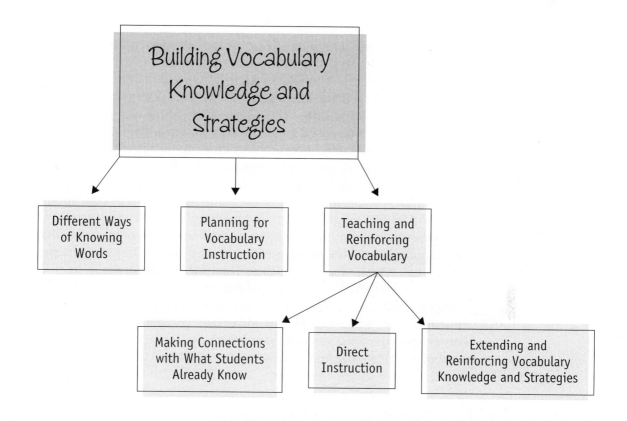

Every content area has its own discourse—the language that is used to communicate, understand, and generate new knowledge (Bruner, 1996). Vocabulary learning is important not just for its own sake. Vocabulary knowledge can play a powerful role in comprehension in a content area (Anderson & Freebody, 1983). If a person reads without knowledge of word meanings, there are few available clues to understanding the Big Ideas. Conversely, vocabulary learning is a way for students to enter the inner circle of a content area. Knowing the word meanings that are integral to a content area empowers students to engage in a content area's language of knowledge and learning.

Conventional approaches to vocabulary teaching are not up to the challenge of teaching vocabulary that matters or of helping students understand vocabulary in-depth. Studying word lists, memorizing, looking up definitions, and writing words in isolated sentences are ways of filling your head with lists of words. Most teachers know from experience that the learning from these activities is shallow, short lived, and lacking in meaningful connections.

Students do not automatically know the vocabulary that matters in a content area. In fact, their vocabulary knowledge in an area can be very limited. Students who lack much experience in a content area will not have much of a frame of reference for figuring out new or unknown words (Graves & Watts-Taffe, 2002). They might also have only a limited understanding of how to gain meanings from words they do not know. Their writing might suffer because they lack experience with words that can help them select words to represent what they know (LaFlamme, 2000). Students with limited proficiency with language generally or with English specifically, such as some students with special educational needs and English language learners, face the dual challenge of acquiring an understanding not only of the forms and structures of an unfamiliar language but also of the nuances of the vocabulary in every content area (Carlo et al., 2004). The challenge in teaching vocabulary is to help *all* students understand why certain vocabulary in a content area is critical to know, what the meanings are behind important words, and, perhaps most essential, how to figure out important vocabulary on their own. This chapter describes research-based teaching activities for developing vocabulary knowledge and vocabulary-learning strategies.

Different Ways of Knowing Words

There are many different ways of knowing a word. Consider your own experiences with language. Think about what comes to mind if someone says:

"What do you think about the *designated hitter rule* in baseball?"
or
"Which do you like better—*hip-hop* or *rhythm and blues*?"
or
"Who are you going to vote for—*a tax and spend liberal* or a *fiscal conservative*?"

Individuals may have differing levels of understanding, depending on previous experiences with these words. For some individuals, these words are thoroughly understood to the point that the person is critical about the meanings and their usage. For some, having encountered these words only briefly, the words might be almost known, yet the person's understanding lacks the detail sufficient to speak or write intelligently about what the words represent. And for some individuals, the words might be completely unfamiliar because of few, if any, encounters in day-to-day conversation, on the Internet, or in print. These dimensions represent the range of possible ways in which we "know" words. Read the Research Brief for a report about the number of words students learn in a given year in school.

Research Brief

How Much Do Vocabularies Grow in a Year?

Research indicates that students' vocabularies grow at a rate of about 3000 words per year. Socioeconomic status appears to play a role. Of students in one study, suburban, middle-class students learned more words than did disadvantaged urban and rural students. One reason for this could be that at the outset, students from different backgrounds vary greatly in their existing vocabularies. The more students know about vocabulary, the better they are able to learn more (Graves & Watts-Taffe, 2002).

Naturally, students come to school with varying levels of word knowledge (Graves, 1984; Graves & Prenn, 1986). Students have a store of **well-established words**—words that they know well enough to use them regularly and appropriately in their daily oral and written language. English language learners may have many well-established words in their native language yet know very few of the English counterparts (Ovando et al., 2003). Students may also know words just on the level of being familiar with them, called **just-acquainted words**. They know the basic meanings of these words, perhaps only in their oral vocabularies, based on their past experiences yet they have not yet acquired the labels that we use in our content areas. Still another level of knowing words concerns **unknown words**, words with which our students have little or no experience, and these words are also sufficiently complicated to be hard to unpack or teach.

Unknown words, sometimes referred to as **technical vocabulary**, are often the center of attention when teachers think about traditional vocabulary teaching. Examples of these words include, from social studies, *cultural relativism* and *ethnocentrism;* from English, *existentialism* and *transcendentalism;* from science, *nanotechnology* and *mechanosynthesis;* and from mathematics, *amplitude* and *platykurtic.* However, some well-known or even just-acquainted words have multiple meanings that students need to know. For example, many middle-school students might have heard or even used the words *rotate* and *translate* many times, but they might never have experienced the specialized meanings these terms have in mathematics, science, or a foreign language.

The classroom might be the first place students have experienced alternative meanings of words that are already established in their vocabularies. Students might know some concepts for which they have not yet learned the labels. For instance English teachers use a number of labels for literary tools, such as *metaphor, irony, euphemism,* or *invective.* We all encounter these concepts in various ways through daily living—having someone hurl invective at us out of anger, for example. Yet we still might not know the labels. So just as there are differing ways of knowing words, different challenges are posed by the technical vocabulary of content areas in relation to what students already know or do not know.

▼ Incorporating new words into puzzles or various word games can help spark students' interest and make learning new words fun.

Be careful in making assumptions about how much students know about words and even which particular students know or do not know the words. The academic meanings of content area vocabulary are usually quite different from students' everyday knowledge. Research has demonstrated that it is really helpful to have students think about what they know about vocabulary and compare their knowledge to the new meanings, especially when words have multiple meanings (Blanchowicz & Fisher, 2000). Though students with special needs and English language learners might be struggling with language, they still might possess life experiences and word knowledge that provides them with an initial understanding about the vocabulary you are teaching (Carlo et al., 2004). Though knowledge of the most abstract, complex words might be rare, some students still know them on the basis of life experiences, such as having a parent or other relative who works in areas related to these ideas. The reverse is also true: Words that seem commonplace to teachers might be completely unfamiliar to students who have had little experience with or knowledge of, or even misconceptions about, the words.

Planning for Vocabulary Instruction

A traditional approach to planning for vocabulary instruction is to focus on all of the words that are in some way unfamiliar to students. Often, this results in teaching from vocabulary lists of only the most abstract, technical words or words with which students have absolutely no experience. There are a number of drawbacks to selecting and teaching words in this way. First, in many content areas, selecting only the grossly unfamiliar words can lead to massively long word lists. This encourages memorization style teaching with short-term learning and only limited utility for understanding and connecting concepts. Second, this approach misses an important principle about vocabulary teaching: Not all of the words are important, yet some of the words are all important. The Action Research feature discusses one way to identify important words to teach in your content area.

A recommended procedure for selecting words for emphasis during vocabulary teaching involves the following three steps (Graves, 1984; Herber, 1978). One teacher's use of these steps appears in Figure 8.1. This procedure represents one way of prioritizing words for direct teaching

Action Research

What Words Are Important in Your Content Area?

Follow these steps to identify important vocabulary words or terms for your content area and to determine how they are used:

1. Revisit the curriculum standards in your content area. Examine the standards for evidence of important vocabulary within one or two Big Ideas.

   Look for:
   ▶ Repeated words
   ▶ Words or phrases that stand for Big Ideas and connecting concepts
   ▶ Words or phrases that are important on the basis of your own content area knowledge

   List the important words.

2. Examine released items from state tests in your content area for evidence and confirmation that the words you identified are important.

3. Obtain a content area textbook corresponding to the curriculum standards you have already examined. Look for additional evidence that the words that you previously identified are important. Compare usage of the words in the curriculum standards and in the texts. Are there similarities? Are there differences? How does the textbook highlight or otherwise signal the importance of the words?

4. Consider the vocabulary-teaching strategies described in this chapter. Describe how you will teach these words so that students can use them in a variety of appropriate ways.

Figure 8.1

Selecting vocabulary words and phrases for emphasis.

Big Idea: Nationalism means unity for a people, but it can also mean being more isolated from the rest of the world.

Words and Phrases Important to the Big Idea	Unfamiliar to Students?	Repeatedly Appears in the Curriculum?
nationalism	✓	✓
unified as a nation		✓
American problems		✓
American progress		✓
domestic affairs		✓
national government		✓
westward movement		✓
isolationism	✓	✓
foreign policy	✓	✓
settle boundary disputes		✓
Rush-Bagot Agreement	✓	
demilitarization	✓	✓
Convention of 1818	✓	
Adams-Onis Treaty of 1819	✓	
Monroe Doctrine	✓	
no new colonies		✓
no interference in Europe	✓	✓
enforcement power		✓

and emphasis, words for starting lessons, and words for just mentioning. Teachers might wish to practice these steps with pencil and paper, as in Figure 8.1. Ideally, this approach to selecting vocabulary is best accomplished as a think-aloud while planning. It is sometimes helpful for teachers to let students in on the teacher's thinking about which words are important and why.

1. *List the key words that are important to understanding the Big Idea(s).* Do not add or delete any words at this point on the basis of whether they are familiar to students or not. Just list the words that are most important for understanding the Big Idea(s). Depending on the topic or your content area, this could be a fairly lengthy list, or it could be a small set of words. Sometimes, teachers use a text or set of texts in making this list. Other times, the list is based on the teacher's own knowledge about the content.

2. *Check off the words that are unfamiliar to students.* Consider what students know and do not know from their life experiences and backgrounds. Remember that many English language learners are unfamiliar with academic words, even if they use many English words in conversation. This will begin to narrow down the list. Consider words that are just-acquainted words that have a specialized meaning in a content area. Students need to understand how the specialized meaning relates to their rough understanding of the word. Be alert for concepts that students know on some level but for which they do not yet know the technical content area label.

3. *Check off the words that appear frequently in your curriculum.* The rationale for this last step is that if teachers emphasize words that are repeated later in the curriculum, then the understandings will accumulate and pay dividends later. The learning of the targeted words is strengthened through repeated exposures.

Following these steps will identify three kinds of words, as discussed in the next sections.

Words to Start a Conversation

One category of words consists of those that are important to the Big Idea(s) and are already familiar to students. These words are good conversation, discussion, or lesson starters. For instance, the teacher could say, "What does it mean to be *unified*?" or "What does it mean for a country to be *unified*?"

Words Just to Mention or Ignore Altogether

These words are somewhat important to the lesson at hand and are unfamiliar to students, but they do not appear routinely in the curriculum. Either these words can be mentioned in passing, or you can decide to ignore them. If you ignore them, a student might ask about their meaning. But you need to define them only for the immediate lesson and then move on.

Words for Direct Teaching

These are words that deserve direct teaching and explanation. These words meet all three criteria for selection: important to understanding the Big Idea(s), unfamiliar to students, and repeated throughout the curriculum. These are words and phrases that teachers need to teach in depth, offering clear explanations of word meanings and multiple exposures to the words used in context and connecting students' prior knowledge to the new words. Teaching this way takes time, but it is time well spent. These are the words that anchor understandings in a content area that, once taught, reemerge for making connections throughout the curriculum.

Teaching and Reinforcing Vocabulary

There are three families of vocabulary-teaching activities within content area literacy. The first family consists of activities that help students to make connections with what they already know. These activities are full of conversation and rich visual images that are organized to depict connections between familiar and unfamiliar words (Juel et al., 2003). The second family involves direct instruction of vocabulary words and vocabulary strategies. These activities focus on words that are useful to know in many situations, with the teacher providing clear explanations of word meanings and strategies for determining the meanings of words (Beck et al., 2002; Biemiller, 2001). The third family focuses on ways to reinforce and extend the meaning of vocabulary words. These activities connect vocabulary to texts, furnishing repeated opportunities to see words in varied contexts while discovering other interesting and important words (Juel & Deffes, 2004). These approaches are powerful practices for expanding students' vocabularies and improving their word study. See How to Plan for an overview of how these approaches work together in a single lesson or unit.

Making Connections with What Students Already Know

Teachers have used these teaching strategies for gaining knowledge in a content area for many years. A newer challenge is to help students translate experiences with these activities into learning strategies, in which they can learn vocabulary on their own. The implicit message in all of the following activities—which teachers must make explicit—is that it is important for students to think about what they already know, including words and connections among words, and then connect that knowledge to new vocabulary. Teachers can help students to become more independent with vocabulary learning by delivering this message whenever using these activities.

List-Group-Label. The **List-Group-Label** method is designed to help students see connections among familiar and not-so-familiar words (Taba, 1967). The technique gets students talking about Big Ideas, connections among words, and vocabulary before they get into the main components of a lesson. List-Group-Label has the following steps:

1. Select a word or set of words that represent the Big Idea(s) for a lesson and present it to students asking, "What do you think about when I say this word?" Not only does this start the brainstorming, but it also provides teachers with a quick assessment for what students know. To help students learn more about how the strategy can work for them, explain why you selected the target word(s) and how it relates to the Big Idea(s) for the lesson.

2. Have students list all words they think relate to the word or words. Explain that this step helps to gain a better understanding of the big picture for the ideas in the lesson. Figure 8.2 depicts the results of this activity in a science classroom. Write students' responses on the chalkboard or an overhead projector. In situations in which students do

A+RISE

Click on A+RISE – WIDA ELP Standard Strategy in the MyEducationLab (www.myeducationlab .com) for your course. Next, select the Strategy Card Index tab, scroll to Vocabulary for Grades 6–12 and select the Vocabulary Mental Connections strategy.

Big Idea: Life cycles happen differently for different organisms (such as plants, animals, and humans).

Brainstorming word: *life cycle*

Listed Words

stages	phases	living	toads
cats	born	die	reproduce
grow up	people	dogs	going to school
going to college	getting married	having babies	getting old

Groups and Labels

Organisms	Phases or Stages	Life Events
toads	born	going to school
cats	grow up	going to college
dogs	reproduce	getting married
people	living	
	having babies	
	getting old	
	die	

Figure 8.2

A science example of List-Group-Label.

HOW ... for a Vocabulary Lesson
to Plan

The following steps were taken by Ms. Mumby, an art teacher in Washington State, to develop a Big Idea. Notice how she bases her thinking about vocabulary on the Big Idea and then selects vocabulary-teaching activities on the basis of the specific qualities of the words she has chosen to teach. After reading this vignette, describe some ways in which you could follow the same or similar steps to develop vocabulary in your content area.

Selecting a Big Idea

Washington State is developing a state assessment in the arts. One of the Essential Academic Learning Requirements is that students will "Apply a *performance process* in the arts."

The notion of a performance process is further broken down into the following steps:

▶ Identify the audience and purpose.
▶ Select an artistic work (or repertoire) to perform.
▶ Analyze the structure and background of the work.
▶ Interpret by developing a personal interpretation of the work.

▶ Rehearse, adjust, and refine through evaluation and problem solving.
▶ Present the work for others.
▶ Reflect and evaluate.

Selecting and Prioritizing Words

Ms. Mumby decided to use the language in the standard as a starting point for her work with the language of artistic performance. Word such as *performance process, audience, purpose, structure, background,* and *personal interpretation* are all new to her high school students in the context of actually doing an artistic performance.

Making Connections with What Students Already Know

Ms. Mumby knows that many of her students are familiar with the word *performance,* from their experiences in bands or sports. She decided to develop a semantic map with her students. Using performance in sports as a discussion starter, she asked, "What kinds of performance have you experienced?" and "What were those performances like?" Students reported their experiences, including some performance examples from out of

not know as much as anticipated, teachers might need to supply more information or even do some preteaching, as described in Chapter 7.

3. The next steps involve grouping and labeling. Explain that this step is important for seeing and making connections among the words, that making connections is a way to learn vocabulary in-depth, and that vocabulary is easier to remember when words are connected or grouped.

school—garage bands, for example. During the conversation, students mentioned interactions with an audience and the different purposes of various performances. Ms. Mumby listed these ideas on the class' developing semantic map.

Direct Instruction

Ms. Mumby discussed how artistic performance is another kind of performance with an audience and a purpose. She told students how a performance in art can be unique because of its visual structure, background, and purpose for the work. Next, she shared several examples:

► Functional art, including artwork on everyday items such as clocks and furniture
► Art that intends to shock or offend people
► Political art or art with a political perspective
► Religious art
► Art that strives to be aesthetically pleasing

Ms. Mumby shared her own approach—her *personal interpretation*—to understanding different kinds of art by examining the art, considering its structure and possible point of view, and imagining the intent of the artist. She modeled this process with one of her artistic examples. Finally, Ms. Mumby discussed how following this process—examining art, structure, point of view, purpose, and audience—is a way to uncover the artist's *performance process*. Ms. Mumby asked her students whether they experienced any kind of similar process in other kinds of performance besides art.

Extending and Reinforcing Vocabulary Knowledge and Strategies

Ms. Mumby invited students to apply the same process of personal interpretation with the other examples. In doing so, students discussed the performance process of each artistic example. Later in the unit, students embarked on their own performance process, with a specific audience and purpose in mind. Ms. Mumby listened to her students' explanations about their artwork for signs that they were learning and using the new vocabulary as well as meeting the state standard.

Start by showing students how to group and label. For example, in the science lesson in Figure 8.2, the teacher started this step by saying:

"I'm searching for words that have something in common. Let's see, *going to school, going to college,* and *getting married* are pretty similar. Can you see any other words that seem to go together?"

This illustrates the practice of grouping and invites students into further practice. Next, the teacher models how to come up with labels:

> "Now, what do *going to school, going to college,* and *getting married* have in common? Those are pretty important events that happen in our lives, so I'm going to call them *life events.*"

Again, it is time for students to practice and they come up with the other two groupings and labels: *organisms* and *phases or stages.*

There are several ways to use List-Group-Label, either in whole class or in small groups. In using List-Group-Label in a whole class, it is helpful to ask students to talk with one another first, selecting the groups and offering labels, before asking them to volunteer. That way, students can think carefully for themselves before they suggest their own groupings and labels. The same practice is helpful when teachers ask students to construct groups and labels in small groups. Throughout this process, ask students to provide reasons for their decisions after asking themselves the question "What do these grouped words have in common?"

When students discuss their grouping and labeling decisions, they gain many opportunities to make connections and revisions in their thinking, verbalizing what they know, and agreeing and disagreeing with one another. For example, there was a debate in the science teacher's classroom about whether having babies is a life event or a stage in the life cycle. Further reading, writing, and discussion will help to clarify this. Classroom conversations of this kind make students' thinking visible, allowing the teacher to prepare good explanations for vocabulary and eliminate misconceptions. The conversations that build from List-Group-Label can provide a sometimes contentious context for seeing the big picture of a lesson as well as the interconnections of important details and vocabulary.

To transform List-Group-Label into a vocabulary strategy that students can use, explain List-Group-Label clearly—what it is and how it works as a way of learning new vocabulary. Explain how brainstorming, grouping, and labeling are all activities that can help students to expand their thinking about at topic while making connections. Model ways of using List-Group-Label in a variety of situations, and provide students with multiple opportunities for guided practice and feedback. Use occasions when the strategy might break down, such as getting off track or getting stuck, to demonstrate how to refocus using Big Idea(s) and topical words. Remind students about key questions for learning, including "How do these words fit together?" "What labels can we use to say what the words have in common?" and "Which words fit under which group labels?" Observe students closely as they apply List-Group-Label so that you can help them to transform this valuable teaching activity into a way of learning.

▲ Students' vocabulary development is influenced by many different sources. Incorporating these different sources into instruction can help foster a connection with your students.

Semantic Mapping. Semantic mapping is another technique for representing connections among words (Johnson & Pearson, 1984). Like List-Group-Label, a semantic map displays words in categories, indicating how words go together. A key difference is that the resulting diagram or map consists of a central hub or hubs, extending spokes, and subordinate circles with labels for groups of words. An example of a semantic map from social studies appears in Figure 8.3.

Semantic maps are particularly helpful for struggling learners (Blanchowicz & Fisher, 2000), hearing-impaired students (Luckner et al., 2001), and English language learners (Short, 1997). Conversations around the mapping provide support by making public the thinking that goes into making connections among the words. Mapping also offers a powerful visual reference for seeing familiar words in a new light and for connecting new and unfamiliar words to known words.

To create a map with students, follow these procedures (from Heimlich & Pittelman, 1986):

1. Choose a word or topic related to the content you are teaching.

2. List the word on the blackboard, an overhead projector, or a large chart.

3. Ask students to think about as many words as they can that are related to the key word. Write those words on the blackboard, projector, or chart.

4. Encourage students to think about different ways of grouping the words. Offer an example or two of groupings that you see. Ask students to select words that might appear under your sample groupings. Invite students to suggest some additional groups, indicating what words might go under each grouping. Document students' decisions and choices on the blackboard, projector, or chart.

Click on A+RISE – WIDA ELP Standard Strategy in the MyEducationLab (www.myeducationlab .com) for your course. Next, select the Strategy Card Index tab, scroll to Comprehension for Grades 6–12 and select the Comparison Web strategy.

Figure 8.3

A semantic map in social studies.

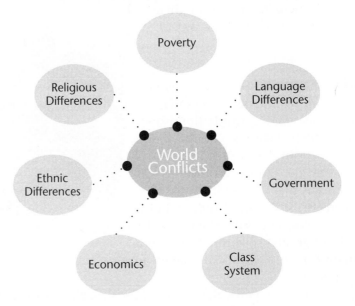

Big Idea: World conflicts are the result of many problems, perceived differences, and special interests.

5. Discuss the semantic map, including the familiar words and relationships. Teach some new words and ask students to add them to the map, providing reasons for their choices.

The cautions for using semantic maps are similar to those for List-Group-Label. Maps work best when students have some available knowledge. The early stages of brainstorming and listing words are a good way to assess how much or how little students know. If you discover that students do not know as much as you anticipated, opt for more explanation and/or preteaching. Also, do not automatically assume that students can do semantic mapping on their own or that simply doing semantic mapping repeatedly will ensure that it becomes a learning strategy for them.

Transforming semantic mapping into a learning strategy requires telling students explicitly about mapping and how it is a good way to visually organize and represent thinking. Share examples of how you have used mapping in the past and how it helped with learning new words and studying. Model different ways of mapping with your students in different situations. Give students ongoing practice with semantic mapping, under your guidance and feedback, so that mapping becomes part of their repertoire for learning vocabulary.

Graphic Organizers. When students encounter new vocabulary, they are faced with making a number of decisions. Their goals in dealing with new information can vary. For instance, sometimes all they need to do is understand the information. Other times, they need to remember it for certain purposes, such as answering questions, talking about it, or writing about it. Graphic organizers are a collection of ways for students to create structures for understanding and remembering new words and ideas (Ausubel, 1968).

Graphic organizers, like those in Figure 8.4, represent an additional level of organization and sophistication in comparison with List-Group-Label and semantic mapping. Students can use graphic organizers to depict ideas in a variety of ways, emphasizing, for example, cause-and-effect relationships, comparisons, time-order relationships, and even Venn diagrams (overlapping ideas).

Students can learn to design their own graphic organizers through a combination of direct teaching of the strategy in different contexts, guided practice with vocabulary and texts, and your own assessment and observations of their efforts, combined with appropriate feedback (Merkley & Jeffries, 2001). Learning to construct and use graphic organizers has been found to be particularly useful for reaching all students but especially students with special needs (Baxendell, 2003; DiCecco & Gleason, 2002) and English language learners (Short, 1997). The combination of conversation and visual display provides all students with multiple hooks for accessing and organizing information.

To get started with graphic organizers, students need to learn the different reasons for using them. First, explain what graphic organizers are for: to help understand new information and to organize information so that students can remember it. Demonstrate how an organizer can be used as a collecting device to answer the question "What is this all about?" or "What is the author conveying?" Show how an organizer helps to depict what one actually understands about a topic and how it helps identify what you may not understand. One of the best ways to do this is to select an organizer, like the ones depicted in Figure 8.4, and show how to list and group words, gathering information from something students are reading. Think out loud while you and your students flesh out an organizer together. Discuss some ways in which you and your students can find out more if work with the organizer reveals some areas that you do not understand. An organizer can also be a useful jumping off point for posing new questions and following up with research.

Show students how an organizer is useful for remembering important information. One way to do this is to help students become aware

A+RISE

Click on A+RISE – WIDA ELP Standard Strategy in the MyEducationLab (www.myeducationlab .com) for your course. Next, select the Strategy Card Index tab, scroll to Vocabulary for Grades 6–12 and select the Fishbone strategy.

Figure 8.4

Common patterns of ideas for graphic organizers.

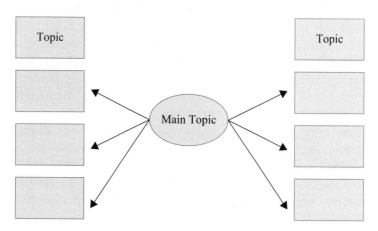

Compare-Contrast Pattern

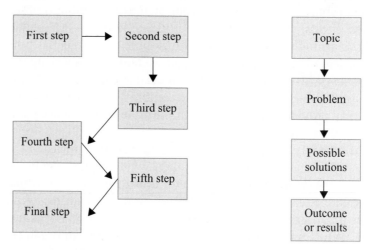

Sequential or Time Order Pattern

Problem-Solution Pattern

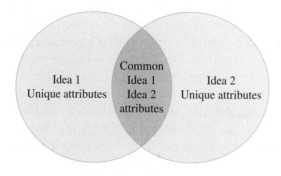

Venn Diagram

Big Ideas	Related Patterns
Skipping steps in algebraic equations can lead to disaster.	sequence of events
Proper conditioning ensures enjoyable participation in a sport or any other physical activity.	cause and effect
The theme of the struggle of good versus evil recurs throughout American literature.	comparison and contrast
Eradicating poverty is the key to ending war in the Middle East.	problem and solution

Figure 8.5

Big Ideas and related patterns.

of patterns that organize and represent important information within Big Ideas. Consider the Big Ideas and their related patterns depicted in Figure 8.5.

Discuss or review with students how to identify Big Ideas. For most people, it involves thinking about what you know about a topic and examining titles, paragraph headings, and topical headings within available reading materials. It also might entail doing some simple research or looking to outside resources, such as the Internet, to see what others have said about the topic and what others have viewed as important.

As students gain an understanding of Big Ideas in an area, they can move on to thinking about how the ideas are organized. The best way to do this is by teacher modeling with different Big Ideas and/or texts as examples. Start by presenting students with a sample list of Big Ideas and asking them to discuss what the ideas may be about. Introduce the concepts of structure and organization by demonstrating how some key words, such as *first-second, cause-effect, if-then,* and *similar-like,* all signal different patterns about important information within various Big Ideas.

Next, introduce some graphical depictions or templates of common patterns within content areas, using examples from Figure 8.4. The software program Inspiration (Inspiration, 2003) contains many other patterns within content areas that teachers might wish to introduce to students. Demonstrate how these graphics can be used to brainstorm and explore concepts and details within Big Ideas as well as to show relationships. Guide students in practicing filling out these graphical patterns based on Big Ideas and selected text passages. Emphasize that the first pattern that is selected is not always the best. As students get more into a topic or idea, they might discover that another pattern is more appropriate. Help students to understand that there are many ways of looking at an idea and seeing how concepts within are organized.

Ultimately, students must learn to create their own graphic organizers for their own purposes. Getting students there requires explicit teacher explanations combined with multiple examples. This teacher-directed work should be gradually replaced by students doing much more of the work on their own. As students move into using graphic organizers for their own purposes, help them to think about why and how they are using them. Ask them periodically, "Is this important? Why?" and "Is this the best way to organize these words or this vocabulary?" These practices will help students to develop a better sense for how graphic organizers can support their own learning.

Direct Instruction

According to research, direct instruction is the most powerful way for students to learn new words and vocabulary strategies (Blanchowicz & Fisher, 2000). This section depicts direct vocabulary instruction. The strategies that are presented—using the context, analyzing words parts, and using the dictionary and technology—are the ones that are most often cited in research for helping students learn new vocabulary (Nagy & Scott, 2000). Each strategy needs to be considered and evaluated carefully with respect to different students, their available knowledge, and the situations in which the strategies are used.

Using the Context. Using the context—examining words surrounding an unfamiliar word to figure out its meaning—is one of the most accessible methods for learning vocabulary. But this works only if an individual has enough knowledge about the surrounding words to determine the meaning. Let's look at a few examples.

Consider the example from geometry shown in Figure 8.6 (from Usiskin et al., 1992). Notice how context is provided here by both the pictures and the language. The pictures provide images of the assembled and unassembled cereal boxes as examples of a rectangular solid. Now consider the assumptions that the writers of this mathematics text are making: that most middle school students have experience with cereal boxes and that some students will even have disassembled a cereal box and noticed the rectangular patterns. That is probably a safe assumption for most students. But what about students with special needs and others who have come from other countries and other cultures? See the Teaching Today's Learners feature on page 248 for ideas and cautions about vocabulary instruction for students with special needs and English language learners.

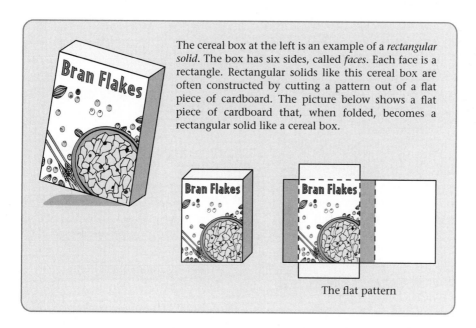

The cereal box at the left is an example of a *rectangular solid*. The box has six sides, called *faces*. Each face is a rectangle. Rectangular solids like this cereal box are often constructed by cutting a pattern out of a flat piece of cardboard. The picture below shows a flat piece of cardboard that, when folded, becomes a rectangular solid like a cereal box.

The flat pattern

Figure 8.6

Vocabulary word used in context: A mathematics text.

To teach students about using contexts to figure out words, teachers and students should gather interesting examples of words used in context. Teachers can provide examples such as this one in which interesting words are used to describe an event or situation:

"The presidential debates last night were nothing more than an *imbroglio,* full of bitter name calling, scathing accusations, and searing glares. Have you ever felt as if you were in the middle of an imbroglio?"

Other interesting words in context can come from students' experiences:

"We were out in our last class, just *kickin' the bobos,* you know what I'm saying? Then this teacher came over and just told us to be quiet. What does it mean to be kickin' the bobos?"

Using these examples, teachers can provide clear explanations and demonstrations for how to use the context to identify unknown words. An advantage of this approach is that it demonstrates how context can play an important role in constructing meaning both in and out of school.

Teaching Today's Learners

About Vocabulary and Vocabulary Strategies

The following ideas have been shown through research to increase vocabulary learning for students with learning disabilities (MacArthur & Haynes, 1995), English language learners, and struggling readers (Reinking & Rickman, 1990).

▶ English language learners and other struggling students might not have enough experience with reading in English to profit much at first from direct instruction with vocabulary strategies (Schmidt & Zimmerman, 2002). Instead, these students need instruction and practice that focuses on developing fluency with words before they work with vocabulary strategies (Juel & Deffes, 2004)

▶ Many English language learners and other students who are struggling with language find that using the context is a very difficult approach to learning new words, because they do not yet understand some word meanings in English and other significant differences due to culture (Carlo et al., 2004). Alternatively, English language learners can make lists of words in their native language that are similar, or have parts that are similar, to some English words.

▶ Keeping a personal dictionary is a good strategy for many struggling students. Having a list of recurring words and definitions at hand reduces the strain on students in applying other vocabulary strategies that require lots of prior knowledge and skill (Yeung, 1999).

▶ English language learners often benefit from pairings of native and nonnative speakers in which each individual can share his or her expertise about a topic while learning new words (Cassidy, 1996). For example, students studying weather patterns and learning the language of meteorology can share experiences with weather in the United States but also weather all over the world.

▶ Students, especially those with learning disabilities, comprehend more of their reading in content areas when they are taught to use software organizers, such as Inspiration (www.inspiration.com) to study new vocabulary (Mastropieri et al., 2003). Vocabulary instruction is most effective when it is accompanied by conversation as well as visual clues to meaning.

Students learn words in context most effectively when they experience the words in use repeatedly in multiple situations (Beck et al., 1983; Graves & Watts-Taffe, 2002). Teachers can provide for multiple encounters with new words by pointing out the words and their use as students use the words for further learning.

Analyzing Word Parts. Another way to figure out unknown words is to analyze parts of words that may be familiar—familiar syllables, such as prefixes and suffixes, and whole words within larger words. For instance, knowing that *therm-* means "heat" can help in constructing the meaning of a number of words, such as *geothermal, thermostat, hypothermia, exothermic,* and *thermos.* Similarly, if you know that the prefix *anti-* means "against" or "opposite," you are in a good position to understand words such as *antiwar, antischool, anticrime, antipollution,* or even *antispam.* Also, if you know that the suffix *-ish* means "related to" or "characterized by," you can figure out the meanings of words such as *babyish, snobbish, yellowish,* and *standoffish.* A past practice involves having students memorize lists of prefixes and suffixes in hopes that somehow, somewhere, they would run into words that contain these items and be able to figure the words out. It is far more effective to help students gain a better understanding of how to analyze word parts on their own. Students who excel at this strategy tend to be better readers (Nagy et al., 1993). The more experience students have with reading, the more knowledge about words they will have available for figuring out new words.

To teach students how to use this strategy, explain that they can figure out the meanings of unfamiliar words sometimes by looking for what might be familiar about them. Model the process by selecting a few words and identifying familiar word parts. List other words that also contain the familiar word parts. Many academic books contain glossaries in which teachers can identify families of words that have the same basic root word but variations in how the word parts or words are used in larger words and phrases. An example appears in Figure 8.7. Review the glossary of a textbook with students, or pull out some words with similar parts to show how many words in a discipline share similar features and meanings. Use occasions when certain words and word parts reappear to remind students about watching for familiar patterns in words.

To get students in the process of analyzing words, ask them to brainstorm and discuss words from their own lives that are familiar in some way. Many words from popular culture are shorter versions of larger words or a combination of several words, such as the following:

props—giving proper respect
24/7—going on all of the time
za—pizza
cell—cell phone, or to call someone on a cell phone
freepy—something that is both freaky and creepy

Figure 8.7 Word families in textbook glossaries.

Science -tions (a process)	Social Studies -isms (set of beliefs, especially within a system)	Mathematics angle words and phrases	English -ogue (a record or form of reporting)	Foreign Language in (means "un" or not)	Health Education -tion (a process)
adaptation	federalism	triangle	epilogue	inactive	prevention
alternation	nationalism	altitude of a triangle	dialogue	inacceptable	intervention
ammonifica- tion	communism	central angle of a circle	apologue	inadequate	nutrition
bacterial transformation	populism	corresponding angles	monologue	inadmissible	addiction
respiration	abolitionism	equilateral triangle	catalogue	inevitable	pollution
	suffragism and feminism	rectangle	prologue	inertia	prescription
	commensalism				

Discuss how these words or word fragments get understood and used by so many people. Discuss experiences about figuring out whole words from familiar fragments. The explicit message needs to be this: Play with the meanings of familiar word parts and words, think creatively about what you know, and you might just figure out their meaning.

Using the Dictionary and Thesaurus. Dictionaries, a thesaurus, and other such resources offer explicit help in ways that are clearly different from the strategies discussed so far. Dictionaries and thesauruses provide lists of clear definitions and word alternatives, in comparison with activities involving context and word parts in which the meaning of a word has to be inferred on the basis of what you know. However, going to a dictionary or thesaurus is not useful without first considering the context (Nagy & Scott, 2000). Knowing how a word is being used in a particular context is a prerequisite for selecting a definition or choosing an alternative word as a way of figuring out a word's meaning. The strategic use of a dictionary and thesaurus—once students construct a hunch about a word's meaning in context—is what teachers need to help their students to understand.

With this description of the strategic use of a dictionary or a thesaurus, it is easy see why exercises dedicated to just looking up words can be pretty limited in value. Although it can be useful to familiarize students with the dictionary or thesaurus, how often do individuals look up words from a list or words presented in isolation? Real life is much more likely to involve developing an educated guess about a word, sometimes trying a strategy like looking for familiar words in context or even asking someone about its meaning, before deciding to look it up (Blanchowicz & Fisher, 2000). This real-life approach is the one espoused here.

To help students develop the appropriate, real-life use of the dictionary and thesaurus, talk with them about your own experiences looking up words. Use a real example of a word that you did not know, and discuss how you went about forming a hunch about the word.

> "They said I needed *collateral* when I was taking out a loan for my car. I had no idea what it meant. They said I had to put down two thousand dollars at a minimum or I could not get a car loan. I figured that the word meant my down payment. But I was still curious, so I went to the dictionary. In the dictionary, I found five definitions (from Hyperdictionary, 2004)."

1. A security (merchandise and/or down payment) pledged for the re-payment of a loan
2. Descended from a common ancestor but through different lines: "cousins are collateral relatives"; "an indirect descendant of the Stuarts"
3. Situated or running side by side: "collateral ridges of mountains"
4. Accompaniment to something else: "collateral target damage from a bombing run"
5. Serving to support or corroborate: "collateral evidence"

> "The first definition fit what I was doing. I didn't realize that the car itself was collateral. I was amazed at the other ways that *collateral* gets used."

At this point, encourage students to look up words in which they have an interest.

Another popular option, once students are familiar with dictionaries and thesauruses, is to have students keep their own personal dictionaries. A personal dictionary can be kept on three- by five-inch cards, in a notebook, or in a computer file, simply by listing recurring, important words, or words of interest, and their corresponding definitions.

Using Technology for Word Study. There are many different options when it comes to having students learn word meanings through

▲ Websites and educational games greatly expand young people's opportunities for vocabulary development.

technology. For example, **assistive technology** assists students with disabilities, including students with learning disabilities, hearing loss, visual impairments, and mobility impairments (Hetzroni & Shrieber, 2004). Some assistive technology software programs offer definitions for words in context or break words down into familiar parts. Some of these programs require students to highlight an unknown word for which the program provides an oral definition or an animation depicting the word's meaning.

Many universities support research centers in assistive technology for diverse students, including the Indiana University Adaptive Technology Center (www.indiana.edu/~iuadapts), a website that is worth visiting to learn more. The following websites represent companies that make software and other assistive technology tools for students with special educational needs, including those with learning disabilities as well as visual and hearing impairments. Some of these websites, such as Intellitools, provide technology resources for English language learners.

▶ Don Johnston: www.donjohnston.com

▶ Intellitools: www.intellitools.com

▶ Kurzweil Educational Systems: www.kurzweiledu.com

▶ Freedom Scientific: www.freedomscientific.com

Technology opens up entire worlds of exploration and conversation that are great for vocabulary learning. Consider recent controversies over submissions to Wikipedia (www.en.wikipedia.org), the free encyclopedia that anyone can edit. Teachers can engage students in debate about which words are more appropriate, in an environment in which anyone can submit his or her point of view. The Internet also contains a vast array of resources for word investigation and word play. For example, Fun with Words (www.fun-with-words.com) is a website that offers hundreds of word puzzles, histories, and interesting stories. Email, instant messaging, blogs, and web forums all offer practice with learning and using new words. And why should students look up words in an old paper dictionary when they can find much more information instantaneously by using these Internet resources?

▶ Hyperdictionary: www.hyperdictionary.com

▶ Merriam Webster Online: http://www.merriam-webster.com

▶ Onelook Dictionary Search: http://www.onelook.com

▶ Cambridge Dictionaries Online: http://www.dictionary.cambridge.org

Using technology in these ways to play with and learn new words can be tremendously motivating (Blanchowicz & Fisher, 2000).

Integrating technology into the classroom for vocabulary learning requires a critical look at the available programs as well as considering how to teach students to use technology wisely. Providing students with knowledge and practice with vocabulary strategies is the best preparation for students using technology for vocabulary learning.

Extending and Reinforcing Vocabulary Knowledge and Strategies

The research on vocabulary learning is clear: Students learn words and vocabulary strategies most effectively through repeated and varied exposure and practice (Juel & Deffes, 2004). To extend and reinforce vocabulary knowledge and strategy, make sure students experience important words over and over again. Ask students to verbalize how they are learning new words. The more students revisit strategies for vocabulary learning strategies, the more they will learn to apply them independently. Consider these principles while reading about the following extension and reinforcement activities.

Vocabulary Self-Collection Strategy. The Vocabulary Self-Collection Strategy (VSS) is a way for students to learn how to select and review important words for themselves (Haggard, 1982, 1985). An important assumption with this activity is students have already worked with the words and word meanings.

VSS involves asking three questions:

1. Which words are important to the Big Idea(s) of a lesson?
2. How did we learn the words (thinking about other words we knew, context, familiar parts, dictionary)?
3. What do the words mean, especially in relation to the Big Idea(s)?

VSS works best within a classroom conversation. Students nominate their own lists of words for review and compare their lists and their reasons for studying them. Thinking and talking about how they learned the words provide a recap of how students used vocabulary strategies to figure them out. Teachers observe these conversations, listening for misconceptions and providing feedback. Words that are still confusing or that have conflicting meanings can be studied further. Words that the class selects for review can also be written in students' personal vocabulary dictionaries.

Teachers can reinforce many of the vocabulary strategies students have learned by reemphasizing the following principles during VSS discussions (Haggard, 1997):

▶ Remind students to think about what they know.

▶ Encourage students to make connections among known and new words.

▶ Build awareness that words have multiple meanings and multiple uses in different contexts.

▶ Review strategies for vocabulary learning.

Categorization. Categorization, as a reinforcement activity, engages students in clustering words in meaningful groups (Herber, 1978). This activity capitalizes on earlier work with students' prior knowledge, reviewing different grouping patterns and the reasoning underlying students' vocabulary connections.

There are a number of ways to have students review and extend word meanings through categorization. One way is to have students list words that they think are important one more time and create new groupings using word sorts. Words can be sorted according to key words in Big Ideas, important concepts, and even vocabulary words. Again, doing this activity through conversation is essential. Students will undoubtedly make different choices in words and groupings. Their comparisons provide multiple perspectives on the words and meanings.

Another way for students to categorize is to ask them to think about words that can stand for or provide a way to group all of the important words in a lesson. Sample group labels from a lesson in English appear in Figure 8.8. The group labels are the literary terms students used to understand a short story, Faulkner's "A Rose for Emily." Students used these labels to gather up descriptive words and quotes to review the story. Again, show students some examples for how to do this. Suggest category labels yourself and think aloud with students about why you selected the group labels and how important words could be listed under

Figure 8.8 Grouping words for reviewing a short story.

Character Description Words	Plot Events, Description Words, and Theme(s)
("A Rose for Emily")	
fallen monument	"The next generation, with its more modern ideas."
tradition	"she would have to cling to that which had robbed her"
duty	"I have no taxes in Jefferson"
a care	"she vanquished them"
small, fat woman in black	"that smell"
a resemblance to angels	"people had begun to feel sorry for her"
"poor Emily"	"I want some poison" "For rats"
"disgrace to the town"	"Homer disappeared"
"bad example"	"her gray head propped on a pillow, yellow and moldy"
	"the long sleep that outlasts love"
	"the patient and biding dust"
	"on the pillow, a long strand of iron-gray hair"

the labels. Sometimes, simple categorization exercises can be developed to give students practice, such as those in Figure 8.9. Have students discuss their answers and, more important, their reasons for their answers.

Semantic Feature Analysis. Students can use semantic feature analysis to revisit word meanings, groupings, and relationships among words (Johnson & Pearson, 1984). Semantic feature analysis is a bit different from some of the activities described before in that not only do students consider how words are alike, they also concern themselves with how words are different. This creates frequent opportunities to reinforce and extend the meanings of new words.

To practice semantic feature analysis (see Figure 8.10), students need to go through the following steps:

1. Select a category or group label from words in a lesson (such as *organism* or *living thing*).
2. List in the first column some words in the category (such as *plant, animal, reptile, fish, sponge*).
3. List on the top row some features shared by some of the words (such as *breathes, grows, reproduces, eats, moves*).

Figure 8.9

Sample categorization exercises.

Mathematics

Below is a list of words from our geometry unit. Select words that go together, and tell why they go together.

location	coordinate	size
slope	midpoint	graph
figure		

Social Studies

Place a label over each group of words that best tells what each group is all about

Label_____

workers

natural resources

investors

expertise

---

4. Put pluses or minuses beside each word beneath each feature and discuss reasons.

5. Add additional features.

6. Add more pluses and minuses and discuss reasons.

Word Puzzles. Word puzzles can be designed to encourage word play and flexibility with vocabulary. There are many resources online for creating and playing with word puzzles, including the following:

▶ Discovery School's Puzzlemaker, a website for creating and doing your own crossword puzzles: http://www.puzzlemaker.school .discovery.com

Figure 8.10

Semantic feature analysis chart: Science class.

	lungs	stomach	feet	mouth	fins
plant	−	−	−	−	−
animal	+	+	+	+	−
reptile	+	+	+	+	−
fish	+ and −	+	−	−	+
sponge	−	−	−	−	−

▶ Wordcentral, an activity-filled place for students to learn about new words, submit words and definitions for a student dictionary, play games, and solve puzzles with words: http://www.wordcentral.com

▶ Funbrain, a place for challenging vocabulary games and puzzles: www.funbrain.com

Although these websites are not designed to automatically include the words from a lesson or unit, each is flexible enough that teachers could include these websites in word study.

Connecting Standards and Assessment

The Vocabulary of Assessment

Assessments, particularly large-scale and standardized assessments, have their own vocabulary. Some assessment experts have coined the term *assessment literacy* to refer to the specialized language that is part of assessment. For teachers, this means knowing the difference between concepts such as *standardized test, criterion-referenced test, diagnostic test, IQ test,* and *achievement test.* Because No Child Left Behind mandates the use of tests like these, it is important for teachers to learn all they can about such tests. This includes the kinds of data reported from large-scale tests, such as *percentile ranks, grade equivalents, scaled scores,* and *stanines.* In making sense of students' performance on standardized and large-scale assessments, it is important to examine at least three years' worth of data. Looking at data for two years invites a comparison between just two groups; data for three years can indicate a trend, either in the right direction or toward areas of need. Appropriate comparisons are based on individual schools with respect to the performance of larger groups, such as students across an entire state or the nation. Item analysis of students' performance on these tests can indicate areas of needed instruction.

For their part, students also need help with assessment literacy. The focus here should be on the specialized language that is used for test questions, such as *explain, describe, compare,* and *prove.* For example, when asked to *persuade,* many students *list* or *describe.* Knowledge about the language of assessment can be just as important as the content knowledge required on the tests.

▶ **Read more about the vocabulary of assessment Chapter 10, "Making Sense of Large-Scale Assessment Information," in** *Connecting Standards and Assessment through Literacy* **(Conley, 2005), published by Pearson Education.**

Summary

Teachers and schools play a pivotal role in vocabulary learning. Teachers need to explain, model, and guide students in effective techniques for learning and using vocabulary. Be careful about making assumptions about what students already know or do not know. Use vocabulary teaching as an opportunity for assessment as well as for helping students to gain word knowledge and strategies for learning new vocabulary. The most effective teaching activities for vocabulary help students to connect what they already know with the meanings of new words. Direct teaching builds vocabulary knowledge and vocabulary strategies. Vocabulary words acquire deep meaning only in the context of Big Ideas and repeated exposure and reinforcement.

Special Projects

1. Select textbook or other appropriate curriculum materials from your content area. Identify a Big Idea that you could use to develop a lesson. Using techniques illustrated in this chapter, identify and prioritize words for vocabulary instruction. Next, take your list of words, and design some ways in which you would teach these words. Describe and defend your decisions based on your Big Idea as well as the appropriateness of different teaching and learning techniques for different words and different kinds of student vocabulary knowledge.

2. Using ideas in this chapter, design a teaching activity that helps to connect students' prior knowledge to understandings of new vocabulary words.

3. Using ideas in this chapter, explain how you would use direct instruction to teach a set of vocabulary words. Tell how you would match specific words with different teaching strategies.

4. Using ideas in this chapter, describe how you would reinforce and extend the meanings of new vocabulary words.

5. Explore the websites listed in this chapter for using technology to teach vocabulary, including those that address the use of assistive technology and those that offer word play. Describe some ways in which you could incorporate this technology into your own approach to vocabulary teaching.

Praxis Practice

Working with Questions to Prepare for the Praxis Reading Across the Curriculum Test

Multiple Choice

1. Well established words are:

   a. Words students already know

   b. Words derived from Latin roots

   c. Words that are know and used daily when speaking or writing

   d. Known words that are used correctly when speaking or writing on a daily basis.

2. Unknown words are:

   a. Often, technical vocabulary which are the center of traditional vocabulary teaching.

   b. Derived from foreign words

   c. Never learned by students

   d. Words with which one is familiar with, but unsure how to use in writing.

3. According to research, effective vocabulary instruction integrates new information with the familiar. Students are most likely to achieve that integration by:

   a. using a dictionary

   b. developing a semantic map

   c. analyzing word structure

   d. memorizing words

Constructed Response Question
Read the following passage and then respond to all three tasks.

Space Cooking
The shuttle returns to Earth this week with astronauts having learned a new skill: orbital cooking.

To deal with weightlessness, the astronauts needed to find a way to keep food from floating around in the space station. The astronauts used duct tape while cutting their food. The duct tape sticks to the little pieces and crumbs.

To cook garlic and onions, the astronauts learned to use the foil packets that their dehydrated food comes in. They put the garlic and onions in the foil, add some olive oil, fold the foil over, and place it in the food warmer. After about four or five cycles in the food warmer, the garlic and onions come out completely cooked.

The astronauts add tuna to the mixture along with honey mustard, ginger, and mayonnaise. The astronauts had a great deal of fun learning to cook, but they also had to learn to be creative.

—adapted from Klotz (2009), Astronaut experiments with space cooking. www .msnbc.msn.com/id/29866375/

1. Below, under the heading "Selecting Vocabulary," describe how you will select for teaching students how to comprehend the passage. Next, under the heading "Teaching Vocabulary," describe how you will teach students to understand the new words from the reading passage.

   Selecting Vocabulary
   Teaching Vocabulary

2. Explain how the instructional strategies that you selected in Task 1 would help students develop their capacities within the area of vocabulary learning.

3. Applying your knowledge for how vocabulary supports comprehension, explain how your chosen teaching strategies would effectively support students' comprehension of this passage.

Suggested Readings

Beck, I., McKeown, M., & Kucan, M. (2002). *Bringing words to life: Robust vocabulary instruction.* New York: Guilford.

Graves, M. (2005). *The vocabulary book: Learning & instruction.* New York: Teachers College.

Silverman, R. (2009). A multidimensional approach to vocabulary instruction: Supporting English language learners in inclusive classrooms. http://www.readingrockets.org/article/30098

Go to Topic 6: Vocabulary in the MyEducationLab (www.myeducationlab.com) for your course, where you can:

- Find learning outcomes for Topic 6: Vocabulary along with the national standards that connect to these outcomes.

- Complete Assignments and Activities that can help you more deeply understand the chapter content.

- Apply and practice your understanding of the core teaching skills identified in the chapter with the Building Teaching Skills and Dispositions learning units.

Go to the Topic A+RISE in the MyEducationLab (www.myeducationlab.com) for your course. A+RISE® Standards2Strategy™ is an innovative and interactive online resource that offers new teachers in grades K-12 just in time, research-based instructional strategies that:

- Meet the linguistic needs of ELLs as they learn content

- Differentiate instruction for all grades and abilities

- Offer reading and writing techniques, cooperative learning, use of linguistic and nonlinguistic representations, scaffolding, teacher modeling, higher order thinking, and alternative classroom ELL assessment

- Provide support to help teachers be effective through the integration of listening, speaking, reading, and writing along with the content curriculum

- Improve student achievement

- Are aligned to Common Core Elementary Language Arts standards (for the literacy strategies) and to English language proficiency standards in WIDA, Texas, California, and Florida.

9 Guiding Students during Reading

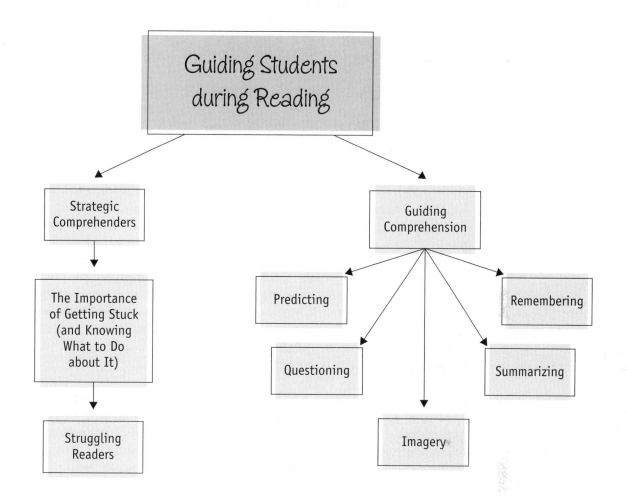

Guiding Students during Reading

- Strategic Comprehenders
  - The Importance of Getting Stuck (and Knowing What to Do about It)
    - Struggling Readers
- Guiding Comprehension
  - Predicting
  - Questioning
  - Imagery
  - Summarizing
  - Remembering

Consider this view of why we read. We read to accomplish many different kinds of tasks: solving problems; learning something new; traveling to distant locations; reflecting on our lives; designing new machines, materials, and spaces; and performing multiple roles as citizens, members of our families, and members of the community. We read to open up packages, pass a test, research a paper, prepare a presentation, assemble a bicycle, fix a meal, repair a piano, maintain a jet, prepare a budget, and build web pages. In other words, we read to gain new knowledge and to learn how to perform all of the tasks that are part of daily living.

The importance of knowing how to read to learn is underscored by state and national tests. For example, performances on various kinds of state tests are used to award diplomas, grant driving privileges, control college entrance, or allow entry into a profession. Tests are crafted using different kinds of texts and tasks. This version of reading to learn says that individuals cannot become a member of the educated, the trades, the business class, or professionals without demonstrating skill in reading to learn.

Knowing how to read to learn is a key component of becoming a successful adult. The more students know about reading to learn, the more likely it is that they will thrive in many adult contexts, including their personal as well as professional lives. This chapter discusses how teachers can guide students in developing research-based strategies for reading to learn.

Comprehension is at the heart of reading to learn. Comprehension is defined as constructing meaning through interactions between a reader and a text (Harris & Hodges, 1995). Depending on a reader's prior knowledge, this interaction can be remarkably simple or incredibly complex. Comprehension sometimes involves starting at a very simple point and building knowledge in small steps over time. In rare situations in which individuals are sufficiently motivated, readers can overcome complexity. Watch what happens, for example, when teachers tell students that they may not read a magazine, web page, or text!

Reading to learn is a **sociocultural activity**. The experience of reading is shaped by the context of different communities and social groups in which reading happens. Content area disciplines represent communities of understanding. Reading to learn is shaped in very particular ways within each area. Compare the symbol systems and meanings in mathematics and music or the ways in which information is organized in social studies and English. Or consider the notion of performances based on reading in foreign language, physical education, art, or music. Reading is deeply embedded within the social interactions and the ways of thinking and knowing within all of the disciplines. The Action Research feature shows how you can explore the ways in which comprehension is represented and used in your content area.

The sociocultural character of reading persists in the world outside of school. Sometimes, individuals read a book or magazine—or even avoid reading—because of the interests or peer pressure from others in a social group. We also read for our own pleasure—to learn about something that is personally satisfying or just for pure enjoyment. Consider your own experiences with reading to learn. How were your reading preferences shaped by your need to know or by your friends and others? Were there situations in which you felt particularly motivated? Were there other situations in which reading to learn was a miserable experience? What made the difference?

Action Research

Comprehension in the Content Areas

Every professional organization across the content areas has created a set of curriculum standards. Locate the Professional Association Standards in your content area. Next, review the standards for what they say or imply about comprehension and reading to learn. In what ways are texts used to teach Big Ideas and content area skills? In what ways are teachers expected to show students how to learn from texts? Having reviewed these standards and considering concepts presented in this chapter, how would you describe the best ways to pursue comprehension and reading to learn in your content area? What are the best ways for you to help your students?

▶ **National Council of Teachers of Mathematics:** www.nctm.org
▶ **National Council of Teachers of English:** www.ncte.org
▶ **National Council for the Social Studies:** www.ncss.org
▶ **The National Science Education Standards:** http://newton.nap.edu/html/nses
▶ **The National Association for Music Education:** www.menc.org
▶ **American Alliance for Health, Physical Education, Recreation and Dance:** http://www.aahperd.org
▶ **American Council of the Teaching of Foreign Languages:** www.actfl.org

Strategic Comprehenders

Good readers are strategic comprehenders; that is, good readers purposefully adjust their interactions with texts according to different goals and purposes. Strategic comprehenders almost always have a goal in mind, be it pleasure, to gather information, or to accomplish a task. They usually read from the beginning to the end of a text. They do not necessarily read all of the words, sometimes jumping around to accomplish their purpose. Strategic comprehenders often look ahead to anticipate information, or they look back to clarify an idea at the beginning. Throughout the experience of reading, strategic comprehenders think about what they already know and use their knowledge to make sense of the text. They monitor what they read, figuring out what parts of the text are important to them depending on their purpose. They discard the parts that are irrelevant. Strategic comprehenders note the parts that are vague and confusing, and if the

▲ **Strategic understanding and comprehension can be enhanced through problem solving with others.**

parts are important enough to them, they apply learning strategies to figure these parts out. Finally, strategic comprehenders continuously reflect on their reading and consider how to use ideas they are gaining from the text (Block & Pressley, 2003).

Think about the ways in which you have interacted with reading since the early hours of this morning. Consider ways in which you have engaged in strategic comprehension. Many individuals start the day with a quick read of the newspaper, skimming and skipping large chunks of text while sipping coffee or tea. Their purpose is not deep comprehension; rather, the purpose is to gain quick bits of information and entertainment. Now, with newspapers on the Internet, this activity can take place within an environment of tabs and links. What were your later encounters with text like? Did the interactions involve web searches and research? Did they entail in-depth reading of informational materials? Or did your interactions engage you in scanning documents such as schedules, rate tables, or graphs of rankings? Consider how your experience of reading changed in each situation as you used your skills as a strategic comprehender. More than likely, as a strategic comprehender, you slowed down or sped up, zeroed in on particular ideas and concepts, or settled for the gist, all depending on your goals and purposes for reading. Strategic comprehenders engage in reading that is purposeful, shaped by motivations, and characterized by multiple, continuous, and deliberate decisions. Have you ever felt exhausted after a day of reading? Your activities as a strategic comprehender could be the reason.

The Importance of Getting Stuck (and Knowing What to Do about It)

Strategic comprehenders know when they get stuck, and they know what to do about it (Sadoski & Paovio, 2001). They continually ask, "Does this make sense?" When meaning gets blocked, strategic comprehenders make a judgment about whether or not it matters. They make this decision on the basis of their overall sense of the text and their goals in gaining meaning. For example, if meaning breaks down during pleasure reading, it might not be as important as a situation in which the information is important for passing a test.

When things do not make sense and it matters, strategic comprehenders know exactly what to do. They engage in any one of a number of comprehension strategies to help themselves out, including the following:

► Figuring out where the meaning is breaking down (e.g., unfamiliar vocabulary, complicated sentences, unfocused writing)

► Selecting a comprehension strategy to address the problem

► Trying out the strategy

► Determining whether or not the comprehension strategy is working

► Trying another strategy if the first one is not successful

Strategic comprehenders ask throughout this process, "Does this make sense?"

Struggling Readers

Contrast the previously described view of strategic comprehenders with this view of struggling readers: Struggling readers are typically inexperienced or lack skills with reading and comprehension. As was discussed in Chapter 2, some students are still struggling with fluency, the automatic ability to read letters and words. These students might be still trying to understand the sound–symbol relationships of language. Some of these readers are students with special needs. Some might be English language learners. Unlike strategic comprehenders, some of these students might not realize when they are stuck with meaning. So much of their attention is focused on the details of the printed page and the challenges of performance with language that they have little left for comprehension. When these students manage to focus on comprehension and realize that they are stuck, they have few options. Some of these students choose to reread without changing their original approach. Rereading without a sense of the problem or what to do about it is one of the least effective ways to comprehend. Some of these students will renew efforts to understand each individual word, again sacrificing comprehension. These students might try and retry ineffective strategies without ever making much sense out of their reading (Allington, 2001; Mastropieri et al., 2003). To learn about reading fluency, struggling readers, and state and national tests, read Connecting Standards and Assessment.

Connecting Standards and Assessment

Promoting Reading Fluency

The research says that reading fluency—the automatic ability to read letters and words—is fundamental in supporting comprehension. Fluency is made up of a number of skills, including phonemic awareness—the ability to focus on and manipulate the smallest units of sound, called phonemes. Fluency also requires phonological awareness, or an understanding of how the alphabet works within spelling patterns and to build sounds and words. Effective fluency means reading with appropriate speed, accuracy, and proper expression. No Child Left Behind has placed greater urgency to promote fluency, especially when many adolescents are appearing in middle and high schools without the ability to practice fluent reading (Rasinski et al., 2005).

There are many ways to assess fluency—from observations to interview to informal and formal standardized tests. There are also a number of ways in which teachers can teach fluency, from modeling fluent reading (yes, adolescent readers still enjoy being read to), and engaging in word play with new vocabulary words. Older students who experience problems with fluency can benefit from audiotaped books, performing plays that are read aloud with expression, poetry readings, and listening to recordings of speeches by inspiring speakers.

▶ **Learn more about building fluency as a support for comprehension in Chapter 9, "Promoting Reading Fluency," in** *Connecting Standards and Assessment through Literacy* **(Conley, 2005), published by Pearson Education.**

A+RISE

Click on A+RISE – WIDA ELP Standard Strategy in the MyEducationLab (www.myeducationlab .com) for your course. Next, select the Strategy Card Index tab, scroll to Comprehension for grades 6–12 and select the Carousel strategy.

Any classroom will consist of different versions of this picture: some students who are already strategic comprehenders, some who are unaware that the point of reading is to comprehend and learn, and some who experience a great deal of difficulty and do not know what to do about it. The goal of guiding reading to learn is to help each of these students grow in his or her expertise as strategic comprehenders. Even the strategic comprehenders can learn more about how to apply their reading to the disciplinary challenges of each content area. Teaching Today's Learners discusses some specific principles to remember and apply in supporting comprehension for students with special needs and English language learners.

Teaching Today's Learners

How to Read, Comprehend, and Learn

Not surprisingly, teaching activities and programs that are designed to help all students work effectively with students with special needs and English language learners. However, there are a few special principles to keep in mind when it comes to supporting students' comprehension. Read the following principles and then describe a lesson in which you would employ several of these principles.

These research-based principles are useful for supporting students with special needs in reading, comprehending, and learning:

▶ Graphic organizers have repeatedly been shown to improve the comprehension of students with learning disabilities. The explicit graphical representations of knowledge help students with learning disabilities by providing additional visual clues besides the text for students to comprehend (Kim et al., 2004).

▶ Teachers who scaffold instruction—that is, show students explicitly how to engage in comprehension strategies—are more effective in teaching students to comprehend than are teachers who simply create assignments (Reid, 1998). Scaffolding has been found to be particularly effective for students with special needs.

▶ Teachers who emphasize multiple forms of literacy—reading, writing, speaking, viewing, and listening—create supportive environments for comprehension for students with special needs (Deshler et al., 2001).

Consider these principles for teaching English language learners to read, comprehend, and learn:

▶ Many culturally diverse students come with a wealth of experiences that can be applied to comprehending and learning if the classroom environment encourages exploration of issues of significance to students' own lives (Garcia, 2001). Although some students might not be quite as proficient in English, teachers can still build on these students' personal backgrounds and experiences to foster comprehension.

▶ Total Physical Response is a technique for making new concepts come alive for students. It involves introducing new concepts through physical demonstrations, diagrams, and pictures of new concepts (Pereogy & Boyle, 2001).

▶ Effective programs in reading and comprehension are ones that involve students in oral language practice, vocabulary development, and direct instruction in comprehension with the goal of transitioning smoothly from proficiency in the first language to proficiency in English (Cheung & Slavin, 2005).

Guiding Comprehension during Reading

The following sections detail specific research-based ways for increasing students' content knowledge and knowledge of comprehension strategies that they can employ during reading. The comprehension strategies that are described here include prediction, asking questions, imagining, summarizing, and remembering. Select lessons that seem right for teaching students about making predictions. Other lessons will present opportunities for teaching about asking questions or summarizing. Teach one comprehension strategy at a time. Name, explain, and model the comprehension strategy. Demonstrate ways for students to assess whether or not the strategy is working. Demonstrate alternatives for students to use when the strategy is not working, including use of another strategy. Finally, provide opportunities for students to practice the strategy, increasingly with less help from you, until they are able to use the strategy on their own. Keep this instructional process in mind as you read the following sections. The How to Plan feature explains how this process works.

Predicting

In Chapter 7, we discussed prediction as a way to activate prior knowledge and motivate students. While predicting, students consider a topic in their reading and make educated guesses about what the topic is all about. In making their predictions, they consider clues in the text, such as titles, key words, and graphics. They also think about their prior knowledge. The goal is to learn how to integrate new information with previous life experiences and texts they have read (Block & Pressley, 2003). What readers think or say while predicting: "Before I start reading, I'm going to look at the text and predict what this will be about and what I already know." The following teaching activity focuses on predicting for comprehension.

The Directed Reading-Thinking Activity. The **Directed Reading-Thinking Activity** (DRTA) was ahead of its time when it was introduced by Russell Stauffer in 1969 (Stauffer, 1969). The DRTA is designed to engage students in very active reading. During this activity, students make predictions and hypotheses, they examine evidence and find proof, and they make decisions based on their prior knowledge and repeated encounters with text. The ability to examine and evaluate information

HOW
TO PLAN ... for Building Content Knowledge and Knowledge about Comprehension

Consider this approach for building lessons around comprehension. After reading these principles and following the decisions of this physical education teacher, plan your own lesson involving Big Ideas and special help with comprehension.

Identify a Big Idea

With state, district, and school curriculum standards in mind, select a Big Idea. For example, consider this Big Idea from the national standards for physical education: Values physical activity for health, enjoyment, challenge, self-expression, and/or social interaction.

Consider Students' Prior Knowledge and Motivation

Consider what students already know or might not know about the Big Idea. For our example from physical education, these questions come to mind:

How much do students value physical activity? How many students practice physical activity for health and enjoyment? How many engage in physical activity for self-expression (dance) or social interaction?

Select Texts and other Resources

What text and other tools are available for teaching about the Big Idea? Are there texts that present opportunities for learning about comprehension strategies (such as texts with clear organizational patterns useful in summarizing)?

A physical education teacher located the following websites to teach students about the positive benefits of physical activity:

Bicycling Magazine: www.bicycling.com
Runners World Online: www.runnersworld.com

Skateboarding and Snowboarding: www.skateboarding.com

Dance Magazine: www.dancemagazine.com

Select a Comprehension Strategy for Teaching

Comprehension strategies and ways of teaching them need to be matched to each instructional situation. In the case of the physical education teacher, she wanted her students to select principles and advice from these magazines and then compare what they found with their own experiences. This created a priority for summarizing important ideas and note taking. This teacher explained the activity: reviewing magazines about favorite physical activities and finding recommendations, comparing them with students' experiences. Next, she demonstrated how to go through the magazine websites, gathering and recording important ideas.

Monitor Students' Progress

As students engage in the activity, watch for misconceptions and occasions when students get stuck. The physical education teacher listened to her students as they worked in pairs examining the information on the magazine websites. She interjected advice about summarizing and note taking when students seemed lost or confused.

on the basis of repeated encounters with text is extremely valuable in reading Internet texts and materials. It is also important for students in learning how to review and respond to information on state and national tests.

To familiarize students with the DRTA, follow these steps:

1. *Select a text.* Choose some reading that students are required to do in your class.

2. *Direct students' attention.* Have students examine the reading for evidence of what it might be about—titles, pictures, formulas, graphs, or other kinds of images.

3. *Predict.* Ask students the following kinds of questions:

   What do you think this is about?

   How do you know? What is your evidence?

   What do you think you already know about this?

4. *Read.* Ask students to read a bit of the information in the text—a paragraph or so.

5. *Revisit Predictions.* Ask students to revisit their predictions for evidence that confirms or refutes what they originally thought. Some teachers like to have their students close their books or cover the reading materials while they revisit their predictions. Ask:

   Were you correct?

   What do you think this is about now?

   How do you know? What is your evidence?

   While asking these questions, have students open their books or uncover their materials so that they can refer specifically to their evidence for their opinions. Give them opportunities to share their observations so that they can engage each other in thinking about their predictions and conclusions.

6. *Summarize.* Ask students to summarize what they are learning with questions such as:

   "What do we know now?"

Have students share what they know as a way of strengthening their understandings.

The DRTA and the Internet. Opportunities for practicing the DRTA on the Internet can be particularly useful (Valmont, 2000). Help students to understand what they need to learn before getting online. For a particular topic, brainstorm predictions about what students might discover. Have students scour the Internet for relevant information to test their predictions while continually evaluating what they find. Give students opportunities to monitor their own thinking with questions such as: "What do you know about this topic now?" and "How do you know?" Providing students with opportunities to discuss their findings with others can be a way for them to clarify, challenge, and extend their ideas. Further Internet searches offer more practice and insight. Provide students with guided practice and observe them for evidence that they are using the DRTA effectively.

Transforming the DRTA from a Teaching Activity into a Comprehension Strategy. To turn the DRTA into a comprehension strategy, teachers need to clearly explain the activity, what it is, and how it works as a way of learning. For example, explain how to make predictions based on the evidence at hand, the information in the text, and what you already know. Model for students how you make predictions, using examples from your own learning. Demonstrate also occasions when prediction might not work very well, such as in situations where one has very little prior knowledge or the topic is particularly abstract. Discuss alternatives, when this happens, such as summarizing or paraphrasing. Emphasize throughout that the purpose for engaging in the DRTA is to make sense of text. Finally, provide students with plenty of guided practice in using this activity on their own so that you can evaluate their transformation of this activity into a learning strategy and they can eventually master it for their own purposes. Include discussion and conversation throughout so that students can compare what they are learning and ways in which they are developing and confirming their predictions. Students should show evidence of increased motivation as they use this process successfully while learning.

Questioning

Students can learn to create their own questions, predict the answers to those questions, search for answers as they read, and paraphrase the answers to themselves. When students learn to ask and answer their own questions, they become more active with their reading (Singer & Donlan, 1982). But this happens only when students learn to ask and answer good or significant questions. Teaching students how to ask and answer their own questions helps students to perform better in the classroom as well as on high-stakes tests (Conley & Gritter, 2007; Rosenshine et al.,

A+RISE

Click on A+RISE – WIDA ELP Standard Strategy in the MyEducationLab (www.myeducationlab .com) for your course. Next, select the Strategy Card Index tab, scroll to Comprehension for grades 6–12 and select the Comprehension Level strategy.

1996). Students should think or say while questioning, "What are some good questions that I could ask about the reading?" and "Does this make sense to me?" The following teaching activities can develop students' questioning as a comprehension strategy.

Three-Level Guides. **Three-level guides** were originally developed for students who experience difficulty with questions. In fact, the guides were referred to as a prequestioning activity for students who could not handle questions very well (Herber, 1978; Herber & Nelson-Herber, 1993). Figure 9.1 depicts the levels of comprehension that underlie the construction of three-level guides. Most people understand the three levels as the difference between facts, interpretations, and applications or themes. When inexperienced readers enter the experience of reading a text, they do not know how to pick out the important facts, form essential interpretations, or construct ideas that represent applications of the information. Three-level guides do not show students how to perform

Figure 9.1 Levels of comprehension.

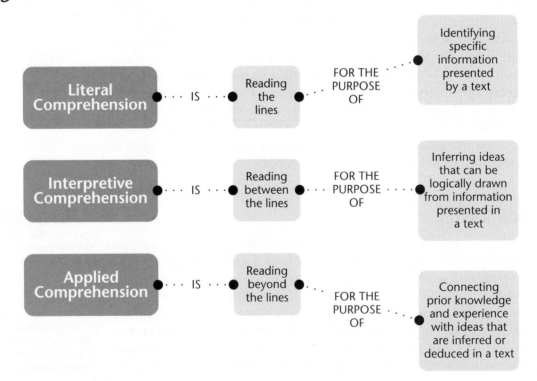

these comprehension skills, but they are a way to help students mentally organize important information from their reading.

Three-level guides are often used during paired or small-group discussions. The added benefit of conversation is to create a situation in which students can help one another but also have available multiple ways to gain access to the knowledge from the reading and conversation. Even students who are struggling with foundational literacy skills can still participate through discussion of the study guide.

Constructing a Three-Level Guide. Constructing a three-level guide is relatively simple (Herber, 1978; Herber & Nelson-Herber, 1993). Start by identifying a Big Idea, ideally one that is connected to a curriculum standard. The next task is to select a text that is useful in developing knowledge about the Big Idea. In this example, the Big Idea is "Miscalculations add up when it comes to planetary exploration." This idea is based on mathematics standards dealing with measurement conversions as well as science standards focusing on speed and momentum. Figure 9.2 consists of a passage about miscalculations and a destroyed Mars orbiter. This brief text nicely represents the problem of accurately calculating speed and momentum for planetary exploration.

The Big Idea is the criterion for writing the statements for the guide. Statements on the guide are written at each of three levels (see Figure 9.1). For the literal level, write statements that identify important factual information from the reading, according to the Big Idea. Interpretive statements represent concepts and relationships among the facts, again in reference to the Big Idea. Finally, applied statements are generalizations that one could deduce from the reading and students' prior knowledge and experiences. Of course, not many students have had experience with interplanetary travel. But statements at this level often encourage discussion about current events, past readings and learnings, and what others say. Figure 9.3 depicts a three-level guide based on our Big Idea about interplanetary miscalculation.

Using Three-Level Guides to Build Comprehension Strategies.
Three-level study guides are all about making connections within the text and beyond the text, but students will not automatically see these connections. Emphasize the need for students to consider (sometimes writing down) the evidence for their decisions about the statements. When students share their decisions, frequently ask, "How do you know that?" and "Does that make sense?" Over time, this will develop a habit of mind in students that it is important to justify their interpretations and points of view with specific facts and concepts.

Figure 9.2

Teaching a Big
Idea about
interplanetary
mismeasurement.

Today's Science   Spring 2007 Issue

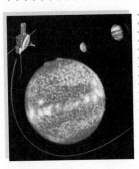

METRIC MEASUREMENT CONFUSION RUINS A NASA MISSION

A mix-up over metric and English measurements likely caused the loss of the $125-million Mars Climate Orbiter as it started to circle the planet last week, officials said Thursday. The error caused the probe to fly too close to the Red Planet, causing the spacecraft to break up or burn up in the Martian atmosphere that it had been designed to study, mission controllers at NASA's Jet Propulsion Laboratory said.

Metric measurements are typically used in navigating spacecraft as well as most scientific studies. Laboratory officials said their preliminary findings showed that Lockheed Martin Astronautics in Colorado submitted acceleration data in English units of pounds of force instead of the metric unit called *newtons*. At the laboratory, the numbers were entered into a computer that assumed metric measurements. Quality control failed to notice the discrepancy. The bad numbers had been used ever since the spacecraft's launch last December, but the effect was so small that it went unnoticed. The difference added up over the months as the spacecraft journeyed toward Mars. The spacecraft was flying way too fast as it entered the Martian atmosphere.

Two separate review committees are investigating the incident at the laboratory; a third board will be formed shortly by NASA. A report is expected in mid-November.

The orbiter's sibling spacecraft, Mars Polar Lander, is scheduled to arrive Dec. 3. The now destroyed orbiter was to have acted as a relay for the lander. With the loss of the orbiter, mission controllers will have to rely on direct communications with Earth as well as relaying information via the Mars Global Surveyor, which has been orbiting Mars since 1997. The lander is equipped with instruments to study Mars' climate history and weather. Its goal is to find what happened to water on the red planet. It is equipped with a robotic arm that will collect samples for testing inside the spacecraft.

After working with the guides for a while, have students write one or more statements at each level on their own. Talk about what it means to select *important* facts versus nonessential ones. Discuss with students what it takes to make a *good* interpretation. Model and give students practice with ways of forming and evaluating generalization-type statements from what they are reading. Doing these things can elevate the three-level guide from just a study guide to a learning experience that lays the groundwork for helping students to generate their own questions as a comprehension strategy.

Big Idea: Miscalculations add up when it comes to planetary exploration.

1. Directions: Check the statements that you believe say what the author says. Sometimes, the exact words are used; at other times, other words may be used.

_____ a. The Mars Orbiter flew too close to the Red Planet.

_____ b. Metric measurements are used in navigating spacecraft.

_____ c. Lockheed Martin submitted acceleration data in English units of pound force.

_____ d. The laboratory should have submitted metric units called newtons.

_____ e. The Mars Polar Lander no longer can use the orbiter for communications with the Earth.

2. Directions: Check the statements that you believe represent the author's intended meaning.

_____ a. Because of the mix-up over English versus metric measurements, the orbiter slammed into the surface of Mars.

_____ b. The main reason for the disaster is that quality control failed to notice the error.

_____ c. Calculations of speed in English units probably mean a faster speed than calculations in metric newtons.

_____ d. The review committees will probably get to the bottom of what destroyed the orbiter.

3. Directions: Check the statements you agree with, and be ready to support your choices with ideas from the reading and your own knowledge and beliefs.

_____ a. Some people think that the space program is an enormous waste of money.

_____ b. Learning new ideas sometimes involves great risk.

_____ c. Science thrives on precision.

_____ d. Studying a mistake can prevent the same mistake from happening again.

Figure 9.3

A three-level guide.

Question-Answer Relationships. Teachers ask a lot of questions, a practice that directs students to information in texts but does not necessarily help them to learn from texts. A far better approach is to help students learn to ask and answer important questions for themselves. This is the premise of activities under the heading of **Question-Answer Relationships** (QARs). Teaching students distinctions among different kinds of questions—what they are asking for and how to answer them—can be very effective for students' performance on classroom and high-stakes tests (Conley, 2005; Conley & Gritter, 2007; Raphael & Pearson, 1985).

Many questions begin with the words *what, how, why, who, when,* and *where.* Amazing as it sounds, many students do not understand what is implied by a question that begins with *what* versus another question that begins with *why.* Teachers discover this when they ask a *why* question only to have a student respond either with a factual answer or an answer

Figure 9.4 Question-answer relationships and classifying questions and their answers.

Right There: Words used to create the question and words used for the answer are "right there" in the same sentence. (Factual, *What* and *When* questions)

Think and Search: The answer is in the text, but words used to create the question and those used for an appropriate answer are found in two or more sentences. You need to "think and search" for an answer across sentences and paragraphs. (Interpretive, *Why* and *How* questions)

Author and Me: The answer is not directly in the text. However, the author has given you information in the text that you have to put together with what you already know and fit all this together to come up with an answer. You have to think to yourself, "What do I know about the text and what I know?" to come up with an answer. (Applied type and predictions, *Why, For what reason, What will happen next*)

On My Own: The answer is not found in the text. You have to think to yourself that "I have to find the answer on my own." (Prior knowledge and belief, *What do you think, Have you ever experienced*)

that simply restates the question without providing an answer. QARs involve building students' knowledge about different kinds of questions, how to ask them, and how to answer them. Figure 9.4 depicts the QAR definitions for types of questions and how to answer them. There are also several examples of the types of words that signal different types of questions. Notice how the signal word *why* appears in several places to signal interpretations or applications.

There have been numerous applications of QARs in various subject areas. For example, the activity has been redefined for the special challenges of mathematics (McIntosh & Draper, 1995):

▶ *Right there questions* are where the question and answer are in the same sentence.

▶ *Think and search questions* involve a question in the text that is like an example but uses different numbers.

▶ *Author and me questions* invite integration across several previously read chapters and previously solved problems with new mathematical knowledge.

▶ *On my own questions* can be answered purely from prior knowledge and experience with mathematics.

Using QARs to Develop Questioning. To use QARs for developing questioning as a comprehension strategy, start by determining what students already know about questions and questioning. Ask students to write down what they consider to be a good question and its answer.

When teachers do this, students often provide extremely factual, right there questions with trivia answers (e.g., "Who is the author of the engraving on page 234?"). This is evidence for why working on questioning as a comprehension strategy for students is worthwhile. Students need to develop a much richer picture of questions and how to deal with them.

The next step is to share the chart in Figure 9.4 with students, perhaps with an example or two for each category of questions and answers that commonly appear in your content area. Developing a comprehension strategy with students happens through teacher demonstration, modeling, and then guided practice. Show students, perhaps by discussing questions in their textbook, how some questions call for *right there* answers while others call for *a think and search* approach. Have students pick out different kinds of questions and answers so that they can practice with the questioning categories. As students appear to be getting the right idea, ask them to write and answer their own questions once again. Teachers should see a much richer set of questions, allowing the class to discuss in more depth what makes a good question, and, importantly, the best answer to a question. This activity can be especially valuable when applied just before a test. Ask students, "If you were going to write questions for the test, what would they look like?" To motivate students, consider using some of their questions on the actual test.

▼ Comprehension is strategic. Learning to ask questions and asking for help are important elements in strategic comprehension.

ReQuest. ReQuest is a teaching technique for helping students to ask their own questions as they read (Manzo & Manzo, 1990). This procedure works on two levels: (1) Teachers model for students how to ask and answer questions, and (2) students are provided with opportunities to practice generating and answering their own questions. This second step also affords teachers a way to observe how well their students are learning how to ask and answer questions and the opportunity to provide reteaching if needed. Teachers could use this procedure either before or after using QARs. The advantage of using ReQuest after a few QAR sessions is that the class will have developed some language for questions and answers that might be useful during ReQuest. Keep in mind here that the

central purpose of this teaching technique is to develop questioning as a comprehension strategy.

The steps for ReQuest are as follows:

1. *Read.* You and your students silently read the same passage from a text. The passage could be from a core classroom text or from a newspaper or magazine. Using just a paragraph or two is a good way to start.

2. *The teacher asks students about the reading.* With the reading closed or covered, you get to ask your students some questions. The class checks the reading to judge the accuracy of responses. Discuss with students why you chose the questions that you did (as good questions to ask) and the answers to the questions.

3. *The students ask the teacher questions about the reading.* Close the book or cover the reading again. Now the students get to ask you the questions. As you answer, students review the reading to check whether your answers are right or defensible.

4. *Repeat the cycle.* Repeat this cycle several times, creating opportunities to talk about good questions and appropriate answers.

5. *Students read the remaining text and ask questions on their own.* A follow-up discussion is effective here to review the content of the text and highlight effective question and answering techniques.

For extra support, teachers can have students prepare their questions in teams. Make sure students prepare questions as well as answers so that they continue to gain practice with relating questions to appropriate answers. Follow-up discussions can sharpen students' understandings of types of questions and how to answer them.

Using ReQuest to Develop Questioning. Be careful about balancing questioning activities with the need for students to continually ask: Does this make sense? Teachers can overdo an emphasis on question strategies to the point at which students lose interest and misplace the reason for asking question in the first place: to grow in knowledge about the content. In teaching about questioning, use lots of examples of good questions and appropriate responses to questions. Gather examples of questions that are not as effective so that you can demonstrate to students the differences between good and less effective questions. As always, offer guided practice and feedback as students ask and answer questions. Balance the need to teach students how to ask questions with the difficulty of text materials. Start with familiar, less complicated materials. From there, teachers can gradually build up students' experiences with questioning accompanied by increasing levels of complicated texts.

Imagery

Imagery is an often neglected but no less powerful comprehension strategy compared with others discussed so far. Before reading about teaching that builds imagery as a comprehension strategy, read the Research Brief.

Research Brief

Imagery

Readers create mental movies. For stories, readers visualize the characters, the action, and the scenes. For informational materials, readers picture how concepts fit together. While this comprehension strategy is excellent for helping all students see in their minds what they are reading and learning (Sadoski & Paovio, 2001), it has been shown to be particularly effective with strug- gling readers and special needs students (Gambrell & Bales, 1986). Bilingual students can use imagery to address the challenges of thinking in two languages (Chamot & O'Malley, 1994). Teachers can help students with imagery by saying, "One good way to understand and remember what you read is to make pictures in your mind" and then demonstrating how to use imagery to comprehend.

Guided Imagery. If you are an avid reader, then you are no stranger to the power of imagery with comprehension. Imagery—visualizing in our mind's eye—is one way in which we make connections. Imagery can evoke some very forceful emotional responses (Sadoski et al., 1988). That is why guiding students in learning how to create images for themselves can result in such a powerful learning strategy. The stronger the imagery we can create about what we are learning, the greater is our ability to comprehend and remember what we read. Imagery works by making reading an active rather than a passive process, stimulating the mental interaction of new ideas with past experiences. Visual imagery is particularly effective for students with special needs (Deshler et al., 2001).

Let's consider several classroom examples of how imagery might work as a learning strategy. In foreign language learning, it can be easier to learn vocabulary when new words are linked to specific places, such as

A+RISE

Click on A+RISE – WIDA ELP Standard Strategy in the MyEducationLab (www.myeducationlab .com) for your course. Next, select the Strategy Card Index tab, scroll to Comprehension for Grades 6–12 and select the Venn Diagram, T Chart strategy.

verbs in a sports arena (running, walking, playing), adjectives in the park (colors, sights, smells), or nouns in the town (books in a library, bread in a bakery, vegetables in the grocery). By visualizing the place—sports arena, park, or town—students can recall the clusters of words that are found there. The semantic map in Figure 9.5 depicts one class's experiences with imagery.

Here's another example. In geometry, the challenge is often to help students understand geometric figures—such as squares, rectangles, circles, and parallelograms—in two and three dimensions. Many students find it difficult to "see" the features of individual figures or discriminate among various figures, especially when they find themselves mired in the visual details. To assist students with this, have students visualize the geometric figures in buildings. By visualizing the geometric figures in, for example, a local 7–11, fire station, theater, or church, students can connect the figures to tangible objects, seeing how various figures go together to make up the buildings they see every day. This can build familiarity with the figures as well as feeding students' curiosity about their everyday surroundings.

Developing Imagery as a Comprehension Strategy. The **Visual Imagery Strategy** supports students in creating a mental image, rich in

Figure 9.5

A semantic map depicting imagery for remembering new words in Spanish.

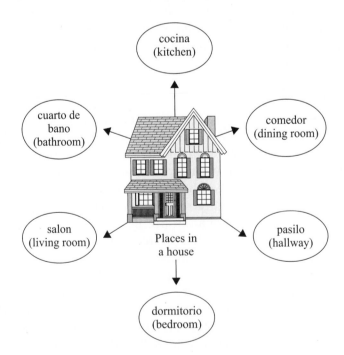

sensory content (sight, sound, smell, touch, and taste) of the content of a reading selection (Deshler et al., 2001; Samples, 1977). Most often, the mental picture will draw from a student's past experiences, connecting the content of the reading selection to the reader's prior knowledge. To develop the Visual Imagery Strategy, follow these steps:

1. Select a passage for students to read that is rich in visual and other sensory details.

2. Explain that students will be learning to use imagery as an aid to learning.

3. Read the selected passage aloud to students.

4. Stop periodically and share with students your own visualizations from the text.

5. Stop periodically and ask students to visualize specific text details. Have students share their sensory impressions with one another. If necessary, prompt student responses with specific questions such as "What do you hear?" and "What do you smell?"

6. Have students compare their visualizations. Point out common images and the specific text passages that produced them. Challenge students to explain the differences in their visualizations, especially those that depart radically from the shared images.

7. Practice imagery with other content area texts.

8. Provide feedback for students as they use imagery on their own.

Summarizing

A simple summary is just the main points, only the ones worth remembering. This raises the question: Do students understand how to identify the most important or main points? In cases where students have a great deal of experience with reading and summarizing, they might already know. But for other students, the notion of most important or main points might be completely unfamiliar. There are many ways to teach students how to summarize.

Using Text Patterns to Summarize. All texts—print-based or digital—depend on structural patterns to guide readers and communicate. Stories, for example, are constructed around characters and/or plot lines. Informational texts depict information in any number of ways, from simple lists and descriptions all the way up to complex cause-and-effect and

Research Brief

Summarizing

Students search out the most important information in their reading and rephrase the content in their own words. Summarizing involves mapping out the Big Ideas in a text and sometimes involves relating the Big Ideas to the smaller details. Students who learned how to summarize wrote better essays and answered questions more effectively than did students who were not shown how to summarize (Armbruster et al., 1987). The ability to summarize is an important skill on many high-stakes state tests (Block & Pressley, 2003; Conley, 2005). What students need to think or say is "What are the main points in the reading?" and "What are the important details?"

problem-and-solution patterns. Digital texts reveal any and all of these patterns but also incorporate features of documents, with graphs, charts, and menus of all kinds. An understanding of these patterns can aid in summarizing if students know where to look and gain experience understanding and using text patterns.

Figure 9.6 contains a list of typical text patterns with some brief examples (Meyer et al., 1980). Using these patterns for summarizing involves several steps. First, students need to understand what text patterns are and what they look like. Labeling and explaining different kinds of patterns within short text segments or passages are ways to do this. Sometimes, it helps to sensitize students to the presence of words that signal text patterns. In narrative and some kinds of informational text, the following signal words sometimes appear:

▶ *Description:* is like, above, below, across, behind, over, under

▶ *Sequence:* first, later, after, before, during, until

▶ *Compare and contrast:* but, although, compared with, however, in common, on the other hand

▶ *Cause and effect:* as a result, for this reason, leads to, if-then, because

▶ *Problem and solution:* the problem, dilemma, predicament; the solution, resolution, result

Figure 9.6 Common text patterns with examples.

Description: This text pattern provides locations, qualities, or characteristics.
A bicycle is an efficient mode of transportation. The drive train consists of two wheels, pedals, and gears. The wheels spin on hubs and are wrapped with air-filled tires.

Sequence: A text pattern in which concepts, events, or procedures are represented in the order in which they occur.
Making a batch of chocolate chip cookies involves a precise order. First, you mix the wet ingredients—eggs, butter, vanilla, and sugar. Next, you mix the dry ingredients—flour, baking soda, baking powder, and salt. Third, you combine the dry ingredients with the wet ingredients and mix. Finally, you add the chocolate chips.

Comparison and contrast: Ways in which people, ideas, concepts, and events are similar and different.
The last president was much more careful with the federal budget than the current president. The last president cut spending. The current president is spending much more money. But like a lot of politicians, they both have strong personalities.

Cause and effect: Text pattern in which one concept or event is the cause of another concept or event.
The roof trusses had strained for years under the weight of the snow. The trusses were bowed and uneven from the weight. The wood was rotted from leaking water. The roof could stand no more and collapsed in a heap.

Problem and solution: A text pattern relationships between a problem and possible or actual solutions.
The decline in test scores had been going on for years. Would better teaching help? Better-qualified teachers? Better parenting? All of these reasons were considered for confronting the problem.

Once students understand the idea of text patterns, teachers can work on helping them learn to use text patterns to summarize.

Using Text Patterns as a Comprehension Strategy. One way to incorporate text patterns into a summarizing comprehension strategy is to work with different text patterns to summarize. A very simple way to do this is with graphic organizers. For example, select a text pattern for the following passage about Boeing 747s.

The Boeing 747 was so much larger than any of its predecessors that an entirely new hangar had to be built. The fuselage is enormous, with a main deck seating of nine across each row plus an upper deck lounge just behind the flight deck. To operate such a heavy aircraft over existing runways, the weight of the plane had to be dispersed over 18 wheels on five landing gear units. Despite its bulk, the 747 was designed to be similar to smaller Boeing designs, such as the 707 and 727, to ease crew familiarization and airport compatibility. Current 747 production models employ powered control systems and advanced navigation technologies to reduce the flight crew to two. Although the 747 typically carries 300 to 500 passengers, this represents only a fraction of the aircraft's lifting capability. High-density versions flown in East Asia routinely carry up to 800, and one Israeli 747 airlifted a staggering 1,087 refugees from Ethiopia in 1991.

A description text pattern is most appropriate, given that the text offers details of the size of a Boeing 747. A graphic organizer depicting this pattern appears in Figure 9.7. Notice how the organizer summarizes the content of the text.

Now consider an example in which students need to summarize a text that consists of a cause and effect pattern. This time, the summary looks more like Figure 9.8.

Again, to teach students how to create summaries like this, demonstrate using graphic organizers in shapes that represent the text patterns. Then show students how to fill out the shapes with important information from the texts. Provide opportunities for students to practice on their own until summarizing via text patterns becomes integrated into their knowledge about comprehension strategies.

Guided Reading Procedure. In the **Guided Reading Procedure** (Manzo, 1975; Manzo & Manzo, 1990), students practice reading and

Figure 9.7 A graphic organizer depicting a description pattern summary.

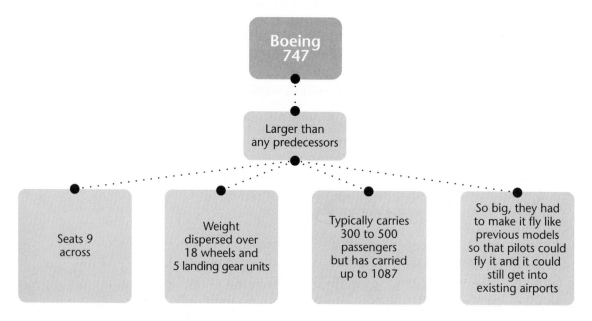

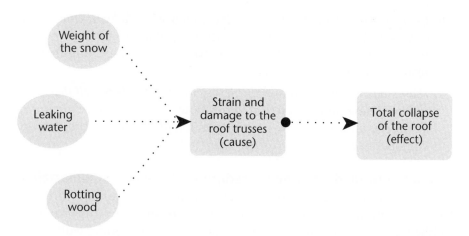

Figure 9.8

A graphic organizer summary based on a cause-and-effect text pattern.

recalling everything that they can, as fast as they can. This technique was first used with adolescents in urban schools as a way to help them intensify their efforts at reading and comprehending. The designers of this procedure claim that it is an effective test preparation strategy, since students start slowly but gradually increase their focus and build up their speed while reading.

The steps in the Guided Reading Procedure are as follows:

1. *Prepare students.* Ask students to examine the text for signs of what it is about or provide a brief introduction of the concepts in the text. Ask students what they already know about the text topic.

2. *Assign the reading.* Select a manageable and appropriate reading selection for your students. This could mean a few paragraphs in a mathematics book for middle school students or a section of a mathematics chapter for high school students. Figure on about five to seven minutes of reading for middle school students and about ten minutes for high school students.

3. *Ask students to recall and retell what they have read.* Have students turn their books face down or cover up their reading. Students can write down all that they remember, or they can retell orally what they read while you write what they say on the chalkboard.

4. *Have students prioritize the ideas in their retellings.* Ask, "Which ideas are most important?" and "Which facts support the main points?" Using students' answers to these questions, build an outline of the new information from the reading.

5. *Redirect students to reread, correct inconsistencies, and add information.* Ask students what they would change in their retellings.

6. *Compare the new information from the reading with students' prior knowledge.* Ask students whether they encountered anything new in their reading or whether what they read connected to anything they already knew about.

7. *Have students self-assess how much they learned and how well they summarized.* Have students reflect about how they used summarizing as a strategy and what they might do differently to make the strategy work better for them.

Using the Guided Reading Procedure for Effective Summarizing.
This technique has a number of uses and potential misuses. One important caution concerns the flexible use of reading and summarizing. While one is reading for pleasure, it is not a time for reading with intensity and speed. On the other hand, there are situations, such as timed tests, in which rapid summarizing is an asset. Be careful, when using this activity, that students do not get the message that this is the way to read all the time. Helping students use this activity for effective summarizing means teaching students how to be flexible, given the opportunities and demands of different reading situations.

Remembering

The strategy of remembering brings together many of the strategies discussed so far, including predicting, questioning, and summarizing. The strategies presented here are commonly referred to as **study strategies**. Studying affects comprehension by directing attention to important ideas and organizing information for later remembering (Roediger & Karpicke, 2006).

Research Brief

Remembering

Remembering is the process of identifying important information and then organizing it for later recall and use. Strategies that emphasize remembering have been found to be particularly effective for learning-disabled students (Bulgren et al., 1997). Strategies for remembering are effective only if they are focused specifically on assignments and assessments that students are required to perform (Anderson & Armbruster, 1984; Deshler et al., 2001).

Note Taking. Note taking is effective for remembering only if it is well matched to what students are expected to do with the information later, when they recall it. Just taking notes for the sake of taking notes does not focus specifically on later assignments or tests. Note taking should support remembering for later recall of important information.

Several understandings are essential if students are to take notes well. First, they need to be able to determine which information is important. As a result, any note taking should not commence without some consideration about the Big Ideas of a lesson or unit, the purpose of a lesson or unit, or the expectations for performance on assignments and tests. Have you ever tried to take notes in a class in which you did not know much about the Big Ideas or the purposes of the class? The experience can feel pretty unfocused. Once teachers have worked with students to gain awareness of what ideas and purposes are important, it is a good time to introduce different note-taking techniques.

The Cornell System. The Cornell System works by dividing up an 8½- by 11-inch piece of paper in the manner depicted in Figure 9.9 (Pauk, 2000). Teachers can have students draw the lines or copy a set of Cornell-style notepaper that you create yourself. It can also be helpful to place the labels Note-Taking Area, Recall Area, and Summarizing Area on the page for the first few times that students use the technique.

To demonstrate the use of the Cornell System, follow these steps. First, discuss reasons for taking notes and introduce several alternatives—gathering up main ideas and details, creating graphic organizers—whatever it takes to record information for later recall. Share your own experiences with note taking, taking special care to provide examples in which the notes were important for accomplishing different kinds of tasks, like completing projects or passing tests.

Next, demonstrate some ways of taking notes for the Note Taking Area of Cornell notes. This can be done in any one of a number of contexts, including note taking:

▶ During a class lecture or demonstration
▶ Based on reading
▶ Accompanying a media presentation
▶ For web-based research

Have students practice note taking, sharing their efforts with others. Provide feedback about note taking. Watch for students who try to write all of the words down or those who fixate on nonessential details. Students

A+RISE

Click on A+RISE –WIDA ELP Standard Strategy in the MyEducationLab (www.myeducationlab .com) for your course. Next, select the Strategy Card Index tab, scroll to Writing for Grades 6-12 and select Content Flipbook: A Note-taking Strategy.

Figure 9.9 The Cornell System for taking notes.

Recall Area	*Note Taking Area*

What are the three branches of the government?	*Branches of the government*
	   - legislative—make laws
	   - judicial—interpret laws
	   - executive—enforce laws

What do each of the branches do?	

Jell-O reminds me of judicial, executive, and legislative.	*Reasons for the branches*
	   - separation of powers
	   - checks and balances

	- need a central government
Why was the government created with separate branches?	*- but not too strong a central government*

	Legislative branch
	   - Congress (Senate, House of
	     Representatives)

What do the branches look like? *Who works in each branch?*	*Judicial branch* *- judges, the Supreme Court*

	Executive branch
	   - President, Vice President
	   - Government agencies and departments

Summarizing Area

   There are three branches of government so that each branch can do a special job but also so that no part of the government can be stronger than another part.

can help each other by asking questions such as "Are these the most important notes?" and "Are there notes that I should have included but missed?"

To develop the Recall Area, students need to have practiced asking and answering their own questions. Teach questioning as a learning strategy, if you have not already done so, or review questioning in the context of the note taking. Some teachers introduce this idea by making a comparison with the game show *Jeopardy*. The Jeopardy answers are in the Note Taking area, while students need to create the Jeopardy questions to represent the key words in the Recall Area.

The Summarizing Area is a place for creating a summary of the notes. Again, if students have little experience, you will need to teach them how to summarize as a learning strategy. Start with the ideas developed earlier in this chapter: Demonstrate and model summarizing and have your students practice. Next, work with summaries in the context of note taking. Show students how summaries from notes pick up on only the most essential information, even approximating the Big Idea for a lesson.

Digital Note Taking. The digital age has created the need to rethink note taking, how students take notes, and what they do with them. New issues have emerged about plagiarism and the need for students to document and paraphrase their notes (Bruce, 2003). As easy as it is for students to cut and paste from various digital media and the web, the new challenge is to help students understand how cutting and pasting are not the same as documenting and paraphrasing. Some teachers construct digital note cards, like the one that appears in Figure 9.10, to address this new opportunity and challenge.

▲ Gathering information for research papers and projects has been made much easier with the Internet. But the ease with which a student can collect this information has raised a number of issues about plagiarism.

The note card can be copied in a paper format or produced digitally, as on a web page, for students to gather and paraphrase their notes. The advantage of this note card is that it provides students with the steps for cutting and pasting according to particular purposes (e.g., the lesson Big Idea), citing the source of the information and then restating the information in one's own words. If you show students how to use this approach with their print and digital texts, you will prepare them for a future world of comprehension and research that might be very different from that of today.

Mnemonics. Sometimes, students can create key words to help with recall of important information. Notice in Figure 9.9 how the student wrote in the Recall Area that thinking about *Jell-O* as a way to remember the *judicial, executive,* and *legislative branches.* Selecting or even making up a word in this fashion is called a **mnemonic**—a special way to remember by associating a word with an acronym, another word, or an image. Teaching students how to create their own mnemonics to remember information can be very effective, especially for special needs students (Lenz & Deshler, 2004). You might be familiar with

Figure 9.10

Digital note taking template.

Big Idea or Question   *How do satellites stay in orbit?*

Quotation

A satellite's orbit works because of a balance between two forces — speed and the gravitational pull of the earth. The orbit is a combination of the satellite's velocity — the speed it is traveling in a straight line — and the force of the Earth's gravitational pull on the satellite. Basically, gravity keeps the satellite's velocity from sending the satellite flying out in a straight line away from the Earth, and the satellite's velocity keeps the force of gravity from pulling the satellite back to Earth.

To illustrate this concept, think of a yo-yo. There is a long string that holds the weight of the yo-yo ball at the end. The yo-yo ball is the satellite, and your hand holding the end of the string is the Earth (not to scale of course). If you swung that yo-yo in a circle, then the string would act as the gravity. Without the string, the yo-yo  ball would fly off into space, but without the weight and forward motion of the yo-yo ball, the string would flop towards the ground.

Web address for the Quotation   **www.spaceplace.nasa.gov**

Paraphrasing in your own words

Satellites stay up because they are going too fast to fall down. If they slowed down, the earth's gravitational pull would take over, and the satellite would fall. You can test this theory out with a yo-yo.

---

mnemonics from *ROY G. BIV,* the way of remembering the colors of the spectrum (red, orange, yellow, green, blue, indigo, violet). Teachers can accomplish similar kinds of association by having students draw pictures.

Developing Remembering as a Comprehension Strategy. The research is quite clear that just taking notes is not enough to aid in remembering. Students need to spend time working with and manipulating the notes for various purposes. There are very general ways to do this, such as with the **five R's of note taking** (Pauk, 2000):

▶ *Record:* Students use the note-taking column to record their notes while reading, during instruction, whenever they need to record important information.

▶ *Recall:* As soon as possible after taking notes, students generate questions and record key words based on their notes. Their questions and key words go into the recall column. Completing this step helps to clarify meanings, reveal relationships, establish continuity, and strengthen memory.

▶ *Recite:* Students cover the note-taking column with a sheet of paper. Then, looking at the key words and questions they wrote in the recall column, they answer the questions and define the key words. This is also a good time to write a brief summary that captures the essence of the notes.

▶ *Reflect:* Students reflect on the notes by thinking about connections between concepts and ideas. Sometimes, they write new questions to help them remember the information.

▶ *Review:* Students are encouraged to review previous notes frequently, especially as they are asked to complete assignments and perform on tests.

Another effective plan is to help students relate their notes to specific assignments and assessments. For example, teachers can ask students to select from their notes the most important questions or key words that should go into an assignment or test. This will accomplish two purposes: (1) connecting in students' minds their notes with tasks they are expected to perform, and (2) motivating and involving students in their own assessment.

Summary

Good readers are strategic comprehenders. They read with specific purposes in mind, and they know what to do for themselves when they get stuck. Teachers play a significant role in guiding students so that they increase not only in their content knowledge but also in their knowledge about comprehension strategies, such as predicting, questioning, using imagery, summarizing, and remembering. Rather than simply rehearsing students through teaching activities designed for these strategies, take time to directly teach students, sharing examples from your own experiences with reading and learning. Remember that the goal is for students to learn how to use comprehension strategies on their own.

Special Projects

1. Select one of the learning strategies described in this chapter: predicting, questioning, imagery, summarizing, and remembering. Design a lesson around a Big Idea in your content area. Then select one of these comprehension strategies. Describe how you will teach the strategy during reading while developing content knowledge about the Big Idea. How will you assess students' knowledge about the content and the comprehension strategy?

2. Select a teaching technique with which you are familiar in your content area. Evaluate its strengths and weaknesses with regard to developing and understanding how to learn in your content area. Suggest some modifications that would make the technique work more effectively with your students. Consider the comprehension strategies described in this chapter as a source of potential modifications.

3. Locate several released test items from the state tests in your content area. Consider how you would prepare students to perform successfully on the state tests by using the comprehension strategies described in this chapter.

Praxis Practice

Working with Questions to Prepare for the Praxis Reading Across the Curriculum Test

Multiple Choice

1. Which of the following teaching strategies uses students' prior knowledge and questioning?

   a. QAR's

   b. KWL

   c. Graphic Organizers

   d. Context Clues

2. Comprehension is best defined as:

   a. Reading and answering assigned questions

   b. Constructing meaning through interactions between a reader and a text

   c. Interactions between a reader and a text

   d. Effective summarizing of a particular assigned reading

3. Strategic comprehenders engage in reading that is (circle all that apply):

   a. Purposeful

   b. Shaped by motivation

   c. Assigned

   d. Characterized by multiple, continuous and deliberate decisions

Constructed Response Questions

1. Mr. Han always begins the school year by discussing the patterns present in expository writing. For example, he points out that the class' history textbook often presents a problem, or root cause, and then explores the solutions and effects of these solutions upon society. Which comprehension strategy is Mr. Lee exploring to help teach his students to read to learn?

2. Ms. Arthur prefers to actively guide her students through text before allowing them to work independently. Today she prepares students by introducing the topic, allows them to read a small section independently for a short amount of time, asks students to retell what they have read, asks students to prioritize the ideas in their retellings, redirects students to reread and correct inconsistencies, asks students to compare information gathered in their second reading of the text with information pulled from the first reading, and finally has student assess their learning and final summaries. Which comprehension strategy is Ms. Arthur teaching her students?

3. Before instructing a lesson on condensation, Mr. Chavez reads to his eighth-grade physical science class a children's book about a lone water molecule traveling through the water cycle. While he is reading, the class is instructed to close their eyes and imagine the experiences of the water molecule. Which comprehension strategy is Mr. Chavez using?

Suggested Readings

Block, C., & Pressley, M. (2003). Best practices in comprehension instruction. In L. Morrow, L. Gambrell, & M. Pressley (Eds.), *Best practices in literacy instruction* (pp. 111–126). New York: Guilford.

Pauk, W. (2000). *How to study in college.* New York: Houghton Mifflin.

Reading for Understanding, the Rand Report on Reading Comprehension. Downloadable from www.rand.org/multi/achievementforall/reading/readreport.html. This report describes comprehension from a research perspective and what teachers and students need to know about comprehension.

The Power of Classroom Practice

A+RISE

Go to Topic 5: Comprehension, and Topic 7: Planning for Instruction, in the MyEducationLab (www.myeducationlab.com) for your course, where you can:

- Find learning outcomes for Topic 5: Comprehension, and Topic 7: Planning for Instruction along with the national standards that connect to these outcomes.

- Complete Assignments and Activities that can help you more deeply understand the chapter content.

- Apply and practice your understanding of the core teaching skills identified in the chapter with the Building Teaching Skills and Dispositions learning units.

- Examine challenging situations and cases presented in the IRIS Center Resources.

Go to the Topic A+RISE in the MyEducationLab (www.myeducationlab.com) for your course. A+RISE® Standards2Strategy™ is an innovative and interactive online resource that offers new teachers in grades K-12 just in time, research-based instructional strategies that:

- Meet the linguistic needs of ELLs as they learn content

- Differentiate instruction for all grades and abilities

- Offer reading and writing techniques, cooperative learning, use of linguistic and nonlinguistic representations, scaffolding, teacher modeling, higher order thinking, and alternative classroom ELL assessment

- Provide support to help teachers be effective through the integration of listening, speaking, reading, and writing along with the content curriculum

- Improve student achievement

- Are aligned to Common Core Elementary Language Arts standards (for the literacy strategies) and to English language proficiency standards in WIDA, Texas, California, and Florida.

10 Guiding Students' Critical Literacy

▶ What view of the world is put forth by the ideas in this text? What views are not?

▶ What are other possible perspectives on the information in the text?

The power of these questions emerges in different ways across the content areas. In mathematics, these questions produce insights that mathematical ideas are shaped by ways in which numbers and data are represented: in graphs, charts, or formulas. Mathematical texts impart human perspectives rather than just cold, objective data (Cobb, 2004). In history, critical literacy produces the idea that expert reading in history involves exploring the motivations of historical writers, examining evidence for conclusions, and developing a healthy skepticism about historical claims (Vansledright, 2004). In science, critical literacy is responsible for the realization that scientific theories are the products of scientific inquiry, conducted by communities of scientist who reason that there is a preponderance of evidence to support the theories (Yore et al., 2004). Critical literacy in arts underlies the notion that participation in the arts and artistic "texts" is an important part of how adolescents build their identities (Heath, 2004).

Critical literacy has the potential to open up the entire world of knowledge and information. Rather than just extracting meaning from text, critical literacy says that students are on the same playing field as writers and producers of texts. Critical literacy says that texts are almost always created with the intent to convince and persuade. Students and anybody else can construct multiple meanings from texts that go well beyond an author's intent. Critical literacy recognizes knowledge production and consumption as a very human activity, ranging from unbridled error to complex understanding.

Language as a Powerful Way of Knowing and Valuing

Suppose that you are in charge of assessment in your state. You are responsible for creating a test in your content area according to what you consider to be high standards. You start out with a blank piece of paper or computer screen. Now you begin designing the test. Think about the words and symbols that you are likely to choose to put on the page. Undoubtedly, they will come from your own knowledge and experience in your content area. Now consider the students who will be taking your test. How are they diverse, and how is their preparation in your content area different across your state?

Thinking about this task in regard to Michigan, you would encounter an incredible range of diversity: European and African Americans who have made their living in the auto factories; recently arrived immigrants from Africa and Asia; seasonal workers, many of whom are Hispanic; and people with all kinds of backgrounds and experience gathering to build the state's technological capacity. Many, if not all, of these individuals want schools to prepare their children for the world of tomorrow. Then there are the politicians and businesspeople who say that they are concerned about education and the economy and that the education system needs reforming. Does this description resemble your region in any way? Suddenly, your test is an important instrument for many different stakeholders. It had better be a good one!

So you proceed to write the test. You meet with political and business leaders and gather their ideas. You talk to a wide range of teachers. You have a limited budget and not much time, so you cannot get to everybody. You manage to write a test that gains approval from the state board of education. On the basis of your test, high school students will be deemed proficient, satisfactorily performing, meeting standards, or exceeding standards in English, mathematics, science, social studies, the arts, or physical fitness.

Is your test objective? Certainly not. You made choices all along the way, according to your knowledge and experience and your conversations with certain individuals and groups. In reality, no test is objective. Every test maker starts out the way you did: with a blank piece of paper or computer screen and a set of assumptions that do not necessarily agree with everyone's set of assumptions. The language of your test reflects your knowledge and values and not necessarily everyone's knowledge and values. But your test has the weight of the state government behind it. Everyone has to do well, or else. This little thought experiment is a good example of how language—in this case, the language of assessment—reflects ways of knowing and valuing some kinds of knowledge over others. Connecting Standards and Assessments offers some examples of how state standards and assessments create opportunities for teaching students about critical literacy.

Let's change the view a bit. Consider the language that students know, use, and value. It is the language of families, the school, neighborhoods, and peers. It is the language of the media—television, movies, and songs. It is the language of the Internet—instant messages, email, and web pages.

YW to go with us. ATM we have room in our car. ATM it is NBD. L8R

Connecting Standards and Assessment

Designing Lessons That Focus on Standards, State Tests, and Reasoning

Teachers who focus only on standards or only on state tests are missing an important point. Although standards say many things about the content of the curriculum, tests raise the bar with respect to expectations for reasoning. Many state tests provide a rich context for critical literacy by asking students to analyze questions, take a stand, support positions with content knowledge, consider prior knowledge, and present organized, reasoned responses. But all of this occurs in the rich context of content-driven standards. To perform well, students must engage in high levels of critical literacy within the context of important and meaningful Big Ideas.

Teachers can create lessons that integrate Big Ideas and critical literacy skills. By identifying the Big Ideas from curriculum standards and then considering the accompanying critical literacy skills, teachers can approximate the challenging questions and issues that appear on the state test. Doing this requires that teachers be knowledgeable about the standards and tests and look for opportunities for taking an integrated approach to lesson planning. Opportunities for reading, writing, and reasoning come from instances in which standards and test-taking skills intersect. These can also be natural occasions for generating controversy in ways that motivate students.

▶ **Read more about ways to promote critical literacy in this era of standards and tests in Chapter 8, "Integrating Standards and Assessment through Daily Practice," in *Connecting Standards and Assessment through Literacy* (Conley, 2005), published by Pearson Education.**

It is the language adolescents use to create and explore their own identity, powerful in its own right (Gee & Crawford, 1998).

What is appropriate and powerful language in one context might not work very well in another. Consider what would happen if an adolescent quoted Shakespeare all the time while instant messaging or talking with friends or used some of the language from cable television in school or at the dinner table. Consider also the type of language that is required to pass a state test—the concepts and symbol systems in mathematics, the ways in which language is used uniquely to understand history, English, and science. Clearly, adolescents—like successful adults—need to use language in a variety of ways that are well matched to particular contexts. Knowing how to shape, shift, and adapt language in multiple ways for multiple contexts and audiences is one very important aspect of critical literacy (Gee, 2000).

Let's shift perspective once more. You are the teacher. The traditional view of your job is that you are to "standardize" students, their language, and their school experiences, emphasizing academic language and ways of knowing. Students who do not go along or use language in the dominant ways are labeled *remedial* or *at-risk of school failure*. Think about the worlds of language that get left out by this view—from families, neighborhoods, the media, and the Internet: the languages that our students explore and use to learn about themselves. Think about the students who are labeled *at-risk* who use language in powerful ways through music or poetry outside of school to gain and celebrate knowledge that they value.

Would acknowledging students' experiences with language outside of school help them to do better academically and pass our test? The research says it would (Moje et al., 2004). Adolescents who learn to use their out-of-school literacies to grow in their in-school literacies can be very successful academically. Teachers who include students' ways of knowing and valuing language open up opportunities for students to use what they know to increase their knowledge about language and its use in multiple contexts. Including students' understandings of language can increase their academic knowledge and even help them pass your state test. There is evidence that everyday experiences with language involve the similar kinds of analytic thinking required by more official texts, such as state assessments (Conley, 2005). Teaching Today's Learners discusses how you can work on critical literacy with all students, including those with special needs and English language learners.

The potential of critical literacy can be summed up as follows: Students can learn to use their everyday experiences with language as a powerful force to engage in multiple literacies—the language of academic work, the language of state assessments, and the language of a yet-to-be-envisioned future workplace. Teachers become a powerful force in students' lives by helping them to use critical literacy to move through multiple worlds of language, texts, and context and for understanding themselves.

Promoting Critical Literacy

So how can you promote critical literacy in your students? Here are some general principles to follow (Moje et al., 2000).

Teaching Today's Learners

Creating a Safe Place for Critical Literacy for All Learners

A common misconception is that students who struggle as readers and writers cannot engage in critical literacy because of difficulties with language, including reading, writing, and communicating. Nothing could be farther from the truth. Consider these principles in creating a supportive place for critical literacy for students with special needs and English language learners (Brenner, 1998; Jitendra et al., 2005):

► All students can learn to think critically when they are immersed in authentic, real-life learning contexts.
► Students learn best when they spend time considering and developing prior knowledge.
► Students can learn to think critically when teachers take the time to show them how to think critically.

► English language learners and others who are struggling with language can learn to read and communicate much more critically during small-group discussions than during whole-class discussions. Small-group discussions provide a much more supportive environment for students to test out and examine ideas.
► The effectiveness of small-group discussions for supporting critical thinking depends upon teachers showing students how to function productively in small groups.

Considering these principles, design a lesson in your content area in which you plan support for critical thinking for all learners.

Pay Attention to the Personal Dimensions of Literacy and Learning

This starts with getting to know students well and knowing what they know and value. It continues with finding ways to include what students know and value as part of teaching and assessment. Keep in mind that language, in the classroom and outside the classroom, plays a huge role in how students construct their own identities. Hopefully, across the range of these experiences, students can learn to make choices that will lead them to construct a unique place for themselves later in life. Guide students to understand that as much as they are shaped by the contexts in which they live, they also can make choices that help them to be what they want to be in life. Help students to define who they want to become (Tatum, 2005).

Promote a Questioning Attitude

To deal with the ongoing information explosion and the barrage of points of view and biases, guide students in developing a questioning attitude. Help students to realize that every text is created for a purpose. Sometimes, students will find these purposes worthwhile and valuable, while other times, texts will be fraught with errors and bias. Whenever possible and appropriate, engage students in conversations about the motivations of authors (e.g., to inform, persuade, dissuade, sell, or malign), their choice of language (e.g., academic, formal, informal, or graphic) and assumptions about audience (e.g., gullible, resistant, adolescent, mature, wealthy, or poor).

Observe Adolescents in a Variety of Contexts to Determine What They Can Do—And Use It

▼ Popular culture plays an important role in shaping young peoples' identities and language. Learning to question sources of information helps them to become critical learners.

Performing in school is a single role, albeit an important one. Keep in mind that students experience all sorts of other roles, as sons or daughters, friends, employees, church members, and neighbors. Though some students are marginalized in school because of academic failure or behavior problems, these same students may appear completely different and ready to learn in other contexts.

For example, a student who was believed to be suffering from attention deficit disorder, on the basis of his classroom behavior, blossomed in a class devoted to African dance (Moje et al., 2001). Some disengaged students might be fluent in several languages, navigate the Internet with ease, communicate scientific information gained from television viewing, or be able to interweave readings in adolescent literature with personal family stories. To help students become more engaged in school, bring students' other lives and experiences in whenever you can. More than just activating prior knowledge, this demonstrates that you and the other students value who they are and what they know and value.

Draw from Multiple Kinds of Texts That Students Respect

Students' outside-of-school readings might consist of comic books, zines, games, and web pages. Use these texts as jumping off points for helping students to gain knowledge. The materials from popular culture often depict real-world problems and questions that are of concern to many adolescents (Alvermann et al., 1999). In designing lesson plans and units, select a range of texts that reflect students' current preferences as well as other texts that will provide more of a challenge. This is particularly important for students with special needs who might be fluent in and excited about reading popular texts but not do as well with academic texts. Blending popular culture and school texts is a way to help students feel supported in confronting the challenges of academic texts. Project-based assignments are a good way to incorporate multiple kinds of texts and encourage student interaction around issues they care about.

Encourage and Support Multiple, Alternative Representations of Knowledge

Adolescents often engage in creating a variety of popular texts, including drawings, cartoons, comics, and graphics. Encouraging students to use these alternatives to enrich and demonstrate their learning can be another way to pull marginalized or poorly performing students into the classroom conversation. For example, a student who bombs out on the five-paragraph essay in English might be a whiz at navigating the Internet. Perhaps she or he can produce a flowchart of steps in finding something with a web search. The organizational details of a flowchart can lead to talking about ways to organize a piece of writing. As students learn to compare different ways of representing what they know, they can consider the limitations and biases of texts and other representations of knowledge. Action Research explores new ways students are representing their knowledge through blogs and podcasts.

Guiding Critical Literacy

The following sections detail ways for teachers to guide students' critical literacy. The learning strategies that are explained here are (1) constructing and evaluating perspectives, and (2) considering and evaluating

Action Research

Exploring Critical Literacy in the Adolescent World

Visit a local shopping mall or place where adolescents gather and interact (including schools). You might also wish to visit places on the Internet designed for and by adolescents. Web logs, referred to as blogs, and podcasts are the new kids on the block when it comes critical literacy. Blogs are usually a record of what is happening in a person's life and what is happening on the web, a kind of hybrid website for personal and public kinds of sharing. Podcasting is the creation and use of audio and video files to share information, most often on MP3 players or on the Internet. These technologies are fast emerging as centers for adolescents to engage in many types of communication, sometimes involving critical literacy. They are also springboards for planning and goal setting for student writing.

Popular websites for blogs include My Space (www.myspace.com), Blogger (www.blogger.com), Livejournal (www.livejournal.com), Xanga (www.xanga.com), and Facebook (www.facebook.com). There are many ways in which a blog could be used to brainstorm and gather information, develop projects, and communicate findings from research.

Suppose, for example, that a science teacher wanted students to do some research on global warming. A blog might already exist, or the teacher and students could create a blog, gathering up and commenting on websites that deal with their chosen issue. Another teacher might want students to study violence on television. Again, a blog could be developed that would capture students' thinking and research. A science teacher in North Carolina developed a blog to accompany many of the science concepts he was going to teach during the year. On Mr. Blake's blog (http://ccmug.blogspot.com), students gather their ideas on blogs but also share what they are learning through podcasts. Be aware that students may encounter inappropriate material on websites or blogs. Advise students to avoid blogs and websites that might contain inappropriate materials, and always visit blogs and websites yourself before asking students to complete assignments involving the web.

Several websites provide extensive resources on using blogs and podcasts for brainstorming and research. Educational Weblogs (http://educational.blogs.com) portray many ideas for classroom-based blogs and serve as a portal for many educational bloggers and podcasters. Searching many of the blog and podcast websites is a good way for teachers to get started with helping students use these new technological tools for critical literacy, including research and writing. Visit the websites listed here, and make a list of the ways in which you could use blogs and podcasts in your content area.

evidence. Many of the lesson ideas presented here lend themselves to use with the Internet (see How to Plan).

Constructing and Evaluating Perspectives

There are so many ways in which students are called upon to form an opinion and evaluate other points of view in school, in the community, and through the media. Constructing a critical perspective is an active, challenging approach to literacy. It involves the critical reading

HOW
TO PLAN
. . . for Internet-Based Critical Literacy Lessons

Many of the ideas in this chapter are adaptable for use with the Internet. Here are a few ideas.

Questioning the Author—Online!
Questioning the Author is obviously a valuable activity for use with Internet content. Design a set of questions that you could use for Questioning the Author online. Then locate one of your favorite websites and apply your questions. What did you learn about your favorite website that you had not noticed before? Were there any hidden biases or unproven assumptions and interpretations?

Critical Media Lessons
Visit the Billboard website (www.billboard.com) and research the top ten to twenty songs. What conclusions can you draw about which songs, singers, and bands are more popular than others? Which themes or topics tend to be mostly represented in comparison with others? What inferences can you draw about the artists' perceptions of adolescents as their primary audience?

Next, create a survey that you could administer to a group of students to find out about their musical preferences. One useful approach to designing the survey would be to ask for a list of students' top ten songs accompanied by questions such as "What is this song about?" and "What do you like about this song?"

If possible, administer your survey to a group of students. Discuss with students similarities and differences in their lists. Compare students' responses to the Billboard list. Ask, "What makes certain kinds of music or a singer or band popular?" Follow up by having students write their own songs, describe their ideal singer or band, and create CD artwork for their band's release. (From Alvermann, D., Moon, J., & Hagood, M. [1999]. *Popular Culture in the Classroom*. Newark, DE: International Reading Association.)

of texts, which enables students to become more aware of the ways texts are constructed, by whom, and how texts direct the reader to respond in certain ways. A critical perspective is one in which the reader considers and evaluates the ideas in texts and then crafts a perspective about the reading (McLaughlin & DeVoogd, 2004).

Questioning the Author.

Questioning the Author is a teaching technique for building and evaluating ideas from texts (Beck et al., 1996; Beck & McKeown, 2002). Originally devised as a way for students to overcome obstacles to understanding in the form of poorly written texts, this approach is intended as a way for students to question an author's message, motivation for writing, and biases. Questioning the Author consists of three tools in building and evaluating information from texts: texts, questions, and discussion.

A goal of Questioning the Author is to help students learn to view texts as just someone's ideas written down. These ideas might be neither clear nor complete. Instead of placing a text on a pedestal, this approach assumes that the text is fallible. This positioning of the reader changes the task of comprehension from one of extracting meaning from a text to the more interesting challenge of understanding and evaluating the author's attempt at communicating.

Questions are used to explore that author's message, connect pieces of information, identify difficulties and/or biases, and verify assumptions and understandings. Figure 10.1 depicts questions developed to guide Questioning the Author discussions.

▲ Critical literacy involves questioning the author as a way of evaluating information provided in the text. Questioning can be used with informational texts, as well as fiction

The spirit of the questions is to focus on meaning—not just the text's meaning or the author's meaning, but also the meanings that you and the students construct together. This helps to reinforce the idea that what the author intended to communicate might be different from the meanings that readers construct. Questioning the Author discussions involve you and your students in collaborative work as you interact to grapple with ideas and build meaning. Students contribute by responding to the questions and to each other. You can help by building upon, refining, or challenging what students say.

Goal	Questions
Initiate discussion and explore the author's message	*What is the author trying to say?* *What is the author's message?* *What is the author talking about?* *That's what the author says, but what does it mean?*
Connect pieces of information	*How does that connect with what the author already told us?* *What information has the author added here that connects to or fits in with _____ ?*
Identify difficulties and/or biases	*What information or points of view does the author include?* *What information or points of view are left out?*
Verify assumptions and interpretations, clear up misinterpretations	*Does the author explain that idea clearly? Why or why not? What is missing? What else do we need to figure it out or find out?* *Did the author tell us that?* *Did the author give us the answer to that?*

Figure 10.1

Questions that guide Questioning the Author discussions.

A Social Studies Example. Consider this example from a social studies class that is studying the Minnesota content standard "How institutions in society change over time." The specific case is women's suffrage. Many social studies textbooks cover the women's rights movement. In one high school textbook, the section on women's rights appears in a chapter called "The Spirit of Reform" (Bragdon, 1998). After discussing the male-dominated world of voting and the American women's tendency to experience fainting spells caused by tight clothing, the author writes:

> Yet foreigners noted the deference paid to women in America and their relative freedom as compared with European women. Particularly in the west, women had a high station. The life of a frontier woman was one of endless toil, but she was a partner in the work of the settlement. In frontier regions, there was such a surplus of men that women had a high scarcity value. (p. 282)

What is the author's message here? It appears to be that women did not need the right to vote because they were fragile but already well cared for and worshipped by men. What are the connections we can make? Men liked things the way they were and did not have a reason to change. What points of view are included or excluded? Interestingly, in this brief segment, this author manages to generalize about what all men supposedly believed or felt and totally ignored what women might have felt or believed at the time. The curious result is that women are portrayed as being in charge of and quite satisfied with the status quo. This makes the next sentence of the text all the more puzzling: "The feelings of women about their place and position in the world came to a head in 1848 when Lucretia Mott and Elizabeth Cady Stanton organized a convention to draw up a 'Declaration of Sentiments and Resolutions' echoing the Declaration of Independence." (Bragdon, 1998, p. 282). The text never makes clear why women, with such an already high standing, would want to organize a movement to press for their rights! Questioning the Author helps students to see these inconsistencies.

Using Questioning the Author to Develop Perspective Taking. The questions for Questioning the Author are very useful for developing a strategy in which students learn to continuously question and evaluate information from texts, including an author's motivation and point of view. Teachers should explain this purpose of Questioning the Author and why it is a good idea to question texts all the time. Show students how to use the questions with various kinds of texts, even ones that they create. Finally, provide opportunities for practice and feedback.

Critical Media Literacy Lessons: Examining Points of View. Critical media literacy lessons help students think seriously about how they construct meaning from the media (Pailliotet, 2001). Critical Media Literacy Lessons have the following characteristics:

▶ Connections to a phenomenon, problem, or issue in the real world.

▶ Assignments or tasks that encourage students to explore real-world texts, such as Internet, newspaper and magazine articles and ads, and television or movie representations.

▶ Culminating activities that allow students to use alternative media representations to showcase the results of their explorations.

To prepare for this kind of lesson, select a Big Idea. Then consider the potential for building in a critical media literacy lesson. What are some ways to connect the Big Idea to real-world issues and texts? How can assignments be crafted to encourage students to examine points of view?

There are a number of ways to create a critical media literacy lesson. For example, in mathematics classes, students can examine data within popular media, including the Billboard music charts. Students scan the charts for evidence of bias, asking questions such as the following: What points of view are represented? What are the messages about gender, age, and race? What songs or song titles represent biased, simplified, or distorted images? What views are left out? Students can tally responses to these questions and represent their findings in various ways, including charts and graphs. Students can create their own popular music charts that more accurately represent their own preferences. These kinds of activities help students to examine real-world applications of mathematics as well as understand how mathematical techniques are used to convey information.

Another example, useful in a health class, is to have students examine the messages in alcohol and tobacco advertisements and public service announcements (Pailliotet, 2001). The purpose of this project is to build students' awareness of how producers of alcohol and tobacco ads use marketing devices and values to appeal to young people. The project, completed in small groups or at home with parents and siblings, looks like this:

▶ Analyze one or more tobacco or alcohol advertisements.

▶ List instances of smoking, alcohol use, and drug use in popular movies. What devices do producers use to make these behaviors seem desirable? What purposes do these behaviors serve (e.g., to make the behaviors seem glamorous, mature, elite, etc.)?

▶ Research effects of substance abuse on the Internet.

▶ Interview peers to determine attitudes about smoking, drinking or drug use.

Students can represent the results of their findings through parodies of the ads, music videos, mock radio announcements, comic strips, skits, or movie posters.

Taking a Stand. As Figure 10.2 illustrates, taking a stand is one of the most common strategies required on many state tests (Conley, 2005). But this is also a strategy that serves as a very important life skill. How many times have you found yourself in situations in which you had to stand up for yourself and your opinions? The teaching ideas presented here will help students to learn this valuable strategy.

Figure 10.2 State test items that require students to take a stand.

Social Studies

Should the United States government require manufacturers to produce more fuel-efficient vehicles?

You may either support or oppose the manufacture of more fuel-efficient vehicles. Write a letter to your senator. You will be graded on the following criteria. Your letter must include

- a clear and supported statement of your position;
- supporting information using a core democratic value of American constitutional democracy;
- supporting knowledge from history, geography, civics (other than the core democratic values), or economics (it is **NOT** enough to only state your opinion);
- supporting information from the data section;
- a credible argument someone with the opposite point of view could use; and
- an explanation that reveals the flaw in his or her argument.

Mathematics

The owner of an automobile dealership selected a sample from a population of 750 customers who received maintenance services last year. Due to time limitations, she sampled only 20 customers.

    A. The owner used the last 20 customers who received repair service as the sample. Explain why that sample would NOT be suitable.

    B. Describe a method of sampling 20 customers in a way that maximizes the probability the sample will fairly represent the population.

Explain your answers, including supporting calculations, tables, diagrams, charts, drawings/graphs in your answer booklet.

English

Scenario: Your school announces that the new high school for arts and science will be opening in the fall. You and your friends are excited about this special opportunity and agree that the new high school will give you an advantage when it comes to future career choices, because it has special facilities with new innovative programs. You make a commitment to attend the new high school. In August, when school begins, you find that none of your friends are enrolled in the new school. When you call them to find out why they chose not to attend the new school, you are told that they did not want to leave their other friends or miss some of the social and athletic events that occur during the senior year.

Scenario Question: Even though you know the advantages of the new school, should you drop out and go to the other school to be with your friends? Why?

Science

According to the article provided, what is the cause of changes in the exercisers? What other factors, not mentioned in the article, could account for the results? In your response, be sure to give two alternative explanations that could account for the increase in muscle size and strength.

To help students develop reasoned or responsible stands, start with forming opinions. A series of topics around which students might form an opinion might include the following (Conley, 2005):

What do you think about . . .
Parents' rules
Television shows with swearing and nudity
Violent video games
Overpaid athletes
The criminal justice system
Crooked politicians
Wars overseas
Drunk driving laws
High car insurance rates for teens
Rich entertainers or athletes accused of a crime

For each topic, you might ask, "What do you think? What do you believe? How do you feel about that? Is it right? Is it wrong?" Explain that these are fundamental questions that help individuals to take a stand.

Once students have gained some practice in generating points of view around various issues, it is important to help them to distinguish points of view from reasons or facts. When confronted with the task of taking a stand in response to a test item, many students produce lists of facts without connecting them to a point of view. Solving this problem requires a couple of different approaches.

One useful approach is to give students practice in distinguishing points of view from facts in especially biased writing. For instance, what is the point of view in the following passage? And what are the reasons or facts?

> *Drilling for oil in the Arctic National Wildlife Refuge is an excellent idea. Since the wildlife area has a potential to produce 1.5 million barrels of oil per day, it has more than enough to supply all of the needs of the United States for the next 50 years. We could stop importing foreign oil. Nobody has ever proven that oil spills have harmed the environment or, more particularly, wildlife in any oil-rich areas. Everybody in the United States is in favor of drilling for oil in the Wildlife Refuge.*

(Source: Bigbucks Oilmen's Society)

Using a chart like the one in Figure 10.3, students can separate the point of view in this paragraph from the supposed facts and then search for whether the facts effectively support the point of view. Teachers can also help students to see that the chosen reasons and facts do not represent all of the reasons and facts that the author could have selected.

Another approach is to have students revise writing from different perspectives. For instance, how would the point of view about drilling in

▲ When presenting in front of a group, students become familiar with the concept of "taking a stand." The practice can help students gain the perspective of authors and to practice considering multiple points of view.

the wildlife refuge change if you were a concerned environmentalist? A scientist? A Native Alaskan living near the refuge? A worker in the oil industry? Select one of these perspectives, and model for students how to think about that person's point of view. Then select facts that the person might use to support his or her view. After that, students can practice with one of the other points of view while you provide feedback.

To build taking a stand into a learning strategy for perspective taking, follow these steps: First, assume that students already know how to take a position on something—the music on VH1, their favorite (or least favorite) teacher, their friends. Even very young children stamping their feet and screaming at the top of their lungs in the middle of a supermarket are demonstrating how well they can take a stand. The missing ingredient, especially for adolescents, is how to construct or connect a stand to something responsible, such as good reasons, especially in

Figure 10.3 Taking a stand, distinguishing points of view from "facts."

Point of View	Drilling for oil in the Arctic National Wildlife Refuge (ANWR) is an excellent idea.

Supporting "Facts"

Since the wildlife area has a potential to produce 1.5 million barrels of oil per day, it has more than enough to supply all of the needs of the United States for the next 50 years. We could stop importing foreign oil.

Not true: Daily oil consumption in the United States is well over 20 million gallons per day. 55 percent is imported foreign oil. Nobody knows how much oil is in the Wildlife Refuge.

Nobody has ever proven that oil spills have harmed the environment or, more particularly, wildlife in any oil-rich areas.

Not true: Nearly 11 million barrels of oil spilled onto the Alaska coastline in 1989, destroying lots of wildlife and ruining prime fishing areas.

Everybody in the United States is in favor of drilling for oil in the Wildlife Refuge.

Not true: The Senate vote allowing drilling in ANWR was 51 in favor to 49 opposed—that's not exactly a mandate!

testing situations. Explain that taking a stand is more than spouting off or accepting uninformed opinions. Provide students with experiences with opinionated texts in which not all of the reasons or facts are believable. Ask students to consider different texts from multiple points of view. The idea here is to help transform students' perspective taking from off-the-cuff opinions to well-reasoned and supported points of view.

WebQuests. A WebQuest is "an inquiry-oriented activity in which most or all of the information used by learners is drawn from the Web" (Dodge, 2001). It is an excellent tool for helping students to construct and evaluate different points of view. WebQuests are designed around important and interesting Big Ideas or questions. Figure 10.4 contains an example of a WebQuest for a recent topic in the news—the use of steroids in the modern baseball era—and how it affects comparisons with the golden era of baseball.

Designing a WebQuest can be a fun activity, especially if teachers are already comfortable with the Internet and search engines. WebQuests involve digital literacy as well as perspective taking. The teacher demonstrates all of the tasks that students will perform so that they can learn how to use the digital media and become proficient at building and evaluating perspectives. To construct and implement a WebQuest, follow these steps (from (Dodge, 2001):

▶ *Find great websites.* Select websites that are readable and interesting to your students. Use search engines (e.g., Google, Altavista, Yahoo!, and Dogpile). Search deeply, going several pages into the results of your search to find more interesting and unique content. Bernie Dodge, the developer of WebQuests, maintains a web page entitled Specialized Search Engines and Directories (http://webquest.sdsu .edu/searching/specialized.html) to assist with deeper web searching for WebQuests. Bookmark websites that you find most interesting and useful, organizing them in special folders for different WebQuest topics.

▶ *Organize your resources, and prepare your learners.* Organize the computer resources that are available to the maximum benefit. If you have only one computer, use it to support whole-class discussion and exploration. Ten computers can be used at once, but plan for the other students to be completing other parts of the WebQuest. If students are working regularly in a computer lab, they need to do a great deal of preparatory work before they go to the lab so that work in the lab will be most productive.

Prepare students by thinking ahead about the assignments that they will need to complete for their WebQuest. Discuss and model ways

Figure 10.4

A Sample WebQuest.

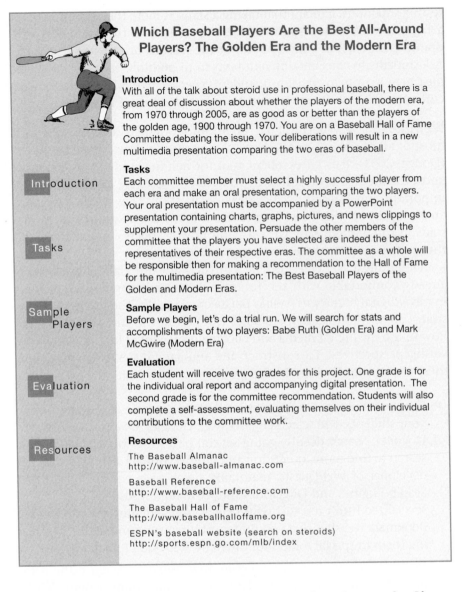

Which Baseball Players Are the Best All-Around Players? The Golden Era and the Modern Era

Introduction
With all of the talk about steroid use in professional baseball, there is a great deal of discussion about whether the players of the modern era, from 1970 through 2005, are as good as or better than the players of the golden age, 1900 through 1970. You are on a Baseball Hall of Fame Committee debating the issue. Your deliberations will result in a new multimedia presentation comparing the two eras of baseball.

Introduction

Tasks
Each committee member must select a highly successful player from each era and make an oral presentation, comparing the two players. Your oral presentation must be accompanied by a PowerPoint presentation containing charts, graphs, pictures, and news clippings to supplement your presentation. Persuade the other members of the committee that the players you have selected are indeed the best representatives of their respective eras. The committee as a whole will be responsible then for making a recommendation to the Hall of Fame for the multimedia presentation: The Best Baseball Players of the Golden and Modern Eras.

Tasks

Sample Players
Before we begin, let's do a trial run. We will search for stats and accomplishments of two players: Babe Ruth (Golden Era) and Mark McGwire (Modern Era)

Sample Players

Evaluation
Each student will receive two grades for this project. One grade is for the individual oral report and accompanying digital presentation. The second grade is for the committee recommendation. Students will also complete a self-assessment, evaluating themselves on their individual contributions to the committee work.

Evaluation

Resources
The Baseball Almanac
http://www.baseball-almanac.com

Baseball Reference
http://www.baseball-reference.com

The Baseball Hall of Fame
http://www.baseballhalloffame.org

ESPN's baseball website (search on steroids)
http://sports.espn.go.com/mlb/index

Resources

in which you would like students to complete these tasks. If you are going to have students work in teams, discuss and role-play the different ways in which you would like students to work together.

▶ *Challenge learners to think.* WebQuests are a waste of time and energy if all you are doing is have students locate and memorize information. Organize WebQuests around Big Ideas and interesting questions to make the most of thinking with the Internet. For instance, in a mathematics class, students researched possible destinations for a two-week vacation. They were given a budget and could select anywhere in the world for their vacation. In making their plans, students explored the destination and the costs of housing, food, tours, and entertainment. Their reports reflected an understanding both of what things cost in another locale and also conversions to the local currency. Rather than using the Internet to record lists of facts, these students made discoveries about what it would actually be like to travel to another country.

▶ *Use the technology to its fullest.* It would be a shame to do the research for a WebQuest only to miss opportunities to report by using digital tools such as instant messaging, blogs, and discussion forums.

▶ *Scaffold high expectations.* This happens in three ways. First, be aware that students might encounter resources on the web that they have not viewed before. As a result, model for students how to locate and think about the different resources they might come across. Second, WebQuests commonly require students to transform what they research into a new medium. Show students how to convert their research into other forms, such as PowerPoint presentations, web pages, and other kinds of digital reports. Focus especially on showing students how to design these alternative products, helping them to compare and contrast different ways of representing what they understand.

Considering and Evaluating Evidence

The sister skill to perspective taking involves considering and evaluating evidence. On many state tests, students take a stand and then are required to support their stand with evidence.

Research Brief

Considering and Evaluating Evidence

Critical literacy thrives on a concern for evidence—students considering and evaluating evidence as part of solving interesting and engaging problems, perspective taking, hypothesis testing, inquiry, and all forms of reasoning (Skaggs, 2004). Proving your point through consideration of evidence is a major learning strategy for being successful on many state assessments (Conley, 2005).

Reaction Guides. **Reaction guides** invite students to consider evidence for Big Ideas and connecting concepts. Examples of reaction guides for mathematics, music, and English appear in Figure 10.5. Reaction guides are created in much the same way as anticipation guides (see Chapter 7) with several important differences, most notably that students use the guides to react to rather than anticipate the content of a lesson. To design and teach using a reaction guide, follow these steps:

▶ Select a curriculum standard and/or Big Idea for a lesson.

▶ Identify sources of information (e.g., readings, media, Internet material) that you want students to consider.

Figure 10.5 Examples of reaction guides.

---

a) Mathematics

Directions: Based on our work with multiplication, for each of the statements, write whether the statement is **"Always true,"** **"Sometimes true and sometimes false,"** or **"Always false."** Provide a number example beneath the statement as evidence for your decisions.

_____ A. Multiplication of a positive number by a number greater than 1 always increases the number.

_____ B. Multiplication of a positive number by a positive number between 0 and 1 always increases the number.

_____ C. Multiplication of a negative number by a positive number always increases the first number.

b) Music

Directions: Write the words _Beethoven_, _Rock and Roll_, or _Hip Hop_ next to each of the following statements if you believe each of the types of music is evidence that the statement is true. Sometimes, more than one kind of music can be used to support the statement. Beneath each statement, write reasons for your decisions.

_____ 1. Only some kinds of music qualify as good music.

_____ 2. Good music is in the ears of the listener.

_____ 3. Sometimes, the most popular music is not the best music.

_____ 4. Sometimes, the simplest music is the best music.

c) English

Directions: For each of the following statements, place a **T** for _true_ or an **F** for _false_, based on the story "The Silent Couple" and your experiences. Write reasons for your decisions beneath each statement.

"The Silent Couple"		**Your Experiences**
_____	Cooperation improves a relationship.	_____
_____	No crime ever goes unpunished.	_____
_____	It is good to forgive those who try to harm you.	_____
_____	Sometimes, all you can do is make the best out of a bad situation.	_____

▶ Analyze the sources of information. Decide what is most important. For reaction guides, consider information that supports or conflicts with the Big Idea of the lesson.

▶ Write declarative statements to which students will react and about which they will find evidence.

▶ Prepare students to read or view the text information for the lesson.

▶ Have students read and view the information.

▶ Discuss with students the meaning of each statement on the reaction guide.

▶ Ask students to respond to the statements on the reaction guide, agreeing or disagreeing and using evidence from the readings to support their decisions.

▶ Compare and contrast students' decisions and the evidence they use to support their decisions.

Keep in mind that an important goal here is to help students learn how to think about, compare, and evaluate evidence. It is especially helpful to use a statement or two on the reaction guide to model how to do this. Engage students in discussions of what counts as good evidence and what would be contradictory or even bad evidence. Have students compare different kinds of evidence and form their own defensible conclusions. These activities will prepare students to become more successful on state tests that require students to consider and apply different kinds of evidence.

Discussion Webs. Discussion webs provide a framework for students to explore evidence with respect to important questions (Gregory & Lipsyte, 1984). Explain to students that every issue has several sides to be considered. Use examples of controversial issues, such as the death penalty, rules for teenage driving, and underage drinking to help students understand that there are many different reasons, both pro and con, that make it difficult for individuals to make decisions. Use a controversial topic when you introduce a discussion web to demonstrate for students how they can think about the different sides of an issue or question.

The steps in using a discussion web are as follows:

1. Prepare students to read or research a topic, using examples and demonstrating Internet searches. For example, if you wanted to use the discussion web in Figure 10.6, which is based on the story "Not Poor, Just Broke" (Gregory & Lipsyte, 1984), you might discuss a Big Idea of the story: what it means to be poor or broke, how someone

Figure 10.6 Discussion web for "Not Poor, Just Broke" by Dick Gregory.

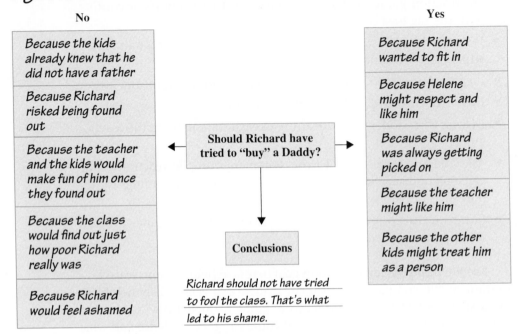

might feel if he or she were poor, and what the person might do to fit in with everyone else.

2. Ask students to read. After they have read the story, introduce the discussion web with the question "Should Richard have tried to buy a Daddy?" In this case, it is especially important to talk about the question and what it means in the story. (Richard, who has no father, tried to put money into the class collection as if he had a father who had given him the money.)

3. Place students in pairs and ask them to discuss. In this case, the discussion is about the pros and cons of Richard's decision. Explain that students should take turns recording their evidence in the spaces but that not all the spaces need to be filled in.

4. Combine the pairs into groups of four to compare responses, work toward consensus, and try to reach a conclusion.

5. Follow up the class discussion by having individuals write their own responses to the discussion web question.

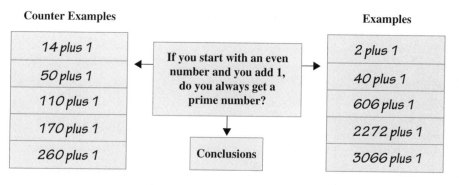

Figure 10.7

Discussion web for number patterns: adding 1 to an even number.

Counter Examples

| 14 plus 1 |
| 50 plus 1 |
| 110 plus 1 |
| 170 plus 1 |
| 260 plus 1 |

If you start with an even number and you add 1, do you always get a prime number?

Examples

| 2 plus 1 |
| 40 plus 1 |
| 606 plus 1 |
| 2272 plus 1 |
| 3066 plus 1 |

Conclusions

Sometimes, you get a prime number and sometimes you do not. Numbers that are not prime are usually divisible by 3 and another number that ends in 7.

An advantage of using discussion webs is that students are afforded the opportunity to think and discuss in pairs and small groups before committing themselves to what they think and know. This contrasts with traditional class discussions, in which teachers or a few vocal students can monopolize discussions. In smaller groups, there are multiple opportunities to interact.

Discussion webs can be used in mathematics to test hypotheses about number patterns. The discussion web in Figure 10.7 is structured in reference to tables of prime numbers from the University of Tennessee (www.utm.edu/research/primes/). To use this discussion web, students search for examples and counterexamples for the question "If you start with an even number and you add 1, do you always get a prime number?"

Another use for discussion webs can be found in health education. Figure 10.8 depicts a discussion web for exploring evidence of good nutrition at fast-food restaurants. This time, the evidence for the exploration comes from the McDonald's Nutrition Information website (www.mcdonalds.com/usa/eat/nutrition_info.html).

Critical Media Literacy Lessons: Evaluating Evidence. The content and images in the media are also good places for students to consider and evaluate evidence. Newspapers, magazines, commercials, and ads are all full of claims that can be subjected to evidence-based scrutiny. Figure 10.9 portrays a number of teaching activities that can be used to

Figure 10.8 Discussion web for a health lesson about fast-food nutrition.

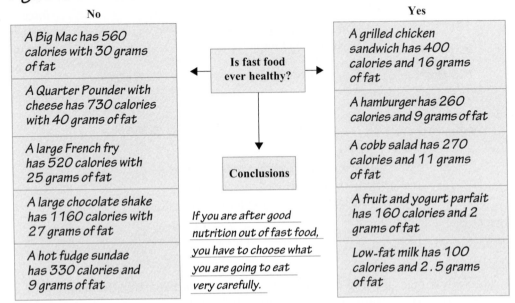

No		Yes
A Big Mac has 560 calories with 30 grams of fat	**Is fast food ever healthy?**	A grilled chicken sandwich has 400 calories and 16 grams of fat
A Quarter Pounder with cheese has 730 calories with 40 grams of fat		A hamburger has 260 calories and 9 grams of fat
A large French fry has 520 calories with 25 grams of fat	**Conclusions**	A cobb salad has 270 calories and 11 grams of fat
A large chocolate shake has 1160 calories with 27 grams of fat	*If you are after good nutrition out of fast food,*	A fruit and yogurt parfait has 160 calories and 2 grams of fat
A hot fudge sundae has 330 calories and 9 grams of fat	*you have to choose what you are going to eat very carefully.*	Low-fat milk has 100 calories and 2.5 grams of fat

promote the evaluation of evidence as a learning strategy. These activities can be incorporated into different content areas in a variety of ways.

For instance, a mathematics class could track news stories for evidence of the accurate versus inaccurate use of numbers. English and music classes could explore evidence of media bias and imagery in media autobiographies. A history class could use the question "Who is my hero?" to investigate evidence underlying assumptions about heroes in various historical periods. Physical education classes could discuss what it means to be heroic in physical activities such as sports. Remember that the point here is to help students understand how to work with evidence as a way of examining assumptions, assertions, and images, particularly as the media embarks on ways to alter images about their own identities.

Figure 10.9 Teaching activities for exploring evidence about beliefs and values in the media.

Teaching Activity	What It Does	How It Works
Adbusters	Gathers and evaluates the messages in advertisements. Seeks evidence for the impact of ads.	What do we like to buy and why? Log time spent watching ads on television and money spent on purchasing related to the ads. Identify favorite advertisements. Create ad parodies—print, video, web pages.
News Story Tracking	Gathers evidence of bias in the news media.	Follow a news story's coverage over a period of time. Whose point of view is covered? Whose is left out? Collect news magazines. Ask students to list where most news stories occur. (Certain areas and people are left out.) Research facts for a news story. Revise the news story to reflect greater accuracy.
Media Autobiographies	Students collect and evaluate media representations of people who are like them in terms of age, race, and gender.	Gather images from television shows and magazines aimed at teens. What products are advertised? How do these products shape students' beliefs about who they are, what they should have, and how they should act? What images dominate? How accurate are the images of gender roles, body image, dress, and lifestyle? Do students really act this way? How do these images affect how students feel about themselves?
Who Is My Hero?	Explores value differences among celebrities, heroes, and real role models or leaders.	Define what students mean by "hero." List traits. Who are my heroes? Brainstorm heroes by category—male, female, race, age, occupation. Identify traits of these heroes. What does the hero look like? Say? Do? Believe? What problems does the hero encounter? Do you agree with how he or she resolves problems? Why or why not? Would you want this person to be your friend? Why or why not? Would you like to be this person? Why or why not?

Summary

Critical literacy is the process of constructing many different kinds of meaning. It is a means for understanding who we are as well as the images that others create of and for us. Language is a powerful way of knowing and valuing, whether it is in the ways in which policymakers create tests, how students instant message one another, or adults' use of language in the workplace. Teachers are at the center of it all, mindful of literacies in use inside the school, in content area classrooms, as well as outside, in communities and families, and with students and their peers. Critical literacy can be a way to interweave these literacies into an ongoing critique of perspectives in school and society as well as the evidence used to support particular points of view. Teaching students the learning strategies for critical literacy—constructing and evaluating perspectives and considering evidence—is a way to help students thrive in many different real-life contexts.

Special Projects

1. Consider your own knowledge and practice of critical literacy. Describe a time when you felt that you used critical literacy effectively. Describe another time when you wish you could have been more critically literate. How can you use your own experiences with critical literacy to help your students?

2. Explore the messages about teachers, schools, and adolescents that are communicated in the media. Make a list of the media images and messages that are reflected in television ads, newspapers, and magazines.

3. Select a topic in your content area or a set of Big Ideas. Describe ways in which you would personalize this topic and develop critical literacy with a group of students.

4. Select a controversial topic in your content area. Next, select one of the teaching activities in this chapter. Describe how you would use this topic and method of teaching to teach your students how to evaluate perspectives and/or consider evidence.

Praxis Practice

Working with Questions to Prepare for the Praxis Reading Across the Curriculum Test

Multiple Choice Questions

1. Reading to evaluate the information in a text is referred to as:

   a. critical reading.

   b. critical literacy.

   c. reading for facts.

   d. reading for opinions.

2. Reading to consider multiple points of view is referred to as:

   a. critical reading.

   b. critical literacy.

   c. reading for facts.

   d. reading for opinions.

3. A literacy skill that is typically found on state assessments is:

   a. Answering literal questions.

   b. Taking a stand and supporting it.

   c. Filling in bubble sheets.

   d. Answering constructed response questions.

Constructed Response Question

1. Describe some ways you can have readers learn to consider alternative points of view in while reading and through writing.

Suggested Readings

Cobb, P. (2004). Mathematics, literacies and identity. *Reading Research Quarterly, 39*(3), 333–337.

Heath, S. (2004). Learning language and strategic thinking through the arts. *Reading Research Quarterly, 39*(3), 338–342.

Heffernan, L. (2004). *Critical literacy and writer's workshop: Bringing purpose and passion to student writing.* Newark, DE: International Reading Association.

Moje, E., Young, J., Readance, J., & Moore, D. (2000). Reinventing adolescent literacy for new times: Perennial and millennial issues. *Journal of Adolescent and Adult Literacy, 13*(5), 4–14.

Pailliotet, A. (2001). Critical media literacy and values: Connecting with the 5 w's. In P. Schmidt & A. Pailliotet (Eds.), *Exploring values through literature, multimedia, and literacy events* (pp. 20–45). Newark, DE: International Reading Association.

Sox, A., & Rubinstein-Avila, E. (2009). Webquests for English language learners: Essential elements for design. *Journal of Adolescent and Adult Literacy, 53*(1), 38–48.

Vansledright, B. (2004). What does it mean to read history? Fertile ground for cross-disciplinary collaborations? *Reading Research Quarterly, 39*(3), 342–346.

Yore, L., Hand, B., Goldman, S., Hildebrand, G., Osborne, J., Treagust, D., et al. (2004). New directions in language and science education. *Reading Research Quarterly, 39*(3), 347–352.

The Power of Classroom Practice

A+RISE

Go to Topic 5: Comprehension, and Topic 7: Planning for Instruction, in the MyEducationLab (www.myeducationlab.com) for your course, where you can:

- Find learning outcomes for Topic 5: Comprehension, and Topic 7: Planning for Instruction along with the national standards that connect to these outcomes.

- Complete Assignments and Activities that can help you more deeply understand the chapter content.

- Apply and practice your understanding of the core teaching skills identified in the chapter with the Building Teaching Skills and Dispositions learning units.

- Examine challenging situations and cases presented in the IRIS Center Resources.

Go to the Topic A+RISE in the MyEducationLab (www.myeducationlab.com) for your course. A+RISE® Standards2Strategy™ is an innovative and interactive online resource that offers new teachers in grades K-12 just in time, research-based instructional strategies that:

- Meet the linguistic needs of ELLs as they learn content

- Differentiate instruction for all grades and abilities

- Offer reading and writing techniques, cooperative learning, use of linguistic and nonlinguistic representations, scaffolding, teacher modeling, higher order thinking, and alternative classroom ELL assessment

- Provide support to help teachers be effective through the integration of listening, speaking, reading, and writing along with the content curriculum

- Improve student achievement

- Are aligned to Common Core Elementary Language Arts standards (for the literacy strategies) and to English language proficiency standards in WIDA, Texas, California, and Florida.

11 Developing Content Area Writers

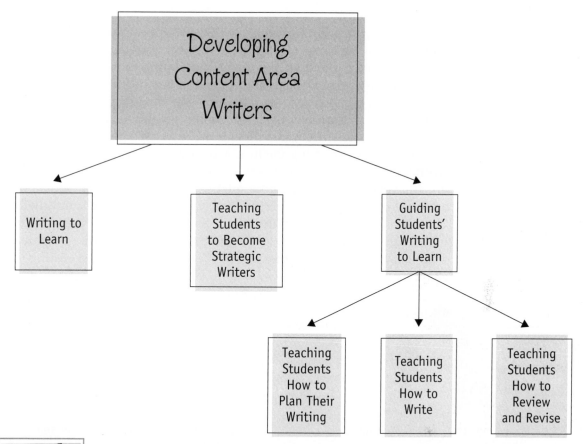

Writing is one of the most important ways to learn and demonstrate learning in content areas. Consider the kinds of writing and ways in which writing functions in your content area. Whether it takes the form of lab reports, solving equations, responding to literature, defending a political position, guiding musical performance, or educating about nutrition, writing is a critical tool in any school subject. Writing is also interwoven into everyday experiences outside of school. It is a way to explore and develop one's identity. It is a vehicle for communicating within families, among friends, and throughout increasingly broad worldwide communities. The prevalence of email, instant messaging, and blogs has made writing as prevalent as face-to-face communication. This chapter is designed to develop students' knowledge of and skill with writing.

Although there are some similarities between writing in the content areas in school and everyday writing, there are also important differences (Daiute, 2000). Any kind of writing is shaped by its context, the purposes for writing, and the audience. For example, writing for purposes of learning a new concept in English or social studies or for demonstrating understanding on a mathematics or history test is different from instant messaging a best friend. In the classroom, writing to learn the content is essential. Writing can be used to support students as they learn, making meaning, organizing ideas into more complex understandings, and building on past learnings. On a test, students might be tuned in to what the teacher-as-audience wants them to write to get a good grade. Everyday or cyberspace writing might not be nearly as focused; instead, the writing is often devoted to emotional and social connections with others. In cyberspace writing, some might not even care much about the audience reaction, despite the awareness that the audience is out there. Once an individual posts an instant message, an opinion on a discussion board, or a comment on a blog, she or he can just turn off the computer. The Research Brief points out how the Internet has changed writing in some classrooms.

Research Brief

How the Internet Is Changing Writing in Many Classrooms

Leu (2000) has the following findings on the uses of the Internet in many classrooms:

- Students who read and write on the Internet report greater interest and motivation for learning.
- Students are often more engaged when writing in digital environments because the Internet promotes a more active orientation to learning.
- Internet-based reading and writing meets a wide range of social and emotional needs, making these activities more creative and playful at times.
- Students often report a greater sense of control over their reading and writing during Internet-related experiences.
- Students who have engaged in Internet-based writing projects report confidence in their work, despite using new and sometimes unfamiliar technology.

Although students may be immersed in many kinds of writing, it does not mean that they know how to use writing in very sophisticated ways (Graham, 2006). Many kinds of formal writing in school and outside of school require knowledge about how to plan for specific purposes and audiences, how to convert plans into writing, and how to revise and edit.

Students need to learn to use this knowledge strategically to pass state and national tests (Conley, 2005) and succeed in college and careers (Achieve Inc., 2005). Research has shown that students can already demonstrate quite a bit of talent in their out-of-school literacies, especially writing (Moje et al., 2001). Any strategy instruction in writing needs to expand on what students know to help them become expert writers in a whole range of in-person, digital, and print venues in our rapidly changing world.

Writing to Learn

Many students who have graduated from high school report that they were not well prepared for the kinds of writing that are expected in college and in the workplace. College instructors representing diverse content areas and many different kinds of employers report that graduating students are ill prepared for the writing demands they face (Achieve, Inc., 2005). How can it be that so many students are so ill prepared to use writing effectively?

▼ Today, almost all jobs require familiarity with technology and good writing skills. Even the most basic entry level jobs often require competent communication skills in various mediums.

Different Demands of High School and College Writing

One answer to this question concerns differences between typical school assignments and writing tasks and demands in colleges and the workplace. Remember the five-paragraph essay, still popular in many middle and high schools? An introduction, three main points with supporting evidence, a conclusion—and you are done. College writing often requires ten- or twenty-page papers. In addition, college writing frequently involves complex interpretations based on varying ways of organizing the writing. No single structure—such as a five-paragraph essay—is up to the task of satisfying all the writing demands in college. College students need to use writing to tackle ambitious topics and devise convincing arguments while entertaining opposing interpretations and evidence (O'Brien et al., 2004). What do you recall about your own transition from high school to college writing? Did you feel that you were well prepared? Read the How to Plan feature (page 334)

HOW ... for Reducing the Achievement Gap with Writing
TO PLAN

In 2002, the writing scores for eighth graders on the National Assessment of Educational Progress in diverse communities such as New York City, Atlanta, Chicago, Houston, Los Angeles, and Washington, D.C., showed these trends (U.S. Department of Education, 2003):

▶ Students in the big-city schools scored considerably lower than the national average.

▶ Student performance at the basic writing level ranged from 64 percent in Los Angeles to 74 percent in Houston, compared with 84 percent across the nation.

▶ White eighth graders had higher average scores than Black and Hispanic eighth graders in Chicago, Houston, and Los Angeles.

▶ Students who were eligible for free and reduced-price lunch because of low family incomes scored lower than did students who were not eligible for these programs.

Direct, explicit instruction in writing and guided practice could be the key to reversing this picture. The research suggests the following principles as promising ideas for building the writing skills of students with special educational needs (Troia & Graham, 2002):

▶ Teach students how to use strategies for writing, including goal setting, brainstorming, and organizing.

▶ Provide students with practice in applying writing strategies in different kinds of situations and for different purposes (e.g., writing stories, writing informational texts, and responding to different kinds of class assignments).

▶ Assign homework in which students can practice and apply writing strategies, accompanied by advice and feedback from the teacher.

Following are some possible approaches to use with English language learners (Ball, 2006):

▶ Create opportunities for extended writing as opposed to worksheets with one-word answers.

▶ Teach and demonstrate how to create argument and analyses through writing.

▶ Use multicultural stories, poems, and plays to stimulate writing.

▶ Critically examine texts that contain information about different cultures.

▶ Start a book club to develop discussion and writing about books that interest students.

Looking at these options, can you think of several more examples for how you can help diverse writers in your classroom?

about the achievement gap that exists for writing achievement and how to help today's diverse students with their writing.

Demands of Workplace Writing

The demands of the workplace writing can also be complex. Figure 11.1 depicts the results of a survey of people in entry-level (stock clerks, bookkeeper, bartender, receptionist, truck driver), skilled (fire inspector, nurse's aide, account manager, dental assistant, news photographer), and professional (high school principal, dental hygienist, auditor, pediatrician, professor, pastor, meteorologist, special education teacher) occupations. Individuals were asked, "What kinds of writing are required in your job?" "What are the purposes for the writing?" and "What are the audiences?" As depicted in Figure 11.1, the workplace demands skill in a range of types of writing for varied purposes and audiences (Craig, 2001). How many of these kinds of writing did you learn and practice in school?

Figure 11.1

Occupational writing.

Types of Writing
- Memos
- Letters
- Charts, tables, and schedules
- Policy and procedure documents

Purposes for Writing
- Share general information
- Share ideas with colleagues
- Compose professional letters
- Compose assigned reports
- Convince a colleague of a new idea
- Compose scientific and technical reports

Audiences
- Superiors
- Clients and customers
- Employees
- Teenagers, children, and other specific populations
- General public
- Trainees
- Colleagues and peers
- Providers of related business services

Reforming Writing Instruction in the Digital Age

Some educators argue that the school curriculum needs to be revamped radically to incorporate the kinds of writing that are needed in higher education and the workplace. For example, one idea would be to take the tasks from the list in Figure 11.1 and use them to create a middle and high school writing curriculum. However, this is not a very realistic solution. The forms, functions, and roles of writing—like those of all of the ways we communicate—are rapidly changing, especially with changes in technology (Leu, 2000). Consider the many ways of communicating in the digital age that are not represented in Figure 11.1. See the Action Research feature for ideas about researching the ways writing has changed and continues to change in the modern world.

Action Research   Exploring Writing in the Real World

Research the ways in which people write and types of writing people use everyday and in the workplace. You can do this in one of several ways:

► Conduct a web search, making a list of the different types of writing that are on the web or are described on the web. Describe ways in which teachers can incorporate this kind of writing into your content area. How will you prepare students to write in the new world of technology?

► Interview friends or relatives about the types of writing required for their daily activities, including work and leisure. Once you have identified different kinds of writing from daily activity and the workplace, ask yourself, "How can teachers (especially in your content area) prepare students for the kinds of writing they will encounter later in life?"

► Keep a log of the kinds of writing in which you engage in a single day. How did you learn to write in these ways? What are some ways in which you can prepare your students for these kinds of writing?

► Observe a classroom and log the kinds of writing that you observe. Describe ways in which students are helped to perform in their writing. For example, how do teachers model what they expect to see in students' writing? How do they provide for practice and feedback? Describe how you will assign writing and offer students help with being successful.

Compare the results of your study with those of others who are reading this book.

As quickly as we prepare students for writing in today's world, the demands of writing change, and we and our students must adapt to the changes. Writing these days, individuals alternate between typing in web addresses, selecting addresses from a Favorites folder, or doing Internet-based library and web research. Sometimes, we select journal articles from lists of electronic journals and download articles appropriate to the learning project or task. Once the documents have been captured on the computer, we highlight or copy information from the articles for later use. Later, this information gets incorporated into a final project text, complete with graphic and other digital representations. How do students learn how to adapt to writing in this technological environment? The answer to this question is to teach students strategies for writing to learn.

Building Bridges: An Example of Writing to Learn

Writing to learn requires clear goals and expectations, a strong sense of purpose, a good understanding of audience, and lots and lots of explanation, demonstration, and guided practice (Graham, 2006). Consider this content area example: A science teacher wants her students to use writing to represent their ideas and conclusions in a lesson about bridges. The students are studying what makes bridges strong and beautiful. Their assignment is to write a recommendation and set of plans to build a bridge over a river to connect two local communities. The culmination of this project is a report in front of a real panel consisting of an engineer, an architect, and a city planner, who will react to the students' recommendations and plans.

To make their recommendations, the students visit the PBS website for the program *Building Big: Bridges* (www.pbs.org/wgbh/buildingbig/bridge). This website contains volumes of information about types of bridges, geometric figures that are the building blocks of various bridges, and people's preferences for bridges used for different purposes. There are also web links to sites related to bridges from all over the world.

Before turning her students loose to do this assignment, the teacher takes some time to offer some advice and ask some important questions:

"To do this assignment well, you are going to have to be very thorough in analyzing and comparing different bridge designs. So, let's think about how you are going to collect the information that you are going to need."

The teacher demonstrates different ways of keeping notes and drawing pictures, using her laptop computer and an overhead projector. She then discusses ways in which students can record data in their notebooks or on their laptops, demonstrating notes and sketching pictures of bridges and bridge components.

Next, the teacher turns her students' attention to the purpose and audience for the writing:

"Now, remember, you are trying to convince our panel about the best kind of bridge. What kinds of things should you focus on to convince them?"

The teacher directs discussion to what makes bridges beautiful as well as what makes them expensive. She also discusses the jobs of the individual panel members—the audience for their reports. The teacher records the students' hunches, using the overhead projector. Next, students write down their observations in their notebooks or on their laptops.

Now it is time for students to launch their own investigations. While students are working, the teacher circulates to answer questions and make sure students remain focused on the writing task (take a position on what would be the best bridge for the communities), the purpose (convince the community members about the better bridge), and the audience (various community members who are concerned about the appearance and cost of the bridge). When students become confused or go off track, the teacher redirects them, sometimes offering a new example or way of thinking about the assignment.

By now, this pattern of instruction should be very familiar. Writing skill—like vocabulary, comprehension, and reasoning skills—benefits from direct instruction, demonstration, feedback, and practice. In short, do not just assign writing. Take time to show students how to write to learn.

Teaching Students to Become Strategic Writers

Strategic writers are able to do these three things:

1. Apply knowledge about writing and powerful skills and strategies involved in the writing process, including planning, writing, revising, and editing

2. Monitor and manage their own writing

3. Maintain positive attitudes about writing and themselves as writers (Harris et al., 2003)

So the effective teaching of writing is anything that helps students to develop greater knowledge about writing, increases their ability to manage writing, and promotes positive attitudes about writing. The following research-based principles promote these goals for students:

▶ *Whenever assigning writing, talk with students about how they are going to respond to the assignment.* If possible, demonstrate different ways to approach writing assignments. Writing out a proof in geometry, analyzing an experiment, composing the lyrics for a song, and writing a persuasive essay all require different ways of thinking and responding. Share with students some ways in which you have learned to write in response to these tasks.

▲ Building opportunities for students to review each other's writing and providing feedback when ever possible encourages them to think critically about their own writing.

▶ *Ask students to write for real purposes and audiences.* Authentic writing is the writing that takes place all around us. For example, a teacher might say, "I'm asking you to write a persuasive essay, trying to convince the assistant principal to use the soda machine money for something the school really needs. What are some reasons we could use? What needs would we want to satisfy?"

Help students to break free of the idea that writing is just an academic event. To do this, consider email, the media (television, newspapers, and magazines), feature articles, editorials, reviews, critiques, or even instant messaging as fair game for writing in your content area. Think about occupations that grow from study in your content area—musicians, scientists, lawyers, teachers, computer scientists, politicians, medical workers, professional writers and programmers, and tool and die makers, to name just a few—and incorporate the writing that individuals perform in those occupations: reviews, detailed reports and descriptions, directions, persuasive speeches and essays, and personal narratives.

▶ *Provide many opportunities for individualized feedback and conversation about writing.* Frequent opportunities for your students to write, to respond to each other's writing, and to talk about what they are writing will help them to become better writers. Doing this can seem like a nearly impossible task for secondary school teachers who deal with 140-plus students each day. But remember that you are not the only audience. In fact, you should not serve as the only audience if you want students to get used to writing for many different audiences. Give informal feedback whenever you are walking around while students are writing. Build opportunities for students to give each other feedback into your writing assignments. To consider these principles in action, go back and review the example about building bridges in the previous section. How did the science teacher explain the assignment in ways that would help her students as writers? In what ways were her students writing for real purposes and audiences? How did the teacher provide opportunities for individualized feedback and conversation? Teaching Today's Learners offers some ways to create a positive environment for writing for students with special needs.

Guiding Students' Writing to Learn

The following sections explain many ways for guiding students' writing to learn in your content area. The sections are organized according to the different research-based learning strategies used for writing to learn: planning, writing, reviewing, and revising. Refer to the graphic overviews of learning and teaching strategies for writing as you read.

Teaching Students How to Plan Their Writing

A plan consists of goals and ways of achieving our goals. When we write, it helps tremendously if we are clear about the task at hand, our audience, and the potential product. Good writers formulate specific goals while sketching out a mental road map for how they will write. As a successful student, you probably have lots of experiences with planning for writing. By sharing your experiences in planning, you can help your students to learn what you know. The following sections detail a number of specific approaches for teaching planning. Remember that your ultimate goal for developing learning strategies for planning should be to help students increase their knowledge and ability to plan for writing on their own.

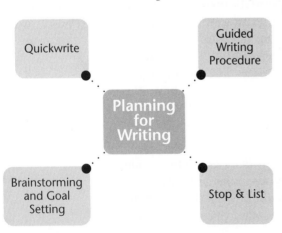

Teaching Today's Learners

Qualities of Classrooms That Support Special Needs Learners with Their Writing

Select one or two of the following principles and explain how you would implement them specifically in your classroom:

▶ A literate classroom environment in which students' written work is prominently displayed, the room is packed with reading and writing material, and word lists adorn the walls

▶ Daily writing with students working on a wide range of writing tasks for multiple audiences, including writing at home

▶ Extensive efforts to make writing motivating by setting an exciting mood, creating a risk-free environment, allowing students to select their own writing topics or modify teacher assignments, developing assigned topics that are compatible with students' interests, reinforcing students' accomplishments, specifying the goal for each lesson, and promoting an "I can" attitude

▶ Regular teacher-student conferences concerning the writing topic the student is currently working on, including the establishment of goals or criteria to guide the student's writing and revising efforts

▶ A predictable writing routine in which students are encouraged to think, reflect, and revise

▶ Overt teacher modeling of the process of writing as well as positive attitudes toward writing

▶ Cooperative arrangements by which students help each other plan, draft, revise, edit, or publish their written work

▶ Group or individual sharing in which students present work in progress or completed papers to their peers for feedback

▶ Instruction covering a broad range of skills, knowledge, and strategies

▶ Follow-up instruction to ensure mastery of targeted writing skills, knowledge, and strategies

▶ Integration of writing activities across the curriculum and the use of reading to support writing development

▶ Frequent opportunities for students to self-regulate their behavior during writing, including working independently, arranging their own writing space, and seeking help from others

▶ Teacher and student assessment of writing progress, strengths, and needs

▶ Periodic conferences with parents and frequent communications with home about the writing program and students' progress as writers

Source: Graham, S., Harris, K., & Larsen, L. (2001). Prevention and intervention of writing difficulties for students with learning disabilities. *Learning Disabilities Research and Practice, 16*(2), 74–84.

Quick-Writes. A Quick-Write is a form of impromptu writing that stimulates brainstorming (Moore et al., 2003). Quick-Writes help students to quickly put ideas and emotions down on paper. The writing itself is an unpolished draft that is often produced in response to some stimulus, such as a picture, brief text, or a discussion. Controversial writing from the Internet and magazine articles and even your own writing can all be the source of Quick-Writes. Quick-Writes can be a good way to start a lesson ("Let's quickly write down everything we know about the federal government") or to end a lesson ("Now let's use a Quick-Write to summarize everything we know about mathematical patterns").

Brainstorming and Goal Setting. The purpose of brainstorming and goal-setting activities is to make writing much more informed and goal-directed right from the start. In Chapter 8, we examined techniques that are useful for brainstorming as an aid to reading, such as List-Group-Label, semantic mapping, and graphic organizers. The same kinds of activities can be put to work to promote brainstorming and goal setting for writing.

Figure 11.2 depicts the results of a brainstorming session around the topic of the value of space travel. The science teacher who constructed

Figure 11.2

Brainstorming for writing about the value of space travel.

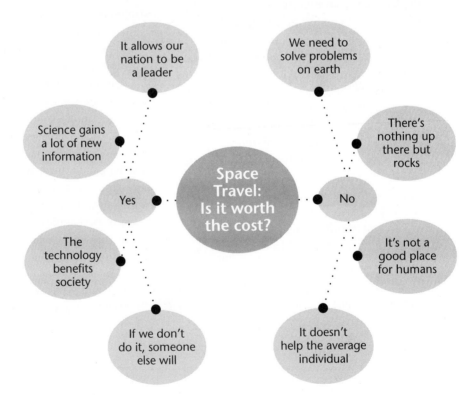

this semantic map with her students wanted to create an opportunity for them to consider the science underlying space travel but also the implications of the science for individuals and society as a whole. She also wanted her students to consider both sides of the issue.

The teacher began the brainstorming session with a quick review of the science content that students had already studied: scientific discoveries and consumer byproducts that have been developed because of space travel in the past. Next, she introduced the central question for the writing: Is space travel worth the cost? The teacher asked students to brainstorm about the question, considering "yes" and "no" to be two different ways to answer the question. She explained that brainstorming and mapping were particularly useful for planning in advance of writing, particularly when the writing can get complicated, as with this question. As students offered answers, their responses were clustered according to positive and negative responses to the question. Notice in this example how the teacher is demonstrating effective practices for strategy instruction: naming the strategy—brainstorming—and modeling for students how to use the strategy for a particular purpose: writing.

The teacher next explained how the brainstorming placed students in a good position to set goals for their writing. She asked them to consider writing an opinion letter to the editor of the local newspaper about funding for NASA. The class discussed whether the readers of the newspaper might be in favor of or against funding more space travel. Next, the teacher explained, students needed to decide which side of the question they would argue: in favor of or against more space travel. Finally, though students would argue one position over another, the teacher suggested that they still needed to acknowledge the opposing opinion in their essay.

The teacher wrote a sample letter with the class to model ways for students to translate the brainstorming chart into their own letters. Over time, students learned to brainstorm, set goals, and transform their ideas into other kinds of writing with other kinds of topics and audiences. Whenever her students were working on their writing, this teacher observed and provided feedback and guidance. The sequence demonstrated here (explain and model the strategy, provide practice and feedback) is the best way to turn students into experts with brainstorming and goal setting in support of their writing.

The Guided Writing Procedure. The Guided Writing Procedure (GWP) is designed to activate students' prior knowledge and thinking about a topic before they write (Smith & Bean, 1980). The GWP has been shown to be particularly useful for English language learners who are trying to relate their oral language to writing in English (Searfoss et al.,

1981). The goals of the GWP are to stimulate students' thinking about what they know and to get students to consider the relative importance of Big Ideas and supporting details before they write. In short, the GWP takes off where brainstorming ends, by helping students learn how to prioritize and support their ideas.

Begin the GWP by asking students to brainstorm any ideas they have related to a particular topic. For example, a music teacher initiated her students to this technique by asking them to listen to the Led Zeppelin song "Stairway to Heaven" to help them understand musical expression and appreciation. The students were asked to come up with words that captured their reactions to the music. Some of the students compared the song to a "beautiful symphony," some thought parts of it sounded like "church music," and still others felt that the entire song was "garbage." Next, students were asked to point to particular parts of the song that were responsible for their impressions. Some students pointed to the change in movements or melodies that reminded them of a symphony. The flute at the beginning reminded some students of the folk music at their local church. A more disapproving group of students said that it sounded like the school band when they were warming up.

Next, the teacher asked students to decide which ideas were major ones and which were details. The major ideas, the students agreed, were their opinions about the song: the song sounds like a symphony, the song sounds like a church hymn, and the song sounds terrible. The supporting details consisted of features of the song that contributed to students' impressions—the song has many movements or changes like a symphony, the song uses flutes like folk music in a church hymn, and the song suffers from a lot of loud banging around and shrill guitars and vocals. The teacher worked with her students to organize these ideas into several graphic organizers (see Figure 11.3).

The teacher then asked her students to write a paragraph or two based on their ideas now represented on the organizer. Each paragraph, she suggested, should specify at least one Big Idea supported by several details. Students chose one organizer that reflected their individual opinion and then wrote their paragraph.

Numerous follow-up or extension activities are possible with the Guided Writing Procedure. Some teachers prefer to have students evaluate their writing using a simple checklist like the one in Figure 11.4. Some use this experience as a springboard to other teaching and learning experiences, such as listening to other kinds of music, reading, or doing research. An extremely useful follow-up would be to have students brainstorm on yet another topic, followed by paragraph writing that builds on

A+RISE

Click on A+RISE–WIDA ELP Standard Strategy in the MyEducationLab (www.myeducationlab .com) for your course. Next, select the Strategy Card Index tab, scroll to Writing for Grades 6–12 and select the Guided Writing for ELLs strategy.

Figure 11.3 Graphic organizers depicting opinions and supporting details about "Stairway to Heaven."

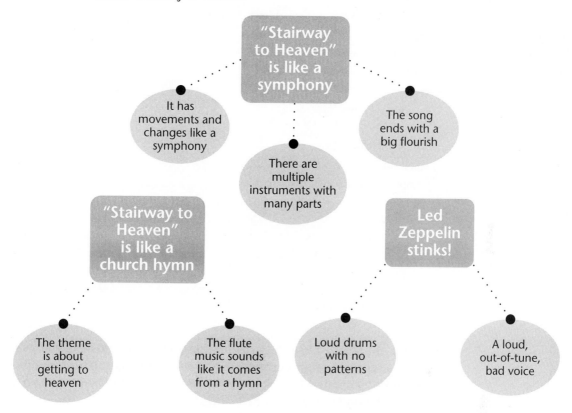

this planning technique. This will give students more practice with the transition from thinking and planning to writing.

Stop & List. **Stop & List** was developed to teach students with learning disabilities how to analyze writing assignments and how to plan and organize their responses (Troia & Graham, 2002). Though beneficial for students with learning disabilities, Stop & List is a good way to help all students stop and think before they rush into completing a writing assignment. Practice with this kind of instructional activity could also help students to become more organized in their responses to writing tasks on state competency and proficiency tests (Conley, 2005; Conley & Gritter, 2007).

Click on A+RISE – WIDA ELP Standard Strategy in the MyEducationLab (www.myeducationlab .com) for your course. Next, select the Strategy Card Index tab, scroll to Writing for Grades 6–12 and select the Graphic Organizers strategy.

Figure 11.4

A simple checklist for evaluating Guided Writing Procedure paragraphs.

Writing Checklist

(✔ = OK; 0 = Needs improvement; ? = Can't tell)

Ideas

Clear topic or opinion _____

Clear supporting details _____

Style _____

Shows variety in:

Word choice _____

Sentence length _____

Mechanics

Complete sentences _____

Capitalization _____

Punctuation _____

Spelling _____

The term *Stop & List* is an acronym for steps in identifying the purposes of a writing assignment, setting appropriate goals, brainstorming ideas, and organizing ideas. Some teachers spell out the acronyms on a chart like the one in Figure 11.5.

Figure 11.6 depicts a mathematics test item from a state test. Let's consider ways to use Stop & List to help students prepare to write in response to the test item. Notice first how the test item has many different parts. The first job is to stop and analyze the question. Students do not automatically know how to do this. So the "Stop" part of looking at this mathematics task involves demonstrating how to uncover all of the purposes and major ideas underlying the question, as in the following example:

Purpose:

Andrea, the cashier, is stuck with a broken cash register.

Andrea has to calculate the price for the customer on a calculator.

The customer has one way to calculate the price, but it might not be correct.

SO ... To answer the questions, the student needs to help Andrea find the correct price to charge the customer.

Stop and	**L**ist
Think	**I**deas and
Of	**S**equence
Purposes	**T**hem

Figure 11.5

Stop & List chart.

The next job is to "List" the mathematical ideas (numbers and related concepts) and sequence them. Here are the givens:

1. The CD is normally 14 dollars.
2. The CD is on sale for 15 percent off.
3. Andrea needs to add 7 percent sales tax to the sales price.

The customer thinks that taking away 8 percent from the total price will save time, since 15 percent (discount) minus 7 percent (the sales tax) leaves only 8 percent left as the discount.

Andrea works as a cashier in a music store. A customer wants to pay for a CD that is on sale for 15% off the regular price of $14.00. The cash register is broken, and Andrea must calculate the price of the CD using only a calculator.

   A What is the sale price of the CD? Show or explain how you got your answer.
   B Andrea needs to add 7% sales tax to the sale price of the CD. What should Andrea charge the customer for the CD, including tax? Show or explain how you got your answer.
   C The customer told Andrea that she could save time by just taking 8% off the regular price of the CD, because 15% minus 7% is 8%. Is the customer right?

Explain your reasoning.

Figure 11.6

Using Stop & List with a mathematics problem.

Source: Massachusetts Comprehensive Assessment System.

In short, we need to calculate the price in order (take away 15 percent and add 7 percent) and then compare that price to taking away only 8 percent (the customer's suggestion). Once the test item has been broken down in this way, it becomes easier to appreciate the complexity of the item. But it also provides a list of steps to perform to successfully write in response to the question.

Consider another example, this time, from social studies (see Figure 11.7). *Stopping* and considering the purpose, the essay assignment asks students to take a position on whether or not a gas tax should be imposed to encourage fuel conservation. The form of the writing is a letter, and the audience is a congressional representative.

Listing the ideas for responding is relatively easy, since the ideas are listed in the essay assignment in a logical sequence:

1. Make a clear statement of your position.

2. Support your position with reasons, consisting of knowledge from history, geography, civics, or economics.

3. Explain your reasons in detail.

4. State a point of view opposite to your own and argue against it.

Figure 11.7

Using Stop & List with a social studies writing assignment.

Take a stand on the following public policy issue:

Should the United States Congress pass a tax that gradually raises the price of gasoline to 6 dollars per gallon, to encourage fuel conservation?

You may either support or oppose the tax to increase the price of gasoline. Write a letter to your congressional representative.

> You will be graded on the following criteria. Your letter must include
>
> - a clear and supported statement of your position;
> - supporting knowledge from history, geography, civics, or economics (it is not enough to state only your opinion);
> - a credible argument someone with the opposite point of view could use and an explanation that reveals the flaw in his or her argument.

Remember to: Use complete sentences.

State your position on the issue.

Explain your reasons in detail.

Explain how your supporting knowledge connects to your position.

Taking the opportunity to map out assignments in this fashion lays a foundation for students to understand how to Stop & List on their own. However, it is also important to provide students with plenty of guided practice and feedback as they learn the process. Teachers might wish to spend some time having students Stop & List a number of times without worrying about answering questions at first. Later, they can practice this strategy by using Stop & List and then connecting it to specific ways in which they are answering the questions.

Notice in both examples how there are opportunities to talk with students about how they are going to respond to the writing assignments. Notice also how the writing tasks represent real situations and/or involve real purposes and audiences. Providing practice and feedback is also essential for students to learn how to write on their own. Some students, particularly those who are experiencing learning difficulties, might need help with identifying purposes. When listing different parts of a writing assignment, students might not know the difference, for example, between taking a stand, supporting with evidence, summarizing, or explaining. It would help these students if teachers identify some specific purposes at first, offering less support as students get the idea about how to do this on their own. Writing instruction that does these things will pay off not only on classroom writing assignments but also on state tests and many kinds of future writing challenges.

Teaching Students How to Write

The students have a plan. They have brainstormed a topic. They have a mental image of what to write. What happens now? Experienced writers have strategies for translating their ideas into words, from referring back to their original plan to writing until their ideas get back on track. This is yet another point at which inexperienced or less skilled writers can stumble. How many times do writers start writing, only to feel as if they have fallen off a cliff with nowhere else to go? The following teaching activities deal with different ways of approaching writing, including strategies for getting unstuck when the words do not seem to flow.

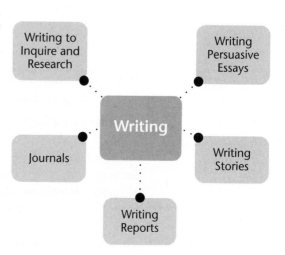

Research Brief

Writing

Translating plans into written language, better known as writing, makes a lot of demands on writers—word choice, syntax, textual connections, maintaining a sense of purpose, organization, clarity, consideration of possible readers' reactions, spelling, punctuation, and using the computer. Skilled writers make many different choices as well as frequent mental revisions in word choice and structure while translating ideas into written language (McCutchen, 2006). Students who get stuck on one area, such as handwriting for young children or word choice with older students, find it difficult to put all of the pieces together (Graham & Harris, 2005).

Journals. Journals were originally considered a very personal form of creative writing, useful only in English or social studies classes (Fulwiler, 1980). But journals can also be focused more narrowly on gathering and responding to the content of a lesson. Journal writing can be used to capture the "what" or the knowledge students are gaining from their studies. Research suggests that journals, especially those that summarize what students are learning, are successful means of writing in content areas because of the way in which journals encourage engagement with a subject (Newell, 2006).

One example of using journals to summarize learning originally comes from mathematics (Burns & Silbey, 2001). Teachers can ask students to write in their journals in response to these prompts:

▶ What I know about _____ so far is _____.

▶ What I am still not sure about is _____.

▶ What I would like to know more about is _____.

As should be clear, these prompts are useful in any content area in which teachers want to give students opportunities to write about what they know but also assess where students are in their learning.

Before deciding to use journals, it is important to consider specific purposes in using them, especially what students will gain from the experience. This step will support clear explanations about journals, what they are, their purpose, and how they will be used. For example, take some time to describe the desired format for the journal. Some teachers prefer more of a freehand approach without word or page limitations, focusing mostly on the journal prompts. Other teachers prefer a more highly structured approach, with specific questions tied to the content under study. Discuss with students how their journals will be used in class. The use of journals is greatly enhanced if teachers provide class time for students to write in them. Will they be read out loud and shared? Will they be graded in any way? Here are three approaches to using journals, followed by suggestions for responding and grading.

Learning Logs.   Learning logs are a form of journal writing that focuses specifically on what students are learning but also on how they are learning (Commander & Smith, 1996). For example, while asking students to write about *what* they know, teachers can also ask students to provide evidence or tell *how* they know or learned what they know. As Figure 11.8 illustrates, there are many useful alternatives for prompting students' reflections and writings, including debriefings after tests as well as reflections on personal behavior.

Figure 11.8 A learning log assignment overview.

Description
Your learning log is a written record of how you are "learning to learn." It is an opportunity for you to reflect on your awareness of how you are learning, rather than just what you are learning. As you will discover, we all learn in many ways. We learn from listening, doing, thinking about ourselves, and watching others. All of these learning activities can be included in your logs.

Topics
The topics for learning log entries will be assigned. Your entry must address the assigned topic. Topics will reflect our class discussions and will include, for example, your thoughts on your notetaking, collaboration with others, and your time management with assignments.

   Reflections on note taking: Reflect on your ability to take notes in our class and from our readings. What problems have you encountered? How have you tried to work out these problems?

   Test debriefing: In your learning log, reflect on your performance and preparation for the test. How was your grade? What kinds of questions did you miss? What will you do differently next time?

   Reflection on personal behavior: Describe a part of you that prevents you from becoming an "A" student. What are your bad habits or poor choices?

   Reading strategies: Describe your strategies for reading and comprehending the readings in our class. How do you organize your reading for long assignments? How do you maintain your concentration? How do you study?

   Work in groups: Throughout the past few weeks, you have been working in groups with fellow students. On the basis of your experiences, what insights have you gained about working in groups? When does it work for you? Why is group work sometimes unsuccessful for you?

Dialogue Journals. **Dialogue journals** are yet another form of journaling. In contrast to personal journals and learning logs, in which the focus is on students and what they are learning, dialogue journals involve partners—teachers and students or students and each other—exchanging information in writing. In the past, dialogue journals were written in notebooks, but more recently, dialogue journals have come to reside on the web through blogs, email, or instant messaging.

Dialogue journals are useful in content area classes because they provide (Holmes & Moulton, 1997) the following:

▶ Interaction about important topics

▶ Enhancement of reading skills

▶ Modeling varied and appropriate uses of language

▶ Interaction in a nonthreatening manner

▼ By incorporating writing into your instruction—whether as part of completing an assignment or to reflect on the content of a lesson—you can reinforce learning by helping students understand *how* they are learning.

These factors make the use of dialogue journals particularly relevant to the needs of second language learners as well as struggling readers and writers.

There are a number of ways to get dialogue journals started. Be sure to describe the purpose for dialogue journals as well as the procedures. For example, one teacher described the purpose for the dialogue journals this way (adapted from Atwell, 1998):

This notebook (dialogue journal) is a place for you and me to talk about what we are learning in our class, the things we are reading, our class discussions and our projects. You're going to write notes to me, and I'm going to write notes back to you.

In your notes, talk with me about what you are learning. Tell me what you are thinking, what you think you know, and why. Ask questions about things that you are uncertain about. Or tell me what you would like to know more about.

Double-Entry Journals. **Double-entry journals** provide a way for students to capture ideas and construct reactions while reading (Bromley, 1999). Double-entry journals help students to remember their reading and are also useful for later studying. Again, it is important to demonstrate for students how you would like them to work with double-entry journals. Explain the purpose:

> *"We're going to use double-entry journals to remember and make connections across the ideas from our reading in this class."*

Next, show students how to use double-entry journals:

> *"First, while you are reading, write down ideas that you think are important. Let me show you how to do this...."*

Demonstrate for students how to determine whether an idea is important, such as connecting to the Big Ideas of a lesson or unit or connecting to previously studied ideas (see Figure 11.9). Share with students the three ways in which they can make connections with the ideas from their reading, including:

▶ Text-to-text connections: "This reminds me of something else that I read ..."

▶ Text-to-self connection: "This reminds me of when I ..."

▶ Text-to-world connection: "This makes me think about ..."

Finally, as with the other teaching activities described throughout this book, provide students with opportunities for practice and feedback. An extension of double-entry journals involves their use with classroom discussions, labs, and projects as a record of the ideas students are learning and their reactions.

Responding to and Grading Journals. Students will also be more willing to write in their journals if teachers maintain a spirit of openness

Ideas from the Text	Reaction/Connection
p. 64 An ecosystem is an assembly of organisms living together in their environment.	*This makes me think about all of the families living in my neighborhood.*
p. 65 Ecosystems can be extremely fragile.	*I remember when we could not swim in our lake because of all of the waste dumping in our area.*
p. 66 The Everglades are an endangered ecosystem.	*I've seen places that remind me of the Everglades, like the wetlands near Lake Michigan. It would be terrible to lose places like that.*

Figure 11.9

A double-entry journal.

to students' questions and perspectives. Several specific practices support the nonthreatening nature of journals, including the following (Kirby & Liner, 1988):

► *Protect the privacy of each journal.* Do not read contributions out loud without permission of the author.

► *Respond actively and sincerely with students.* Avoid the temptation to correct students, responding instead with your own ideas and specific suggestions.

► *Be honest in your responses.* If students share language or situations that make you feel uncomfortable, tell them what you think is not appropriate.

► *Look for something positive.* Encourage students' ideas and avoid being sarcastic.

► *Keep journal writing special and interesting.* Maintain a specific time for journals. When interest wanes, take a break.

► *Do not make promises that you cannot keep.* It is impossible for teachers to respond to every student's journal every time they write. Involve students in responding to each other, responding yourself regularly in a pattern that is convenient.

Many teachers do not grade individual journals but offer credit for completed entries instead. In reviewing journals, focus on the content of the entries and what it tells about individual students and their understanding. Avoid giving students overly general feedback such as "Good job." Instead, give responses that reflect what students write and know.

Writing Reports. One would think that the act of writing a report is straightforward: simply recording or listing ideas or facts for presentation to an interested audience. One just puts the information in a letter, a paragraph, or a summary to convey a simple message. In reality, good reports require that information be gathered, selected, interpreted, and shaped for a particular audience—in short, "a process of translating raw data into meaningful text." (Fennick et al., 1993).

A way to help students with report writing is to follow some examples from the workplace. Recall that workplace writing is quite diverse, especially in comparison with typical school writing (see Figure 11.10). The reports that are required in the workplace range from announcements of upcoming events to detailed accounts of procedures and events. Consider a police report as just one example. An investigative report becomes the basis for legal action. Anyone who has observed police work in real life

The **GREATE ESCAPE!**	The History of the EPA	Some Companies Act Responsibly

How Famous Companies Evade the Environmental Protection Agency and What We Can Do About It!		Who Are the Bad Guys?
	The Problems of Toxic Waste	
		Getting Involved

Figure 11.10

An alternative report style.

or as depicted on reality television shows knows that police reporting can involve multiple forms of analysis, collaboration with others, and uses of computer and other kinds of technology as well as an awareness of multiple audiences. Errors in these kinds of reports can mean a loss of a criminal conviction, loss of a person's freedom, or even loss of life. In short, although real-world reports might not resemble the classic research paper, a report can represent quite a bit of observation and analysis.

To develop good report-writing skills in students, consider the following ideas. Emphasize classroom writing that resembles real work-place writing: brochures, newspapers and newsletters, press releases, official reports to key stakeholders, letters, and even web pages. In a science class, students could write up lab reports as press releases to the local community. Or consider a news account or police blotter report of what happened to the guilty party in a murder mystery. Or how about a report from a math class to Congress about the cost per mile of a trip to Mars? One way to gather ideas about these kinds of assignments is to form partnerships with local businesses so that students can learn about the authentic kinds of report writing that go on in the community.

Select some kinds of report writing that seem authentic and appropriate, and engage students in discussion about the important elements of the reports. Include a consideration of the following:

► Audience

► Collaboration with others

► Attention to timeliness and time constraints for the report

► Quality of editing (especially important for publicly available writing)

► Production of visually informative, appealing text, using available technology

Doing reports in this way with students not only will extend their understanding of content area knowledge but also will prepare them for the world of report writing beyond school.

Writing Stories. Jerome Bruner, a very wise psychologist, wondered what the curriculum would be like if stories continued to be emphasized beyond the elementary grades (Bruner, 1996). "Imagine," he said in a presentation, "if students read the story of Marie Curie's life, rather than just reading about her discoveries in a textbook." Bruner's idea is that stories better represent the fabric of life and, as such, make content area learning more memorable.

Although many adolescents have heard stories most of their lives and have experienced "stories" though watching television and playing video games, they might require help in developing stories on their own, especially in relation to their content area learning. One home economics teacher worked with stories as a way of helping students to get ready for a test on nutrition. The focus of the test was on what students had learned about proper nutrition, weight control, and physical fitness. Each student, the teacher explained, needed to tell a story about one individual's struggle with weight and nutrition.

To assist students with this task, the teacher spelled out these elements of a well-written story (Troia & Graham, 2002):

► *Setting:* where the story takes place

► *Problems:* the troubles or dilemmas experienced by people in the story

► *Actions:* what people in the story try to do, either successfully or unsuccessfully, to solve their problems

► *Consequences:* what happens as a result of the actions people take

► *Emotions:* how people feel as they experience the events of the story

The teacher explained each of these story elements and then asked students to recount stories, movies, or television shows, labeling the story elements as they retold the stories. After the teacher was convinced that students understood these components of stories, she asked them to prepare their stories about individual struggles with weight and nutrition.

Some of the students wrote about family members and friends and their own heart-wrenching struggles. Some wrote about harmful experiences with fad diets. As the students shared their stories, the teacher was able to observe how well her students understood the content of the weight and nutrition lessons. Consider stories as one way to help your students extend their knowledge while honing their writing skill.

Writing Persuasive Essays. Persuasive writing is writing that convinces or sways. It is about taking a stand and defending it. Many students do not know how to do this well, despite the importance of persuasive writing on state and national tests (Conley, 2005) as well as in success later in life, as in college and in the professional world.

D.A.R.E. is an acronym designed to help students write better persuasive essays (Troia & Graham, 2002). D.A.R.E. stands for the following:

- ▶ Develop a position statement.
- ▶ Add supporting facts or ideas.
- ▶ Report and refute opposite facts or ideas.
- ▶ End with a strong conclusion.

To teach this approach, introduce and explain each of the persuasive essay elements. Then present a sample persuasive essay written by you or a student, and work with students to identify the persuasive essay elements. Third, have students identify the elements on their own with another persuasive essay. Next, ask students to compose an oral essay in response to a persuasive prompt, such as "Should the school allow soft drink sales in the cafeteria?" As they say their response, have students identify each one of the persuasive elements. Finally, have students practice their understandings of persuasive essays in writing based on written essay prompts. The following example is one way of helping students to understand the difference between points of view and supporting evidence. Read the Connecting Standards and Assessment feature for more information about how persuasive writings skills can be important for performing on state tests.

Connecting Standards and Assessment

Persuasive Essays and State Tests

Most, if not all, state tests contain persuasive essays. Many of these essays require students to form points of view about Big Ideas and then support their points of view with smaller supporting details. It can be difficult for many students to understand the differences between big and small ideas. A helpful strategy is to use examples, such as the fingers on a hand, to illustrate Big Ideas (the whole hand) and smaller, supporting details (the fingers). Once students understand this analogy, it is time to transfer this understanding to writing in response to persuasive essay prompts.

Another important skill required for persuasive essays on state tests involves analyzing questions to create an appropriate response. Again, students need help with this skill. Teach students to identify important parts of essay questions and then examine what each part requires with respect to a response.

Yet another skill involves organizing an essay response. Most essay raters look for signs that students are answering the question, so the first sentence needs to use words from the question. Another important principle is to map out answers with respect to parts to the question. That way, students can be sure that they are thorough in their responses.

Many students forget to stop and think about what they know before responding. Teachers can help here by reinforcing a habit of stopping and thinking before putting pencil to paper.

The two most essential skills for persuasive essays on state tests consist of proving your point and providing supporting evidence. Although many students profess opinions, they do not always know how to prove what they think or compare their ideas with what others believe. Teachers need to help students learn these skills as well.

▶ **Learn more about these ideas by reading Chapter 7, "Building Lessons around Test-Taking Skills That Matter," in Connecting Standards and Assessment through Literacy (Conley, 2005), published by Pearson Education.**

Which of the following represent a statement that takes a position? Compare the statements and tell why one is more of a position that one could take than the other.

Passenger jets land at approximately 140 miles per hour.

Airplane travel has gotten increasingly expensive.

For the statement you selected as a position statement, identify two facts or ideas that you could use to support the statement
and two facts or ideas that would refute the statement.

I-Search Writing to Inquire and Research.

I-Search involves
students in investigations of topics in which they have an interest
or about which they have a need to know (Macrorie, 1988). I-Search
is an effective activity for English language learners, since it relies
on students' experiences and allows them to explore what is already
familiar to them (Alejandro, 1989). Investigations using I-Search can
be as broad as interviewing experts and family members, conducting
Internet searches, emailing noted authorities in a topical area, or just
old-fashioned library exploration. The approach is called I-Search because it is intended to help students learn to direct their own search for
information in advance of their writing. An I-Search involves four steps
(see Figure 11.11):

1. *Choose a topic.* Students select topics of personal interest. These topics
   can be related to a unit of study, or a topic could simply come from
   a student's own experiences. Students may falter even on this early
   step. Many students will stare at a blank piece of paper or computer
   screen with no idea about how to choose something to research or
   write about. A solution to this dilemma is to demonstrate with students how you might go about selecting a topic.

   For example, one teacher illustrated ways of choosing a topic
   by listing topics that she knew about: bicycling, running, traveling
   across the country, and preparing a family tree. Next, she compared
   the topics with respect to how much or how little she knew about
   each of the topics. Noting that she had just started biking and running but had more experience with traveling and her family tree, she
   chose to write about traveling. After demonstrating how to list topics
   and choose one that she knew more about, the teacher turned the
   responsibility over to her students. As students listed their own topics and compared them, the teacher circulated and guided them in
   their decisions.

| 1. Choose a Topic | 2. Plan Your Search | 3. Gather Information | 4. Develop a Product |

Figure 11.11

Steps in an
I-Search.

2. *Plan your search.* The emphasis in this approach has always been on taking a very broad perspective on sources of information. Consequently, live interviews, web searches, and traditional library searches are all possible. Of course, students might not be aware of all of the possibilities. Plan to model different ways of exploring a topic.

   The teacher who liked traveling used the Internet as her example of planning to research a topic. Offer students an entire range of possibilities for their research—interviews, magazines, and books, for instance—but also make time for demonstrating how to use these resources, as this teacher did. She demonstrated how several search engines, including Google (www.google.com) and Altavista (www.altavista.com), could be used to investigate different travel locations. She used Travelocity (www.travelocity.com) and Yahoo (www.yahoo.com) to show how she could plan travel to and from different locations. She demonstrated the Internet Public Library for Teens (www.ipl.org/div/teen/aplus), which offers an excellent step-by-step process for writing research papers. This is a website put together by librarians and researchers about how to do library and Internet research. Finally, the teacher modeled ways of taking notes during her search.

3. *Gather information.* The next phase in the I-Search process involves the actual information gathering. Because a great deal of the work has been modeled up to this point, it is time for the teacher to assume a different role, going from director to facilitator. Provide students with opportunities to do their research—on the Internet, in the library, or through interviews. Observe how well students emulate the ways you have demonstrated the brainstorming and research process. Offer feedback whenever necessary so that students can stay on track. Some students might discover that there is very little conventional or formally published writing on their topic. Guide students into exploring alternative sources, including the Internet or local experts. Use these times as opportunities to ask questions about what counts as authoritative or reliable information and what might be untrue or misleading.

4. *Develop a product.* The product of an I-Search can be as varied as the research itself. Remember that whatever the expectations, it is worth the time and effort to explain and demonstrate them. Consider web pages, formal papers, creative writing, poetry, blogs, and podcasts as several of many possible products emanating from an I-Search. The teacher who was interested in traveling, for example,

decided to create a web-based poster documenting her preferred steps in planning and taking a trip. She decided that her audience would be anyone who was interested in taking a trip on their own. She created her electronic poster while her students observed. She thought out loud as she designed each of the travel components. She wanted her students to see exactly how she made her choices among all of her available information. Next, students prepared and shared their own I-Search products. At the end of each product, the students listed their sources of information and briefly described what they had done to brainstorm and research their product.

An issue that sometimes emerges with projects such as the I-Search involves plagiarism. Plagiarism is the practice of claiming or implying original authorship of material that one has not actually created, such as when a person incorporates material from someone else's work into his or her own work without citing its source. With computer access and cutting and pasting so prevalent these days, not every student gets the idea about putting things in his or her own words or attributing quotes accurately to original sources. Students need to be taught the differences between plagiarism and appropriately using quotations and citations. Therefore, spend some time during the I-Search sequence showing students how to select information but also how to rephrase, quote, and provide proper citation for any researched information.

Teaching Students How to Review and Revise

Reviewing and revising can be one of the most difficult areas of writing for teachers as well as students. This is especially true if students see little reason for their writing other than handing it in to get a grade. A number of suggestions have already been provided for responding to students' journals and for guiding students as they practice various forms of writing. This section offers specific ways of focusing students' attention as they review and revise. Read the Research Brief for recent research on this important topic.

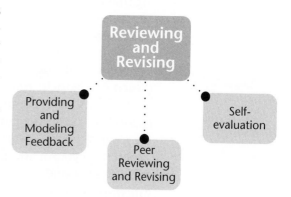

Reviewing and Revising

Reviewing is rereading to see whether the words on the page capture the original intent, to see where one is with the original plan, and to see whether more writing is needed. Nearly all writers review, but less experienced writers are often confused about what to look for. Experienced writers often revisit their original intent. Less experienced writers can get lost in the details or add extraneous ideas. **Revising** is changing one's mind while changing the text, noticing mismatches between the intent and the text and making changes, a process of restructuring and reshaping the writing, reconsidering the audience. Inexperienced writers often confuse revising (restructuring and reshaping ideas) with editing (correcting spelling and grammar). Inexperienced writers will simply recopy or retype when asked to revise because they are not very engaged with the messages in their writing or how to communicate well (Fitzgerald, 1992). Most students will not bother to review or revise or will do so ineffectively without effective feedback from teachers or peers (Beach & Friedrich, 2006).

Providing and Modeling Effective Feedback. The most familiar kind of feedback from a student's perspective comes from teachers. Many teachers agonize over how to provide effective feedback and how much feedback is enough. Keep in mind that the goal of your feedback should be to help students become more independent writers.

To model effective writing, teachers can demonstrate strategies for coping with common writing problems, such as confusing writing, writing that fails to adequately explain, or presenting unsupported opinions. Teachers do not help when they only mark problems with a red pen. Instead, it is important to show students how to address these problems—by adding clarifying details, providing elaboration for information or events, or learning how to supply supporting evidence for opinions (Beach & Friedrich, 2006).

Students prefer comments from teachers that explain why something is good or bad in their writing and that suggest specific ways for making improvements. Overly general comments are things like "awkward," "tighten up your writing," or "unsupported idea." Instead, focus on specific ways for students to improve, such as pointing to places where they can provide more information or make changes. An effective way to model ways of dealing with common writing problems in your class is to use a sample of students' writing, with permission from the students, to demonstrate issues such as poorly supported opinions or confusing writing. After a few sessions of reviewing writing in this way, provide students with practice in reviewing their writing with each other.

Another way to provide and model effective feedback is through teacher conferences. During these conferences, teachers can describe reactions to students' writing, their intentions, and their explanations in response to written feedback. For their part, students can share their purposes for writing, practice self-assessment, and develop alternative revisions (Frank, 2001). Often, teachers divide up these conferences for various purposes: prewriting (developing strategies for gathering ideas), writing or drafting (translating ideas into written words), and editing (focusing on clarity and proofreading). The thought of having conferences with a full day's complement of 140 students has been daunting. But technology, particularly in the form of online comments through email attachments, instant messaging, or blogs, has made prospects for regular conferences much brighter.

Peer Reviewing and Revising. Because teachers often do not have adequate time to provide feedback for all of their students' writing and because students need practice evaluating writing, peer reviewing and revising are useful options. Two cautions need to be expressed here: Peers are not a substitute for explicit teacher feedback, and peer reviewing and revising are effective only when students are trained (Simmons, 2003). Without training, students might give overly general or judgmental feedback, or they might hold back criticism for fear of jeopardizing their friendships.

One form of effective training involves teacher modeling, as discussed in the preceding section. Teachers need to show students how to provide constructive feedback, and constructive feedback can lead to substantive revisions. If you have already been providing students with a great deal of modeling for reviewing and revising their own papers, the priority becomes showing students how to do with each other what you have taught them.

A second form of training involves working cooperatively with peers. Explain to students that the purpose of peer revising is to help one another get better at writing. Engage students in role-playing different situations in which writing problems and solutions are discussed. Then provide feedback as students move into collaborating with one another on their writing.

Self-evaluation. Not all approaches to student self-evaluation are equally effective. True, it can be very easy to design a self-assessment with very simple writing projects. For example, asking students to write

A+RISE

Click on A+RISE – WIDA ELP Standard Strategy in the MyEducationLab (www.myeducationlab .com) for your course. Next, select the Strategy Card Index tab, scroll to Writing for Grades 6–12 and select the Revising Techniques strategy.

a five-sentence paragraph about their favorite topic could yield a very simple self-evaluation: Did you write five sentences and was the paragraph about your favorite topic? Teachers could create a simple chart or checklist to ensure that all of the elements of the writing assignment are complete.

However, this kind of self-evaluation says more about *completing* the assignment than it does about whether the assignment was completed *effectively*. Engaging students in self-evaluation of the quality of their writing requires a different approach. As they assign writing, teachers need to remind students that the focus is on producing a well-written product. To do this, ask students, "If you do this writing well, what will it look like?" or "What are you going to need to think about and write about to do this writing well?" Questions like these introduce the notion of quality into students' self-evaluation.

Teachers need to model effective reviewing and revising strategies all along, reminding students to use these strategies with their own writing. Students may also benefit from web-based resources such as Paradigm Online Writing Assistant (www.powa.org), Online Resources for Writers from Boise State University (www.ccc.commnet.edu/writing/writing.htm), and the University of Kansas Writing Center (www.writing.ku.edu). Other websites provide guidance with topic selection, word choice, and sentence, paragraph and essay construction (see Figure 11.12).

Figure 11.12 Online resources for student writing, reviewing, and revising.

- Dictionary.com (www.dictionary.com): allows students to search multiple dictionaries at the same time
- Merriam-Webster Dictionary (www.m-w.com\dictionary)
- LookWAYup Dictionary/Thesaurus and Translation (lookwayup.com/free/dictionary): is a large online English dictionary that tolerates small spelling errors.
- iTools (www.itools.com): contains links to a number of dictionaries, thesauruses, and other language tools.
- Roget's Thesaurus (http://thesaurus.reference.com): facilitates comparisons among many different words.
- Your Dictionary (www.yourdictionary.com): provides a source of definitions as well as word games.
- Webgrammar (www.webgrammar.com): is a website devoted to grammar.
- The Editorial Department (www.editorialdepartment.com): offers online help with self-editing.
- The Writer's Block (www.pvc.maricopa.edu/%7Ebutler): contains links to resources for writing, grammar, research, and reference.
- Word Surfing (www.wordsurfing.co.uk): provides numerous links for language learning and use in writing, especially for English language learners.

Grading Students' Writing

One of the challenges that naturally comes from getting more students to write and having them generate more written products concerns how to grade all of the writing. The first response to this dilemma should be some careful deliberation about what needs to be graded and which kinds of writing serve more of a learning purpose. For example, writing like I-Search serves an instructional purpose, to guide research. Teachers might not choose to grade instructional writing, or even some kinds of journal writing, deciding to focus more on students' development and dispositions. Writing assignments, on the other hand, like a research paper, a persuasive essay, or a research paper lend themselves readily to evaluation and grading. So, first decide which kinds of writing should be graded and why.

The next decision concerns how to grade students' writing. The desired approach is to first closely examine the writing assignment, like this one in a mathematics class:

> *Now that you each have built a model dream house, and you have reviewed other students' houses, write a persuasive essay about the best way to plan, design, and build a dream house. Include as your reasons considerations for cost, size of the house, and the materials you chose for your house versus other ways you could have built your house. You must take a stand about the best way to build a dream house, give three reasons for your opinion, and support your opinion with your experiences building your dream house and observing other houses.*

Notice how the writing assignment has some recognizable parts: Students must:

1. Take a stand.
2. Support their stand with three reasons.
3. Support their reasons with experiences building their dream house.
4. Support their reasons based on observations of other houses.

Ideally, the teacher will want to discuss the question and these components with students, perhaps even having students generate the list. An important part of the conversation before students write can be discussion about what an essay might look like if it did each of these things really well. This will sharpen students' sense for what a quality response might look like as students start to write. The teacher could then construct an evaluation rubric.

	Not Evident	Sometimes but not clear	Clearly Evident
Take a stand	1	3	5
Support the stand with three reasons.	1	3	5
Support reasons with experiences building their own house.	1	3	5
Support reasons with observations of others' houses.	1	3	5

Note how the evaluation rubric also contains points for scoring. The conversation with students helps clarify exactly how the rubric will be applied. The point values are arbitrary; a teacher could use numbers on a 10 point scale—3, 5, and 10—or even a one hundred point scale—0, 50, and 100. Another choice is to have more columns to make even finer distinctions. A goal should be to create a functional evaluation tool that everyone—both teachers and their student—all understand. Doing so makes the evaluation process run much smoother. Students gain a better idea about what is expected of them and teachers have clear criteria to use for grading, and so can get right to the point when assigning grades. Approaching grading in this manner can help teachers avoid grading overload when it comes to writing.

Summary

These days, writing to learn means more than just an ordinary school term paper. It involves using writing to learn in various ways across the curriculum and in preparation for everyday writing, including writing that will be required in the workplace and throughout the digital world. Students must learn how to be strategic in their writing, altering their approach according to different genres, purposes, situations, and tasks. Learning to do this requires instruction and modeling from teachers and peers in planning, writing, reviewing, and revising. There are many different approaches and different kinds of writing activities that should be part of every teacher's writing instruction. Remember that the goal is for students to develop into independent, strategic writers.

Special Projects

1. Consider what it means to be a skilled writer in your content area. Make a list of the writing skills that you use routinely to be a successful student. Make another list of ways in which you can help your students to acquire those skills.

2. Gather examples of writing from your own content area. These examples should come from writing that occurs in the outside world. Discuss how you could use these examples to acquaint students with real-world writing in your content area.

3. Select several of the writing activities described in this chapter, and incorporate them into a lesson or unit of study in your content area. In doing this, what have you learned about ways to integrate writing into your content area teaching?

4. Journals and the variations of journals described in this chapter (learning logs, dialogue journals, double-entry journals) are often easily incorporated into many content areas. Describe how you would use journals in your classroom.

5. Writing is an important part of many state and national tests. Gather some sample writing items from the state or national tests in your content area. What are some ways in which you can help your students with writing and these tests?

Praxis Practice

Working with Questions to Prepare for the Praxis Reading across the Curriculum Test

Multiple Choice Questions

1. What are some key features of journal writing?

   a. All journaling should be open ended.

   b. Journals should only be for keeping notes.

   c. Journals should never be shared in the classroom.

   d. Journal writing can be for many different purposes.

2. Students should be shown how to write strategically because:

    a. Teachers do not always know what they want from students.

    b. Writing is handed in to teachers who have specific ideas in mind.

    c. Writing can differ according to different purposes and genres.

    d. College writing is demanding and very uniform.

3. What are the best ways to assign writing to students?

    a. Have students do a lot of writing warm-ups before you assign the writing.

    b. Write an answer to your writing assignment before assigning the writing.

    c. Make sure the assignment has clearly specified expectations.

    d. Utilize writing assignments that come from the teacher's manual.

Constructed Response Question

1. Ms. Angeline wants her students to complete a research paper but needs to consider a number of ways to get her students ready to write. Describe the approach you would recommend to her for preparing her students through the process all the way to creating and evaluating a written product.

Suggested Readings

Graham, S., & Harris, K. (2005). *Writing better: Effective strategies for teaching students with learning difficulties.* Baltimore: Brooks.

Samway, K. (2006). *When English language learners write.* Portsmouth, NH: Heinemann.

Trefethen, M., & Smart, R. (2005). *Direct from the disciplines: Writing across the curriculum.* Portsmouth, NH: Boynton Cook.

Go to Topic 4: Writing in the MyEducationLab (www.myeducationlab.com) for your course, where you can:

- Find learning outcomes for Topic 4: Writing along with the national standards that connect to these outcomes.

- Complete Assignments and Activities that can help you more deeply understand the chapter content.

- Apply and practice your understanding of the core teaching skills identified in the chapter with the Building Teaching Skills and Dispositions learning units.

- Examine challenging situations and cases presented in the IRIS Center Resources.

Go to the Topic A+RISE in the MyEducationLab (www.myeducationlab.com) for your course. A+RISE® Standards2Strategy™ is an innovative and interactive online resource that offers new teachers in grades K-12 just in time, research-based instructional strategies that:

- Meet the linguistic needs of ELLs as they learn content

- Differentiate instruction for all grades and abilities

- Offer reading and writing techniques, cooperative learning, use of linguistic and nonlinguistic representations, scaffolding, teacher modeling, higher order thinking, and alternative classroom ELL assessment

- Provide support to help teachers be effective through the integration of listening, speaking, reading, and writing along with the content curriculum

- Improve student achievement

- Are aligned to Common Core Elementary Language Arts standards (for the literacy strategies) and to English language proficiency standards in WIDA, Texas, California, and Florida.

12 Building Literacy and Community from Inside and Outside the Classroom

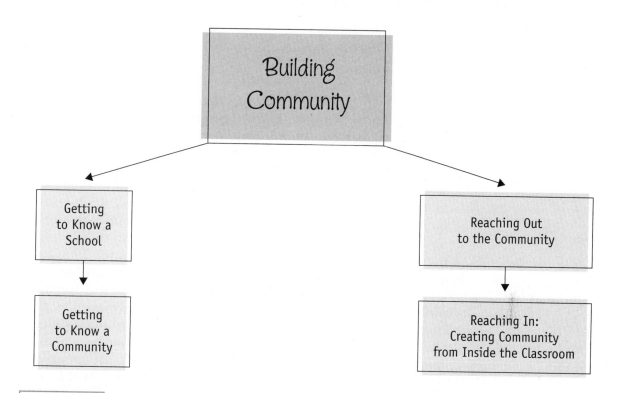

Think about what the words *family* and *community* mean to you. If you are in an undergraduate or graduate class, the students around you probably have different kinds of associations with those words. Now consider what *school* has meant to you. Did you feel that your family and community experiences were supportive of what happened in school? Were your school experiences confirming and compatible with your family and community? If the answers to both questions are "yes," then you were indeed fortunate.

Parents and other community members provide unique contributions to students' education. Research shows that the more parents are involved in their children's education, the more likely are the chances of the children's success in school (Epstein et al., 2002; Henderson & Berla, 1994; Miedel & Reynolds, 1999). Classrooms are places where notions about family, community, and curriculum can come together.

There are a number of reasons why this vision does not always approach reality, however. Despite the value of including parents as partners in their children's education, it can take a long time to build the trust necessary for parents to feel like partners in their children's education. There can be little, if any, connection or contact between home and school. In fact, tremendous gaps can emerge between home and school (e.g., "My Dad and Mom say this is so, but my teacher says that is so"). Some critics argue that these gaps pose insurmountable challenges to students, especially when they are forced to make painful decisions about their families, their communities, and their own identities (McCaleb, 1994). Some students, whose homes are fraught with poverty, where the language is not English, where the culture is different from the dominant culture, experience a devaluing of their home and community when they come to school. Far too often, parent conferences become battle zones that are symptomatic of the conflicts between school and community.

So how can teachers build community within the classroom—one that values family, community, and school alike? Not surprisingly, one answer to this question involves opening up communication with students, parents, and community members. It means exchanging the traditional role of teacher as ultimate authority for a role that is more collaborative and guiding. It means communicating clearly about goals and how goals are connected to students. It means welcoming insights, knowledge, and feelings that come from students, their families, and the community and finding opportunities to value students' backgrounds. Again, literacy is at the center here: the languages and literacies of families and communities and how teachers invite those literacies in so that all of today's students grow and learn. This chapter is about building community.

Research Brief

Partnering with Parents and the Community

Though developing effective approaches to parent involvement can be challenging, particularly in middle school and high school, it can be well worth the effort (Sanders et al., 1999). In a study of 423 parents at six high schools in Maryland—two rural, two urban, and two suburban—the results were as follows:

▶ Parents appreciated efforts by the schools to assist parenting, including learning how to interact with adolescents and work together on learning activities such as homework.

▶ Parents tended to participate more at school when school practices encouraged volunteering and participation in school decision making.

▶ Good communication between home and school was a key factor in home and community involvement.

Getting to Know a School and the Community

For many teachers, learning about a school and the community is a prudent step in preparing for a job interview. However, the task of learning about a school and the community does not end with getting the teaching job. Given the complexity of school and community relationships and the likelihood of change in schools and communities, this learning needs to be an ongoing process. The more you know about your school and the community, the better prepared you are to build on the experiences of students and their families.

Getting to Know a School

Let's start with the process of learning about schools through websites, newsletters, interviews, and onsite visits and interviews.

School Websites. Consider the home page for the Lansing School District (Figure 12.1). Notice how the website incorporates an invitation for the local community to participate in the schools, references to the world of technology, and connections to career possibilities. The website also contains inviting pictures and has a clear organizational scheme to depict the school district's priorities: students, parents, administrators, teachers, and the outside world. By following this district's links, you will find useful information, including library and Internet resources for teachers and students, tips for parents in helping their children, important parent and community organizations, and important dates for school and community meetings. Inspired by national and state legislation aimed at accountability, many websites provide information about their goals, curriculum standards, and test scores. Some websites include online chats and threaded discussions about school issues. School websites can offer a perspective about the unique character of a school and district as well as what educators and others in the community consider to be important.

School Newsletters. School newsletters also offer special insights into the priorities of a school. Consider the newsletter in Figure 12.2 on pages 376–377. It depicts a mix of topics from the reality of schools: state funding, a vignette about a teacher who went the extra mile for a student, and information about student-led portfolios and science, music, and drama events. It says nothing about sports, which are covered in

Figure 12.1

Learning about a school or school district by visiting websites.

a separate newsletter in this school and district. The newsletter depicts considerable support for teachers. It also suggests that the administrators care about keeping the public informed about impending financial challenges and their commitment to maintain high standards, regardless. Notice also the announcement about the Homework Hotline that appears before the information about the National Honor Society, indicating a concern not only for successful students but also for those who are struggling. In presenting a realistic picture, this newsletter demonstrates a sincere commitment to education, both in confronting dilemmas and in providing opportunities for students. In what ways does the content of this newsletter reflect the realities faced by schools you attended?

Schools and Curriculum Standards. Though all schools face similar pressure from current educational reforms and increased testing, there still can be considerable diversity in the curriculum standards from school to school. For example, Figure 12.3 on page 378 compares the science standards from two different districts. Notice how the different versions of the standards suggest differences in what students are expected to know. The first set of standards focuses on reasoning, observation, modeling, and experimental procedures for biology and chemistry. The second set of standards emphasizes the connections between science, other disciplines, and real-life situations. For the first set of standards, one can envision more of a detailed, analytic approach to teaching and learning. The second set of standards poses more of an open-ended exploration of science through reading and writing. How might classrooms appear different if teachers followed one set of standards versus the other? What would the teaching look like? What would the tests look like? Describe a typical classroom day in Buffalo organized around the science standards. Next, describe a typical science classroom day in Austin. The point here is that every set of standards poses different implications with respect to teaching and literacy. Knowing how to translate standards into classroom practices is an important skill for any teacher.

School Visits and Interviews. Of course, the best way to learn about a school is to go there and talk with teachers, administrators, and students. Websites and standards documents say little about the actual lived experiences inside the school—what it is like to teach in the school every day, how teachers and students relate with one another, and what learning looks like when kids are engaged and/or finally "get it." If possible, talk with a broad range of individuals, including the district superintendent, the district curriculum coordinator, and school-based department chairs as well as teachers in your content area and parents. Consider asking such questions as the following: What do students learn in the elementary grades? What do students find challenging to learn? What were the best ways to teach and for students to learn? How are students tested? What happens to students who fall behind? What are ways in which teachers and parents communicate with one another? Compare the responses. It should come as no surprise that answers to these questions can reflect various and sometimes conflicting points of view. But this approach will help you to develop your own opinions and approaches to being a teacher in the school.

Figure 12.2

A sample school newsletter.

FORT IOWA

JUNIOR & SENIOR HIGH SCHOOL NEWSLETTER

March 2007

SUPERINTENDENT'S NOTES

The legislature is in full session, and the Education Committee public hearings are almost completed for the session. The next step will involve the senators selecting their priority bills. The governor's budget shows a decrease in state aid to schools, and the bills being talked about in the legislature have anywhere between 10% and 13% reduction in dollars going to the state aid formula. One of the Department of Education printouts shows that our K–12 system could

lose more than 50%, or $200,000 in state aid. In their current form, some of the bills being watched could restructure the method used in distributing state aid to school districts, allow for levy exclusions to make up for the lost state aid or special building funds, and revise the student fees act passed last year. Your Board of Education is watching this very carefully and will be forced to make some tough decisions in the near future. Do we drastically reduce the programs for our students, or do we find some other sources of revenue? Hard decisions will be made concerning our program and services to students. Any cuts made will adversely affect some students. How

we address these troublesome times will be played out in the next few months; however, it can safely be said that there will be some changes and just how those changes will affect our students is of utmost importance! Let me assure you that the board's number one goal remains to maintain our focus on high academic achievement. Tuesday, March 4th, is Teacher Appreciation Day. Teachers are special people who work with our nation's most important commodity: your children. Teachers, just like all people, like to be told that they are appreciated. Take time on Tuesday to thank a current or past teacher for his or her efforts. I know they will appreciate it.

HOMEWORK HOTLINE

The homework hotline will be fully staffed this week, with help available for Algebra, Geometry, Biology and all kinds of writing. To ask questions on the hotline, dial 555-8732 or visit the district website at www.fortiowa.k12.ia.us

FROM THE PRINCIPAL'S DESK

March marks the end of our third quarter and the beginning of the fourth and final segment of the 2006/2007 school year. I want to again notify parents

that they should be getting progress reports about their child's academic performance from each class they are in, even if your child is passing the class. These reports are sent out about every three

weeks, give or take a couple of days. If your child is failing, we are sending those out weekly through the mail. If you are not receiving these reports, please give me a call. The next Progress

Getting to Know the Community

As was discussed earlier in this book, adolescents inhabit many worlds out of school, including neighborhoods, families, and society as a whole. When the in-school and out-of-school worlds are complementary and reinforcing, adolescents develop into productive citizens and adults. But this match-up often escapes many adolescents, particularly those from poverty, those of color (Edwards et al., 2001), and those who

FROM THE PRINCIPAL'S DESK CONTINUED...

Reports are due to come home during the week of April 1–4 and again during the week of April 28–May 2.

I recently read an article in the Sunday newspaper that some of you may have also read. For those who didn't, it was both interesting and represents the teaching profession. The article told about a retired teacher who donated a kidney to a former student. The student, now 35, has been spending the last few months on a dialysis machine awaiting a donor. Her comment upon hearing about the generosity of her former teacher was, "You've got to be kidding me, giving a body part to someone not related to you. It's overwhelming! How can you ever thank a person like that enough?" It surprises me somewhat that she would be that amazed, because that is what teachers do. If not a kidney, it is their love, their dedication, their time. Sometimes, I don't think people really fully understand how much teachers care and want the best for each of their students. I hope that the next time a parent comes out to school or calls to complain about a teacher for keeping their child after school to get some work done, for giving their child a detention because he/she acted inappropriately, or if the teacher talked to their child about the choices they are making, the parent first thanks the teacher for caring.

IMPORTANT MUSIC DATES

March 27: Music Booster meeting 7:00 p.m.
April 17: District Music Contest
April 23: Fine Arts program for invited elementary schools 1:15 p.m. (held in gym)
April 26: Fine Arts Awards Dinner 6:30 p.m.
April 28: Middle School Concert 7:00 p.m.
May 1: Senior High Concert 7:00 p.m.

STUDENT-LED CONFERENCES AT MIDDLE SCHOOL

Students from the middle school will be conducting portfolio conferences on March 23rd and March 24th. Middle school students will lead their own conferences by presenting portfolios to their parents or guardians. The teachers will monitor and facilitate the conferences, but each student will be in charge of leading his or her portfolio conference. What is a portfolio? A portfolio is a meaningful collection of student work that illustrates each student's efforts, progress, and achievements. Each student will show academic work and explain his or her report card grades. Each student will also share various personal strengths and weaknesses in learning and discuss the goals he or she has set for the future. The students have worked hard to prepare for this conference. We believe that students grow through this process and gain a sense of pride in their learning.

feel disengaged from family, school, community, and even themselves (Guthrie & Alvermann, 1998). Knowing about the community is good background for relating to students. The more teachers can make connections based on knowledge about the backgrounds, cultures, languages, aspirations, and motivations of students, the more teachers are able to challenge and inspire students and the more students will want to learn.

It is almost always a mistake to characterize a community as being of a single mind or character. Research is full of overgeneralizations

Figure 12.3 Two different approaches to curriculum standards in science.

Content	Skills students will be able to do:	Vocabulary
Designing a scientific experiment	Design and carryout a scientific experiment	Scientific method, hypothesis, variable, control, theory
Observing the mealworm cycle	Observe the stages in the life cycle of a mealworm	Observation, life cycle
Butterfly conservatory	Observe butterfly behaviors at the Niagara Falls Botanical Gardens	Observation, life cycle
Analyzing a chemical reaction	Observe the effects of meat tenderizer on starch, fat, and protein	Digestion, organic molecules, proteins, starches, amino acids, simple sugars
Carbohydrate chemistry	Use models to learn to interpret the structural formulas of some carbohydrates	Organic molecules, simple sugars
Chemistry of fats and proteins	Use structural formulas and models of glycerol and fatty acids to show how protein molecules form	Organic molecules, building blocks, proteins, amino acids
Proof of enzyme action	Use iodine to test for starch, use Benedict's solution to test for glucose, and test for enzyme action using amylase	Energy, enzyme, simple sugars
Cell energy ATP-ADP	Use paper models of ATP and ADP to determine similarities and differences between the two	Energy, building blocks

Source: Buffalo Public Schools.

The purpose of the Austin ISD Science Program is to graduate responsible, productive, scientifically literate citizens who are empowered to make informed decisions based on sound science knowledge.

Belief Statements about Science Education

We believe that the science program is for all students. Therefore, this program:

- reflects real life situations.
- utilizes relevant, interdisciplinary curricula that ensures quality over quantity.
- creates an environment that encourages divergent thinking, emphasizes hands-on/minds-on experiences, and applies ever-changing technology.
- fosters cooperative and independent problem solving using scientific inquiry, critical thinking skills, and effective communication.
- assures equitable access to appropriate resources, facilities, and ongoing professional development.

Source: Austin Independent School District.

about what happens and does not happen in families to support children and adolescents in schools. Communities often reflect a widely diverse range of histories, races, cultures, and languages. There is a long and unfortunate history of treating differences within a community as a deficit or problem to be solved. Economic hardship, abuse and neglect, family breakups, and racial discrimination are all ways in which students can be singled out for unfair treatment. A common misconception is that families who are experiencing these hardships do not care about supporting their adolescent children and that their children will not succeed in school.

On the contrary, the homes of families living under the most difficult circumstances can sometimes be places that are rich in print and daily literate activities. Families who face hardships may value literacy and learning as much as, if not sometimes more than, occurs at school. For example, families that enjoy a high quality of meaning and interaction in their native language often provide tremendous support for students who are acquiring English as a second language (Ovando et al., 2003). Many families see school as one avenue for their children to get ahead and therefore are willing to support their children in any way they can. They might not know how to support their children, or they might see the school as an uninviting place (McCaleb, 1994). Knowing something about the community and its families can help you to build many kinds of bridges so that families and others in the community can be there for their kids. Following are some ways to find out about a community.

▲ Everyday activities out in the community can help a teacher get a feel for the people and the community. This knowledge can be brought back into the classroom and used in lessons.

Community Organizations. Like schools, many community organizations can be identified from research on the Internet. Some community organizations, such as parent-teacher organizations (PTOs or PTAs), neighborhood associations, and partnership organizations (such as business and civic groups) are likely to be listed on school and district websites. In increasing numbers, community organizations have their own websites.

Community organizations can provide useful insights into local expectations and resources. The old way of looking at schools and communities is that they function totally apart: The school educates while the community supports, disciplines, and otherwise raises the children.

Figure 12.4

Community organizations are good places to learn about a community and its families.

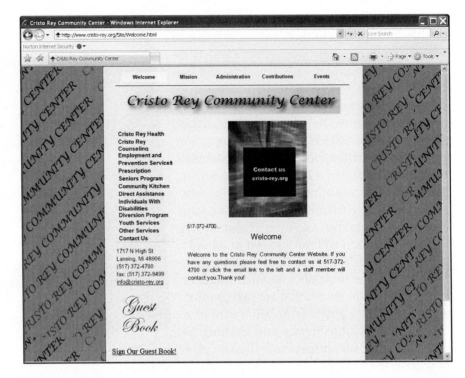

This has been particularly true of secondary schools, where adolescents sometimes work hard to keep their school life separate from their home life. This separation is sometimes perpetuated by impersonal, mass-produced communication from schools in the form of progress reports, information sheets, and report cards.

Some schools and districts have taken up the challenge to form a common culture in support of teachers, children, and families. Where partnerships exist, there are often "action teams," parent-teacher organizations or comparable groups that are responsible for negotiating educational standards, the role(s) of parents, appropriate communication, learning at school and at home, school decisions, and collaboration with the community (Epstein et al., 2002). These groups can be excellent sources of information about literacy resources in the community, concerns about literacy learning, as well as ways for communicating with parents.

Touring the Community. Another approach is to simply walk and drive around a community to see what people do for a living and observe where students live. Attend sports and musical events. These simple steps will give you an initial perspective of what it is like to be in the community, how people live and work, and what they care about. Teachers sometimes participate in home visits, a daunting task when you consider that many secondary school teachers have 140 or more students. The purpose of these visits is to develop a rich fund of knowledge about the community that can be used as a resource for teaching and learning (Rodriquez-Brown, 2001). Though it might not be feasible to do individual home visits, it might be possible to gather information about students, families, and the community during the numerous public opportunities that occur for teachers to interact with parents and the community, such as parent-teacher organization and community meetings, parent-teacher conferences, student club meetings, and student awards presentations.

Researching Community and Family Histories. It is important to keep in mind that you are searching not only for knowledge *about* families and the community, but also for knowledge *within* families and the community. Take some time to research the history of the community and, if possible, find out about the personal histories of some of the families. Seek an understanding of the resources—cultural, linguistic, and familial, such as values and aspirations—that the families and community bring with them. What do the families know and what does the community know that can be a resource for teaching in your content area? Taking this approach will give teachers an important perspective on the community, one that will help them to see students and their parents as real human beings trying to live productive lives. It will also help teachers relate to students better from a perspective of who the students are rather than just what teachers are trying to teach them. The Action Research feature provides information about exploring schools and communities.

▼ Schools that develop a strong partnership with the community create an atmosphere that promotes the value of educating its youth. Students as well as the community benefit from such a partnership in the long run.

Building Community: Reaching Out and Reaching In

The process of building community needs to be multifaceted, with lots of different approaches both inside the classroom and between the school and the community. Not every recommended approach is going to work well in every situation. Focusing on getting parents to help with

Action Research

Exploring Schools and Communities

Many kinds of information are important in finding out about a school. Pupil-teacher ratios, percentages of economically disadvantaged students, test scores, and graduation rates offer clues to a school's challenges and priorities. School Matters (www.schoolmatters.com) is a website sponsored by Standard and Poor that depicts many different kinds of data about individual schools across the United States. Select three schools that differ in geographic location and economic base (urban, rural, and suburban). What comparisons can you make across these schools? What, if any, are the similarities? In what ways could the demographic characteristics of these schools (e.g., pupil-teacher ratios, percentages of disadvantaged students) be used to explain the test scores? How might these characteristics affect your work as a teacher? How might they affect conditions for your students' learning? How might students' experiences with literacy differ according to the differences you observe?

Explore a school that is different from the one that you attended. Explore the district and school websites. If possible, interview someone who works at the school—a teacher, an administrator, or a paraprofessional. Ask about the school's history, including significant achievements, challenges, expectations for students, connections with the community, and anything else that you consider important. Ask also about the impact of state standards and testing as well as national laws and policies on the school, its teachers, administrators, and students. Write the school's

story. Consider the following questions: What roles do reading and writing play in this school? What are the criteria for students to be successful in this school? What would it be like for you to be a teacher in this school? What challenges would you face? What special talents would you bring?

Explore a community that is different from the one in which you grew up, preferably the community that surrounds the school you explored earlier. If possible, interview someone who lives in the community—a parent, a businessperson, a politician, a person who works at a community center, or a pastor of a local church. Ask about the nature of the community, its families, local cultures and languages, how people make a living, the values placed on education, the history, relationships with the schools, community priorities, and anything else you think might be important. Ask the following questions: How does the community think the school is doing? How is the school doing in comparison with other schools? What are ways in which the community has an impact on the schools? Write the community's story. Consider the following questions: What kinds of cultures and languages are integral to this community? What roles do reading and writing play in this community? What would it be like for you to be a teacher in this community? What challenges would you face? What special talents would you bring? In what ways could the community help its local schools to come closer to the ideal described earlier in this chapter?

homework, for instance, is not going to work particularly well if parents are working two or even three jobs to make a living wage or if parents speak a language other than English and all the assignments come home only in English. Adjustments need to be made for every situation.

Reaching Out to the Community

Because of old traditions, fear, or their own negative experiences in the past, many parents feel locked out of the school. Yet many of these parents love their children and wish they could find ways to be supportive. Here are some ways to help parents feel more included in educating their child and more informed about what is going on in school.

Asking Parents about Their Children.   Parents can be an invaluable resource for information about students. Parents know a great deal about their likes and dislikes, their experiences at home and at school, and possibly their future aspirations. Use any occasion for interacting with parents, such as parent conferences and school and community events, to ask parents about students. This will help parents to feel involved but can also provide insights upon which good teaching decisions are based.

Do not be surprised, however, if some parents are less than enthusiastic about providing this information or getting more involved with schools. Some parents hold the culturally shaped view that direct involvement in schooling is not part of their role as parents. For example, many Asian American families have high expectations for their children's academic success but tend to view education as the responsibility of the school (Fuller & Olson, 1998). Similarly, many Latinos greatly value education, but they might limit their role in schooling to ensuring that their children attend, respect the teacher, and behave well (Chrispeels & Rivero, 2000). Do not make the mistake of assuming that lack of participation, even in providing information about students, means that these parents do not care about school or their children.

Sending Messages Home.   Many kinds of messages are transmitted from the school to the home, from progress and failing reports to schedules of school dances and parent-teacher association meetings. Parents frequently complain that information is skimpy or negative, and teachers retort that parents never read anything that they send home. In reality, not nearly enough attention is given to the messages that go home. Messages sent home are important opportunities to create meaningful exchanges with parents about classrooms, special events, and students' progress.

Figure 12.5

Brochures informing parents about your class.

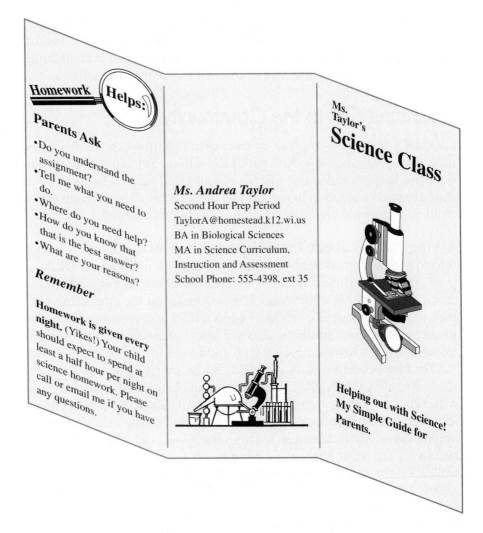

Figure 12.5 depicts two brochures that a teacher created for her students' parents. Notice how the brochures provide useful information about the class topics and assignments. They also suggest some simple ways in which parents can help.

Figure 12.6 shows an example of an announcement for a parents' information night. The night's activities include meeting teachers, following students' schedules, and learning how to become involved in the school. Notice how the announcement is given in English and Spanish, a sign of consideration and respect for the multilingual members of the community. Teachers can enlist the help of a supportive parent for translating messages like this.

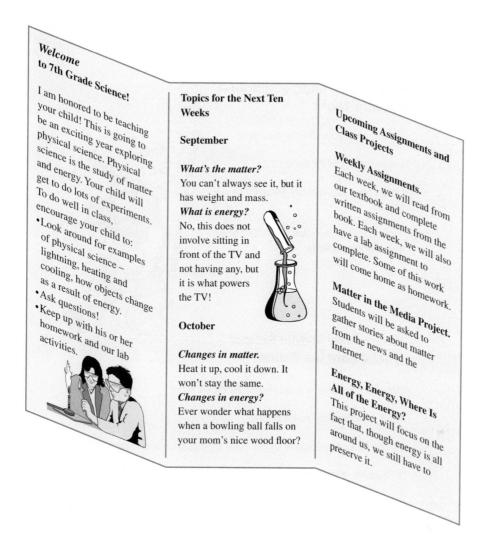

Welcome to 7th Grade Science!

I am honored to be teaching your child! This is going to be an exciting year exploring physical science. Physical science is the study of matter and energy. Your child will get to do lots of experiments. To do well in class, I encourage your child to:

• Look around for examples of physical science – lightning, heating and cooling, how objects change as a result of energy.
• Ask questions!
• Keep up with his or her homework and our lab activities.

Topics for the Next Ten Weeks

September

What's the matter?
You can't always see it, but it has weight and mass.
What is energy?
No, this does not involve sitting in front of the TV and not having any, but it is what powers the TV!

October

Changes in matter.
Heat it up, cool it down. It won't stay the same.
Changes in energy?
Ever wonder what happens when a bowling ball falls on your mom's nice wood floor?

Upcoming Assignments and Class Projects

Weekly Assignments.
Each week, we will read from our textbook and complete written assignments from the book. Each week, we will also have a lab assignment to complete. Some of this work will come home as homework.

Matter in the Media Project.
Students will be asked to gather stories about matter from the news and the Internet.

Energy, Energy, Where Is All of the Energy?
This project will focus on the fact that, though energy is all around us, we still have to preserve it.

In one innovative program, students composed and performed poetry with their families as a way of making home and school connections (Wiseman, 2010). Not only did the program help break down barriers between home and school, it also helped students feel more connected with their families.

Finally, Figure 12.7 contains a sample letter for sending good news home. Parents who dislike school, either because of their own experiences with failure at school or because of frustrations over negative experiences with their own children and school, can be delightfully surprised to receive a sincere report of a job well done. As one mother tearfully informed my wife, a teacher at the time, "I have never received good news about my child!"

Figure 12.6

Parents' Night announcement.

Washtenaw Middle School – Parents' Night

Come meet your child's teachers!

Follow your child's schedule.

Learn how you can get involved in our school.

Thursday, October 4th, at 8:00 P.M. in the school cafeteria

Washtenaw Middle School – Noche para los Padres

¡Venga y consosca a los maestros de su niño!

Siga el horario de su niño.

Aprenda a cómo puede usted estar envuelto enla escuela.

El Jueves, 4 de Octubre a las 8:00 P.M. en la cafeteria

Source: Thank you to Rosario Garcia.

Supporting Parent Involvement through Homework Assistance. A number of barriers can interfere with homework, especially when students fail to understand assignments, forget to accurately record what they need to do, neglect to bring materials home, do not take the time to do the work, or are unsuccessful in remembering to take their work back to school (Bryan et al., 2001). Although these problems especially plague students with learning disabilities, they are experienced by many other students as well. Procrastination,

Dear Mrs. Wilcox:

I just wanted you to know what a good job your son, James, did this week on his science project. He worked extremely well in his project group, offering many ideas and suggestions. When we did Internet research, James was very resourceful in selecting information for his project and team. Thanks for all of your help with James and the project!

Sincerely,

The Dream Team

Goshen Middle School

Figure 12.7

A sample letter sharing good news.

forgetfulness, and poor understanding of classroom assignments all conspire to make homework not as less effective as than it could be. With appropriate support, parents can change this picture. Parents can help their adolescent children to do the following:

▶ Review and practice what has been learned

▶ Get ready for the next day's class

▶ Learn to use resources, such as libraries, reference materials, and even the Internet

▶ Explore subjects more fully than time permits in the classroom (Paulu, 1995)

To make this happen, teachers need to communicate with parents about the curriculum. For example, on parents' nights, share information about upcoming topics, projects, and assignments. If parents are aware of assignments and schedules, they are in a better position to offer some assistance. Even if parents feel ill prepared academically to help with homework, at least they can help their children by monitoring when assignments need to get completed.

Assignment books and logs that are produced and maintained by students can be the focus for parents and their children as they complete schoolwork together. With the increasing availability of Internet-based resources, teachers can post assignments on school or class websites so that students and their parents can access their homework remotely. Figure 12.8 depicts a handout that teachers can use to share some general tips with

Figure 12.8

Helping parents to help their children with homework.

Twelve Ways You Can Help Your Child with Homework

1. Set aside a regular time for starting homework.
2. Reserve a quiet, well-lit place.
3. Remove distractions.
4. Provide supplies (pens, paper, pencils, rulers, etc.) and identify resources (dictionary, encyclopedia, library, Internet).
5. Read the directions for the assignments.
6. Make sure your child understands what she or he is expected to do.
7. Help your child get started when she or he has to do research reports or other big assignments.
8. Help your child structure time, pacing himself or herself, so that he or she can complete assignments. Help your child understand why waiting until the last minute is not a particularly effective approach!
9. Set a good example by reading, writing, and doing things that require thought and effort on your part.
10. Look over assignments and make sure they are complete.
11. Balance homework with television watching and other leisure activities (Internet, video games etc.).
12. Give praise (and sometimes, constructive criticism). If you give a suggestion and your child does better, be sure to let them know.

Source: Paulu, N. (1995). *Helping your child with homework*. Washington, DC: U.S. Department of Education.

parents for helping their children with homework. In addition, you might share with parents some very simple questions they can ask that will help students break big assignments into smaller, more manageable parts:

▶ Do you understand what you are supposed to do?

▶ What do you need to do to finish the assignment?

▶ Where do you need help in understanding how to do your work?

▶ Have you ever done any assignments like the ones you are supposed to do right now?

▶ Do you have everything you need to do the assignment?

▶ Do your answers make sense to you?

Much free material is available for downloading from Internet sites. *Helping Your Child with Homework* (www.ed.gov/parents/academic/help/homework/homework.pdf) is a U.S. government publication available in English and Spanish that gives parents additional ideas for communicating with teachers about homework. There are also subject-specific resources for parents who want to dig in and help with homework. For example, *How to Help with Math Homework When the Answers Are Not in the Book* by William Blatner is available at www.mathimp.org/downloads/resources/ParentBrochure(MASS).pdf. Ideas for involving parents in an entire range of content areas are available from the National Network of Partnership Schools at Johns Hopkins University (www.csos.jhu.edu/p2000). For a more extensive approach to supporting parents with homework assistance, read the How to Plan feature.

Planning Effective Parent Conferences. Parent conferences are opportunities for teachers to showcase their goals, the instructional activities upon which students have been working, samples of student work,

How
TO PLAN
. . . for Parents' Assistance with Homework

Teachers Involve Parents in Schoolwork (TIPS) is a special project within the National Network of Partnership Schools that provides teachers and parents with resources for homework help. Research on the TIPS project has shown promising results with regard to students' homework and related achievement in English, mathematics, and science classrooms (Epstein & Voorhis, 2001).

Homework sheets designed using guidelines from TIPS include the following:

▶ A brief message to parent, guardian, or family partner that explains the purpose of the activity. The student writes in the due date and signs the letter.

▶ Objectives explaining the learning goal of the activity (if this is not clear from the title and letter).

▶ Materials listed if more than paper and pen are needed.

▶ Space to complete the specific assignment activities.

▶ Interactions such as a family survey or an interview, a guide for the student to interview someone for ideas or memories, reading work aloud for reactions, monitoring their work, or taking turns with each other in giving ideas.

▶ Home-to-school communication that invites the family partner to share comments and observations with teachers about whether the child understood the homework, whether they both enjoyed the activity, and whether the parent gained information about the student's work in language arts.

Following is sample TIPS guide sheet for a homework assignment about persuasive writing (adapted from Epstein et al., 2000). Using an assignment that is appropriate for your content area, design a TIPS guide sheet for a homework assignment in your content area.

continued

Student's Name _____ **Date** _____

Dear Family Partner,

We are writing paragraphs that persuade, convince, and argue. I need to support my argument with specific reasons and details. I hope you enjoy this activity with me. This assignment is due _____

Sincerely,

_____
(Student's signature)

THINGS TO REMEMBER:

Persuasive writing:
- States a position
- Includes reasons to support the position
- Uses details to support the reasons

PROCEDURE:

1. Read the following prompt. You may discuss it with your family member.

? **PROMPT: The BIG Question** **?**

Many successful people, both famous and unknown, have taken action to follow their dreams and accomplish their goals, regardless of what other people said or did. You have been asked to contribute an essay for a brochure that your school guidance department plans to publish about choosing a career.

Before you write, think about someone you know who has followed his dream. Think about what other people said to him and what happened to his dream.

2. Complete the following prewriting chart:

Topic: _____   Purpose: _____

Audience: _____   Form: _____

QUESTIONS	ANSWERS	DETAILS
Who was successful?		
What did they dream?		
1. Reasons they were successful?		
2. Reasons they were successful?		
3. Reasons they were successful?		

3. Now write a rough draft of your essay. Remember your topic sentence and closing sentence.

_____

_____

_____

_____

_____

_____

4. Read your essay to your family member.

Who is listening to you?_____

Add or delete details, or make changes to improve your work.

FAMILY SURVEY— Ask: "How did you become successful in your life?" Write the example that your family partner shares. Use complete sentences.

_____

_____

_____

_____

HOME-TO-SCHOOL COMMUNICATION

Dear Parent,

    Please share your reactions to your child's work on this activity. Write YES or NO for each of the following statements.

_____ 1. My child understood the homework and was able to discuss it.

_____ 2. My child and I enjoyed this activity.

_____ 3. The assignment helped me know what my child is learning in English class.

Any other comments?

_____

_____

_____

_____

Parent signature_____

and plans for helping students to learn more effectively. During conferences, parents expect answers to three questions (Conley, 2005):

- ► What are you trying to accomplish with my child?
- ► How is my child doing?
- ► What are you doing to help my child do better?

The first question, "What are you trying to accomplish with my child?" is about goals. Parent conferences provide a perfect opportunity to explain curriculum goals, both short and long term, and teaching practices for achieving them. This would be a good time to hand out a parent brochure or information sheet about the class. Many parents, sitting on the outside of the school and classroom, can only imagine what is going on based on old memories or what their adolescent children report about their experiences. Parent conferences provide the opportunity to correct any misconceptions and build tangible images of what your class is all about.

The second question, "How is my child doing?" is a question about class assignments and a student's progress. Be mindful that many adolescents and even some parents experience difficulty in connecting student effort with grades earned. Be ready with sample assignments and examples of student work so that you can offer explanations and evidence both for your expectations and students' performance.

The third question, "What are you doing to help my child?" gets at the heart of a teacher's responsibilities. Most parents care deeply that their children will do better and become successful. Many expect teachers to have the expertise and desire to create conditions for children to succeed. Parents are reassured when teachers can communicate effectively about learning problems experienced by students and how teachers plan to help. Of course, students and their parents also have a role. Parent conferences are a good time to solicit parents' observations about how their child is doing (and why) as well as suggest ways in which parents can get involved with their child's learning.

Challenges and Dilemmas for Parent Conferences. These recommendations for parent conferences are not without some challenges and dilemmas. For example, it is essential to be sensitive to cultural differences in communication styles (Weinstein et al., 2003). During parent conferences, many teachers immediately launch into a discussion of the student's progress, especially in high schools where meetings are scheduled only fifteen minutes apart. This can appear cold and unfriendly to parents who are generally accustomed to exchanging pleasantries (such as asking about the health of family members) before getting down to the business at hand (Brown & Kysilka, 2002). Likewise, when teachers sometimes wait only a very short time after asking a question, but individuals from some cultures, including Native Americans, are generally accustomed to longer pauses (Swap, 1999). Teachers who rush into conferences without sensitivity to these differences might be dismissed as rude or uninterested in parents' perspectives.

Parents also may disagree with teachers about the teacher's goals and how the teacher is going about achieving them. Parents will often refer back to their own memories of schooling to criticize what teachers are doing today. When this happens, take the opportunity to explain how the curriculum is different today, because of new curriculum and assessment demands as well as updated methods and ideas about teaching, learning, and assessment.

Other parents who have experienced long-term frustration over their child's performance might continue to feel frustrated, even taking out their frustration on teachers, when the news about their child continues to be bad. Some parents inappropriately ask teachers to compare their child's performance with that of their neighbor's child or others in the class. They might get angry when teachers, appropriately, tell parents that privacy laws prohibit releasing information about anyone other than their own child. Remembering to focus on answering the three questions parents ask is a way to address these dilemmas responsibly. For more information about effectively communicating with parents, read the Connecting Standards and Assessment feature.

Coping with Conflicts with Parents. By following many of the ideas presented in this chapter, teachers will have laid the groundwork for parents' understanding and cooperation. However, at some point, you will be in the difficult position of delivering bad news (Edwards, 2004). Start the conversation with a positive ("Your child is caught up on homework") before delivering the bad news ("She is still struggling with algebra"). Be factual and provide examples of what you are trying to accomplish with your student—their child—and how the student is doing. Enlist parents' insights into what they have observed about their children and school.

When conflicts with parents emerge, it is important to listen. Parents of a student with a lengthy history of problems in school are likely already to be already frustrated and sensitive to criticism. Just listening

Connecting Standards and Assessment

Communicating about Student Progress

Imagine that you are a parent in a community where the teachers' communication with parents has been inconsistent from the early elementary grades all the way through high school. In the elementary grades, your child received descriptive grades that are unlike any you received: *emerging, developing,* or *mastery.* In the middle school, it was back to familiar letter grades: "A's," "B's," "C's," and "D's." You noticed your child waiting until the last week of the marking period to complete schoolwork. But it was okay, because many of the teachers accepted make-up work, no matter how late it came in. Most, if not all, of the students, got "A's" and "B's." It took more than an hour to read the students' names at the A-Honor Roll Assembly.

Now your child is in the high school. Teachers have informed the students that make-up work is no longer allowed. At the end of the ten-week marking period, the grading lists all look like bell curves—with very few "A's," some "B's," a large number of "C's," and a dribble of "D's" and "F's." Students ask what they can do to improve and get better grades. Teachers tell them to just work harder. Parents are frustrated because they want their children to get into good colleges. Parent conferences are battles over grades and teachers' grading practices.

It is frightening to consider this true story and the potential for its reoccurrence throughout the educational world. But the reality is that communication around assessment is inconsistent and often arbitrary. The clearer teachers can be with parents about goals, how students are performing, and how they are helping students to achieve, the fewer conflicts will emerge. Equally important is for teachers to talk with one another about grading practices so that entire schools can present consistent and clear messages.

▶ Read more about these ideas in Chapter 12, "Communicating Assessment Information," in *Connecting Standards and Assessment through Literacy* (Conley, 2005), published by Pearson Education.

can be a way to diffuse some of their frustration and send the message that you are open to input. Remain focused on the problem at hand: the child's behavior or school performance. Some parents might try to move the focus off of their child by blaming you or the school. Getting a teacher angry is one way for a parent to take control of a meeting and avoid dealing with their child's problems.

If possible, guide the conversation to a common set of understandings. For instance, if you and the parents can agree on the problems a student is experiencing, suggest some ways in which you can work together to confront the problems. In some cases, it might not be possible to arrive at common goals or solutions. Still, the exchange might at some later time lead to changes in communication and partnerships with the parents or help the student to improve. Despite the stress of conflict with some parents, teachers can still gain some insight or make some progress that will eventually help students.

Reaching In: Creating Community from Inside the Classroom

Community building is just as important from inside your classroom. Three important principles involved in building a classroom community are creating a respectful and caring classroom, practicing responsive pedagogy, and striving for clear, fair, and effective communication.

Creating a Respectful and Caring Classroom. Safe and caring classrooms are characterized by mutual respect and understanding. This practice starts with teachers. If teachers make no attempt to learn about students, to respect them, or to create expectations for mutual respect and caring in your classroom, how will students ever learn to do these things with teachers or each other? Research suggests that students are particularly frustrated by teachers who do not take time to get to know them but just impose assignments without explanation or emotion or who give directions carelessly, expecting students to figure things out on their own. The reverse picture is also true: Students tend to appreciate teachers who communicate their expectations well, with consideration for who they are and what they care about, and who go out of their way to help students become successful (Brophy & Good, 1986; Pressley et al., 2003).

This same research suggests that respectful and caring classrooms are well managed. Well-managed classrooms are those in which students are deeply involved in their work, students know what is expected of them, there is relatively little wasted time, and the climate is relaxed but work-oriented (Weinstein, 2003). Respect and caring are experienced in well-managed classrooms because students feel that they are supported in becoming successful learners. Classrooms that are not well managed are often full of confusing directives and assignments, with teachers making up rules and punishments as they go, and insincere praise or no praise at all. Building community from inside the

▲ Building community within the classroom starts with creating an environment where students are engaged in their work and feel supported and respected.

classroom starts with building an environment in which students are engaged in interesting work, assignments and grading are clear and relatively predictable, and students feel supported. Can you recall some times when the classroom you were in was a particularly supportive, respectful, and caring place?

Practicing Responsive Pedagogy.
Recall from Chapter 6 our discussion about culturally responsive pedagogy. Recall that culturally responsive pedagogy involves learning about students and their backgrounds, cultures, and languages and then using that information to form relationships and create opportunities for learning. Here, we will discuss two important cases in which these practices can be used: students with special needs and English language learners. Consider how elements of these cases are applicable for building community among all students.

For Students with Special Needs. Responsive pedagogy for students with special needs takes the following form (Soodak, 2003). First, it is important to promote membership and acceptance in class and throughout a school's programs, settings, and events. Students with special needs often feel isolated, frequently as a result of efforts to provide them with special instruction. The more teachers can create an inviting atmosphere for these students, the less the students will feel isolated.

Another role that teachers can play in supporting students with special needs is by facilitating friendships. Although this can be a tricky issue for adolescents, teachers can support friendships by incorporating activities that involve cooperation and collaboration. Teachers can create rituals that involve all members of the class, including class meetings and limited social time, once work has been completed.

For students with special needs, it is also important to set up classroom rules that encourage respect, such as requiring turn taking and not permitting any student to be left out of classroom activities. Praise for performing an activity well or for behaving well also goes a long way toward building community. In cases of misbehavior, these students, like many adolescents, do much better when they are given choices in how to make amends for misbehavior.

For English Language Learners. The experience of being an English language learner among adolescents in a classroom where only English is spoken can be frightening and even embarrassing. It is important to keep the potential for these feelings in mind in considering responsive pedagogy for English language learners.

Teachers need to understand, expect, and feel comfortable with natural responses (e.g., laughter, first language use, silence, and fatigue) that occur when English language learners participate in classroom language interactions in which they are not completely proficient (Curran, 2003). Teachers can support English language learners by expressing admiration for a student's bilingual ability, by commenting enthusiastically about the number of different languages that are represented in class, and by including examples and content from a variety of cultures in their teaching (Weinstein et al., 2003).

To help English language learners feel included, it is also important to structure classroom activities and use strategies in support of language acquisition and comprehension. When English language learners feel forgotten or ignored, they might misbehave. The more that teachers use a variety of materials and emphasize many literacies, the more these students are likely to be engaged.

English language learners also benefit when teachers build a strong sense of community (see Teaching Today's Learners, page 398). Practices that build community for English language learners as well as all other students include the following (Brown, 2003):

▶ Talking with students about their families

▶ Learning about students' interests, strengths, and needs

▶ Demonstrating caring about students as individuals

▶ Practicing good communication, especially listening

▶ Using knowledge about students and their families to create environments for learning (such as friendliness and caring in ways practiced by families)

▶ Forming trusting and respectful relationships with students

▶ Maintaining an assertive stance, especially with regard to expectations and inappropriate behaviors

A+RISE

Click on A+RISE – WIDA ELP Standard Strategy in the MyEducationLab (www.myeducationlab .com) for your course. Next, select the Strategy Card Index tab, scroll to Language and Content for Grades 6–12 and select the Cooperative Learning Roles strategy.

Teaching Today's Learners

Culturally Responsive Teaching Practices across Content Areas

Consider this list of culturally responsive practices from many different content areas (Ladson-Billings, 1994). What ideas can you add to this list?

▶ Surveying all of the ways in which families use mathematics in their daily lives so that students can build on what they already know and practice

▶ Encouraging students to make observations about their natural environment so that students can make connections in science

▶ Inviting parents in to share life histories and experiences as a way of building a richer picture of history

▶ Asking students to gather and record favorite family stories as a way of building relationships with literature in school

▶ Conducting surveys of families' favorite music, musical styles, and musical periods as a way of planning the music curriculum for the year

▶ Engaging students in discussions about jobs and careers in students' families as a way of opening up discussion about future career choices

▶ Discussing the physical activities and food choices experienced by students and family members to increase knowledge about healthy lifestyle choices

▶ Accepting alternative communication styles, such as the tendency in some cultures to speak out loud in response while a teacher is talking or the tendency of some recent immigrants to listen to other conversations rather than speaking up

▶ Providing opportunities for socialization and conversation during instructional activities

Striving for Clear, Fair, and Effective Communication. Have you ever been a student in a class in which the goals were murky, the teacher made little or not attempt to help you learn, and you struggled on anyway? To add insult to injury, perhaps you received a grade yet had no clue about what you did or did not do to receive it. That is exactly the opposite of what is being recommended here. To build classroom community, teachers need to practice clear, fair, and effective communication with students.

Students will work harder for the teacher and for themselves if they know the goals for learning, how to achieve the goals, and how they will be evaluated. A very simple idea—yet a very important one—is to involve your students in their own assessment (Conley, 2005; Stiggins, 2005). Whenever you start a new assignment, lesson, or unit, talk with students about expectations—what students should know and be able to do—and about the kinds of teaching activities and assignments that will be required and ways of doing those assignments successfully. For example, when students are given a problem to solve, a writing assignment, a research project, an experiment to perform, a new musical piece, an exercise routine, or a new mode of artwork, ask, "If you do this well, what will it look like?" Then, solicit students' points of view about how they will need to perform.

This invitation to consider the quality of the work is important for a number of reasons. One reason is that so many students have a "do it once and turn it in" mentality. Many students rarely stop to think about the quality of their work. Another reason is that asking this question gives you and your students the opportunity to practice clear and effective communication about expectations and strategies for success. This focus on clear communication is eminently fair: Students are given every opportunity to be successful—from clear expectations to supportive instruction and student-involved assessment. Clear communication can be responsible for a "we are all in this together" attitude that can be the basis for a very positive classroom community.

Summary

Getting to know schools and communities is one of the best ways for teachers to reduce the gap between home and school and to build on the knowledge and experiences of students and their families. Every school and community is different, so take the time to review websites, locate community organizations, and visit local community sites and events to gain insights. Once teachers understand what makes a school and the community unique, they are in an excellent position to enlist support from and communicate effectively with students and their parents.

Community building takes place when teachers reach out to the community and when they build relationships within the classroom. Respectful, informative, and inviting messages home can entice parents to become involved. Respectful, caring, and responsive classrooms are places where students really want to learn. Teachers who adopt these principles create opportunities to genuinely help adolescents learn accompanied by parents' enthusiastic support.

Special Projects

1. Think back to your own parents' involvement in school. Were your parents more likely to participate or not? If they did participate, how did they become involved? What kinds of communication do you remember coming from the school to invite your parents in?

2. Consider teachers you have known who were particularly involved in the community. In what kinds of activities were they engaged? Describe some ways in which you can learn more about the community surrounding your school and some ways in which you can become involved in the community.

3. Design a brochure for your content area class. Describe other ways in which you will communicate with parents (e.g., messages home, homework help).

4. Interview several teachers about how they communicate with parents, including parent conferences. In what ways do they satisfy parents' concerns about how their children are doing? In what ways do they enlist parents' help in working with students?

5. Draft a plan for a parent conference. Describe the artifacts and examples that you will bring to the conferences, including goals for your class, sample activities, and samples of student work.

6. Create a plan to create community in your classroom. In what ways will you model caring and respect as well as involving students?

7. Write an assignment in your content area and adapt it using the ideas presented in this chapter for guiding parents in helping their child to do the assignment successfully.

Praxis Practice

Working with Questions to Prepare for the Praxis Reading Across the Curriculum Test

Multiple Choice Questions

1. Some of the best ways to get to know a school and its community are:

   a. Look at the test scores.

   b. Visit the school website.

   c. Attend local music and sporting events.

   d. All of the above.

2. Which ideas about literacy are most important for learning?

   a. Ideas that are taught in school.

   b. Ideas that come from the community.

   c. Ideas and values that come from the school and community.

   d. Ideas that local businesspersons have for how to succeed.

3. What information are parents looking for when they attend school conferences?

   a. Their child's grades.

   b. Their child's behavior.

   c. What you are teaching, how the child is doing, and what you are doing to help.

   d. Whether or not what you are doing will help their child get to college.

Constructed Response Question

1. Describe ways you will use ideas about literacy to reach out to parents but also make use of your students' experiences in teaching and learning.

Suggested Readings

Curran, E. (2003). Linguistic diversity and classroom management. *Theory into Practice, 44*(4), 334–340.

Edwards, P. (2004). *Children's literacy development: Making it happen through school, family, and community involvement.* New York: Pearson.

Epstein, J., Sanders, M., Simon, B., Salinas, K., Jansorn, N., & Van Voorhis, F. (2002). *School, family, and community partnerships: Your handbook for action* (2nd ed.). Thousand Oaks, CA: Corwin Press.

Singer, J., & Shagoury, R. (2005). Stirring up justice: Adolescents reading, writing, and changing the world. *Journal of Adolescent and Adult Literacy, 49*(4), 318–340.

Soodak, L. (2003). Classroom management in inclusive settings. *Theory into Practice, 42*(4), 327–333.

Weinstein, C., Curran, M., & Tomlinson-Clark, S. (2003). Culturally responsive classroom management: Awareness into action. *Theory into Practice, 42*(4), 269–276.

Wiseman, A. (2010). "When you do your best, there's someone to encourage you:" Adolescents' views of family literacy. *Journal of Adolescent and Adult Literacy, 53*(2), 132–142.

Helpful Websites

Even Start Family Literacy Initiatives: www.evenstart.org/

National Center for Family Literacy: www.famlit.org

Rhode Island Family Literacy Initiative: www.nelrc.org/practice/rifamily.html

Go to Topic 9: Integrating Technology in the MyEducationLab (www.myeducationlab.com) for your course, where you can:

- Find learning outcomes for Topic 9: Integrating Technology along with the national standards that connect to these outcomes.

- Complete Assignments and Activities that can help you more deeply understand the chapter content.

- Apply and practice your understanding of the core teaching skills identified in the chapter with the Building Teaching Skills and Dispositions learning units.

- Examine challenging situations and cases presented in the IRIS Center Resources.

Go to the Topic A+RISE in the MyEducationLab (www.myeducationlab.com) for your course. A+RISE® Standards2Strategy™ is an innovative and interactive online resource that offers new teachers in grades K-12 just in time, research-based instructional strategies that:

- Meet the linguistic needs of ELLs as they learn content

- Differentiate instruction for all grades and abilities

- Offer reading and writing techniques, cooperative learning, use of linguistic and nonlinguistic representations, scaffolding, teacher modeling, higher order thinking, and alternative classroom ELL assessment

- Provide support to help teachers be effective through the integration of listening, speaking, reading, and writing along with the content curriculum

- Improve student achievement

- Are aligned to Common Core Elementary Language Arts standards (for the literacy strategies) and to English language proficiency standards in WIDA, Texas, California, and Florida.

References

Abedi, J. (2004). The no child left behind act and English language learners: Assessment and accountability issues. *Educational Researcher, 33*(1), 4–14.

Abedi, J., Lord, C., Hofstetter, C., & Baker, E. (2000). Impact of accommodation strategies on English language learners' test performance. *Educational Measurement: Issues and Practice, 19*(3), 16–26.

Achieve, Inc. (2005). *Rising to the challenge: Are high school graduates prepared for college and work?* Washington, DC: Author.

Alejandro, A. (1989). Cars: A culturally integrated "I-Search" module. *English Journal, 78,* 41–44.

Alexander, P., & Jetton, T. (2000). Learning from text: A multidimensional and developmental perspective. In M. Kamil, P. Mosenthal, P. Pearson, & R. Barr (Eds.), *Handbook of Reading Research,* (Vol. 3, pp. 285–310). Mahwah, NJ: Erlbaum.

Allington, R. (2001). *What really matters for struggling readers.* New York: Longman.

Allsup, R., & Baxter, M. (2004). Talk about music: Better questions? *Music Educators Journal, 91*(2), 29–33.

Alvermann, D., & Hagood, M. (2000). Critical media literacy: Research, theory and practice in "new times." *Journal of Educational Research, 93,* 193–205.

Alvermann, D., Moon, J., & Hagood, M. (1999). *Popular culture in the classroom: Teaching and researching critical media literacy.* Newark, DE: International Reading Association.

Anderson, R., & Freebody, P. (1983). Reading comprehension and the assessment and acquisition of word knowledge. In B. Hutton (Ed.), *Reading/language research: A research annual* (pp. 231–256). Greenwich, CT: JAI Press.

Anderson, R., & Pearson, P. (1984). A schema-theoretic view of basic processes in reading. In P. Pearson, R. Barr, M. Kamil, & P. Mosenthal (Eds.), *Handbook of reading research* (Vol. 1, pp. 255–291). New York: Longman.

Anderson, T., & Armbruster, B. (1984) Studying. In P. Pearson, R. Barr M. Kamil & P. Mosenthal (Eds.), *Handbook of Reading Research* (Vol. 1, pp. 657–679). New York: Longman.

Armbruster, B., Anderson, T., & Ostertag, J. (1987). Does text structure/summarization facilitate learning from expository text? *Reading Research Quarterly, 22,* 3331–3346.

Atwell, N. (1998). *In the middle.* Portsmouth, NH: Boynton Cook.

Ausubel, D. (1968). *Educational psychology: A cognitive view.* New York: Holt, Rinehart and Winston.

Ball, A. (2006). Teaching writing in culturally diverse classrooms. In C. MacArthur, S. Graham, & J. Fitzgerald (Eds.), *Handbook of writing research* (pp. 293–310). New York: Guilford.

Barton, P. (2005). *One-third of a nation: Rising dropout rates and declining opportunities.* Princeton, NJ: Educational Testing Service.

Baxendell, B. (2003). Consistent, coherent, creative: The 3 c's of graphic organizers. *Teaching Exceptional Children, 35*(3), 46–53.

Beach, R., & Friedrich, T. (2006). Response to writing. In C. MacArthur, S. Graham, & J. Fitzgerald (Eds.), *Handbook of writing research* (pp. 222–223). New York: Guilford.

Beck, I., & McKeown, M. (2002). Questioning the author: Making sense of social studies. *Educational Leadership, 60*(3), 44–47.

Beck, I., McKeown, M., & Kucan, L. (2002). *Bringing words to life: Robust vocabulary instruction.* New York: Guilford.

Beck, I., McKeown, M., & McCaslin, E. (1983). All contexts are not created equal. *Elementary School Journal, 83,* 177–181.

Beck, I., McKeown, M., Sandora, C., Kucan, L., & Worthy, J. (1996). Questioning the author: A yearlong classroom implementation to engage students with text. *Elementary School Journal, 96*(4), 385–414.

Biancarosa, G., & Snow, C. (2004). *Reading next: A vision for action and research in middle and high school literacy: A report from Carnegie Corporation of New York.* Washington, DC: Alliance for Excellent Education.

Biemiller, A. (2001). Teaching vocabulary. *Perspectives, 26*(4), 143–148.

Blanchowicz, S., & Fisher, P. (2000). Vocabulary instruction. In M. Kamil, P. Mosenthal, P. Pearson, & R. Barr (Eds.), *Handbook of reading research* (Vol. 3, pp. 503–523). Mahwah, NJ: Erlbaum.

Block, C., & Pressley, M. (2003). Best practices in comprehension instruction. In L. Morrow, L. Gambrell, & M. Pressley (Eds.), *Best practices in literacy instruction* (pp. 111–126). New York: Guilford.

Boatright, M. (2010). Graphic novels: Graphic novels representations of immigrant experiences. *Journal of Adolescent and Adult Literacy, 53*(8), 468–476.

Bond, G., & Wagner, E. (1966). *Teaching the child to read.* New York: Macmillan.

Bragdon, H. (1998). *History of a free nation.* New York: McGraw Hill/Glencoe.

Brenner, M. (1998). Development of mathematical communication in problem solving groups by language minority students. *Bilingual Research Journal, 22*(2), 103–128.

Bromley, K. (1999). *Journaling.* Chicago: Scholastic.

Brophy, J. (1985). Teacher-student interaction. In J. Dusek (Ed.), *Teacher expectancies* (pp. 308–328). Hillsdale, NJ: Erlbaum.

Brophy, J., & Good, T. (1986). Teacher behavior and student achievement. In M. C. Wittrock (Ed.), *Handbook of research on teaching* (3rd ed., pp. 328–375). New York: Macmillan.

Brown, D. (2003). Urban teachers' use of culturally responsive management strategies. *Theory into Practice, 42*(4), 277–282.

Brown, J., & Pardun, C. (2004). Little in common: Racial and gender differences in adolescents' television diets. *Journal of Broadcasting and Electronic Media, 48*(2), 2004.

Brown, S. (2004). *Mass layoff statistics data in the united states and domestic and overseas relocation.* Washington, DC: Bureau of Labor Statistics.

Brown, S., & Kysilka, M. (2002). *Applying multicultural and global concepts in the classroom and beyond.* Boston: Allyn and Bacon.

Brozo, W. (2002). *To be a boy, to be a reader.* Newark, DE: International Reading Association.

Bruce, B. (2003). What kind of library is the World Wide Web? In B. Bruce (Ed.), *Literacy in the information age: Inquiries into making meaning with new technologies* (pp. 71–77). Newark, DE: International Reading Association.

Bruner, J. (1996). *The culture of education.* Cambridge, MA: Harvard University Press.

Bryan, T., Burstein, K., & Bryan, J. (2001). Students with learning disabilities: Homework problems and promising practices. *Educational Psychologist, 36*(3), 167–180.

Bulgren, J., Oeshler, D., & Schumaker, B. (1997). Use of a recall enhancement routine and strategies in inclusive secondary classes. *Learning Disabilities Research and Practice, 12*(4), 198–208.

Burns, M., & Silbey, R. (2001). Math journals boost real learning. *Instructor, 110*(7), 18–21.

Butler, F., & Stevens, R. (1997). *Accommodation strategies for English language learners on large-scale assessments: Students' characteristics and other considerations.* Los Angeles: University of California, National Center for Research on Evaluation, Standards, and Student Testing.

Cain, K., & Oakhill, J. (2004). Reading comprehension difficulties. In T. Nunes & P. Bryant (Eds.), *Handbook of children's literacy* (pp. 313–338). Dordrecht, The Netherlands: Kluwer Academic.

Carlo, M., August, D., McLaughlin, B., Snow, C., Dressler, C., Lippman, D., et al. (2004). Closing the gap: Addressing the vocabulary needs of English language learners in bilingual and mainstream classrooms. *Reading Research Quarterly, 39*(2), 188–215.

Carver, R. (1990). *Reading rate: A review of research and theory.* San Diego: Academic Press.

Cassidy, J. (1996). Computer assisted language arts instruction for the ESL learner. *English Journal, 85*(9), 55–57.

CAST. (2004). Pathways to learning for students with extreme cognitive challenges. Retrieved March 14, 2006, from www. cast. org

Cervetti, G., Pardales, M., & Damico, J. (2001). A tale of differences: Comparing the traditions, perspectives, and educational goals of critical reading and critical literacy. *Reading Online, 4*(9). Retrieved October 14, 2006, from www.readingonline.org/articles/art_index .asp?HREF=/articles/cervetti/index.html

Chamot, A., & O'Malley, J. (1994). *The CALLA handbook: Implementing the cognitive academic language learning approach.* Reading, MA: Addison-Wesley.

Cheung, A., & Slavin, R. (2005). Effective reading programs for English language learners and other language minority students. *Bilingual Research Journal, 29*(2), 241–270.

Cho, S., & Ahn, D. (2003). Strategy acquisition and maintenance of gifted and nongifted young children. *Exceptional Children, 69*(4), 497–504.

Chrispeels, J., & Rivero, E. (2000). *Engaging Latino families for student success: Understanding the process and impact of providing training to parents.* Paper presented at the American Educational Research Association, New Orleans, LA.

Cipielewski, J., & Stanovich, K. (1992). Predicting growth in reading ability from children's exposure to print. *Journal of Experimental Child Psychology, 54,* 74–89.

Cobb, P. (2004). Mathematics, literacies and identity. *Reading Research Quarterly, 39*(3), 333–337.

Coiro, J. (2006). Exploring changes to reading comprehension on the internet: Paradoxes and possibilities for diverse adolescent readers. Dissertation, University of Connecticut, Storrs.

Collins, A. (1987). A sample dialogue based on a theory of inquiry teaching. In C. Reigeluth (Ed.), *Instructional theories in action: Lessons illustrating selected theories and models* (pp. 181–199). Hillsdale, NJ: Erlbaum.

Commander, N., & Smith, B. (1996). Learning logs: A tool for cognitive monitoring. *Journal of Adolescent and Adult Literacy, 39*(6), 446–453.

Conley, M. (1995). *Content reading instruction: A communication approach.* New York: McGraw-Hill.

Conley, M. (2005). *Connecting standards and assessment though literacy.* Boston: Allyn and Bacon.

Conley, M. (2007). Reconsidering adolescent literacy: From competing agendas to shared commitment. In M. Pressley (Ed.), *Research we have, research we need.* New York: Guilford.

Conley, M., & Gritter, K. (2007). A pathway for connecting standards with assessment: Backwards mapping of assessment tasks. In J. Paratore & R. McCormack (Eds.), *Classroom Literacy Assessment: Making Sense of What Students Know and Do.* New York: Guilford.

Craig, J. (2001). The missing link between school and work: Knowing the demands of the workplace. *The English Journal, 91*(2), 46–50.

Curran, E. (2003). Linguistic diversity and classroom management. *Theory into Practice, 44*(4), 334–340.

Daiute, C. (2000). Writing and communication technologies. In R. Indrisano & J. Squire (Eds.), *Perspectives on writing: Research, theory and practice* (pp. 251–276). Newark, DE: International Reading Association.

Daly, A. (1994). Gender issues in dance history pedagogy. *Journal of Physical Education, Recreation and Dance, 65*(2), 34–39.

DeBoer, G. (1991). *A history of ideas in science education.* New York: Teachers College Press.

Deshler, D., Schumaker, B., Lenz, K., Bulgren, J., Hock, M., Knight, J., et al. (2001). Ensuring content-area learning by secondary students with learning disabilities. *Learning Disabilities Research and Practice, 16*(2), 96–108.

DiCecco, V., & Gleason, M. (2002). Using graphic organizers to attain relational knowledge from expository text. *Journal of Learning Disabilities, 35*(4), 306–320.

Dodge, B. (2001). Focus: Five rules for writing a great webquest. *Learning and Leading with Technology, 28*(8), 6–10.

Dole, J., Duffy, G., Roehler, L. & Pearson, P.D. (1991). Moving from the old to the new: Research on reading comprehension instruction. *Review of Educational Research, 61*(2), 239–264,

Edwards, P. (2004). *Children's literacy development: Making it happen through school, family, and community involvement.* New York: Pearson.

Edwards, P., Dandridge, J., McMillon, G., & Pleasants, H. (2001). Taking ownership of literacy: Who has the power. In P. Schmidt & P. Mosenthal (Eds.), *Reconceptualizing literacy in the new age of multiculturalism and pluralism* (pp. 111–136). Greenwich, CT: Information Age.

Epstein, J., & Voorhis, F. (2001). More than minutes: Teachers' roles in designing homework. *Educational Psychologist, 36*(3), 181–193.

Epstein, J., Salinas, K., Jackson, V., & Voorhis, F. (2000). *Teachers involve parents in schoolwork (tips) interactive homework for the middle grades.* Baltimore: Johns Hopkins University, Baltimore Center on School, Family and Community Partnerships.

Epstein, J., Sanders, M., Simon, B., Salinas, K., Jansorn, N., & Van Voorhis, F. (2002). *School, family, and community partnerships: Your handbook for action* (2nd ed.). Thousand Oaks, CA: Corwin Press.

Eskey, D. (2005). Reading in a second language. In E. Hinkel (Ed.), *Handbook of research in second language teaching and learning* (pp. 563–579). Mahwah, NJ: Erlbaum.

Espy, K., Molfese, D., Molfese, V., & Modglin, A. (2004). Development of auditory event-related potentials in young children and relations to word-level reading abilities at 8 years. *Annals of Dyslexia, 54*, 9–38.

Fehring, H., & Green, P. (2001). *Critical literacy: A collection of articles from the Australian Literacy Educators' Association.* Newark, DE: International Reading Association.

Fennick, R., Peters, M., & Guyon, L. (1993). Solving problems in twenty-first century academic and workplace writing. *English Journal, 82*(3), 46–53.

Finders, M. (1997). *Just girls.* New York: Teachers College Press.

Fitzgerald, J. (1992). *Towards knowledge in writing.* New York: Springer-Verlag.

Frank, C. (2001). What new things these words can do for you: A focus on one writing-project teacher and writing instruction. *Journal of Literacy Research, 33*(3), 467–506.

Fuller, M., & Olson, G. (1998). *Home-school relations: Working successfully with parents and families.* Boston: Allyn and Bacon.

Fulwiler, T. (1980). Journals across the disciplines. *English Journal, 69*, 14–19.

Gagne, R., Wagner, W., Keller, J., & Golas, K. (2004). *Principles of instructional design.* New York: Wadsworth.

Gambrell, L. (2001). What we know about motivation to read. In R., Flippo (Ed.), *Reading researchers in search of common ground.* (pp. 129–143). Newark, DE: International Reading Association.

Gambrell, L., & Bales, R. (1986). Mental imagery and the comprehension-monitoring performance of fourth and fifth grade poor readers. *Reading Research Quarterly, 21*(4), 454–464.

Garcia, E. (2001). *Student cultural diversity: Understanding and meeting the challenge.* Boston: Houghton Mifflin.

Gay, G. (2000). *Culturally responsive teaching: Theory, research, and practice.* New York: Teachers College Press.

Gee, J. (1996). *Social linguistics and literacies: Ideology in discourse.* London: Falmer.

Gee, J. (2000). Teenagers in new times. *Journal of Adolescent and Adult Literacy, 43*(5), 15–23.

Gee, J. (2003). *What video games have to teach us about learning and literacy.* New York: Macmillan.

Gee, J., & Crawford, V. (1998). Two kinds of teenagers: Language, identity and social class. In D. Alvermann, K. Hinchman, D. Moore, S. Phelps, & D. Waff (Eds.), *Reconceptualizing the literacies in adolescents' lives* (pp. 225–246).

Goodman, Y. M., Watson, D. J., & Burke, C. L. (1987). *Reading miscue inventory: Alternative procedures.* New York: Owen.

Gough, P. (1984). Word recognition. In P. Pearson, R. Barr, M. Kamil, & P. Mosenthal (Eds.), *Handbook of reading research* (Vol. I, pp. 203–211). New York: Longman.

Gove, P. (2002). *Webster's third international dictionary.* Springfield, MA: Merriam-Webster.

Graham, S. (2006). Strategy instruction and the teaching of writing. In C. MacArthur, S. Graham, & J. Fitzgerald (Eds.), *Handbook of writing research* (pp. 187–207). New York: Guilford.

Graham, S. & Harris, K. (2005). *Writing better: Effective strategies for teaching students with learning difficulties.* Baltimore: Brooks Publishing.

Graves, M. (1984). Selecting vocabulary to teach in the intermediate and secondary grades. In J. Flood (Ed.), *Promoting reading comprehension* (pp. 245–260). Newark, DE: International Reading Association.

Graves, M., & Prenn, M. (1986). Costs and benefits of various methods of teaching vocabulary. *Journal of Reading, 29,* 596–609.

Graves, M., & Watts-Taffe, S. (2002). The place of word consciousness in a research-based vocabulary program. In A. Farstrup & S. J. Samuels (Eds.), *What research has to say about reading instruction* (pp. 140–165). Newark, DE: International Reading Association.

Gregory, D., & Lipsyte, R. (1984). *Nigger: An autobiography.* New York: E.P. Dutton.

Guthrie, J., & Alvermann, D. (1998). *Engaged reading: Processes, practices, and policy implications.* New York: Teachers College Press.

Guthrie, J., Wigfield, A., & Perencevich, K. C. (2004). *Motivating reading instruction: Concept-oriented reading instruction.* Mahwah, NJ: Erlbaum.

Haggard, M. (1982). The vocabulary self-selection strategy: An active approach to word learning. *Journal of Reading, 26,* 634–642.

Haggard, M. (1985). An interactive strategies approach to content reading. *Journal of Reading, 29,* 204–210.

Haggard, M. (1997). *Teaching content reading and writing* (2nd ed.). Boston: Allyn and Bacon.

Harris, K., Graham, S., & Mason, L. (2003). Self-regulated strategy development in the classroom: Part of a balanced approach to writing instruction for students with disabilities. *Focus on Exceptional Children, 35*(7), 1–16.

Harris, T., & Hodges, R. (1995). *The literacy dictionary: The vocabulary of reading and writing.* Newark, DE: International Reading Association.

Heath, S. (1983). *Ways with words: Language, life, and work in communities and classrooms.* Cambridge, England: Cambridge University Press.

Heath, S. (1991). The sense of being literate: Historical and cross-cultural features. In R. Barr, M. Kamil, P. Mosenthal, & P. Pearson (Eds.), *Handbook of reading research* (Vol. 2, pp. 3–25). New York: Longman.

Heath, S. (2004). Learning language and strategic thinking through the arts. *Reading Research Quarterly, 39*(3), 338–342.

Heimlich, J., & Pittelman, S. (1986). *Semantic mapping: Classroom applications.* Newark, DE: International Reading Association.

Henderson, A., & Berla, N. (1994). *A new generation of evidence: The family is critical to student achievement.* Washington, DC: Center for Law and Education.

Herber, H. (1978). *Teaching reading in content areas* (2nd ed.). New York: Prentice Hall.

Herber, H., & Nelson-Herber, J. (1993). *Teaching in content areas with reading, writing and reasoning.* Boston: Allyn and Bacon.

Hetzroni, O., & Shrieber, B. (2004). Word processing as an assistive technology tool for enhancing academic outcomes of students with writing disabilities in the general classroom. *Journal of Learning Disabilities, 34*(2), 143–155.

Holmes, V., & Moulton, M. (1997). Dialogue journals as an ESL learning strategy. *Journal of Adolescent and Adult Literacy, 40*(8), 616–621.

Hyperdictionary. (2004). Hyperdictionary. Retrieved March 4, 2004, from www. hyperdictionary. com/.

Inspiration. (2003). *Inspiration 7.5.* Portland, OR: Author.

Irwin, J., & Davis, C. (1980). Assessing readability: The checklist approach. *Journal of Reading, 24,* 124–130.

Jitendra, A., Griffin, C., Deatline-Buchman, A., Dipipi-Hoy, C., Sczesniak, E., Sokol, N., et al. (2005). Adherence to mathematics professional standards and instructional design criteria for problem-solving in mathematics. *Exceptional Children, 71*(3), 319–337.

Johannessen, L. (2004). Helping "struggling" students achieve success. *Journal of Adolescent and Adult Literacy, 47*(8), 638.

Johnson, D., & Johnson, R. (1985). Conflict in the classroom: Controversy over the debate in learning groups. *American Educational Research Journal, 22,* 51–70.

Johnson, D., & Pearson, P. (1984). *Teaching reading vocabulary.* New York: Holt, Rinehart and Winston.

Juel, C., & Deffes, R. (2004). Making words stick. *Educational Leadership, 61*(6), 30–34.

Juel, C., Biancarosa, G., Coker, D., & Deffes, R. (2003). Walking with Rosie: A cautionary tale of literacy instruction. *Educational Leadership, 60*(7), 12–18.

Kim, A., Vaughn, S., Wanzek, J., & Wei, S. (2004). Graphic organizers and their effects on the comprehension of students with learning disabilities. *Journal of Learning Disabilities, 37*(2), 105–119.

Kintsch, W. (1989). Learning from text. In L. Resnick (Ed.), *Knowing, learning, and instruction.* (pp. 25–46). Hillsdale, NJ: Erlbaum.

Kirby, D., & Liner, T. (1988). *Inside out.* Portsmouth, NH: Heinemann.

Kiyama, H. (1999). *The four immigrants manga: A Japanese experience in San Francisco.* Berkeley, CA: Stone Bridge.

Kohn, A. (2000). *The case against standardized testing: Raising the scores, ruining the schools.* Portsmouth, NH: Heinemann.

Koss, M., & Teale, W. (2009). What's happening in YA literature: Trends in books for adolescents. *Journal of Adolescent and Adult Literacy, 52*(7), 563–572.

Krashen, S. (1996). *Under attack: The case against bilingual education.* Culver City, CA: Language Education Associates.

Krashen, S. (2004). *Applying the comprehension hypothesis.* Paper presented at the 13th Annual Symposium on Language Teaching, Taipei, Taiwan.

Ladson-Billings, G. (1994). *The dreamkeepers: Successful teachers of African American children.* San Francisco: Jossey Bass.

LaFlamme, J. (2000). The effect of multiple exposure vocabulary method and the target reading/writing strategy on test scores. *Journal of Adolescent and Adult Literacy, 40*(5), 372–384.

Landis, D. (2002). Reading engaged readers: A cross-cultural perspective. *Journal of Adolescent and Adult Literacy, 45*(6), 472–478.

Landrum, T., Tankersley, M., & Kauffman, J. (2003). What is special about special education students with emotional or behavioral disorders? *Journal of Special Education, 37*(3), 148–156.

Langer, J. (1982). Facilitating text processing. In J. Langer & T. Smith-Burke (Eds.), *Reader meets author/bridging the gap* (pp. 149–162). Newark, DE: International Reading Association.

Langer, J. (1999). *Beating the odds: Teaching middle and high school students to read and write well* (No. 12014). Albany, NY: Research Center on English Learning and Achievement, the University of Albany.

Learning Disabilities Association of America. (2005). *Summer reading tips for parents.* Pittsburgh, PA: Author.

Lenz, K., & Deshler, D. (2004). *Teaching content to all: Evidence-based inclusive practices in middle and secondary schools.* New York: Allyn and Bacon.

Leonard, L. (1998). *Children with specific language impairment.* Cambridge, MA: MIT Press.

Leu, D. (2000). Literacy and technology: Dietic consequences for literacy education in an information age. In M. Kamil, P. Mosenthal, P. Pearson, & R. Barr (Eds.), *Handbook of reading research* (Vol. 3, pp. 743–770). Mahwah, NJ: Erlbaum.

Leu, D., Kinzer, C., Coiro, J., & Cammack, D. (2004). Toward a theory of new literacies emerging from the internet and other information and communication technologies. In R. Ruddell & N. Unrau (Eds.), *Theoretical models and processes of reading* (pp. 1570–1616). Newark, DE: International Reading Association.

Leu, D., Zawilinski, L., Castek, J., Banerjee, M., Housand, B., Liu, Y., et al. (2007). What is new about the new literacies of online reading comprehension? In A. Berger, L. Rush, & J. Eakle (Eds.), *Secondary school reading and writing: What research reveals for classroom practices.* Chicago, IL: NCTE/NCRLL.

Lloyd, C. (1998). Engaging students at the top (without leaving the rest behind). *Journal of Adolescent and Adult Literacy, 42*(3), 184–192.

Lou, Y., Abrami, P., Spence, J., Poulsen, C., Chambers, B., & d'Apollonia, S. (1996). Within-class grouping: A meta-analysis. *Review of Educational Research, 66,* 423–458.

Lowery, N. (2002). Construction of teacher knowledge in context: Preparing elementary teachers to teach mathematics and science. *School Science and Mathematics, 102*(2), 68–80.

Luckner, J., Bowen, S., & Carter, K. (2001). Visual teaching strategies for students who are deaf or hard of hearing. *Exceptional Children, 33*(3), 38–44.

Lyon, R., Shaywitz, S., & Shaywitz, B. (2003). A definition of dyslexia. *Annals of Dyslexia, 53,* 1–15.

MacArthur, C., & Haynes, J. (1995). Student assistant for learning from text (SALT): A hypermedia reading aid. *Journal of Learning Disabilities, 28,* 150–159.

Macrorie, K. (1988). *The I-Search paper.* Portsmouth, NH: Heinemann.

Manzo, A. (1975). Guided reading procedure. *Journal of Reading, 18,* 287–297.

Manzo, A., & Manzo, U. (1990). *Content area reading: A heuristic approach.* Columbus, OH: Merrill.

Marshall, J. (2000). Research on response to literature. In M. Kamil, P. Mosenthal, P. Pearson, & R. Barr (Eds.), *Handbook of Reading Research* (pp. 381–402) Mahwah, NJ: Erlbaum.

Marx, R., Blumenfeld, P., Krajcik, J., Fishman, B., Soloway, E., Geier, R., et al. (2004). Inquiry-based science in the middle grades: Assessment of learning in urban systemic reform. *Journal of Research in Science Teaching, 41*(10), 1063–1080.

Mastropieri, M., Scruggs, T., & Graetz, J. (2003). Reading comprehension instruction for secondary students: Challenges for struggling students and teachers. *Learning Disability Quarterly, 26*(2), 103–116.

Mayer, J., Perkins, D., Caruso, D., & Salovey, P. (2001). Emotional intelligence and giftedness. *Roeper Review, 23*(3), 131–139.

McCaleb, S. (1994). *Building communities of learners: A collaboration among teachers, families and community.* New York: St. Martin's Press.

McCutchen, D. (2006). Cognitive factors in the development of children's writing. In C. MacArthur, S. Graham, & J. Fitzgerald (Eds.), *Handbook of writing research* (pp. 115–130). New York: Guilford.

McGraw-Hill, C. (2003). *Glossary of assessment terms.* Monterey, CA: CTB/McGraw-Hill.

McIntosh, M., & Draper, R. (1995). Applying the question-answer relationship strategy in mathematics. *Journal of Adolescent and Adult Literacy, 39*(2), 120–131.

McKenna, M. C., Kear, D. J., & Ellsworth, R. A. (1995). "Children's attitudes toward reading: A national survey." *Reading Research Quarterly 30*(4), 934–956.

McKenna, M., & Robinson, R. (1990). Content literacy: A definition and implications. *Journal of Adolescent and Adult Literacy, 34*(3), 184–186.

McLaughlin, M., & DeVoogd, G. (2004). Critical literacy as comprehension: Expanding reader response. *Journal of Adolescent and Adult Literacy, 48*(1), 52–63.

Merkley, D., & Jeffries, D. (2001). Guidelines for implementing a graphic organizer. *Reading Teacher, 54*(4), 350–357.

Meyer, B., Brandt, D., & Bluth, G. (1980). Use of top-level structure in text: Key for reading comprehension of ninth grade students. *Reading Research Quarterly, 16,* 72–103.

Miedel, W., & Reynolds, A. (1999). Parent involvement in early intervention for disadvantaged children: Does it matter? *Journal of School Psychology, 37*(4), 379–402.

Mikulecky, L., & Kirley, J. (1998). Changing workplaces, changing classes: The new role of technology in workplace literacy. In D. Reinking, M. McKenna, L. Labbo, & R. Kieffer (Eds.), *Handbook of literacy and technology: Transformations in a post-typographic world* (pp. 303–320). Mahwah, NJ: Erlbaum.

Moje, E. (2002). Re-framing adolescent literacy research for new times: Studying youth as a resource. *Reading Research and Instruction, 41*(3), 211–228.

Moje, E. B., McIntosh Ciechanowski, K., Kramer, K., Ellis, L., Carrillo, R., & Collazo, T. (2004). Working toward third space in content area literacy. An examination of everyday funds of knowledge and discourse. *Reading Research Quarterly 39*(1), 38–71.

Moje, E., & Hinchman, K. (2004). Culturally responsive practices for youth literacy learning. In T. Jetton & J. Dole (Eds.), *Adolescent literacy research and practice* (pp. 321–350). New York: Guilford.

Moje, E., & Tysvaer, N. (2010). *Adolescent literacy development in out of school time: A practitioner's guidebook.* New York: Carnegie.

Moje, E., Willes, D., & Fassio, K. (2001). Constructing and negotiating literacy in a writer's workshop: Literacy teaching and learning in the seventh-grade. In E. Moje & D. O'Brien (Eds.), *Constructions of literacy: Studies of literacy teaching and learning in secondary classrooms and schools* (pp. 193–212). Mahwah, NJ: Erlbaum.

Moje, E., Young, J., Readance, J., & Moore, D. (2000). Reinventing adolescent literacy for new times: Perennial and millennial issues. *Journal of Adolescent and Adult Literacy, 13*(5), 4–14.

Moll, L. (1992a). Bilingual classroom studies and community analysis: Some recent trends. *Educational Researcher, 21*(2), 20–24.

Moll, L. (1992b). Funds of knowledge for teaching: Using a qualitative approach to connect homes and classrooms. *Theory into Practice, 31*(2), 132–141.

Moore, D., Moore, S., Cunningham, P., & Cunningham, J. (2003). *Developing readers and writers in content areas: K-12* (4th ed.). Dubuque, IA: Kendall Hunt.

Morrell, E. (2004). *Linking literacy and popular culture.* Norwood, MA: Christopher Gordon.

Mosenthal, P., & Kirsch, I. (1989). Lists: The building blocks of documents. *Journal of Reading, 33*(1), 58–60.

Mosenthal, P., & Kirsch, I. (1998). A new measure of assessing document complexity: The PMOSE/IKIRSCH document readability formula. *Journal of Adolescent and Adult Literacy, 41*(8), 638–657.

Nagy, W., Diakidoy, A., & Anderson, R. (1993). The acquisition of morphology: Learning the contribution of suffixes to the meanings of derivatives. *Journal of Reading Behavior, 25,* 155–170.

Nagy, W., & Scott, J. (2000). Vocabulary processes. In M. Kamil, P. Mosenthal, P. Pearson, & R. Barr (Eds.), *Handbook of reading research* (Vol. 3, pp. 269–284). Mahwah, NJ: Erlbaum.

National Center for Education Statistics. (1999). *Highlights from TIMMS: Overview and key findings.* Washington, DC: Office of Educational Research and Improvement, U.S. Department of Education.

National Center for Education Statistics. (2005a). *Contexts of elementary and secondary education.* Washington, DC: Author.

National Center for Education Statistics. (2005b). *Number and percent of children served under individuals with disabilities education act.* Washington, DC: U.S. Department of Education.

National Center on Educational Outcomes. (1997). *Providing assessment accommodations for students with disabilities in state and district assessments.* Minneapolis, MN: Author.

National Governor's Association Center for Best Practices. (2005). *Reading to achieve: A governor's guide to adolescent literacy.* Washington, DC: Author.

National Reading Panel. (2000). *Report of the national reading panel: An evidence-based assessment of the scientific research literature on reading and its implications for reading instruction.* Washington, DC: National Institute of Child Health and Human Development, National Institutes of Health.

Newell, G. (2006). Writing to learn. In C. Mac Arthur, S. Graham, & J. Fitzgerald (Eds.), *Handbook of writing research* (pp. 235–247). New York: Guilford.

Noddings, N. (1984). *Caring: A feminine approach to ethics and moral education.* Berkeley: University of California Press.

Nokes, J., & Dole, J. (2004). Helping adolescent readers through explicit strategy instruction. In T. Jetton & J. Dole (Eds.), *Adolescent literacy research and practice* (pp. 162–182). New York: Guilford.

O'Brien, E., Rosenzweig, J., & Sommers, N. (2004). *Making the most of college writing.* Cambridge, MA: Harvard College.

Ovando, C., Combs, M. C., & Collier, V. (2003). *Bilingual and ESL classrooms: Teaching in multicultural contexts.* (3rd Ed.) New York: McGraw-Hill.

Pailliotet, A. (2001). Critical media literacy and values: Connecting with the 5 w's. In P. Schmidt & A. Pailliotet (Eds.), *Exploring values through literature, multimedia, and literacy events* (pp. 20–45). Newark, DE: International Reading Association.

Pauk, W. (2000). *How to study in college.* New York: Houghton Mifflin.

Paulu, N. (1995). *Helping your child with homework.* Washington, DC: U.S. Department of Education.

Payne, R. (2001). *A framework for understanding poverty.* Highlands, TX: Aha Process.

Pereogy, S., & Boyle, O. (2001). *Reading, writing, and learning in ESL: A resource book for K-12 teachers.* New York: Longman.

Perfetti, C. (1985). *Reading ability.* New York: Oxford University Press.

Pipher, M. (1994). *Reviving Ophelia: Saving the selves of adolescent girls.* New York: Ballantine Books.

Popham, W. (2003). "The seductive allure of data." *Educational Leadership 60*(5), 48–51.

Pressley, M. (1998). *Reading instruction that works: The case for balanced teaching.* New York: Guilford.

Pressley, M. (2000). What should comprehension instruction be the instruction of? In M. Kamil, P. Mosenthal, P. Pearson, & R. Barr (Eds.), *Handbook of reading research* (Vol. 3, pp. 545–561). Mahwah, NJ: Erlbaum.

Pressley, M. (2006). *Reading instruction that works: The case for balanced teaching* (3rd ed.). New York: Guilford.

Pressley, M., Dolezal Kersey, S. E., Bogaert, L. R., Mohan, L., Roehrig, A. D., & Warzon, K. B. (2003). *Motivating primary-grade students.* New York: Guilford.

Pressley, M., Raphael, L., Gallagher, J. D., & DiBella, J. (2004). Providence-St. Mel School: How a school that works for African American students works. *Journal of Educational Psychology, 96*(2), 216–235.

Rackow, S. (1986). *Teaching science as inquiry.* Bloomington, IN: Phi Delta Kappa.

Raphael, T., & Pearson, P. (1985). Increasing student awareness of sources of information for answering questions. *American Educational Research Journal, 22,* 217–237.

Rasinski, T., Padak, N., McKeon, C., Wilfong, L., Friedauer, J., & Heim, P. (2005). Is reading fluency a key to successful high school reading? *Journal of Adolescent and Adult Literacy, 49*(1), 22–28.

Ravitch, D. (2010). *The death and life of the great American school system: How testing and choice are undermining education.* New York: Basic Books.

Reed, J., Schallert, D., Beth, A. & Woodruff, A. (2004). Motivated reader, engaged writer: The role of motivation in the literate acts of adolescents. T. Jetton & J. Dole (Eds.), *Adolescent literacy research and practice* (pp. 251–282). New York: Guilford.

Reeves, D. (2000). The 90/90/90 schools: A case study. In D. Reeves (Ed.), *Accountability in action: A blueprint for learning organizations.* Englewood, CO: Advanced Learning Press.

Reid, D. (1998). Scaffolding: A broader view. *Journal of Learning Disabilities, 31*(4), 386–397.

Reinking, D., & Rickman, S. (1990). The effects of computer-mediated texts on the vocabulary learning and comprehension of intermediate-grade readers. *Journal of Reading Behavior, 22,* 395–411.

Ridgway, T. (2003). Literacy and foreign language reading. *Reading in a Foreign Language,* 117–129.

Roberts, D. (2000). Media and the youth: Access, exposure, and privatization. *Journal of Adolescent Health, 27*(2), 8–14.

Rodriquez-Brown, F. (2001). Home-school collaboration: Successful models in the Hispanic community. In P. Schmidt & P. Mosenthal (Eds.), *Reconceptualizing literacy in the new age of multiculturalism and pluralism* (pp. 273–288). Greenwich, CT: Information Age.

Roe, K. (1998). "Boys will be boys and girls will be girls": Changes in children's media use. *European Journal of Communication, 23*(1), 5–25.

Roediger, H., & Karpicke, J. (2006). Test-enhanced learning: Taking memory tests improves long-term retention. *Psychological Science, 17*(3), 249–255.

Rosenshine, B., Meister, C., & Chapman, S. (1996). Teaching students to generate questions: A review of the intervention studies. *Review of Educational Research, 66,* 181–221.

Rumelhart, D. (1994). Toward an interactive model of reading. In R. Ruddell, M. Ruddell, & H. Singer (Eds.), *Theoretical models and processes of reading* (4th ed., pp. 359–380). Newark, DE: International Reading Association.

Rycik, J., & Irvin, J. (2001). *What adolescents deserve: A commitment to students' literacy learning.* Newark, DE: International Reading Association.

Sadowski, M. (2003). *Adolescents at school: Perspectives on youth, identity, and education.* Boston: Harvard Education Publishers.

Sadoski, M., Goetz, E., & Kangiser, S. (1988). Imagination in story response: Relationships between imagery, affect, and structural importance. *Reading Research Quarterly, 23*(3), 330–336.

Sadoski, M., & Paovio, A. (2001). *Imagery and text: A dual coding theory of reading and writing.* Mahwah, NJ: Erlbaum.

Sainsbury, M., & Schagen, I. (2004). Attitudes to reading at ages 9 and 11. *Journal of Research in Reading, 27*(4), 373–386.

Samples, R. (1977). *The whole school book.* Reading, MA: Addison-Wesley.

Sanders, M., Epstein, J., & Connors-Tadros. (1999). *Partnerships with high schools: The parents' perspective.* Baltimore: Johns Hopkins University, Center for Research on the Education of Students Placed at Risk.

Satrapi, M. (2003). *Persepolis: The story of a childhood.* New York: Pantheon.

Satrapi, M. (2004). *Persepolis 2: The story of a return.* New York: Pantheon.

Savignon, S. (2005). Communicative language teaching: Strategies and goals. In E. Hinkel (Ed.), *Handbook of research in second language teaching and learning* (pp. 635–651). Mahwah, NJ: Erlbaum.

Savoie, J., & Hughes, A. (1994). Problem-based learning as classroom solution. *Educational Leadership, 52*(3), 54–57.

Schmidt, N., & Zimmerman, C. (2002). Derivative word forms: What do learners know? *TESOL Quarterly, 36*(2), 145–171.

Schumm, J., & Mangrum, C. (1991). FLIP: A framework for content area reading. *Journal of Reading, 35*(2), 120–124.

Searfoss, L., Smith, C., & Bean, T. (1981). An integrated strategy for second language learners in content area subjects. *TESOL Quarterly, 15,* 383–389.

Shanahan, T. (2006). Relations among oral language, reading, and writing development. In C. MacArthur, S. Graham, & J. Fitzgerald (Eds.), *Handbook of writing research* (pp. 171–183). New York: Guilford.

Short, D. (1997). Reading, 'riting, and social studies: Research in integrated language and content secondary classrooms. In D. Brinton & M. Snow (Eds.), *The content-based* classroom: *Perspectives on integrating language and content* (pp. 213–232). Reading, MA: Addison-Wesley.

Short, D., & Echevarria, J. (2005). Teacher skills to support English language learning. *Educational Leadership, 62*(4), 8–13.

Simmons, J. (2003). Responders are taught, not born. *Journal of Adolescent and Adult Literacy, 46*(8), 684–693.

Singer, H., & Donlan, D. (1982). Active comprehension: Problem-solving schema with question generation for comprehension of complex short stories. *Reading Research Quarterly, 17*(2), 166–186.

Skaggs, K. (2004). Childhood and adolescence. In J. Kircheloe & D. Weil (Eds.) *Critical thinking and learning* (pp. 83–87). Westport, CT: Greenwood Press.

Smith, C., & Bean, T. (1980). The guided writing procedure: Integrating content reading and writing improvement. *Reading World, 19*, 290–298.

Snow, C., & Biancarosa, G. (2003). *Adolescent literacy and the achievement gap: What do we know and where do we go from here?* New York: Carnegie Corporation.

Snow, C., Burns, S., & Griffin, P. (1998). *Preventing reading difficulties in young children.* Washington, DC: National Academy Press.

Soodak, L. (2003). Classroom management in inclusive settings. *Theory into Practice, 42*(4), 327–333.

Sox, A., & Rubinstein-Avila, E. (2009). Webquests for English language learners: Essential elements for design. *Journal of Adolescent and Adult Literacy, 53*(1), 38–48.

Stauffer, R. (1969). *Teaching reading as a thinking process.* New York: Harper & Row.

Stepien, W., & Gallagher, S. (1993). Problem-based learning: As authentic as it gets. *Educational Leadership, 50*(7), 25–28.

Stiggins, R. (2005). *Student-involved assessment for learning.* Upper Saddle River, NJ: Prentice Hall.

Swan, E. (2004). Motivating adolescent readers through Concept Oriented Reading Instruction. In T. Jetton & J. Dole (Eds.), *Adolescent*

literacy research and practice (pp. 283–303). New York: Guilford.

Swap, S. (1999). *Developing home-school partnerships: From concepts to practice.* New York: Teachers College Press.

Taba, H. (1967). *Teacher's handbook for elementary social studies.* Reading, MA: Addison-Wesley.

Tan, S. (2007). *The arrival.* New York: Arthur Levine.

Tatum, A. (2005). *Teaching reading to black adolescent males.* New York: Stenhouse.

Tomlinson, C. (2004). Differentiating instruction. In T. Jetton & J. Dole (Eds.), *Adolescent literacy research and practice* (pp. 228–250). New York: Guilford.

Troia, G., & Graham, S. (2002). The effectiveness of a highly explicit, teacher-directed strategy instruction routine: Changing the writing performance of students with learning disabilities. *Journal of Learning Disabilities, 35*(4), 290–305.

U.S. Department of Education. (2003). *National assessment of educational progress trial urban district assessment.* Washington, DC: U.S. Department of Education, Office of Educational Research and Improvement.

U.S. Department of Education. (2010). *Race to the Top Program Description.* Washington, DC: U.S. Office of Education, Office of Elementary and Secondary Education.

Usiskin, Z., Flanders, J., Hynes, C., Polonsky, L., Porter, S., & Viktora, S. (1992). *Transition mathematics.* Glenview, IL: Scott Foresman.

Vacca, R., & Vacca, J. (2004). *Content area reading: Literacy and learning across content areas.* (8th ed.) Boston: Allyn and Bacon.

Valencia, S. (1990). A portfolio approach to classroom reading assessment: The whys, the whats and the hows. *Reading teacher 43*(4), 338–340.

Valmont, W. (2000). What teachers do in technology rich classrooms. In S. Wepner, W. Valmont, & R. Thurlow (Eds.), *Linking literacy and technology.* Newark, DE: International Reading Association.

Vansledright, B. (2004). What does it mean to read history? Fertile ground for cross-disciplinary collaborations? *Reading Research Quarterly, 39*(3), 342–346.

Vellutino, F., & Scanlon, D. (2001). Emergent literacy skills, early instruction, and individual differences as determinants of difficulties in learning to read: The case for early intervention. In S. Neuman & D. Dickinson (Eds.), *Handbook of early literacy research* (pp. 295–321). New York: Guilford.

Vizyak, L. (1999). Student portfolios: Building self-reflection in a first-grade classroom. In S. J. Barrentine (Ed.), *Reading assessment: Principles and practices for elementary teachers.* (pp. 135–139). Newark, DE, International Reading Association.

Weinstein, C. (2003). *Secondary classroom management.* New York: McGraw-Hill.

Weinstein, C., Curran, M., & Tomlinson-Clark, S. (2003). Culturally responsive classroom management: Awareness into action. *Theory into Practice, 42*(4), 269–276.

Wilhelm, J., & Smith, M. (2002). *Reading don't fix no Chevy's: Literacy in the lives of young men.* Portsmouth, NH: Heinemann.

Wiseman, A. (2010). "When you do your best, there's someone to encourage you:" Adolescents' views of family literacy. *Journal of Adolescent and Adult Literacy, 53*(2), 132–142.

Worthy, J., Moorman, M., & Turner, M. (1999). "What Johnny likes to read is hard to find in school." *Reading Research Quarterly 34*(1), 12–27.

Yamashita, J. (2004). "Reading attitudes in L1 and L2 and their influence on L2 extensive reading." *Reading in a Foreign Language 16*(1), 1–19.

Yang, G. (2006). *American born Chinese.* New York: First Second.

Yeung, A. (1999). Cognitive load and learner expertise: Split attention and redundancy effects in reading comprehension tasks with vocabulary definitions. *Journal of Experimental Education, 67,* 197–217.

Yore, L., Hand, B., Goldman, S., Hildebrand, G., Osborne, J., Treagust, D., & Wallace, C. (2004). *New directions in language and science education. Reading Research Quarterly, 39*(3), 347–352.

Index

Photo Credits